JUDICIAL SYSTEMS OF THE WORLD

Series Editors

DAVID S. LAW
E. James Kelly, Jr., Class of 1965 Research Professor of Law,
University of Virginia
Honorary Professor of Law, University of Hong Kong

and

BRYANT GARTH
Distinguished Professor of Law Emeritus,
University of California-Irvine

The Judicial System of China

JUDICIAL SYSTEMS OF THE WORLD

Series editors
David S. Law
E. James Kelly, Jr., Class of 1965 Research Professor of Law,
University of Virginia

and

Bryant Garth
Distinguished Professor of Law Emeritus,
University of California-Irvine

The Judicial Systems of the World series offers sophisticated and in-depth yet accessible scholarship by leading experts on the practical, day-to-day operation of a wide variety of judicial systems. Each volume offers a convenient point of entry for scholars and practitioners alike seeking to understand the courts in a particular country, such as the internal dynamics of the judiciary, the training of legal professionals, and the concrete details of how cases are handled. The incorporation of a structured comparative framework into each volume, in the form of a summary table, ensures consistency of coverage across the series and facilitates cross-country comparison.

Other titles in this series

The Judicial System of China

XIN HE

Professor, The University of Hong Kong, Hong Kong

OXFORD
UNIVERSITY PRESS

OXFORD
UNIVERSITY PRESS

Great Clarendon Street, Oxford, OX2 6DP,
United Kingdom

Oxford University Press is a department of the University of Oxford.
It furthers the University's objective of excellence in research, scholarship,
and education by publishing worldwide. Oxford is a registered trade mark of
Oxford University Press in the UK and in certain other countries

Published in the United States of America by Oxford University Press
198 Madison Avenue, New York, NY 10016, United States of America

British Library Cataloguing in Publication Data

Data available

Library of Congress Control Number: 2024943782

ISBN 9780198927785 (hbk.)
ISBN 9780198927778 (pbk.)

DOI: 10.1093/9780198927815.001.0001

Printed and bound by
CPI Group (UK) Ltd, Croydon, CR0 4YY

Contents

Figures

Tables

Abbreviations

ADR	Alternative Dispute Resolution
ALL	Administrative Litigation Law
ARL	Administrative Reconsideration Law
BRI	The Belt and Road Initiative
CCP	Chinese Communist Party
CiPL	Civil Procedure Law
CPC	The Central Party Committee
CrPL	Criminal Procedure Law
HPCs	Higher Provincial Courts
JM	Judicial Master
LLB	Bachelor of Laws
LPA	The Law of People's Assessors
MOJ	The Ministry of Justice
MPS	The Ministry of Public Security
MSS	The Ministry of State Security
NPC	National People's Congress
NPCSC	Standing Committee of the National People's Congress
SOEs	State-owned Enterprises
SPC	The Supreme People's Court
SPP	The Supreme People's Procuratorate

Introduction: The Governance Model

In 2014, an unlicensed physician in Shaanxi, western China, prescribed a drug to a 13-year-old girl, resulting in her death from an allergic reaction. The doctor was sentenced to 14 years in jail and ordered to pay 220,000 yuan in compensation, which he was unable to pay (the *Medical Malpractice Case*). The girl's father launched a petition campaign, but it was futile. On the anniversary of his daughter's death, the father jumped into the Gold Water River in front of Tiananmen Square in Beijing, catching the attention of senior officials, who prompted the local court to reopen the case. After exhausting all efforts, the responsible judge convinced the father to accept a reconciliation deal. The doctor's mother contributed 80,000 yuan from her retirement savings, the court contributed 20,000 yuan to the victim's family, and the doctor's jail time was reduced by four years. The case was eventually closed.

This dramatic incident unfolded amidst China's rapid rise as the world's largest economy. Scholars hold differing opinions on whether China has turned toward or against the law (A. Chen 2016; Minzner 2011), as well as whether it has a thin or thick version of the rule of law (Peerenboom 2002). However, one thing is certain: the laws in China have evolved beyond mere window dressing. In the past 40 years, numerous laws, statutes, ordinances, and amendments have been churned out. The proliferation of law schools and the increasing number of graduates entering the legal field may suggest that the law produces the largest share of college graduates, and the number of lawyers has soared. Legal discourse is evident in official rhetoric and everyday conversations. The state encourages people to utilize the law as a weapon, and many are heeding this advice.

Chinese courts are currently processing 45 million cases annually. On average, each of the nation's 126,000 judges resolves 350 cases per year, or roughly one case per day. The issue of "too many cases, too few judges" is often cited in the work reports of first-instance courts, with efficiency being just one of the concerns. To handle these cases, judges must possess both legal expertise and political acumen. For example, convincing a disgruntled father to accept a reconciliation deal is a time-consuming process. With the current deluge of cases, the role of courts in China has never in the country's history been more prominent.

Characterizing or sketching Chinese courts is a challenge, as they are described as "a strange animal" (Ng and He 2017a, 121). While Chinese courts may share some characteristics with authoritarian systems, they also possess distinct features. Ensuring social stability is a primary policy objective; rules play a prominent

The Judicial System of China. Xin He, Oxford University Press. © Xin He 2025. DOI: 10.1093/9780198927815.003.0001

role, but can be applied flexibly. Mediation is encouraged across all contexts. As the economy transitions from socialism, judges are tasked with addressing the concerns of both litigants and the state. The court system's efficiency is evident in its ability to resolve most cases within three months, making it one of the world's most effective judiciaries. It is hard to find another judicial system that bears similar marks.

The Independence Perspective

Over the past two decades, an expanding body of literature has delved into the unique nature of Chinese courts. One of the most notable perspectives is the "independence perspective," which originates from the Western concepts of the separation of powers, and checks and balances among government branches. In this idealized image, judges take center stage while adjudicating political, policy, or legal cases, and are protected from interference by measures such as life tenure.

Scholars debate the extent and standard by which Chinese courts are independent. Most argue that China's judiciary is either not sufficiently independent or not independent at all (Cohen 1997; Lubman 1999). In Yuwen Li's book (2014), subtitled *Stumbling Towards Justice,* the lack of judicial independence is seen as a primary cause of various judicial shortcomings. Some suggest that China could learn from Singapore's experience and grant its courts more respect and independence (Ang and Wang 2019). In contrast, Peerenboom (2010) contends that Chinese courts are more similar to Western courts than is often assumed, and that critiques about a lack of judicial independence are frequently overstated and based on uncertain premises. Despite their differences, both sides of the debate generally agree that China's courts *should* be independent.

This independence perspective offers valuable insights into the development of Chinese courts and their interactions with various actors. However, this perspective is often based on an ideal of convergence, where Chinese courts are expected to follow a Western model. It is now evident that China is climbing its own ladder, and few reputable scholars believe that Chinese courts would converge with Western courts (Liebman 2017; He 2020; Clarke 2022).

China has never adopted the concepts of separation of powers or checks and balances. Even in its laws, there is no mention that Chinese judges, as *individuals*, are to exercise judicial power independently. Instead, the laws, including the Constitution, state that the courts, only as *institutions*, are to adjudicate cases independently, free from the interference of administrative agencies, social organizations, and individuals (Art. 131). This approach is similar to the internal control exercised by promotions for career judges in many continental systems, such as those in Chile (Hilbank 2007), Japan (Abe 1995), and several European nations (Guarnieri 2001). However, in China, even this type of arrangement does not exist, because no law indicates that the Chinese Communist Party (CCP) is covered by the terms "administrative agencies" or "social organizations." In other words, the CCP can always look into court cases.

In practice, Chinese courts are an integral part of the local party-government coalition, which includes the local congress, the procuratorate, and the government and its branches, all operating under the leadership of the Party. There is no separation of powers among these branches. "Division of labor exists" but "only for purely practical ends" (Clarke 2022, 553). The courts do handle dispute resolution, but they can also be called upon to address any matters deemed appropriate by the authorities. Additionally, the procuratorate, and even the Party itself, wield significant power in supervising the courts. As a result, political influence within the courts is multifaceted and sometimes unavoidable.

Since the 2014 reforms, which elevated personnel and budgetary decisions to the provincial level, Chinese courts have become more horizontally independent (Zhang and Ginsburg 2019). It appears that judges can make most decisions without requiring approval from their supervisors (Sun and Fu 2022; Wang 2020a). However, the aim of these reforms was not to establish a genuinely independent judiciary or anything resembling the model in liberal democracies. The primary goal of the reforms was to sanction undue influence from supervisors or senior officials that could hamper the implementation of Beijing's policies.

The state's control over judges in China has not decreased. Instead, the original hierarchical and direct control by supervisors has been truncated and replaced by a panoptic control mechanism that includes open documents, secret memoranda, citizens' complaints, media reporting, and party discipline (see Chapter 2 for more details). All rank-and-file judges are required to align with the Party's line, and loyalty to the Party is embedded in the system (Liebman 2017). When the regime's interests are at risk, judges know what to do. Chinese judges do not have life tenure, and they can be removed, demoted, disciplined, or even criminalized at *any* time. How can they act against the Party? The senior officials of the courts are, first and foremost, party cadres, and they hold relatively low-ranked administrative positions within the Party. For example, a court president is often regarded as inferior to the vice administrative head of the same jurisdiction. Furthermore, all party cadres are subject to party discipline.

Some scholars, including Fu (2019) and myself (He 2011), propose a dualistic approach to understanding judicial independence in China. According to this approach, judges are subject to Party supervision when dealing with politically sensitive cases, but they can act independently in routine cases where the Party has no interest or capacity to supervise. While this distinction is somewhat useful, the line between politically sensitive and routine cases is never clear-cut: it is constantly shifting, based on factors such as the nature of the cases, the sociopolitical environment, and media reactions. While cases involving mass protests are clearly politically sensitive, it is difficult to predict whether a criminal case, such as the one described at the beginning of the book, will become politically salient during the trial. Therefore, even when handling routine divorce cases, judges lack genuine independence (He 2021a). Judges in all types of cases are subject to ongoing supervision and intervention.

The Rights Approach

Much of the existing literature on Chinese courts focuses on the angle of rights protection (Kellogg 2009; Hand 2011; Liu and Halliday 2016; Pils 2014; O'Brien and Li 2006). This line of research asks questions such as: To what extent do Chinese courts enforce the rights enshrined in the law? How do litigants utilize the law to achieve justice? How do lawyers use the courts as a platform for social change? What tactics does the state use in response? What are the experiences of lawyers and litigants, and what impact do they have?

These questions are essential in understanding how the Chinese judicial system operates and how individuals and groups navigate it to seek justice. Examining the tactics of litigants and their lawyers, the responses of the state, and the outcomes of cases provides valuable insights into the dynamics of the courtroom and state–society relations more broadly. Law and resistance, taking advantage of the ambiguous position of the courts, are critical to understanding judicial politics in authoritarian states. Many scholars studying judicial politics in such states view the courts as a limited yet critical battleground for rights. Asserting rights through legal mobilization is seen as a spark that could ignite the flame of revolution (Moustafa 2007, 41).

In these studies, "law versus the state" is assumed (Moustafa 2007; Ginsburg and Moustafa 2008; El-Ghobashy 2008; Chua 2014). Tamir Moustafa even titled the introductory chapter of his influential book with this phrase. However, while this assumption may be accurate in the context of Egypt and other authoritarian states, it is barely applicable to China.

In China, the law and courts do not oppose the state; instead, they work for the state. After Mao's era, the government has made law an essential tool for governance. As a massive authoritarian regime with multiple administrative layers, China faces a challenging principal–agent problem in its governance (Edin 2003; Minzner 2009; Zhou 2022). The government must control the agents it relies on to control the population. Delegating too much power can lead to corruption, while tightening control reduces incentives (Svolik 2012). Therefore, law and the courts have become critical components of China's statecraft (He 2020).

Specifically, the courts are *one of the agents* of the state, and are under the tight control of the Party. The official narrative states that the courts are one of the state apparatuses. Zheng Tianxiang (1994, 554), the Supreme People's Court (SPC) president from 1983 to 1988, stated: "[T]he courts are the Communist Party's courts." Peng Zhen (1991, 516), the senior leader of political-legal affairs in the 1980s, emphasized that "the political-legal apparatuses," of which the courts are a component, "are armed escorts of the Party, the state, and the people." They are tasked with controlling society and, to some extent, other agents. As part of the government apparatuses, the courts primarily support the governance of the state (Trevaskes 2011; Wang 2022). The state has always tried to control the courts and the Party has always been omnipotent in them (Zhu 2010). Indeed, this level of tight control is unique to China and cannot be found in any country in which "law versus state" is the prevailing theme.

While Chinese courts do protect certain types of rights when resolving disputes and applying laws, it is essential to understand that the concept of rights in China may differ substantively from that in liberal democracies. Scholars have noted that civil and political rights are tightly restricted in China (Fu and Peerenboom 2010, 110). But one must be conscious that in liberal democracies, private rights also differ fundamentally from personal entitlements. Damaska (1986, 83 ,quoted from Clarke 2022, 577) insightfully pointed out that personal claims in authoritarian states are "mislabeled if characterized as rights." Some rights are even turned into obligations (Damaska 1986, 84). These so-called rights are better understood as "conditional privileges" that can be forfeited when in conflict with state interests (Damaska 1986, 84; Creemers 2020, 25).[1]

Overall, rights protection is not the main task of Chinese courts. Their main task is to balance the conditional privileges with "the various interests at stake and choose the resolution that maximizes social utility, as defined by the Party in the pursuit of its mission" (Clarke 2022, 577). Although rights-focused scholarship offers valuable insights into court operations, it may fail to consider the state's objectives for the courts.

In the *Medical Malpractice Case*, the court did not serve as a platform for resistance. Instead, the father's voice was heard through petitioning. He did not present forceful arguments for rights in the courtroom, nor did he receive assistance from a powerful lawyer. It was his dramatic petition behavior that caught the attention of higher-level officials. From the court's perspective, while obtaining monetary compensation for the victim's family may have been seen as a way to uphold rights, the more immediate goal was to pacify the aggrieved father and maintain stability by ending the petition.

---

[1] Scholars have argued that constitutional rights in China have been developed through private laws. For example, dignity is incorporated in China's Civil Code. Yet even advocates of this argument admit that China "has not fully embraced the dignity norm in the way other constitutional systems have" (Stone Sweet and Wan 2023, 433).

The Governance Model

This book presents a governance model. It explores the operation of the courts by paying particular attention to the extent to which the courts strengthen the state's governance. It offers a broader model to connect Chinese courts with the political-legal goals that they are required to achieve.

In line with Gramsci's definition of governance as a tool for establishing and upholding the ruling class's control (Martin 1998: 76), this study adopts a similar understanding. Governance will be treated as a mechanism aimed at "sustaining and enhancing the ruling Party's control." This concept of governance encompasses not only the maintenance of order but also factors essential for preserving the state's legitimacy, which in turn solidifies the ruling status of the Party.

I propose two key characteristics of Chinese courts under the governance model. The first is policy implementation. Judges are required to "respond to a range of policy goals set out by the party-state" (Ng and He 2017, 121). In China, laws are basically the policy statements of the Party state. According to Peng Zhen (1991, 493), "the Party's policy shall be transformed into the state's policy through the form of the state, and the policy proven correct in reality shall be solidified into law." Xi Jinping (2014) emphasizes that the judiciary, as part of the political-legal apparatus, must consciously maintain the authority of both the Party's policies and the state's laws, ensuring that they are implemented consistently and correctly. Chinese courts must implement both legal rules and policies, with the latter often taking priority over the former. Judges must consider the consequences of their decisions and are often required to apply legal rules flexibly. As Ng (2019, 811) notes, "the judiciary uses decisions and, in some cases, non-decisions, to advance the *policy* intent of the party state" rather than interpreting laws based on legality criteria (emphasis added).

If policy implementation is to realize the state's goals to manage society, legitimacy enhancement makes sure that this way of policy implementation is accepted. Legitimacy is crucial, as it enhances governance by creating trust in authorities. Legitimacy, in this context, refers to "social trust or credibility" (Linz 1978; quoted from Toharia 2003, 26). Chinese courts place special emphasis on legitimacy enhancement because trust in the legal system is low (Ng and He 2017a, 76). There exists a constant tension between the state's reliance on the law as a means to implement policies and the general public's mistrust of the legal system.

In the governance model, there are often contradictions between the courts' efforts to implement policies and their efforts to enhance legitimacy. These tensions arise due to the inherent conflict between laws and policies. While laws are stable, policies respond to sometimes long-term but often short-term needs of the party-state. They are thus often ad hoc, and can vary significantly between central and local authorities. When policy implementation takes precedence over laws, it can be difficult to enhance or even maintain legitimacy. The combination of legal and social effects, a fundamental principle pursued by Chinese courts, is challenging to achieve, resulting in inevitable contradictions. For instance, during the COVID-19 pandemic, disputants were not allowed to file lawsuits, as it was deemed necessary to prioritize combating the pandemic. This practice left a negative impression of inaction on the part of the court and eroded its legitimacy. Such contradictions are an integral part of the courts' operation under the governance model.

Although the governance model shares some similarities with the rule-by-law thesis advocated by Ginsburg and Moustafa (2008), there are significant differences. According to Ng (2019), rule by law fails to capture the complexities of the Chinese legal system. Under rule by law, the law is a tool for authoritarian control and oppression (Krygier 2012, 234, quoted from Ng 2019, 794). The law is a bad rule that provides superficial legitimacy to the regime and is commanding, obscure, and arbitrary. While the Chinese legal system does have some of these characteristics, it would be an exaggeration to say that they are essential. Nowadays, the courts primarily handle civil and commercial cases that aim to resolve personal disputes and facilitate market transactions. Criminal cases constitute only about 3.7 percent of the dockets. Most laws are also quite clear, and the courts have shown an impressive degree of determinacy in many areas of the law.

In the governance model, the courts are seen as an instrument for the Party to promote governance by emphasizing policy implementation and legitimacy enhancement. While the courts may still be commanding in challenges to the state's political authority, they are also flexible and pragmatic in addressing the needs of the socially aggrieved. The policies that the courts are tasked with implementing are multifaceted and aim to enhance effective governance. While the rule-by-law thesis is useful in understanding the repressive aspect of the legal system, it fails to capture many other aspects.

A caveat is in order: In presenting the governance model, I am not seeking to justify or defend the practices of Chinese courts. My intention is to provide a more comprehensive, neutral, and accurate portrayal of the Chinese legal system and offer explanations for its operation. I aim to contextualize the courts within the political and socioeconomic contexts of China. Therefore, the governance model does not assume a dichotomy between law and the state, as the law works for the state, and so do the courts. Additionally, the governance model does not presuppose that individual rights always conflict with the interests of the government, as is commonly found in the rights approach. Under the governance model, there are times when interests collide, while at other times they coexist compatibly with one another.

The status of defense lawyers in the Chinese criminal justice system serves as an example of the conflicts that can arise, within the governance model, between individual interests and those of the state. According to Liu and Halliday (2016), while the Chinese criminal justice system has become more sophisticated and functional, many defense lawyers continue to face significant challenges and live in fear. Some have had their licenses revoked or been physically assaulted, or even arrested and prosecuted.

From the perspective of rights protection, this situation presents a "great puzzle," as the modernization of the Chinese criminal justice system has not significantly improved the working conditions of defense lawyers (Liu and Halliday 2016, 179).

However, under the governance model, the status of China's lawyers may not be as puzzling as it initially appears. In the eyes of the state, defense lawyers who advocate for individual rights may not be viewed as contributing to effective governance. Instead, they may be seen as promoting Western ideology, which could be perceived as a threat to the legitimacy and existence of the state. As a result, the interests of defense lawyers and the state are often in conflict, and the state may have little incentive to safeguard their rights. Instead, efforts may be made to discipline and control them.

The role of the courts in handling labor protests exemplifies the second scenario within the governance model. In what Yang Su and I (Su and He 2010) refer to as the "street as courtroom" phenomenon, the courts and the state did not simply repress labor protestors, but instead redirected them from the streets to the legal system. This approach allowed the state to contain the protests and maintain governance while also ensuring that the interests of the laborers were protected through legal proceedings. In this scenario, the interests of the citizens—in this case, the laborers—were not in direct conflict with those of the state. By providing avenues for laborers to seek remedies through the courts, the state was able to address their concerns while simultaneously maintaining social stability. This approach illustrates that protecting rights can actually contribute to legitimacy and governance. As a result, the governance model offers insights into the evolution of rights—or, more accurately, conditional privileges—which may not be as evident when viewed solely through the lens of the rights approach. Through the governance model, we can gain a more comprehensive understanding of how the Chinese legal system operates and how the interests of both individuals and the state can be addressed simultaneously.

Chinese Distinctiveness

Chinese courts, like courts in any jurisdiction, play a role in governance through policy implementation and legitimacy enhancement (Shapiro 1981; Sweet 1999). However, what sets Chinese courts apart is the *dominant* role of policy implementation.

Chinese courts can be characterized as "policy-implementing courts," due to the dominant role of policy implementation within their function. In contrast to laws, entitlements, privileges, and rights, immediate policy concerns often take precedence in Chinese courts, with these concerns being "explicitly and immediately political" (Ng and He 2017, 121). When the policies of the Party and government conflict with laws, they often supersede the laws. According to Damaska's typology (1986, 181), policy implementation and conflict resolution represent two opposite ideal types for courts' functions. In Chinese courts, policy implementation features so prominently that dispute resolution itself is considered one of many policies to be implemented. For instance, during Mao's era and the early stage of Deng Xiaoping's period, dispute resolution was not a top policy priority for the courts. It only gained significance when more cases were brought before the courts in the late 1980s.

The role of stability-maintenance policy in contemporary Chinese courts provides a striking example of the dominant emphasis on policy implementation. By the early 2000s, stability maintenance had become the primary goal of the public security system, including the courts (Trevaskes et al. 2014). This policy has since permeated every aspect of the Chinese courts' operations, and is often referred to as "stability justice" (Yuqing Feng and Yu Zeng 2022). Under the stability-maintenance policy, courts are "over-responsive," and legal rules are often bent to maintain social stability (Liebman 2011). This policy overshadows the decisions of almost every type of case, emphasizing the importance of maintaining order and stability over other considerations. This focus on stability reinforces the idea of Chinese courts as policy-implementing institutions, where the implementation of state policies takes precedence over other factors.

In contrast to Chinese courts, judges in continental or common law systems do not prioritize stability maintenance. This was also true in authoritarian states like the former German Democratic Republic (Markovits 2002), and under Stalin's rule (Solomon 1996), where the policy of social stability was implicit or barely mentioned. Similarly, Russian courts under Putin do not prioritize stability maintenance (Hendley and Solomon 2023).

Stability maintenance is just one of many policies that Chinese courts are tasked with implementing. Chinese courts are responsible for implementing a wide range of policies, including birth control, economic development, the Belt and Road Initiative, controlling the spread of COVID-19, urban beautification, tax collection, environmental protection, and the eradication of criminal organizations. These policies reflect the broader governance objectives of the Chinese government and highlight the multifaceted role of Chinese courts in policy implementation.

Policy implementation is, in the context of Chinese courts, much broader than just order maintenance. While Clarke (2022) characterizes Chinese legal systems, including the courts, as order-maintenance institutions, it is important to recognize that Chinese courts have multiple policies to implement, often from various sources. Order maintenance connotes a sense of quietude and stillness, which may be applicable to courts in Myanmar where immobilization has been seen as a social ideal (Cheesman 2015). However, in China, there are constant social changes and political turmoil such as those during Mao's period. Chinese courts often face tensions between maintaining the existing order and adapting to social changes. They are frequently tasked with changing the original social order, which is why the concept of policy implementation better characterizes the nature of Chinese courts.

Legitimacy enhancement is another distinct characteristic of Chinese courts. Every judicial system seeks to enhance its legitimacy, but it is the approaches taken by Chinese courts to enhancing legitimacy that differentiate them from other courts. The courts in liberal democracies achieve legitimacy enhancement primarily by rendering a rational decision following the established procedure (Weber 1954; Tyler 2007, 31). Judges are supposed to dispense justice with integrity (Garoupa and Ginsburg 2015). Judicial independence and procedural justice are key. Some courts in authoritarian states also share similar traits in this regard (Markovits 2002; Hendley 2017).

Yet in Chinese courts, neither judicial independence nor procedural justice is crucial. Due to the policy-implementing nature of the courts, they cannot afford to allow Western-style judicial independence. Furthermore, compared to the mushrooming of new laws in substantive areas, procedural rules in China are underdeveloped. This is because the laws in substantive areas are policy statements to be flexibly applied, and procedural rules take discretion away from judges (Ng 2019, 817). If procedural rules were strictly followed, the outcomes may contradict with policy goals. To enhance legitimacy, Chinese courts have to rely upon other means than judicial independence and procedural justice—substantive justice, efficiency, judicial democracy, and judicial transparency. As a result, legitimacy enhancement is diffused in the operation of Chinese courts.

Despite being crucial in liberal democracies, neither judicial independence nor procedural justice is essential in Chinese courts, due to their policy-implementing nature. The courts cannot afford to adopt Western-style judicial independence, and procedural rules in China are underdeveloped compared to the proliferation of new laws in substantive areas. This is because substantive laws are flexible policy statements, while procedural rules restrict judges' discretion (Ng 2019, 817), potentially leading to outcomes that contradict policy goals. Therefore, Chinese courts rely on other means to enhance legitimacy, such as substantive justice, efficiency, judicial democracy, and transparency. Legitimacy enhancement is diffused throughout the operation of Chinese courts through means other than judicial independence and procedural justice.

Chinese courts prioritize achieving substantive justice over strict adherence to procedural rules. Mediation has persisted as a means to achieve acceptable outcomes for litigants with opposing interests. Judges explain the rationale behind their decisions to ensure their acceptance, focusing on substantive justice rather than procedural aspects. They are sensitive to litigants, social groups, and media reactions. Former SPC president Wang Shengjun openly stated that public opinion heavily influences the application of the death penalty (Caijing 2008; Belkin 2018;

Miao 2013a). Xi Jinping consistently emphasizes the importance of fairness, effectiveness, and efficiency in the courts. His words, "it shall let the general public feel
fairness in every case" (2014), are prominently displayed in the lobbies of many
Chinese courthouses. The courts have also invested heavily in artificial intelligence
to improve access to their services.

Judicial democracy has been emphasized, with greater participation of people's
assessors, to increase recognition of court decisions. Judicial transparency has also
been strengthened, with a large number of adjudicatory documents posted online
(Ahl 2016; Harvard Law Review 2020; Liebman et al. 2020; Xi 2022) and court
hearings broadcast live using new technologies (Tang et al. 2022). These measures
increase the legitimacy of both the state and the judiciary while allowing Beijing to
better control the behavior of judges.

Chinese courts stress the legitimacy of both the judiciary and the state, whereas
courts in liberal democracies focus primarily on the legitimacy of the judiciary.
While the legitimacy of the state and courts often overlap, the state's legitimacy
tends to take precedence in conflicts. Strict adherence to the law can enhance the
legitimacy of the courts, but if it threatens social stability, compromises must be
made (Su and He 2010). The courts are expected to prioritize the state's political
goals at all times.

The characteristics of Chinese courts are determined by the policies and approaches used to boost state legitimacy. During Mao's era, the focus was on class
struggles, and ideological indoctrination was a major method used to increase legitimacy. The courts' primary function was to use criminal trials to suppress class
enemies. In the post-Deng Xiaoping era, the characteristics of the courts are closely
linked to policies related to economic development, dispute resolution, and stability maintenance, as this book will demonstrate.

Regional Variations

As argued in a previous work (Ng and He 2017a, 6–14), there are significant regional variations in Chinese courts. In economically developed regions, courts
tend to rely more heavily on laws, while in economically disadvantaged areas fewer
laws are utilized. It is crucial to understand the operation of courts within their
political, administrative, social, and economic contexts. While some forms of embeddedness may have been reduced after the 2014 judicial reforms, they have not
been eliminated entirely. The embedded nature of Chinese courts continues to
persist.

The governance model aligns with this thesis, as it recognizes that while all
courts in China are tasked with implementing policies and enhancing legitimacy,
they are not all in identical positions. Different courts may have varying levels
of professionalism among their judges, operate in social environments where

guanxi (social connections) hold more influence, or possess different logistical and technological resources. Moreover, the policies to be implemented can differ across regions. For some courts, economic development may be prioritized, while for others environmental protection may take precedence. Some courts may need to favor local state-owned enterprises, while others may not consider this significant. In regions like Xinjiang and Tibet, the courts must pay special attention to conflicts related to ethnic minorities.

Indeed, even when courts are tasked with implementing the same policy, their approaches can vary. For instance, while dispute resolution is a common policy goal for all courts in China today, there are regional differences in how cases are resolved. In economically less developed areas, mediation is more extensively employed. The caseload pressure is lower, and judges may have lower levels of professionalism. Therefore, they tend to rely more on mediation, which takes more time and does not require sophisticated legal skills. In contrast, in economically more developed areas, the caseload is heavier, and efficiency is a greater concern. Mediation may still be used, but to a lesser extent. Judges in these regions are often more well-versed in legal analysis, allowing them to render judgments more comfortably. Consequently, a greater reliance on legal principles and laws is observed in these areas.

The policy priorities of local party-states have a significant impact on how the law is used in courts. For example, in less-developed hinterland areas the courts generally receive fewer administrative litigation cases. This is because the major policy goal of the local party-states in these areas is to develop the local economy, and as a result the party-state may prioritize administrative expedience for the execution of development policies over legalistic approaches. In contrast, in more developed areas, an unconstrained administrative power for development becomes less important for the local party-state, and administrative law can become more useful in resolving social conflicts (He 2013). Moreover, the social wealth brought by a developed economy allows local governments and agencies in more developed areas to allocate more resources towards conflict resolution.

Roadmap

Interweaving the law on the books with laws in action, this book draws upon extensive empirical scholarship in both the Chinese and English language. It synergizes, updates, and expands the existing literature, complementing it with fresh research based on court statistics, public opinion polling, and interviews with judges, lawyers, and litigants. It documents not only the institutional rules, but also the behavioral patterns of the judges and other players revolving around the courts.

This book narrates stories about how agents think and behave. The Party may be the director, but many players improvise. There is no preset script for the show.

Here, our cast of characters is large: judges, lawyers, and prosecutors. There is also a shifting cast of amateurs or semiprofessionals: the people's assessors and legal workers. How far can the courts challenge the government's decisions? What are the political and professional "protocols" of the judges? How can the courts control their behavior? How do the judges interact with other political actors—their political bosses, the police, and the prosecutors? The book also explores how the courts make decisions in the major categories of cases—civil, criminal, and administrative. Which actions can be taken and which cannot? Where are the boundaries? How are cases processed? How does the general public, including those men and women who bear the outcomes of court proceedings, view the courts?

Indeed, the courtroom is only a point of entry into selected social disputes that are deeply revealing of Chinese society. This book is as much an account of Chinese courts in action as a social ethnography of China in the midst of momentous social change. Chinese courts are evolving, as are China's society and political landscape. In this sense, the book is as sociological as it is historical: How have Chinese courts come to take the shape they hold today? As the state weighs various governance tactics, Chinese courts change amid the legal and political developments, institutional intricacies, and the forces of social culture. Piecing the changes and all the questions above together are the two pillars that lead to governance: policy implementation and legitimacy enhancement.

Setting the stage for the cast and stories, Chapter 1 begins with an introduction to the structures and jurisdictions of the courts. How has the situation developed historically and what were the recent reforms? What was the situation of the courts after Deng Xiaoping's reforms? What did Xiao Yang (SPC President 1998–2008) achieve? Why did Wang Shengjun (SPC President 2008–13) make a left turn, and what did he launch? What legacies of Xiao Yang were kept intact or even strengthened, and for what reasons? What were the problems of the judiciary before Xi Jinping? What are the goals, major components, and implications of the reforms? Why were some policies intensified during a certain period of time? The chapter highlights the developments of several phases in China's judicial reforms in the midst of the political and social environment over the last four decades.

Chapter 2 puts the work of the judges under the microscope. Who are the judges? What do they do? How are they disciplined and promoted? What are their incentives? What are their inspirations? How have they been affected by current reforms aimed at instilling legal professionalism? The prevailing view is that the reforms have offered the judges more autonomy. This chapter argues instead that the state's control over the judges has been tightened. As state agents, they have become more accountable than independent. The chapter focuses on the reforms' impacts on the judges' workloads, promotions, pressures, and feelings of prestige. In particular, the discussion addresses the extralegal influences that the judges face. It contends that there are two types of influences on them—legitimate and illegitimate—and with the decline of illegitimate influences, the legitimate influences have increased.

The original hierarchical control has been truncated, but the current control has become panoptic.

Chapter 3 turns to the people's assessors, who, according to the law, share the same decision-making power that the judges wield. The people's assessors were a marginal institution in much of the post-Mao period, but their role has recently been strengthened. What does the new Assessors' Law introduce? How have the reform measures been implemented? Does the law enhance the assessors' legitimacy, as intended? The chapter focuses on the impact of "the random selection" of the assessors and their "meaningful participation"—two key reform measures intended to improve the courts' functioning. The discussion reveals a dilemma of this institution: the regime wants it to present an image of judicial democracy but cannot afford not to control it. This dilemma explains why, despite enormous investments and efforts to improve the assessors' role, the desired improvement remains limited.

Chapter 4 explores the roles of lawyers in Chinese courts. Rather than criticize the state's treatment of them, as the literature viewing the courts from the independence perspective or the rights-protection approach does, the chapter explains why this group of court participants remains marginal. The discussion starts from the issue of "unlicensed" legal workers. Why are they allowed? How do they interact with judges and compete against other service providers? Then the discussion moves to formal, licensed lawyers. What roles do these lawyers play in civil and criminal trials? To what extent do they contribute to the case outcomes? What is the fate of *weiquan* (rights-advocating) lawyers, a once widely acclaimed but now almost extinct species? Overall, are Chinese lawyers a profession without professionalism?

The party-state's reliance on the law to govern, and the mistrust of the general public toward the law and the courts, constitute a constant tension. Chapter 5 first discusses Chinese citizens' primary belief in legal consciousness—*guanxi*—when they encounter the law in the courts. It then moves to their second belief—petitioning—that litigants often pursue when they lose their cases. What are the views of petitioners, who protest the court decisions in upper-level courts or government institutions after exhausting their legal remedies? It then examines the extent to which procedural justice factors in civil litigants' views of the courts. Among those who have experienced the courts, which elements determine their impression of the courts? Is it the outcome of the case, or whether they have been treated fairly in the process? I will demonstrate that, unlike in Western societies, procedural justice provides few cushion effects for Chinese litigants when they are required to accept unfavorable outcomes. This chapter concludes after demonstrating the dilemma of Chinese courts in improving public confidence in the judiciary, considering that the courts are employed as a mechanism for governance.

Civil justice is the most important division of the courts, in terms of the volume of cases handled. Chapter 6 begins with the question whether Chinese civil trials have become adversarial. The discussion shows that, under their increased caseloads, the courts have incorporated many elements of adversarialism, but that the state's control over judges has pushed the system back toward inquisitorialism. What, then, is the outcome gap between the haves and the have-nots? Nonetheless, due to the regime's efforts to enhance legitimacy, China's courts' performance in handling civil cases has been greatly improved, with local protectionism declining and the enforcement of judgments becoming more effective.

Chapter 7 focuses on Chinese courts' role in alternative dispute resolution. The courts are deeply engaged in both pretrial and in-trial mediations. The rationale is straightforward: mediation addresses efficiency, stability, and legitimacy concerns. Despite some ups and downs in the state policy on mediation, it continues to permeate the pretrial stage and all in-trial stages of civil trials. Regardless of many problems in due process and equality, mediation is allowed, encouraged, and even preferred. In contrast, the courts' role in arbitration is pretty much in line with international best practices. The inconsistent role of the courts in mediation and arbitration actually indicates that the Party has various policy priorities and employs different approaches to enhance legitimacy.

Traditionally, the iron triangle—the police, the procuratorate, and the courts—has been the underlying model shaping China's criminal justice system. Have trials become of greater substance after the recent reforms? Chapter 8 argues that, due to the concerns of efficiency and stability, the plea leniency system has moved the procuratorate to the center stage and, as a result, the courts have been further marginalized. The death penalty is also manipulated to enhance legitimacy and maintain stability, which is consistent with the trend of leniency.

Chapter 9 demonstrates that administrative litigation has also undergone tremendous changes. After the 2014 amendment to the Administrative Litigation Law (ALL), the traditional three difficulties—"to file the lawsuit, to adjudicate cases, and to enforce judgments"—have been ameliorated. Still, the courts' political status remains rather weak. After all, administrative litigation is a minor instrument in governance. Administrative litigation's development also depends on its interaction with administrative reconsideration. Administrative mediation remains popular. I argue that the relationship between the courts and other state agents is the key to understanding administrative litigation's trajectory and its role in governance.

As this book is being written, the focus on the law in the official discourse of the Chinese party-state is being renewed and heightened. The slogan "ruling the country according to law" has dominated the speeches of Xi Jinping. Is such talk simply a pretext for, and a prelude to, further control from an authoritarian state? Can the rule of law take root in China? In the book's Conclusion, I argue that, whereas judges are likely to become more professional, they are unlikely to deviate from the current, highly instrumentalist, paradigm. Very likely, the policy-implementing nature of Chinese courts will persist. Rights protection, if any, has to be in the service of the state's legitimacy and governance. Even the most professionally minded judges in China are unlikely to embrace a rights-based notion of the rule of law.

1

Historical Background and Judicial Reforms under Xi Jinping

Since the initiation of Deng Xiaoping's reforms in the 1980s, the skeleton of the judiciary has barely changed. In keeping with the civil law model, Chinese courts are, by and large, organized in correspondence with the level of government. At the apex is the Supreme People's Court (SPC), in parallel with the central government. Basic, intermediate, and high courts correspond respectively to the county (district), prefectural (municipal), and provincial administrative levels, and together they are called local courts. In other words, including the SPC, the courts have four tiers. There are also special courts, such as maritime, military, financial, and intellectual property courts, and others (Organic Law of the People's Courts, Art. 15) (see Figure 1.1.), which handle only a minimal proportion of the cases.

The two-tier appellate system has not been changed either. The appeals court's decision is final. According to the laws, only errors in fact and legal application, or the submission of new evidence, can change a decided case. Also left largely unaltered are the courts' jurisdictions: "By level and by territory" has been the general principle, although issues at stake that require higher courts to hear a case at first instance have been shifting across time and space. In most cases, the principle of the defendant applies, which means that civil lawsuits are to be brought at the court of the domicile or habitual residence of the defendant (Civil Procedure Law (CiPL), Art. 22). Procedurally, under the ordinary procedure for civil cases, each case is to be tried by a collegial panel, usually consisting of three judges or people's assessors. However, most civil cases are handled under the simplified procedure, in which only one judge sits on the bench (CiPL, Art. 40).

Nevertheless, the muscle around the skeleton—the internal organization of each court—has been built up. Nowadays, most of the basic-level courts have adjudicative divisions, such as civil and criminal divisions, along with administrative, case-filing, trial-supervision, and enforcement divisions. Non-adjudicatory departments have proliferated, such as the general office, the department of logistics, the political division, and the disciplinary group. Regional variations are palpable. In regions where the caseload is explosively large, a court may have several civil divisions in addition to the specialized divisions of intellectual property, family and adolescence, labor, and foreign-related cases. By contrast, in areas with only a handful of administrative cases, the comprehensive division takes care of all residual types of cases other than civil and criminal ones.

The Judicial System of China. Xin He, Oxford University Press. © Xin He 2025. DOI: 10.1093/9780198927815.003.0002

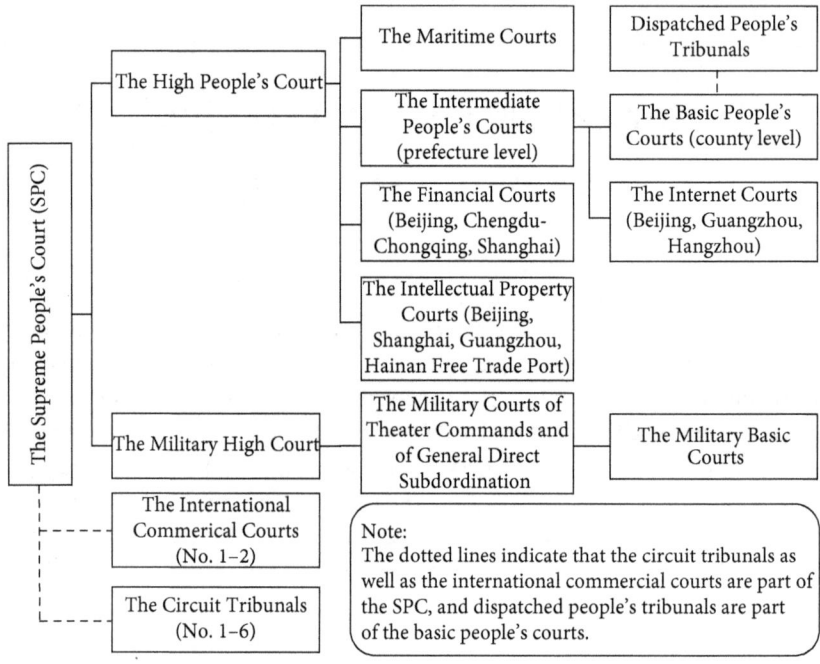

Figure 1.1 Organization of the Chinese Court System

What was the situation of the courts immediately after Deng Xiaoping's reforms? What were the characteristics of the judiciary throughout the course of the reforms? Were there any zigs or zags? What problems was the judiciary facing before Xi Jinping took power? What measures have been taken to overcome those problems? The answers to these questions inform us about how the Chinese court system has taken its current shape.

Policy implementation and legitimacy enhancement are key to understanding the history of the courts. Various policy agendas were weighted differently across the reform period. In the early stages of Deng's reforms, the availability of judges was a major concern, as was the court infrastructure: court officials were worried about the availability of office space, furniture, and telephones, and access to vehicles. These were crucial for effective dispute resolution and a positive image for the legal system. Stability maintenance was not explicitly mentioned, in part because social order was being maintained by the anticrime Strike Hard Campaign.

In Jiang Zemin's era, dispute resolution emerged as the prominent concern, and professionalism was highlighted as a response. Soon, however, the state became worried about social stability. The legitimacy crisis continued, as did many other problems. Since Xi's rise to power, legitimacy enhancement has been stressed, and popularity and political royalty have become the key tenets.

Deng Xiaoping's Era

If the Chinese courts remain politically marginal in today's political landscape, they were almost nonexistent during the tumultuous years of the Cultural Revolution, from 1966 to 1976. The political-legal apparatuses—the police, the procuratorate, and the courts—were "smashed" (Jiang 1989, 9,11). Chinese courts, to the extent that they were still functioning, handled only a few criminal or family cases (Xu 2020, 201–205). After Deng Xiaoping's reforms in the late 1970s, the Chinese courts were literally rebuilt from scratch. Deng personally stated that the reforms should "have one hand on economy and the other on the legal system." Under his auspices, a series of new legislation was passed, such as the Constitution (1978), the Organic Law of the People's Courts (1979), the Criminal Law (1979), the Criminal Procedure Law (CrPL) (1979), and the CiPL (Trial) (1982). However, the existence of these pieces of legislation raised questions—who would be tasked with implementing them? And did the judges themselves understand the laws in the first place?

Manpower

At the early stage of Deng's period, virtually anyone could be appointed as a judge. The Organic Law of the People's Courts of July 1, 1979, stated: "Citizens who have the right to vote and to stand for election and have reached the age of 23 are eligible" (Art. 34). In practice, however, until the 1990s many courts faced a shortage of adjudicating staff. Many appointees had received no formal legal training; indeed, many of them had received no formal education. According to Jiang Hua (1989), the president of the SPC during the period 1975–83, the judiciary across the nation had only 58,000 staff members in 1980, or an average of fewer than 30 for each court. Many dispatched tribunals—court divisions stationed in rural areas for local litigants' easy access—were staffed by only one person (Jiang 1989, 306). Many judges had to act as both the adjudicator and the clerk recording the process, and likewise, many clerks were also adjudicating cases (Ding 2014, 98; Jiang 1989, 306). Of the limited number of staff members, in 1984 not even 3 percent had received systematic legal training (Zheng 1994, 417). A considerable percentage of them were "illiterate or half-illiterate" (Jiang 1989, 307). The statement that "judges were nightclub hostesses and court presidents were illiterate" (Y. He 2018, 218) might be an exaggeration, yet in the Dexing court in Jiangxi Province, none of the 11 court presidents from 1950 to 1992 had completed higher education (Chronicle of the Court at Shangrao Region 1996, 90–91).

To ameliorate the shortage of manpower, the courts used several channels to enhance recruitment. The major channel for recruitment was from society, and high school graduates or factory workers were targeted (Y. He 2018, 57; see also Ding 2014, 95). Some candidates were from other government apparatuses, while others were discharged military officers. Either way, the quality from these sources was by no means good. In a Chongqing court, one-third were of poor physical health. A cadre recruited to court in Hunan Province was so undereducated that he was incapable of minute-taking. The courts were one of the main hosts for the placement of demobilized military officers, an important political task (Jiang 1989, 307–308).

Law schools have mushroomed in China since the 1990s. During the Cultural Revolution, only two law schools—Peking University and Jilin University—were allowed to operate, but by the end of the 1970s law schools had been established across the country and student enrollments had increased dramatically (Liang 2008, 58–59). By 1988, there were 81 law schools. By April 2006, 620 institutes offered an undergraduate major in law (Biddulph 2010, 266). In 2023, the number of students enrolled in LLB programs was more than 700,000 (Ministry of Education 2023). The introduction of the JM (Judicial Master) program—the so-called "Chinese JD"—signaled that Chinese legal education had abandoned the mode of the Soviet Union, with its focus on Marxism and Leninism, and had become more influenced by the US model (Biddulph 2010, 271). In 1996, only eight law schools were licensed to take JM students, but in 2005 the number had jumped to 50 (Zhu 2007, 533), and in 2015 it was 186 (Liu 2016, 418). Indeed, full-time and part-time JM programs, charging from 30,000 to 70,000 yuan for tuition, have become the primary source of income for law schools. Long-distance, evening, self-learning, and correspondence programs have also flourished, and the array of opportunities has opened the gates of legal education to students of various backgrounds and ages. The schools have lowered their entry requirements over time, causing enrollment rates to expand remarkably. Reminiscent of US law schools in the 1950s, the programs take in anyone, as long as they can write the check. Most legal practitioners, including legal workers, lawyers, judges, and prosecutors, who may not have received formal legal training, have had their degrees "upgraded" (i.e., bought) (see the speech given by Zhang Fusen, then the justice minister, quoted in Zhu 2007, 533).

The early shortage of court staff was soon alleviated, and graduates with formal legal training have become the main source of the "new blood". New hires usually start as assistants to the judges, before themselves being promoted to judges. According to Fu and Cullen (2011a, 32), "During the 1980s, more than 80 percent of the law school graduates joined various legal organs. … By the late 1980s, judges in the SPC, HPCs [Higher Provincial Courts] and courts in the coastal, economically advanced cities were highly professionalized."

Courthouses

The physical condition of the courthouses has experienced similar changes. According to Jiang Hua (1989, 310–311), in 1983, more than 100 county courts and a majority of intermediate courts in Yunnan Province did not have courtrooms, and hearings were conducted in classrooms, borrowed auditoriums, courtyards, and even beneath trees. Tables and chairs were set up temporarily. It was common for seven to eight cadres to be crammed into one office, with two or more judicial cadres sharing one table. Due to the lack of space, laying case files on the floor was the solution. Moreover, many dispatched tribunals did not have a fixed location, and adjudicators often carried a bag of case files to be used in the hearings, thus earning nicknames such as "the Handbag Court," or "the Beggars' Court." In Sichuan Province, three-quarters of the courts did not even have a single prison van, and judges ferried criminal suspects from the detention center to the courthouse by public transportation or bicycle. According to Zheng Tianxiang (1994, 394), the SPC president during the period 1983 to 1988, "when criminal defendants were taken to court hearings on foot, their family members would bring them dim sum and fruits at the crossroads; some would embrace and kiss them in public, resulting in vicious repercussions. Isn't it ridiculous that such a scene appears in the People's Republic of China?"

One of the most conspicuous reforms enacted by Deng Xiaoping was the decentralization of power, in which local governments were encouraged to become financially self-reliant. The fiscal policy known as "eating in different kitchens," which sought to separate the central and local governments, was adopted (Young 2000, 1099). Under this policy, the local governments were solely responsible for covering the budgets and operating costs of the local courts. The policy required the separation of the filing fees from the budget: the filing fees were to be handed in to the local governments, and the budget was to be made independent of the filing fees. In developed areas, this arrangement was fine, but in undeveloped areas it was a grave problem. In many courts in Yunnan and Sichuan Provinces in 1983, the annual budget was only large enough to pay for half a year. The cadres' salaries were misappropriated to cover the operating costs, and there was no money for stationery, nor was there paper for judgments. In Jilin Province, the courts could not conduct out-of-court investigations because of the financial constraints; in Henan, three court presidents resigned because of budget deficits (Jiang 1989, 310). These were consequences that Deng may not have anticipated at the time.

Without a sufficient budget from the local governments, the courts were on their own. In 1997, the total budgetary funds for all courts were 790 million yuan, while extrabudgetary funds hit 3.91 billion, or five times the budgetary amount (He 2009b, 466). When one dispatched tribunal eventually gained its own building in the early 2000s, it rented out all of its first-floor rooms for additional income—from a garage to a legal worker's office (for more on legal workers, see Chapter 4), a barbershop, and a China Mobile store (Ding 2014, 83–85). For other courts, the filing fees were the main source of income (He 2009b). This dire financial situation persisted into the 2000s. In 2003, each division of a Hunan court had to share the financial burden, and indeed each of the judicial cadres, whether they were an adjudicating judge or not, was assigned a quota to fulfill. Their salary and bonus were to be withheld should they fail to "meet the target" (He 2009b, 466). Some courts doubled the nationally standardized filing fees. Litigant parties were also charged for enforcement costs, even though the law makes it clear that the courts are fully responsible for these. In Shaanxi Province, a dispatched tribunal was equipped with nothing more than a worn-out minivan. To fuel this gas-guzzler, the tribunal relied on the litigants and, occasionally, a nearby "electrical plant" (Ding 2014, 90). To obtain more filing fees, judges would scout potential cases (Liao and Li 2005, 327), triggering a multitude of corrupt activities and complaints (He 2008).

Relying on these sources of income in addition to funds provided by the local governments, most basic-level courts had managed to obtain their own buildings by the 2000s, but the exact locations were left for the local governments to decide. A Shaanxi local court was built on an abandoned chemical park, far from the city center. Wei Ding describes that, "Public transportation was not available; the smelly tap water looked yellow, undrinkable even after being boiled" (2014, 88). Litigants frequently complained that the court's geographic location was too remote and inaccessible. Some judges heard cases during the weekend in a legal workers' office located in the city center (Ding 2014, 89). The First Intermediate Court of the Beijing Municipality was, notoriously, located in Babaoshan, a suburban area known for being the capital's cemetery. The locations of the courts speak volumes about the marginal political status of the judiciary in China's political landscape.

Nonetheless, due to China's rapid economic development and the central government's decision to reallocate resources to less-developed areas, the office conditions of most courts has quickly improved. For example, in 2007, dispatched tribunals in Guangzhou each had an average area of 2442.65 square meters, and all were equipped with computers. Each tribunal received 5.75 million yuan in infrastructure investment. Today, most court buildings are somewhat grandiose, with an imposing crest and wide steps leading to the main gate, depicting the grandeur of the law.

The Trial-mode Reform

During the 1980s, legal caseloads increased steadily and cases became more complex. Economic cases—those involving at least one institution as a litigating party—increased from 44,000 in 1983 to 690,000 in 1989, or 15.7 times within six years. The 1982 CiPL (trial) (Art. 6) stated that the courts should focus on mediation and adjudicate only after mediation had failed. The process was extremely inquisitorial. The judges had to collect evidence or even conduct investigations by themselves, thereby taking on the role of a lawyer (actually more akin to the role of a prosecutor). They had limited space in which to conduct hearings, and little authority to ensure that court decisions were enforced; the dominant approach to handling civil disputes had to be mediation. Neither litigants nor judges cared as much about procedural justice as they did about substantive justice.

Facing skyrocketing caseloads, the courts would soon have collapsed under this mode of justice. Repetitive mediations, when combined with the inquisitorial approach, were just too time-consuming (Huang 2010). Subsequently, the CiPL was amended in 1991, shifting the burden of proof to the party making the claim. The trial mode was also reformed—the open trial replaced the pretrial phase as the key stage; the evidence presented by the parties became more crucial than that collected by the judges; and adjudication replaced mediation as the dominant approach for civil justice (Ren 2005, 313; cf., Fu 2023, 62). With some adversarial elements, the primary cost of collecting evidence shifted from the courts to the litigants, and the judges conducted themselves more as arbitrators than as lawyers or prosecutors. The formal, procedure-based trial format also made processing the cases more efficient.

By any standard, Deng Xaioping's era set the foundations for Chinese courts today. The courts began to have enough judges (although not necessarily competent ones) and enough office space. The laws and the courts were new, and whether laws could be enforced was a concern for the top leaders. As a result, to "strictly enforce the law," was printed in Peng Zhen's calligraphy on a placard and hung in the lobbies of both the SPC and other courts across the country (see Table 1.1) (Potter 1995, 1). The three sets of procedural laws—criminal, civil, and administrative—were in place alongside the formal adjudication mode. The enforcement department was separated from other divisions of the courts (Ren 2005, 314).

However, the new era also brought about many problems: recruiting judges from various sources and backgrounds led to the formation of a group of unprofessional judges; financially relying on local governments led to an increase in local protectionism; and the frequent use of the Strike Hard Campaign led to the inadequate protection of human rights and an inability to establish the legal principle of due process.

With all of these problems, the courts are continuously being reformed. In 1999, the judiciary launched the first five-year outline for judicial reforms, and in 2024 it is implementing its fifth set of reforms. Those reforms have been compelled by perhaps the most dramatic economic development in human history—no words can overstate the extent to which China has transformed over the last four decades. China's GDP per capita has leaped 231 times—from 385 yuan in 1978 to 89,358 yuan in 2023 (*Xinhua News* 2024). Population mobility, the public's level of education, the mode of medical services, and the forms taken by culture, art, and even

Table 1.1 Outline of the History of Chinese Courts for the Period 1978–2024

The Party Leader	Deng Xiaoping	Jiang Zemin (Hu Jingtao)		Xi Jinping
The SPC Presidents	Jiang Hua (1978–83); Zheng Tianxiang (1983–88); Ren Jianxin (1998–2008)	Xiao Yang (1998–2008)	Wang Shengjun (2008–13)	Zhou Qiang (2013–23) and Zhang Jun (2023–)
Focuses	Judge Recruitment; Court Infrastructure; Adjudicatory Mode Reform; Anti-crime Strike Hard Campaign	Professionalism; Formalism; Judicial Autonomy; Centralized Death Penalty Review	Judicial Activism	Judges Quota Reform; Elevation of Court Budgetary and Personnel Decisions; Smart Courts; the Belt and Road Initiative
Problems	Local Protectionism; Unprofessional Judges	Legitimacy Crisis; Judicial Corruption; Mounting Petitions	Legitimacy Crisis; Judicial Corruption; Mounting Petitions	Pressured Judges
Slogans	Strict Enforcement of the Law	Fairness and Efficiency	Judiciary for the People	To Allow the Masses to Feel Justice in Every Case
Characteristics	Dispute Resolution	Dispute Resolution; Stability Maintenance	Dispute Resolution; Stability Maintenance	Dispute Resolution; Stability Maintenance; Legitimacy Enhancement

freedom have witnessed a sea change (Hessler 2015; Osnos 2012). Numerous and sometimes new genres of conflicts have been generated by the country's increased economic and social activities (He 2007).

Xiao Yang's Westernized Reforms and Setbacks

Xiao Yang, the SPC president during the period 1998 to 2008, left indelible marks that still affect the operation of the courts today. No biography of Xiao Yang has yet been written, but he surely deserves one. He was appointed to the position when the Party's leadership had promoted the separation between the Party and the government. During the 10 years that he served as the SPC president, Chinese society was laden with contentious conflicts that arose from the transition of a planned economy to a market one. It was also a time when social stability became an imminent concern for the state, and the judiciary suffered minimal legitimacy. Facing these challenges, Xiao Yang's responses were to promote professionalism, formalism, anticorruption, transparency, neutrality, and trial independence in the court system (Keith et al. 2014, 24–27).

One of the most significant and lasting achievements of Xiao Yang's tenure as the SPC president was a reform to improve the educational qualifications of judges (Peerenboom 2009, 87). Whereas the first Judges Law (1995) separated judges from other bureaucrats,[1] during Xiao Yang's reign the threshold for judges was raised significantly. The 2001 amended Judges Law states that passing the National Uniform Judicial Exam—an equivalent of the bar exam in the US—is a prerequisite for entry-level judges (Art. 12). "Without legal education, experience, skills, or professional ethics, one can no longer join the force of judges (Xiao 2003, 9)." Xiao also strengthened academic training for incumbent judges (Judges Law 2001 amended, Art. 9). The courts have since recruited more law school graduates to be judges than people from other sources. Discharged military officers, previously a significant source of judicial cadres for decades, ceased to join the courts, largely because most of them were unable to pass the bar examination.

Now, two decades since the educational requirement came into effect, most Chinese judges have received formal legal training. As recently as 1995, the percentage of judges with a college degree was merely 6.9 per cent, whereas since 2005 over half of Chinese judges have earned university degrees (Liebman 2008, 625). Even though some degrees might have been obtained by "writing a check," this achievement was nevertheless remarkable. Today, most newly recruited judges are college educated. In fact, in most cities and coastal areas, a master's degree is a prerequisite for an assistant judgeship. The thresholds have continually been raised. The 2019 Judges Law specifies the educational qualifications for being a judge as follows: either a bachelor's degree in law, a nonlaw bachelor's degree but with a JM or master of laws, or a nonlaw bachelor's degree but with legal expertise (Art. 12.5). "In areas having difficulty in fulfilling such requirements, a bachelor's degree is also allowed, *only if approved by the SPC*." (emphasis added)

With the quality of the judges thus enhanced, Xiao Yang accelerated and systematized the judicial reforms that had previously been launched. A key word was "formalism." Chinese judges now dress in a more Westernized black judicial

---

[1] According to Art. 2 of the Judges Law (1995), judges are "judicial persons who exercise the judicial authority of the State according to law, and they include the presidents, vice-presidents, members of judicial committees, chief judges and associate chief judges of divisions, judges and assistant judges of the Supreme People's Court, local People's Courts at various levels and special People's Courts such as military courts."

gown and have become accustomed to the use of a gavel in the courtroom, both of which were introduced to the Chinese courts under Xiao (Xiao 2003, 7). At the same time, more substantive reforms occurred in both civil and criminal trials (Xiao 2003, 7). In response to the growing volume of civil disputes, civil procedures were strengthened. The prevailing slogans adopted under Xiao were "fairness" and "efficiency," twin terms with unique meanings. Fairness was traditionally defined as substantive justice, but under Xiao it referred more to procedural justice or party autonomy. There has also been a shift from "judge-centric justice" to "party-centric justice" (Fu and Cullen 2011a, 40), in which the judges have been relieved from most of the fact-finding responsibilities and thus can focus on "legal delicacies" (Fu and Cullen 2011a, 40). Core to this reform was the SPC's launch of the new evidence rules for civil justice (2001), which stipulated that the parties are to exchange evidence before the trial and that only new evidence can be submitted after a given time limit (SPC 2001, Art. 43). These rules force the parties to submit evidence in a timely and professional manner (Fu and Cullen 2011a, 41). Xiao believed that fairness, conscience, openness and professionalism were the keys to enhancing legitimacy (A. Chen 2018, 160). Of course, none of this can be achieved without a certain degree of trial independence (Keith et al. 2014, 27).

One measurement of judicial efficiency is the time limit for handling civil cases. Under the CiPL, the court must deliver its decision within either three or six months after receiving a case, depending respectively on whether the Simplified or the Ordinary Procedure was adopted. Another important measurement is the case closure rate, which is a yardstick for the effectiveness and efficiency of court operations. The annual work reports of most courts have indicated an almost 100 percent case closure rate. As was mentioned in the Introduction, China's judiciary is one of the most efficient in the world.

In addition to professionalism and formalism, which Xiao believed were crucial in effective dispute resolution and legitimacy enhancement, he also reconciled stability maintenance with human rights protection. A graduate of the prestigious Renmin Law School, Xiao Yang had been innovative in balancing punishment and social activities in his earlier career as a top prosecutor in Guangdong Province. Within the scope of criminal justice, he had made numerous reforms in relation to human rights protection. Yet, his most noteworthy contribution was the centralized ratification of the death penalty by the SPC. From 1983 to 2006, the ratification power had been held by the Higher Provincial Courts (HPCs), in an effort to punish criminals "severely and swiftly." In 2007, the SPC took that power back—a change that is estimated to have reduced the number of actual executions by a half to two-thirds (Liu 2012, quoted in Li 2014, 115). The change also standardized the criteria for the sentencing of death penalties. Most importantly, however, the change conveyed a message that the application of the death penalty shall be "extremely strict" (Xiao 1999, 20). Xiao insisted that severe punishment must be limited to a tiny proportion of offenders, whose crimes are nothing short of hideous. These criminals are to be sentenced to death in accordance with the policies of "Killing Fewer, Killing Cautiously" (Trevaskes 2010b, 353).

The death penalty reform was no mean feat. For this change, Xiao Yang openly fought against Luo Gan, then a standing member of the politburo and the most senior leader in political-legal affairs. Luo insisted on the Strike Hard policy for social stability, an approach that the Party had adopted upon the establishment of the republic. Taking advantage of the dominant harmonious society policy under Hu Jintao, Xiao forcefully argued that a more humane approach to the death penalty and punishment would lead to a more harmonious society (Trevaskes 2010b, 350, 352–353). In reconciling the tension between stability maintenance and rights protection, Xiao unleashed a new era upon China's criminal justice system.

As a result of Xiao Yang's reforms, Chinese courts and judges at that time looked more like their Western counterparts. Of course, for politically sensitive cases, the streets might still be used as a courtroom (Su and He 2010), but the "Handbag Courts" vanished, and there was a sharp decline in "the courthouse on horseback" (Liu 2006), whereby judges travelled to mountainous villages to resolve disputes. In most cases, the judges examined case files and conducted hearings within the courthouses. Moreover, the number of civil cases that ended with mediation also declined sharply. In the mid-1980s, the mediation rate was 70 percent, but it had dropped to 30 percent by the mid-2000s. Many judges with formal legal training preferred adjudication over mediation because adjudication was considered more efficient and consistent with procedural justice. Under the rigid time limits and the emphasis on case closure rates, there was no time to mediate repetitively (Fu and Cullen 2011a, 38–39). However, the newly introduced adversarial proceedings were confrontational, making settlements rather difficult (He and Ng 2013a).

Nonetheless, Xiao Yang's reforms in formalism and trial independence were quickly put under attack and left largely abandoned. His reforms had occurred during a time when China's social conflicts had mounted as a result of rapid social transformation. Hu Jintao had promoted "the Harmonious Society" for a reason. In the early 2000s, the number of petitions to Beijing had surged (Li et al. 2012). The courts were directly blamed for this upsurge, because a large proportion of petitions to Beijing were related to failures of the lower courts. During the period 1998 to 2002, the courts received 42 million petitions (SPC Work Report 2003), and an official survey estimated that 80 percent of the petitions to the National People's Congress were well-grounded (Wang 2003).

As Peerenboom (2009b, 176) argues, the courts may not be "the proper venue for resolving many of the nation's socially, politically, and economically contentious issues." Some of the problematic issues had arisen as a result of the kinds of political sensitivities that appear in a single-party regime, some were doctrinally difficult, and others were related to problems commonly seen in middle-income countries. Nonetheless, in the eyes of the Party, the courts that failed to close cases were equated with failures of the bureaucratic style of handling cases, exorbitant court fees, and corruption. The Party believed that the court reforms had placed the interests of the courts above those of the Party, thereby indicating a dangerous threat to the Party's political legitimacy. Furthermore, the court's reforms for procedural and judicial formality likely frustrated the litigants (Chapter 5). Formalized procedures and courtroom formalities failed to enhance the legitimacy or the validity of court decisions. Dissatisfied with court decisions, litigants had repeatedly petitioned to upper-level governments, which had the effect of destroying the finality and credibility of court decisions. The Party believed that the growing tensions around dispute resolution, stability maintenance, and legitimacy were on the verge of explosion.

It was not surprising, then, that during Xiao Yang's second term, the Party believed that the Westernized reforms had gone a step too far. In 2006, party authorities launched a "socialist rule-of-law theory" campaign in the courts and other legal institutions, stressing loyalty to the Party and the need to avoid the pernicious influence of Western rule-of-law theories (Minzner 2011). A judiciary serving the needs of the people replaced fairness and efficiency as the tenet of the judiciary (Minzner 2011). Close to the end of his second term, Xiao Yang himself instructed the judges to "mediate cases that could be mediated, adjudicate cases that should be adjudicated, combining mediation with adjudication, concluding the cases and ending the dispute concurrently" (Xiao 2006, 5). Whether this sudden change in policy was a representation of his true will remains unclear.

Wang Shengjun's Accentuated Left Turn

The judiciary's U-turn on formalism only became clearer when Wang Shengjun was appointed as the SPC president in 2008. Without formal legal training, Wang had spent most of his career as a senior bureaucrat serving on the Party's political-legal committee. Within months, Chinese courts were enmeshed in the "Three Supremes" campaign, which emphasized Party developments, the interests of the people, and the Constitution and the law as sources for guiding judicial work. Because it was impossible to have three different elements with equal supremacy simultaneously, the sequence of those elements indicated that the Party's interests were superior to the Constitution and the law. According to Wang, the "fundamental characteristic" of the Chinese judicial system was "the organic unity of the Party's leadership, the people as the master, and rule in accordance of law" (Wang 2011, 14). Once again, rule in accordance of law was placed behind the Party's leadership.

Wang Shengjun's image of a model judge revealed his personal idea, or ideal, of what a judge should be like. Chen Yanping, a district court judge from Jiangsu Province (Minzner 2011, 950), is generously described here:

[She] has handled over 3100 cases in fourteen years; without a *single* complaint or appeal; without a *single* petition by a disgruntled party; without even *one* wrongly decided case. Her decisions are uniformly accepted by all parties ... [h]er correct work ethic, merged with her earnest desire to realize the Confucian ideal of "a world without litigation" *(tianxia wusong)*, helps her achieve the Party's goal of a "harmonious society"*(hexie shehui).*

As any person with knowledge in dispute resolution knows, it would be a fairy tale for all 3,100 court decisions to be "uniformly accepted by all parties." Under Wang's reign, the law was "disdained" (DeLisle 2017, 70). It seemed that the law had failed to fulfill its promise of furthering the state's aims and interests. The trend toward promoting judicial professionalism and formalism, in particular, was reversed. Wang emphasized the judges' political loyalty to the Party over their capabilities in adjudication. Judges were sent into the countryside to interact with the masses, so that they could become more in touch with them. Wang embraced "judicial activism": the judges were expected to forgo bureaucratic styles of adjudication, and especially the impersonal and meticulous maintenance of neutrality, and instead adopt a mass-line stance to gain rapport with the people (Keith et al. 2014, 41). He even required judges to treat litigants as loved ones, steering away from the image of a professional judiciary. Mediation was proposed to be placed above adjudication, painting the picture that one adjudicates only if mediation is out of the question. "Comprehensive coordination shall be adopted, such as education, negotiation, channeling, and remedies, et cetera" (Wang 2009, 9). In achieving a balance between legal effects and social effects, social effects should prevail. Informal dispute resolution replaced the law as the preeminent factor in judicial decision-making. In the early 2010s, the rate of mediated cases rebounded to 70 percent.

According to Wang Shengjun, public opinion should be taken into account in decision-making; the courts should endeavor to improve the level of public satisfaction (Chen 2018, 160). For the death penalty, Wang (in)famously suggested two extralegal considerations (*Caijing* 2008): the first consideration was the overall level of social security and the second was the consensus of society and the general public. This marked the first time that public sentiment, despite the difficulty in measuring it, was officially recognized as a criterion in the sentencing of death penalties—which is arguably the most important decision that a court can make. Wang stressed the severity aspect in the policy of "balancing severity and leniency," stating that, "Nowadays criminal activities are frequent, so we must impose severe punishments for those who deserve them." In the areas of constitutional and administrative disputes, grand mediation was adopted (Hand 2011), involving a multilevel, party-state political consultation in which the judiciary's role was limited.

Ineffective dispute resolutions, a legitimacy crisis, and social instability hounded the courts. A direct consequence of Wang Shengjun's populist policy was that Chinese courts became overresponsive. Litigants still refused to accept the finality of court decisions, and petitions continued to grow. The courts were forced to change their decisions to mollify disgruntled litigants. Specific funds were set aside to satisfy the petitioners (cf., the *Medical Malpractice Case*). "The squeaking wheels get more grease," and nothing was "impermissible" when the courts were influenced by petitioning (Liebman 2011, 307). Social harmony and stability took over from individuals' legal rights as the policy of utmost importance in judicial decision-making (Trevaskes et al. 2014).

Although Wang Shengjun presented and promoted a rather disparate, even weird, image of the courts and the judiciary compared with that of Xiao Yang, upon closer inspection the two had much in common. Xiao's reforms for professionalism, anticorruption, and the centralized ratification of the death penalty had survived, in the form of continuities which look puzzling but are perfectly understandable once the courts are understood to be the agents of the state. It is crystal clear that anticorruption serves the interest of the Party. Professionalism, as will be shown in Chapter 2, also boosts the Party's control over the society and other local agents. The centralized ratification of the death penalty, as Smith argues forcefully (2020, 50), helps the central authorities to regulate local agents, including the courts and the adjacent political-legal apparatuses. In this light, only Xiao Yang's reforms promoting formalism and judicial autonomy had failed, because they did not uniformly seek to boost the Party's superiority (Smith 2020, 50).

In many ways, Xiao Yang's reforms had tried to sculpt a judiciary that was less influenced by the Party. His approaches had partial successes but also created problems, such as an increase in petitions and a general dissatisfaction with the courts. Wang Shengjun, a disciple of Zhou Yongkong (Keith et al. 2014, 39), the political-legal tsar with a reputation for gravitating toward mass mobilization and social stability, allowed the judiciary to be more influenced by the Party. Still, in essence, both leaders knew quite well that, ultimately, the judiciary was to serve the governance of the state.

The Courts' Problems Prior to Xi Jinping's Reforms

On the eve of President Xi Jinping's reforms, many problems remained unrectified. First, the local courts were tightly controlled by the local governments. In addition to controlling the courts' finances, local party and administrative authorities participated prominently in appointing court officials, and as a result, "local courts had become local governments' courts" (Y. He 2018, 198). The local courts were required to support the main tasks of the government, such as economic development or birth control (He 2004). In short, the local courts were taken captive.

One reification of the "local governments' courts" was strong local protectionism or favoritism. The local courts tended to protect the interests of local litigants. Local protectionism appeared in the SPC's work reports from 1988 to 1996, and in the first five-year outline for judicial reforms issued in 1999. This practice was especially severe when state-owned enterprises (SOEs) formed the pillar of the local economy (Lubman 1999), because these were the dominant source of income for local governments. Naturally, under pressure from their local governments, the local courts gravitated toward these SOEs and other local revenue-generating litigants.

In contrast, measures taken by the local courts against nonlocal litigants were striking, and included "restrictions on case filing, fights over jurisdiction, delays on hearings, pressures in mediation, biases in adjudication, abuses in compulsory measures, and obstacles in enforcement" (Liu 2003, 90–94). An intermediate court president stated that, "For enforcement requests by non-local courts, local courts adopted the 'three no policy': no help, no serving, no enforcement. Conflicts between courts intensified. ... Some courts, to protect local litigants, even issued fake decisions, fake judgments, fake bankruptcies." (Zou 1997, 61). This left litigants at a disadvantage, with few to no opportunities for judicial redress and access to justice, purely as a result of not being local.

Relatedly, the courts had difficulties in ensuring that civil judgments were enforced (Li 2014, 156–163). Unlike courts elsewhere, Chinese courts did not just render the decisions; they were also responsible for enforcing them (CiPL 1982, 161). Indeed, prior to the mid-1980s, the adjudicating judge was responsible for enforcing his or her rulings. In the early 1990s, the courts set up an enforcement division (Y. He 2018, 249–250), and the division was subsequently elevated to "the Enforcement Bureau," headed by the court vice president, as part of efforts to combat the difficulties with enforcement. However, those enforcement entities did not provide much help, and the SPC regarded the courts' poor enforcement as their most serious deficiency (Li 2014, 157). One report suggested "Half of China's civil court rulings remain on paper," or unenforced (*People's Daily* 2004). Many reasons stood behind the poor enforcement of judgments, but a leading one was local protectionism: it was "threatening the uniformity of the legal system and damaging the judiciary's reputation," as articulated by Ren Jianxin, the SPC president from 1988 to 1998 (Ren 1989, 9).

Second, while the courts were being plagued by a lack of accountability, judicial corruption was also regarded as rampant (Gong 2004). *Guanxi* and other extralegal influences permeated every corner of the system (Li 2011; He and Ng 2017). Hundreds or perhaps thousands of Chinese judges were punished for inappropriate behavior each year (Li 2014, 76–77; *SPC Work Reports*, various years). A nonexhaustive list showed that, during the period 1995 to 2005, nine high-level court presidents were disciplined for inappropriate behavior or outright corruption (Y. He 2018, 212). In fact, at the time of writing, three former vice presidents of the SPC are currently serving jail sentences for convictions for bribery and embezzlement. Xi Xiaomin, the vice president of the SPC from 2004 to 2015, twisted court decisions in cases in which his son represented clients as the lawyer; 300 million yuan was uncovered in cash in his son's apartment. The vice president himself took bribes totaling as much as 115 million yuan. In 2020, the vice president of Hainan High Court took a bribe of 43.75 million yuan. In May 2022, an SPC judge was sentenced to 14 years in jail for both taking bribes and committing a theft of state secrets in a case involving a coal mine worth billions of yuan. Most of these corrupt activities occurred before President Xi's reforms.

It had been common practice for political leaders, inside and outside of court, to influence court decisions. The judges were also inclined to seek advice from their superiors and the Adjudication Committee, the highest decision-making body consisting of senior court officials (He 2012). The outcomes of these cases were directed by nonlegal factors, some of which were beyond the scope of the courts, and all of which made the courts an unpredictable institution (Wang and Fu 2015, 217–218). Although this may not be characterized as judicial corruption, the general public was largely unaware of how these cases were handled, and these untransparent practices often led people to form a negative impression.

Finally, there was a lack of judicial professionalism. The number of court staff increased by 5.5 times from 1978 to 2008, while the average number of cases per judge decreased (Liu 2012a, 47, 53). Many cases were not handled by frontline judges, and instead most of the deciding judges occupied administrative, logistical, supervisory, and political posts. In the Beijing Municipality in 2005, of 4,374 judicial cadres, only 1,573 were handling cases (Liu 2012a, 50). The courts' management was bureaucratic, cumbersome, and inefficient.

Furthermore, many court decisions were issued without attention to professionalism. Many judges, under pressure to dispose of cases efficiently, were not able to follow the procedural requirements closely. Yulin Fu (2021, 64) commented that, "most judges left procedural 'standardisation' primarily to legal textbooks and the petitions of lawyers." Voluntariness in mediation was seldom observed; coercive settlements were common. Inevitably, some cases were considered unfair by the litigants and the public (He and Feng 2021).

As a result, many litigants refused to accept court decisions, and petitions therefore skyrocketed. A crisis of trust had fermented—each year, dozens of violent incidents stemming from resistance to the courts' enforcement actions had occurred (Xu and Tian 2011, 7), and almost 100 sheriffs died as a result (SPC Work Reports, various years). Judges were met with retaliations for their decisions, and votes of no confidence from the delegates in the local people's congresses increased (Y. He 2018, 277–279).

Judicial Reforms under Xi

In light of all of these problems, Beijing had become increasingly worried about losing control over its agents. The judicial reforms under President Xi Jinping have, therefore, centered on strengthening the central party's leadership. Meanwhile, the central party appeared to have abandoned the grand mediation approach, which had proven only to have the capacity to solve conflicts in the short run, and had unfortunately also demonstrated the potential to create more problems in the long run.

Long-term social stability is real stability. The first obvious target for Xi was the local governments, which had traditionally influenced the courts through their budgetary and staffing decisions. One core goal of Xi's reforms has been to transform the judiciary from being the tool that harbored the stronghold of local protectionism, into an instrument that instead seeks to combat local protectionism. Yulin Fu (2021) calls these efforts "delocalization." Second, and relatedly, the central party's leadership needed a more loyal, capable, and professional judiciary that could faithfully carry out its orders and increase the social perception of fairness. The Party sought to free the judiciary from being controlled by the local governments.

In response to the Fourth Plenum of the Eighteenth Party Central Committee, in October 2014, the SPC, in February 2015, swiftly revised its fourth five-year outline for judicial reforms. These reforms include, among other matters, the elevation of court budgets to the provincial level, setting up the SPC circuit courts, strengthening adjudication powers, and overhauling the people's assessors system. The rest of this chapter will discuss the factors that affect the operations of the courts, and leave those affecting judges to the next chapter.

Elevating Personnel and Budgets to the Provincial Level

As previously mentioned, the courts' financial dependence on local governments was regarded as a primary cause of local protectionism and other local influences. To increase the central party's control over the judiciary, the natural response, via reforms, was to transfer the court budgets to a higher administrative level. The Party's 2014 Decision on the Rule of Law, therefore, moved all judicial budgeting and personnel decisions to the provincial level, in order to "solve the deeper structural problems that impede judicial fairness and limit judicial capacity."

Why was the judicial budgetary decision elevated only to the provincial level rather than all the way to Beijing? Zhang and Ginsburg (2019) argue that, "[R]emoval to Beijing would have entailed vastly greater administrative costs in return for only a moderate boost to judicial independence, which suggests that removal to the provincial level may very well have represented the optimal balance."

In reality, raising the budgetary decision-making to the provincial level has had a smaller effect than the literature suggests. The budget allocation system has helped to alleviate the budgetary gap between courts in China's coastal areas and its hinterland areas, with the central government having allocated 3 to 4 billion yuan per annum to compensate for this shortfall (The General Office of the CCP Central

Committee and the State Council 2009). The reforms to raise the budgets to the provincial level have simply institutionalized the existing practices. Moreover, the budget for support staff, and the distribution of the local allowance, still rely on the local government (Zhang 2019). According to Yueduan Wang (2021, 545), the local party-state still maintains informal influence over the courts, "from appropriating land for new courthouses to providing police protection for remote tribunals."

Elevating the level of personnel in charge of decision-making to the provincial level has brought about only one salient change—the basic-level court president is now approved by the Provincial Party Organic Committee. Other court officials—including the vice presidents of the basic-level courts—are still decided by lower-level party committees. As Ye Meng (2023) points out, the efforts to promote centralization have brought very limited impacts. According to her, the reason for this is not that the courts must rely on the local governments for financial or other material resources, but is due to the internal paradox of the regime's political structure. The Party has largely relied on the *kuai*, or "the horizontal axis," for governance. At this horizontal level, various agencies, including the courts, must co-ordinate with each other to implement policies and achieve good governance. Because the courts are part of the apparatus of that horizontal governance, the centralization of judicial power is thus limited.

Nonetheless, the outrageous practices commonly seen before the reforms, such as inflated filing fees, soliciting lawsuits, or charging litigants for court enforcement and investigations (He 2012) have diminished, if not disappeared.

Truncated Hierarchy inside the Courts

Chinese courts were extremely hierarchical in the past. Under the previous system, both the judicial processes and outcomes were tightly controlled. The hierarchical control was manifested through the courts' internal administrative structure: the case approval system and the adjudication committee.

The case approval system was sophisticated. Depending on the sensitivities, complexities, and influences of the cases, approval was needed before a decision was released (Ng and He 2017a). This practice required a responsible judge to approach their superiors (usually the division head and the president) to sign off on their judgment before releasing it. Responsible judges used a particular form to obtain the required signatures. When a judgment was released, the signature of the responsible judge alone would appear on the decision. The internal, often unwritten, nature of the signing-off process meant that senior judges could often "hide in the dark", despite their influence over case outcomes.

According to Ng and He (2017, 114), the judgment release form was a single-page document consisting of two halves. On the bottom half was a short summary of the case, drafted by the responsible judge. The top half was divided into two parts. In the upper-right quarter would be the division head's comments and signature, and in the upper-left quarter would be the signature of the president, or sometimes the vice president, of the court. The signature of the responsible party would occupy the lower-right quarter, below the case summary. The hierarchy of authority and power is materially manifested in the layout of this simple single-page form. The president's signature would occupy the most prominent space—the upper-left quarter.

Consequently, the adjudicators responsible for handling the cases did not make the decisions, and the decision-makers never heard the cases. From the 1990s onwards, outcries over this phenomenon spread throughout Chinese jurisprudence—the practice was considered an egregious violation of the principle of due process of the law, because it is widely believed that hearing cases in person is crucial to making decisions.

The judicial reforms enacted, beginning in 2014, have targeted this institutional arrangement. According to the new judicial responsibility system, the frontline judges that make the decisions are held responsible for their actions. This reform measure obviates the case approval system. In the words of the SPC (2015), "the system of seeking level-by-level approval has been revoked. Whoever tries the case shall decide the case and be held responsible for it." To ensure that such a reform is effective, the SPC and the Central Party Committee have also prohibited higher-ranking officials, both inside and outside the courts, from making inquiries or intervening in decision-making. The judges are to record any such interference, which will trigger a formal investigation from the SPC, together with the Party Disciplinary Division (SPC 2015a). Although such inquiries or interferences have rarely been recorded, the message conveyed is that the top leaders have displayed a certain sense of seriousness in targeting this matter.

Following the abolishment of this channel of hierarchical control and influence, a judge or judicial panel trying a case is now able to sign off on their decisions without any further approval. Although what constitutes an interference remains ambiguous, a report states that "the elimination of the formal approval system has made it harder—and thus less worthwhile—for leaders to interfere with their subordinates' cases under most circumstances" (Wang 2020a, 751).

At the same time, the role of the Adjudication Committee has been narrowed, despite the Committee having remained at the pinnacle of judicial decision-making within the hierarchy of Chinese courts (see more in He 2012). The Committee consists of the most senior court officials, including the president, vice presidents, and the heads of all major divisions. The Committee adopts a rigid structure of layered and hierarchical authority; power is determined by one's incumbent rank. It reviews only the most influential and difficult cases, although this is vaguely defined, with the true scope of review varying across regions, case types, courts, and levels. In the past, over 90 percent of criminal cases were reviewed in some courts, but it was not surprising for a court to have reviewed less than 15 percent of its criminal docket. Behind closed doors, voting was rare and decisions were usually unanimous, a testimony to the president's influence. Thus, the Adjudication Committee has a history of wielding immense discretion over whether a decision would follow the laws, policies, and due processes, or whether the committee ought to seek external advice. Rather than providing legal analysis or justice to litigants, the cases' social and political repercussions had become the main factors in contemplating case outcomes.

Also fundamentally lacking in the past was an established mechanism for disseminating the Committee's decisions to frontline judges. Previously, the frontline judges and the litigants would be notified of the decisions, but the rationale behind the decisions would not be disclosed. Matters pertinent to the decision-making process were often classified. The Committee's reasoning remained opaque, not just for outsiders, but also for the frontline judges. It is clear that the committee viewed day-to-day supervision and risk management as having greater importance than the development of general principles and rules for judges to follow in the future. All of this suggests, then, that the Adjudication Committee previously functioned as a hierarchical bureaucracy nodding to the power of rankings rather than to professional expertise.

One previous function of the Committee was to control decisions, and another was to dilute responsibility. Once a case had been reviewed by the Committee, the judge or the panel handling the case could be—at least partially—shielded from responsibility, should any adverse consequences occur. This provided certain protections for junior judges. However, in many cases, the protection was limited, since the judgment only showed the names of the responsible judges.

Under the reforms, however, the Adjudication Committee only has to review cases related to "foreign affairs, state security, and social stability" (SPC 2015a). The SPC states that the Adjudication Committee is only in charge of the most influential and complicated cases (SPC 2015a, Art. 32)—in other words, it is not to review cases simply because they "involve large sums of money" (Wang 2020a, 751), nor is it to review most criminal cases. One judge who was interviewed said that, recently, only a few civil and commercial cases have been heard by the Committee each year. But before the reforms, 3.4 percent of such cases were reviewed in one Shaanxi court (He 2012, 689). The SPC further states that all of the Committee members' decisions must be recorded in the minutes. In addition, the Committee is not to interfere with fact-finding. The items processed by the Committee are to be monitored, appropriately addressed, and publicized.

Under the now-truncated hierarchy, Chinese judges do indeed enjoy more autonomy when making decisions. A Guangzhou judge told Ying Sun and Hualing Fu (2022, 879):

> These days even the Political and Legal Committee does not intervene with our cases anymore and administrative departments inside the court cannot tell us

what to do either. The Political and Legal Committee does not ask about the details of a case, and its main role is to coordinate with other departments for us when needed. . . . Now we enjoy autonomy in deciding cases, as long as we follow the unified trial standards.

According to some judges, their responsibilities have become "independent judging," or even "complete independent handling of cases" (Wang 2020a, 754). Some lawyers have suggested that there have been significant improvements, and that there is only interference "if the value of the subject matter is large" (Wang 2020a, 757). Taisu Zhang and Tom Ginsburg (2019, 336) assert that "recent reforms have strengthened both judicial professionalism and judicial independence." This is a remarkable change, in the face of the reality that judicial independence is synonymous with "institutional" and "horizontal" independence from other Party and government entities, and not from the Party's leadership (Zhang and Ginsburg 2019, 332).

Circuit Tribunals of the SPC

Another reform is the SPC's establishment of "circuit tribunals" (巡回法庭) to try cases over different administrative jurisdictions. The decisions of such tribunals are the decisions of the SPC itself. They take administrative, civil, and commercial cases. The purposes of establishing the circuits are threefold: first, to relieve the SPC of being overwhelmed by detailed case processing and petitions; second, to ensure that the laws are applied consistently across the country in a way that maintains the integrity of the legal system; and finally, to provide convenient access to justice at the highest judicial organ. According to the official statement, this has been done to "lower the gravity of judicial activities." Apparently, establishment of the circuit tribunals targets local protectionism by allowing the central authority to penetrate the localities (Fang 2015, 62).

Since 2014, six circuits have been established, leaving the SPC headquarters in Beijing to cover only five neighboring provinces or municipalities. The circuits handled 47 percent of the total number of SPC cases in 2017, and this had increased to 57 percent by 2019. As many as 70 percent of their cases were administrative (Finder 2020a), and they also handled an enormous amount of petitioning. The Number 1 and 2 circuits received a total of 73,000 petitions from the time of their initial establishment in 2015 to the end of 2016. This number is equivalent to the overall annual number received by the SPC in Beijing (Hou 2021, 80–81).

It is clear that social stability in Beijing has been enhanced by this move. The number of petitions in Beijing has decreased sharply. The SPC has also relieved itself from case adjudications and can thus focus more on policymaking. It is less clear, however, whether the establishment of the circuit tribunals has successfully addressed the problem of local protectionism. Of course, because the tribunals' personnel, resources, and funding are controlled by the SPC, technically they should be free from any interference from the local governments. Even so, according to an analysis of the cases handled by the Number 6 circuit, most of its cases were from one province rather than different provinces. Moreover, 70 percent of the cases were administrative, of which 97 percent were rejected. Thus, the circuit tribunals' function in containing local protectionism, which is common in commercial cases, seems to be limited (Finder 2020a).

Smart Courts

Building smart courts has been another major reform for Chinese courts under Xi (Stern et al. 2021). From the governance perspective, this seems an obvious choice. Technology could ease workload and thus increase efficiency, but more importantly, it asserts central oversight over judges.

Under the reforms, the whole judicial process, from case filing to trial preparation and hearing, to judgment issuing, must be digitalized (SPC 2017a). This requirement also covers the back-end processes such as trial management, including file archiving and document serving. As a result, litigants can now file claims and submit evidence via the Internet or automated dockets in court halls. Judges can also find the applicable law and similar cases through automated software. Court officials can also perform real-time monitoring of the work processes of frontline judges.

Until recently, large quantities of adjudicating documents were made available on the Internet. This was intended to enhance judicial transparency. The more fundamental goal was to address the principal–agent problem: the judges knew that they had to make their judgments available and thus place them under more scrutiny (Ng 2019, 819). Yet the state has realized that full disclosure might undermine state legitimacy because their "dirty laundry" would be exposed. It has thus has rolled back the trend, and now only allows the public to access the "excellent" judgments, as defined by the SPC.

It thus created a "digital iron cage" (Papagianneas 2023, 475). For sensitive cases, almost every step of the judges' handling process can be monitored closely. Even for mundane cases, court officials are alerted when there is anything unusual. Judges shall make decisions following the laws and free from personal interferences. At the same time, it also allows the flexibility of intervention when the court and state authorities regard this as necessary. Indeed, according to Papagianneas and Junius (2023), user convenience, internal accountability, and external visibility have been improved. As a result, the judicial process has become fairer and more transparent, and the state's legitimacy has been sustained.

Enhancing the Belt and Road Initiative

A centerpiece of Xi's foreign policy, the Belt and Road Initiative (BRI) is a global infrastructure development strategy to invest in more than 150 countries and international organizations. It calls for China to assume a greater leadership role in global affairs, in accordance with its rising power and status. With a bid to enhance regional connectivity, it contributes to the policy of the great rejuvenation of the Chinese nation.

Chinese courts have played an active role in enhancing the initiative. In 2022, Chinese courts handled 95,000 foreign-related commercial cases (SPC Work Report 2023), almost 20 times higher than the 2013 figure of 5,364. In 2015 and 2019, the SPC issued two specific opinions, requiring that all Chinese courts provide judicial services and guarantees for the BRI. In the 2015 opinions, it stated that it is a "sacred mandate" for Chinese courts to actively serve for, and participate in, the implementation of the BRI.

Furthermore, in 2018 the SPC set up two international commercial courts, one in Shenzhen, and the other in Xi'an. This is expected to "create a stable, fair, transparent, and efficient international business environment based on the rule of law, and serve and guarantee the construction of the BRI." The commercial courts encourage foreign parties to submit disputes to them. As a part of the SPC, they claim to operate as a "one-stop shop" for international dispute resolution, combining services in litigation, arbitration, and mediation. For example, a settlement agreement reached in a mediation conducted or facilitated by the courts' international expert committee can be validated by the courts and thus become enforceable in China. The competitiveness of the courts, however, is limited. They do not accept investor–state or interstate disputes, and require all lawyers and judges to be Chinese nationals, and all proceedings to be conducted in Chinese (Cai and Godwin 2019). Up to September 2023, the two courts had accepted only 27 cases and closed 17 of them (SPC Information Department 2023).

To enhance the BRI, Chinese courts also actively engage in international exchanges. Before the BRI, Chinese judges were regularly trained abroad. The BRI has overturned this trend: judges from the BRI countries have been invited to China. From 2007 to 2019, for example, 10 such "research and study programs" were conducted for judges from Mongolia (Cai and Wang 2021, 163). The visiting judges visit Chinese courts, law firms, and companies. They listen to presentations by Chinese judges and hold seminars with them. In this process, Chinese judges have switched from the trainees to the trainers (Cai and Wang 2021, 161–163). The exchanges disseminate the wisdom of Chinese judges and their experience in judicial administration. Intended to increase the confidence toward China's judicial system, these programs do have some impact. One chief judge from Peru said after their trip that they not only knew more about the Chinese judicial system but also Chinese national development, and that Chinese good judicial practice would benefit Latin American countries. In these programs, BRI judges may also learn much from "smart" courts in China, which have streamlined court procedures and increased judicial transparency.

Conclusions

If Deng Xiaoping's reforms can be characterized as a move toward decentralization, centralization should be the key word for Xi Jinping's intentions. The decentralized reforms led to unprecedented economic development, social and cultural prosperity, technological innovations, and greater individual freedom. With those achievements, however, came rampant corruption and weakened central authority (Landry 2008). The history of the courts comprises parts of those processes—of both decentralization and centralization.

If a Chinese judge who retired in the early 1980s time-traveled to the present day, they would barely be able to recognize the state of today's courts. They would be surprised to see the grand buildings and the modernized offices, equipped with computers, telephones, and Internet access, that have replaced the crammed office rooms. Some hearings are broadcast live. Most of their colleagues would be university graduates with legal training. Judges now rarely conduct out-of-court investigations; instead, they hold hearings and apply the laws which have proliferated over the last four decades. They are also kept busy and put under significant pressure, as will be shown in the next chapter.

The time-traveling judge's modern colleagues would also tell him that even though the two characteristics of the judiciary—policy implementation and legitimacy enhancement—always stood as the underlying themes, the specific policies and approaches have varied during the different stages of judicial evolution over the past four decades. In the first decade following the initiation of Deng's reforms, the courts were concerned with construction, which included placing more focus on both manpower and infrastructure (Zheng 1994, 393). Later, in the 1990s, judicial professionalism and trial-mode reforms were launched to tackle the increased caseloads and more legally challenging cases. Xiao Yang's solutions to the mounting number of disputes, a legitimacy crisis, and social instability were to promote professionalism, formalism, and trial independence. Xiao's slogan of "Fairness and Efficiency" was soon replaced by Wang Shengjun's "the Judiciary for the People" (See Table 1.1). Trial independence and formalism were subsequently discarded. Under President Xi's reforms, various efforts have been put in place to enhance the legitimacy of the judiciary and the state. The judiciary has become a vehicle for leverage by the central authorities in their goal to readjust the power of the local governments. The local courts were originally bound tightly by their local government at the same administrative level, without being influenced by the central authorities in the implementation of national laws. With the personnel and budgetary decisions elevated to the provincial level and the establishment of the SPC's special circuit courts, the courts have become more an agent of the central authorities than of the local governments.

The time-traveling Chinese judge will, however, discover that one thing remains unchanged: the instrumental nature of the judiciary in facilitating the state's governance. For this aspect of the system, he will have a feeling of déjà vu. In particular, he will find one remark by Xi Jinping to sound suspiciously familiar: "The courts, as an integral component of the political-legal apparatuses, are the dagger handle of the Party" (Xinhua News 2014).

2

Judges

On her court's official website, Ms. Feng's picture is spotlighted, along with the pictures of several vice presidents. After graduating from law school, working for the court for two decades, and being rotated to the procuratorate for several years, she has now been appointed president of a basic-level court that has almost 100 judges and 300 support staff, and which processes 40,000 cases per year.

Along the way, she had demonstrated skills in legal analysis, capabilities in management, shrewdness in social relationships, and overall, a nice personality. Ms. Feng is now the fourth-tier senior judge. The Judges Law (2019, Art. 26) classifies judges into four tiers and 12 ranks: chief justice, grand justices, senior judges, and judges. Every judge has his or her own ranking.

The institutional environment under which Ms. Feng has grown and worked differs palpably from a typical courthouse in the US. Even following the 2014 reforms, the organization of China's courts remains bureaucratic. Today, judges are recruited, assessed, and disciplined according to a rubric similar to that of other government and Party entities. Court officials can be appointed to other political-legal apparatuses, and vice versa.

Whether a judge has an administrative post still makes a huge difference in the person's workload, opportunities for promotion, and responsibilities. Officials like Ms. Feng are more concerned with management, in contrast to frontline judges, who tend to be more oriented toward processing cases. Feng and her lieutenants run the courts, supervising junior judges and participating in the adjudication committee to discuss difficult cases. They identify and promote promising young judges and chastise those whose performance is not deemed up to par. They handle the external relationships with other government and Party organizations. They are expected to deal adroitly with vituperative litigants. Lower-ranking court officials, such as division heads and vice division heads, also have to handle a large load of cases.

In the post-Xiao Yang era, the judges' quota reform has arguably been the most influential official reform that has shaped the profession of judges. This chapter will introduce its key components and assess its impact. Can the judges make decisions that are free from extralegal interferences? Have they become a prestigious social group? How has the mode of the state's control been changed? Ultimately, are they judges to adjudicate cases through interpreting laws or bureaucrats to implement policies?

The Judicial System of China. Xin He, Oxford University Press. © Xin He 2025. DOI: 10.1093/9780198927815.003.0003

The Judges' Quota Reform

If the budgetary reform has had fundamental impacts on the operation of the courts, the judges' quota reform has touched a nerve in the judges' lives and work. The judges' quota reform (员额制) has attempted to build an elite profession of judges, in part by adopting a selective process and only admitting to the judge's track those who are deemed highly capable. The quota reform has sought to weed out people who lack sufficient adjudication abilities and thus to lay the foundation for judicial reforms that have the goals of shaping a professional, standardized, and elite court organization.

Specifically, the Supreme People's Court (SPC) has presented several reasons for the judges' quota reform (Xu 2017), the first of which has been to change the original situation, wherein some judges were swamped with many responsibilities while others had little to do. The second reason has been to ensure that the most capable judges are put forward to adjudicate cases and are not assigned to tangential jobs, such as in the logistics departments, or to otherwise be engaged in trivial tasks. The reform has aimed to equip judges with assistants to ease their workloads. Finally, the reformers recognized that only judges who are capable and experienced can be held accountable for their decisions.

Originally, almost all of the staff members of a court were known as judges, and most of them were allowed to adjudicate cases. The quota reform debuted in 2014 (*China News* 2014) and was further discussed at the Fourth Plenary Meeting of the 18th Central Committee Conference, in October 2014. For each province, a maximum of only 39 percent of judicial cadres were to be reappointed as judges after the quota reform, and those who were not readmitted were to be disqualified as judges. However, depending upon caseloads, population, court level, and other socioeconomic factors, this ratio was not implemented consistently across all of the individual courts. Generally, the heavier the caseload was, the higher was the quota (Chen and Bai 2016). Even more important, though, is the fact that the quota reform has been an ongoing process—a court might start with an appointment rate of below 39 percent in the first round of reforms and then readmit other judges later (CPLC 2015). Nonetheless, upon their completion in 2017 (*Xinhua Net* 2017), the judges' quota reforms had reduced the number of Chinese judges from 210,000 to 120,000.

Who was originally allowed in? According to Xu Jiaxin (2018), the head of the SPC's political department, the rigorous standards for being included in the quota evaluated the candidate's work experience, performance, investigative reports, awards, adjudicatory documents, and adjudicatory reports. However, individual courts' definitions of work performance varied, and many courts relied on the recommendations of immediate supervisors. Some courts examined the candidates in person before making their final recommendations. Given the bureaucratic nature of Chinese courts, it was common for the majority of court officials to be accepted, even if they might not recently have adjudicated cases. At the same time, some original frontline judges were not accepted (Zhang 2019).

Article 25 of the Judges Law makes it clear that additional judges can only be appointed when there are vacant quotas. The new judges can be admitted from the pool of original nonquota judges or from those new to the judiciary altogether. Passing the National Judicial Examination is a precondition for an entry-level judge—a necessary but insufficient condition for becoming a judge. The standard for recruitment, as the Judges Law (Art. 14) states, is assessment by both virtue and capability (德才兼备). According to our interviews with senior court officials, the courts prefer those who are "young, single, twenty-something, college educated" (Ng and He 2017a, 67). Such individuals tend to learn things quickly and are better equipped to withstand the long hours expected of frontline judges. The Judges Law also states that entry-level judges are to start from a basic-level court, whereas higher-level courts only recruit from lower-level courts (Art. 17). This protocol makes Chinese courts resemble their continental or Japanese counterparts and is thus another move toward professionalization.

Income

As is the case in most jurisdictions, monetary income is not a decisive motivator for people who aspire to become a judge—prestige, career development, and power are more important concerns. Nonetheless, the judges' quota reform has managed to address the issue of income, and as part of the reforms, the original court staff were classified into three categories: quota judges, support staff, and judicial administrative staff. To increase the court staff's incentives, a separate, higher salary system was created. In Shanghai, for example, the salaries of quota judges, support staff, and judicial administrative staff were supposed to be set respectively at levels 50, 20, and 10 percent higher than the average civil servant of the same rank (Wang 2016; *China Court* 2016). Other jurisdictions made similar arrangements. At the beginning of the reform, these salary changes created tensions between the courts and other government entities, and likewise between quota judges and nonquota judges. Since then, however, the differences have gradually been balanced out.

A judge's income also consists of performance and local allowances, in addition to the base salary, and this has led to a lower actual percentage increase in income than the above-mentioned percentages (Ai 2021). In Shenzhen, the difference in 2016 was only 19 (instead of 50) percent for quota judges (*China Court* 2016). In one hinterland intermediate court, a vice president's income was originally set at 30 percent higher, but in another intermediate court in a developed area the difference was less than 10 percent.

Furthermore, the differences in compensation between quota judges and other civil servants have gradually been narrowed. At the beginning of the reforms, only judges enjoyed salary increases, and the Guangzhou Municipality even announced that its 50 percent difference between the salaries of judges and other civil servants would remain unchanged (*China Court* 2016). Soon, however, the police, the most powerful branch of the political-legal arena, secured a political-legal allowance (Ministry of Human Resources 2017). Local governments with abundant resources have also raised the salaries of other civil servants and Party cadres.

Promotions

Before the reforms, the judges' only opportunity for promotion was through an administrative position, such as a promotion to the position of a deputy division head, and as a result, competition was fierce (Jonathan 2015). For the lower-ranking positions, competition was constant, as individuals sought to prove themselves able to exhibit professional capabilities, in what Wang (2015) dubbed "horse-racing." For higher-ranking positions, local political leaders made their selections in what was dubbed "horse-picking"—a complicated process in which the criteria were always changing (Liu 2019, 83). Therefore, one needed not only to excel in an administrative position but also to establish relationships with the leaders and serve as an effective communicator and liaison. The process became politicized, and the local congress, government, and court officials each possessed influence, but the ultimate decision-making power fell under the discretion of the Party (Liu 2012b). The SPC might offer potential opportunities for promotion, but local Party committees determined ranking and allowance (Ding 2014, 111).

The reforms have changed the formal part—that is, it has become easier for rank-and-file judges to advance in nominal rankings—but for court officials, the practice has remained status quo. Under the new system, however, most rank-and-file judges can be promoted a nominal rank every other year. Although this means higher salaries, it does not come with administrative posts, which are most judges' ultimate goal for their career progression. Through such promotions, a young person beginning a career as a judge at the age of 23 can achieve the third-highest form of judgeship by the age of 40—the equivalent of *zhengchu* (正处), the same nominal rank (or salary grade) as the vice president of an intermediate court (Xu 2018).

In keeping with the above changes, a judicial personnel commission was created at the provincial level to handle the promotions and appointments of the rank-and-file judiciary (SPC 2015a), and alongside that move, the regulation of the salary budget was also elevated to the same level (CPC and State Council 2009; Zhang 2019). Lifting the decisions on the staffing, budgeting, and equipment of the courts to the provincial level was intended to free them from local government interference. However, the appointment and promotion of major court officials has proven to be more symbolic than substantial. The only salient change has been the appointments of basic-level court presidents, which now have to be approved at the provincial level of the Party instead of at the municipal level—the court president has nominally become a province-managed cadre. Even so, the provincial Party's Organization Department lacks the capability to scrutinize presidential candidates from across a province—Guangdong Province alone has more than 200 basic-level courts. Behind the scenes, the weight of that decision still lies at the municipal level. For less important court officials, the original practices have been kept intact.

Workloads

The caseloads for judges in coastal areas were already high before the reforms. A popular saying among Chinese judges aptly captures this: "In courts, women are used as men, and men are used as donkeys" (Zheng et al. 2017, 190). The quota system has only made this worse. The reforms in 2017 cut the number of judges by 40 percent, even though caseloads were increasing—for example, from 143 million cases in 2014 to 250 million in 2018 (Figure 2.1). Sun and Fu (2022) contend that, because the number of the judges before 2017 included non-adjudicating staff, the real size of the pool of adjudicating judges has remained by and large the same after the quota reforms. To an extent, that is true. Still, before the reforms, non-adjudicating staff also helped adjudicate cases in busy courts, whereas now they are not allowed to help. Moreover, the increase in the caseload is indisputable. On average, every quota judge handled 152 cases in 2017—three times the 50 cases handled by a judge in 2008 (*The Paper* 2017). In urban and coastal courts, like that of Ms. Feng, it is common for each judge to close an average of more than 400 cases a year (SPC 2023). Although the SPC hailed this as an improvement in efficiency, never before have Chinese courts had to face such a severe situation of "too many cases, too few personnel" (Zhang 2019; Xia 2018; Chen and Bai 2016).

Moreover, the number of cases does not really tell the whole story of the issue of workloads; nor does comparing the numbers of cases with judges in other jurisdictions make much sense. On average, US judges handle 965 cases per year, and German judges—the least efficient among Western, developed jurisdictions—process 140 cases (Zhu 2010, 196). Even so, a full-scale trial in the US is very rare, with only 3 percent of cases filed in the US federal district court ending up in a complete hearing. The US system has also established special divisions, such as small claims courts and eviction courts, to expedite the process. In China, in contrast, the courts do not divert cases from the trial process—in fact, to maintain governance, they "take in *more* cases" (Ng and He 2017a, 55). Almost every case reaches the hearing stage or is settled by mediation, which can be considered even more time-consuming than a trial. Furthermore, the responsibilities of judges do not end at the point when the decision is handed down. There are "post-judgment

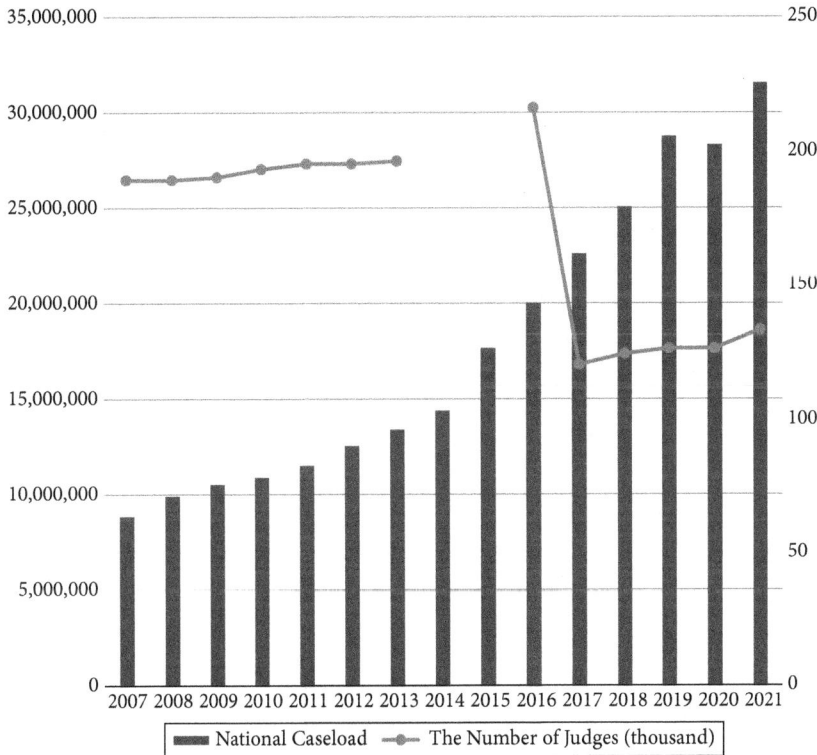

Figure 2.1 The Caseload Changes Contrasted with the Number of Judges in China (2007–21)

Notes: 1. The number of cases closed by People's Courts in China: "Statistics," in *Law Year Book of China* (2008–2022); 2. For the number of Chinese judges in 2007–09, see SPC(2010), Zhu (2012); People's Court Daily (2013), The Central People's Government of the People's Republic of China (2013); 3. For the number of Chinese judges in 2018, see the China Law Society, *Annual Report on the Construction of the Rule of Law in China* (2018); 4. The numbers of judges in 2019, 2020 and 2021 were calculated based on the average number of cases handled per judge mentioned in the 2019, 2020 and 2021 Work Reports of the SPC, along with the total number of cases reported in the *Law Year Book of China* for those years.

jobs" (Ng and He 2017a, 53–54) that make judges responsible for the outcomes of the cases. When litigants are comparatively difficult to handle, the judges have to find a way to deal with them. Judges are expected to explain to litigants such processes as the admission of facts by the courts, and how the legal regulations have been applied. Judges must ensure that unsatisfied litigants with an unfavorable outcome are dissuaded from petitioning and leave the system somewhat satisfied. In this light, handling 200 to 300 cases per year is very demanding for a Chinese judge.

The most immediate reason for the recent spike in case numbers seems to have been the case registration system, under which all cases are accepted without review or filtering (Xia 2018). Other reasons include reclassifications of enforcement cases, which have occupied roughly 40 percent of the overall caseload, along with the problems that arise from socioeconomic development. Zhang and Ginsburg (2019, 342–43) assert that the explosion in cases has been a result of the improved quality of judges and their decisions, but there is little evidence to support that claim.

An uneven distribution of caseloads within individual courts has aggravated the situation. Most court officials, such as the president, vice presidents, and division heads, squeeze themselves onto the judge's track (Zhang 2019) while sharing only a tiny portion of the caseload. According to the SPC guidelines (2017b), in basic- and intermediate-level courts, which process most of the cases, the president should handle only 5 to 10 percent of the frontline judge's average, and the vice president should take 20 to 30 percent at the intermediate level and 30 to 40 percent at the basic level. The division head's rates at both the basic and intermediate courts should stay at 50 to 70 percent of what the frontline judges handle. Furthermore, the court officials can choose to take the more straightforward cases that are easier and less time-consuming. Some court leaders only chair the collegial panel and do no substantial work.

Consequently, the president of a provincial high court may handle only 10 cases per year, while the caseload of a rank-and-file judge at the basic level commonly exceeds 300. It is not surprising that judges in the express division, which deals with routine and straightforward cases, or those with multiple plaintiffs and/or defendants, handle as many as 700 to 800 cases per year. The situation is especially grave in the more economically developed areas, where caseloads are the heaviest (Table 2.1). Numerous basic-level judges have to work overtime, and some consider switching from the judge's track to the judge's assistant's track for a lighter workload (Zhang 2019).

Handling cases, however, forms only a fraction of the judge's full list of roles and responsibilities. Although the State Council and the Judges Law (Art. 54) prohibit the assignment of administrative errands to the judges, the practice has persisted. One judge noted that "non-adjudicatory work has occupied a great deal of my time, such as conferences, poverty alleviation work, political indoctrination, and preparation of reports. To some extent, case handling became a side dish while

Table 2.1 Caseloads across Courts

	Developed Areas	Developing Areas
Lower Courts	Heaviest	Heavy
Higher Courts	Medium	Lightest

non-professional errands were the main course. Often I had to review the cases during my overtime hours" (Zhang 2019).

Performance Evaluations

The judges are also subject to frequent evaluations of their performance. Article 42 of the Judges Law states, "the result of appraisal shall be taken as the basis for award and punishment, dismissal, demotion, and for readjustment of his or her grade." The measurements are often concrete, quantitative, and formal, and they are important because they directly affect the judges' prospects for career advancement.

Although the emphases have evolved over different eras and the courts' practices have varied across different regions, several core elements that are taken into account in the performance assessments have prevailed: the number of cases handled each year, the case closure rate, the appeals rate, the remands rate, the petitions rate, and others (He 2021a, 34–40; Kinkel and Hurst 2015, 942). Before the recent reforms, it was common practice to "have the so-called 'league charts,' i.e., charts that rank courts from top to bottom according to specific indicators" (Ng and He 2017a, 56). An opinion of the SPC (2015) has confirmed the abolition of such so-called ordering practices, and instead called for and supported the continuation of more "scientific" performance evaluations.

Six years after the judges' quota reform was initiated, the SPC (2021a) promulgated a new performance evaluation system that covers "virtue, capability, diligence, and performance." Virtue was placed at the top and refers to the judge's political stance and moral character. However, the most relevant criterion to our discussion here is that of performance, which covers four items (SPC 2021a, Art. 11). First is the number of cases handled, which indicates the overall workload. Second is the quality of cases handled, which is primarily based on the cases being remanded or reversed upon appeal. Third is efficiency, with the primary measurement being the judge's closure rate, or whether the cases have been closed within the stipulated timeline. The final category is that of impacts, with parameters such as the cases' political effects, legal effects, and social effects. Impact assessments include questions such as the extent to which the cases have facilitated state security, social stability, the authority of the law, the people's lawful interests, and the core values of socialism.

This system has only been tightened, compared with the pre-reform period. Efficiency, legitimacy, and social stability remain key concerns. Efficiency has increased in importance in response to the dramatic rise in caseloads, while the number of judges has been chopped by almost a half. "Sitting on unfinished cases without reasons is strongly sanctioned" (Ng and He 2017a, 57). For cases processed under Ordinary Procedures, although the statutory limit specified in the Civil Procedure Law (CiPL) (Art. 149) allows six months, most courts tend to shorten that to 90 days. For cases under "the summary procedure," many courts set 20 days, despite the statutory limit of three months (CiPL, Art. 161).

Indeed, efficiency is a primary focus of court management at the grass roots level. Court officials monitor what cases and how many cases are assigned, and to whom. Each judge's caseload and progress are made known to all colleagues within the same division, via their internal computerized system (He 2021a, 243–244). Judges, therefore, know their own performance, as well as that of their peers, thus highlighting that "peer pressure is built in to push judges to work harder" (Ng and He 2017a, 57). Consistently falling short of deadlines signifies incapability, which will "certainly affect career development." The pressure is most palpable for young judges who are in the early stages of their judicial careers.

"The first thing I do when I get into my office is to turn on my computer and check out the cases waiting for me on that day," said Judge Tan, who has been working as a judge for 20 years in a major city in Guangdong. "Just looking at the case list on my computer sometimes gives me a headache. When the title of a case blinks yellow, it means its deadline is approaching. When it blinks red, it means I failed to close the case before the deadline set out by my court" (Ng and He 2017a, 56).

Impacts are another important concern that include several indices. Judges' performances are downgraded, and judges are even punished, if litigants file a successful complaint against them. In 2002, the SPC instructed all Chinese courts to focus on resolving complaints raised in petitions and to treat those complaints as if their importance was equal to that of a court trial (Liebman 2011, 295). The SPC also instructed lower courts to take a careful approach to handling petitions arising from the litigation process, in which judges are to persuade and guide petitioners and rectify the judgments on which they have erred. The SPC itself has as many as 80 judges working on petitions (Liebman 2011, 295). As a result, some courts have set "zero petition" targets.

In fact, the number of malicious incidents has become a major criterion in assessing judges' performance, and they are held personally accountable for it. A "malicious incident" usually refers to collective sit-ins, demonstrations, or unnatural deaths resulting from court behavior, and such incidents will taint the political future of the court directors, no matter the merits of the courts' behavior. This is so because social stability has become a defining sociopolitical goal, with protests and disputes over socially sensitive issues, such as land, labor, and environmental protection, being viewed as threats not only to the growth of China's economic agenda but also to the nation's political life and the Party's future (Wang and Minzner 2015). How local courts and government apparatuses marshal the forces of the laws to resolve disputes and pacify protests has thus emerged as a central political issue in the minds of China's authorities.

All of these indicators are predominantly quantitative. In Solomon's words (Solomon 2012, 915, 917), such performance criteria constitute "bureaucratic accountability," following the systems adopted by Russian courts under Putin, and by many European courts before the second half of the twentieth century. This approach to performance assessment is used in contrast to professional account-ability, which focuses on the judges' skills. The judges' knowledge of substantive and procedural laws and their ability to conduct trials can only be assessed quali-tatively, such as by reading their judgments. The current quantitative approach is another indicator, then, that the bureaucratic nature of Chinese courts has barely changed.

Impacts of the Quota Reforms

The recent judges' quota reforms have scarcely elevated the prestige of the judicial profession. Prestige depends upon a high level of dignity, a high income, and social respect. In reality, however, the caseloads of rank-and-file judges have increased at a rate between 50 and 100 percent, while their overall income has only increased by 10 to 30 percent. "The judge is no mandarin," my informants kept saying, "We are cogs in a huge bureaucratic machine." Several judges called themselves "judi-cial *min'gong*," where *min'gong* literally means "peasant worker" and is a derogatory term that stigmatizes farmers who migrate to cities for temporary jobs (Solinger 1999). Calling themselves judicial migrant workers puts the judges at the bottom of Chinese society and denigrates their self-worth. A female judge said, "[j]udging is entry level work linked to routine, repetitive and mechanical work, as a house wife does the dirty laundry day in and day out" (Sun and Fu 2022, 871). The term "frontline judge" also carries inferior connotations.

The judges' increased chances for promotion do not serve to elevate their pres-tige either—their promotions bring about only monetary benefits without a gain in substantive power (see also Liu 2019). As the saying goes, no one pays atten-tion to a mandarin who has no administrative power. The judges have little sense of pride when comparing themselves with their colleagues in the political, super-visory, staffing, and even logistics departments. These colleagues have been af-forded a large amount of leverage—they can assign judges to remote villages to work on poverty alleviation, they could ask them to check residents' temperatures in dilapidated neighborhoods during the coronavirus outbreak, they can initiate an investigation based on complaints against the judges, and their review reports on the judges can affect the judges' chances for promotions and salary increases.

Nor have the reforms granted life tenure to the judges—instead, they have been landed with the lifelong responsibility of always being held liable for their court judgments. In a state that prioritizes social stability, wherein a populist ideology that responds to the people's feelings has been reinvigorated (Lin and Trevaskes 2019; Trevaskes et al. 2014), the judges have been made more vulnerable. Many cases that can be examined retrospectively for judicial errors sleep like time bombs, and no one knows when they might explode. A litigant's petition, an investigation triggered by other cases, or an inspection by the appellate court could trigger an "explosion." With the average annual caseload hitting 300 cases per judge, it is hard to be free of mistakes, especially when the definition of "mistake" is vague. Due to the heavy caseloads, judges have to rely on their support staff, who are not always reliable, and they must also bear the responsibility for any mistakes made by the support staff. One scholar argues that "a lifetime accountability system has become a sword of Damocles hanging over judicial minds" (Wang 2016, 75). Remarkably, even concerns about personal safety loom large—judges often face threats, sometimes even of a physical nature, from resentful litigants, especially following controversial judicial decisions (Li 2022; Zheng et al. 2017).

The requirement of judicial transparency only aggravates the situation (*Harvard Law Review* 2020; Ahl and Sprick 2018). Massive investments allow hearings to be live-streamed (Finder 2020b), and until recently most of the adjudication documents were made accessible online. This visibility allows the creation of big data analytics on every judge's propensities, traits, and streaks.

The lack of prestige among judges is evident through the spatial arrangements of their workplaces. "Frontline judges in many grassroots courts work in offices that resemble anything but the quiet, solitary antechamber of an Anglo-American common law judge" (Ng and He 2017a, 31). Their offices are often crowded, with two, three, or even four judges sharing one office space. In some courts, the clerks are seated in front of the judges, literally sitting and working next to each other—"[t]heir desks are closely aligned," and "[t]hey move freely and frequently into and out of each other's workspace" (Ng and He 2017a, 32). Conversations between judges and litigants, family members, or friends can easily be overheard by colleagues.

If that is the situation for rank-and-file judges, do court officials fare any better? The officials control the quota reforms' implementation; it is within the discretion of the higher-level courts to decide how the quotas are to be distributed within their jurisdictions. Whereas the presidents and division heads are required to handle cases, they can always choose the easier ones. They are also able to interpret the rules promulgated by the SPC and can determine the criteria for assessing the rank-and-file judges. Overall, then, the presidents and division heads are far more well-respected in the courts.

Therefore, the court officials tend to fare better than ordinary judges do—but overall, not much better. One indication of this is their having had to surrender their originally spacious and extravagant offices—they now sit in private yet modest offices, similar to those of judges in Hong Kong. More substantively, the government and Party leaders continue to exert influence on them. Moreover, since the reforms, the court officials' promotion channels into other government and Party organs have been blocked on the grounds that they can be promoted within the judicial system. The court officials' frequent aspirations to be transferred into other branches suggests that the judicial profession is far from prestigious.

Ultimately, the recent reforms have failed to make the judicial profession more competitive, because of "the pressure imposed by the heavier-than-ever caseload, demands for judicial accountability and reduction in the number of judges," "the insignificant salary increase," and an overall lack of protection (Fu 2023, 73). The judicial profession has, therefore, been unable to attract new blood.

In addition, although leaving a governmental post is a risky move, the brain drain of judges has continued. Immediately before the implementation of the judges' quota system, the number of judges leaving the courts was "unprecedented" Fu (2021, 74). That exodus was the result of the judges' overriding fear of not being accepted onto the judge's track, and the "disproportionately" low salary increases compared with the increasing responsibilities. Interestingly, the attrition rate may not seem high if one looks only at the ratio for the judiciary as a whole—the post-reform rate of resigning judges was only 0.35 percent, much lower than the 1 percent in US federal courts for the same period (Liu 2019, 78, 81). However, the judges that have left were often "the cream of the crop" (Ng and He 2017a, 77). Mostly young or middle-aged, they were competitive in the judicial profession, and even in private practice. The SPC Work Report of 2019 states that because "the caseloads in some courts are enormously heavy, some judges perennially have to work beyond their limits, and some courts suffer serious losses in talent." In explaining the brain drain, and especially in addressing why mid-career male judges tend to leave the judicial profession, three eminent scholars have argued that there is "a general decline of professional honor" (Zheng et al. 2017, 190). According to another scholar, courts in the largest metropolitan areas face the most serious talent losses because of their heavy caseloads, the contrast between their judges' incomes and prohibitively high housing prices, and the lucrative opportunities open to lawyers in private practices (Xia 2018). Still, for many, under the new ideology that stresses political loyalty, judges are often afraid to tender their resignations because it may invite investigations by the supervision commission. Furthermore, to avoid a negative impression, some courts have refused to approve some resignations.

Despite the heavy workload and demanding responsibilities, however, most of the young personnel have felt pressured to seek admission to the judge's track. Without aspirations to become a judge, career prospects in the judicial system are bleak. One judge said, "getting into the track is to a judge what a license is to a lawyer." An implicit reason is power—as one judge put it bluntly, "the power of a quota judge is what they are after. If one does not have any say on cases, you have little to exchange in a society full of *guanxi*." Some court personnel, especially those with better job alternatives, chose to quit right after failing to get on to the track (Liu 2015). In some areas, the courts had already faced an exodus of middle-career judges who left for better prospects in law firms or other private-sector institutions

(Zheng et al. 2017). The quota reform has triggered another mini exodus—mid-career judges, fearful of being left out and worried about the future, have often chosen to leave. To stop the trend, some courts have made explicit internal rules to restrict or prohibit judges' resignations (Sun and Fu 2022).

Illegitimate Influences

Chinese courts are embedded in a complex network. Ng and He (2017) list four types of embeddedness—administrative, political, social, and economic—and, in a sense, the recent quota reforms have been targeting many of these. Elevating budgetary and personnel decisions, including the previous efforts to transfer more resources to help hinterland courts that have insufficient operating funds, are efforts to address economic embeddedness and, to some extent, political embeddedness. Efforts to truncate the hierarchy within the courts, and particularly to allow frontline judges to make their own decisions, have been put forward to reduce administrative embeddedness. The Party's battle against corruption should have brought a seismic impact on social embeddedness. Here, then, is the most important question: To what extent have the reforms reduced the different forms of court embeddedness?

There are two types of influences on courts, one of which is allowed, preferred, and even urged by the state. In the official rhetoric, that influence is called "supervision," "management," and "carrying out duties." It can be openly discussed in the courts' internal meetings, recorded in the minutes of those meetings, and subjected to further scrutiny by the Party and the higher-level courts or governments. These are deemed "legitimate influences." In other words, according to the current Chinese laws and political rules, certain influences over Chinese courts are not only declared to be legally and politically legitimate but are *required* and even hailed as the key to achieving effective governance (Peng 1991). Nobody should be punished or held responsible for exerting or acting under such influences—on the contrary, failing to act on or obstructing them will be penalized. For example, both the court officials and the government or Party leaders are expected to instruct the responsible judge on how to handle politically sensitive or influential cases, such as those affecting social stability. In keeping with this responsibility, the media, and especially the official media, can comment on case decisions, and their comments have even affected how the courts decide cases (Li 2018, 327).

The second type of influence on the courts comprises influences that permeate through informal, private channels to support personal interests and are disapproved of or forbidden. Exemplifying these influences is *guanxi*, or social ties (He and Ng 2017). These may be exercised through the structural channels of Chinese courts, in which patron–client relationships between superiors and subordinates may lead to abuses of power. *Guanxi* is sometimes exerted through broad, diffused, and deeply rooted cultural influences that are prevalent in Chinese society, and while these influences may coexist with the rule of law (Potter 2002), they lack legal and political justification and cannot be openly cited by the courts when making decisions. No official rhetoric praises them, nor can they be recorded in the formal minutes of any meeting. They are illegitimate influences.

However, the line between legitimate and illegitimate is sometimes blurred, and there is always a gray area. For one thing, the Party's policies and politics are always changing. After a policy change, an originally legitimate practice may be denounced as illegitimate. Furthermore, regional variations prevent a clear-cut line, and a practice that is legitimate in one region may be illegitimate in another. Furthermore, it is sometimes unclear whether the officials are acting out of the state's interests or their own personal interests. More often, illegitimate influences are exerted through the individual, personal channels, whereas the legitimate influences infiltrate through the collective, formal channels (Fu 2023, 71). A court president can intervene in a politically sensitive case through multiple means, such as the adjudication committee, a remanded case through the case management system, or a case complained about by litigants through the disciplinary division. Still, though, that president is strictly barred from making a private inquiry about a case related to their relatives.

How have the quota reforms altered the illegitimate influences on Chinese judges? According to the "SPC Opinions on the Judge's Quota Reform," the judges must sign off on their own decisions, and the court leaders cannot meddle or interfere in them (SPC 2015b). The reforms further require that the judges record any external or internal interference; failure to do so will incur a penalty (SPC 2015b, Art 33). Similar warnings prohibit improper interventions by political leaders outside of the courts (CPC and State Council 2015).

According to judges that I have interviewed, rarely had they heard of recorded instances of leaders exerting undue interference (*Xinhua Net* 2016)—but that may be because the court officials and political leaders remain powerful. Court officials have immense discretion over the judges' perks, not to mention control over the allocation of their promotions and positions. Recording instances of interference can lead to reprisals against a judge. If the judges have recorded these interferences, that would trigger formal investigations, covering both the interference itself and a thorough review of the case-handling process. In one instance, where a judge had mistakenly recorded a government official's participation in a case related to social stability, which should have been a legitimate interference, excessive efforts from both the local leaders and the court officials in the upper-level court were required to rectify the error. Extra work is one thing; letting things spin out of control is another.

Nonetheless, the prohibitions against leaders exerting illegitimate influence have seen palpable results. The omnipresent statement that was typical of leaders' instructions prior to the reforms—"please take this seriously in accordance to the law"—has almost vanished. After the reforms, leaving a written record of such a statement in the file would be labeled as interference and could conceivably wreck its author's political future. The prohibitions have certainly repressed the previous rampant presence of illegitimate influences in hinterland areas. According to the interviewees, such incidents have become even rarer in the more developed coastal areas.

An example of an incident that did indeed arise is revealing. In a basic-level court located in a coastal area, a special member of the adjudication committee (equivalent to the vice president) contacted a division head about a commercial case represented by a law firm with which his son was affiliated (the *Son's Case*). In response, the division head invited the special member and the responsible judge to his office. The division head then left the room, leaving the special member alone with the judge, who was a female in her 30s. When the special member made his intentions known, the judge was unconvinced. After all, she was neither the special member's direct supervisee nor his friend. Humiliated, the special member orchestrated a complaint to the court's political department, accusing the judge of malfeasance. The move cornered the judge, who revealed the whole story.

What would have been a trivial matter before the reforms had spiraled into a full-scale political incident. The nature of the intentions of the special member was revealed, and he was removed from his position and ousted from the judge's track. Both the judge and the division head were criticized for not recording the interference. A note of criticism was circulated across the jurisdiction, and all of the judges were rattled.

The impacts of the reforms were evident. The division head had left the office to avoid bearing the responsibility for the incident, the judge had ignored the—albeit illegitimate—instructions of a court official, and the judge and division head had been publicly shamed for simply failing to record the interference! Because this occurred in a developed area, where *guanxi* had not permeated the judicial system as much as it has in many other places (He and Ng 2017), one wonders what the situation would be in the hinterland areas.

Although the issue of illegitimate influences has been targeted, such influences continue to exist in a surreptitious form. When a hinterland court leader approaches a judge, the leader does it in a more circumspect and sociable fashion than was previously the case, and the judge, while responding to the request, has also had to become more careful. Thus, the parties have learned to channel their interferences through more personal interactions, rather than through institutions or conduits. For instance, an interviewee had noted a case in which a vice president of a suburban basic-level court in a hinterland area had summoned a judge to his office. The vice president was polite and, while showing his detailed notes, said:

> The president of the intermediate court called yesterday. One of his relatives was in your hands, sued for back wages (the Wage Case). This is the president's phone

number. You may register it as well. I've been caught by this. You know, he is the president of our upper-level court, and this was the first time he asked me for a favor. I cannot just go without responding. See what you can do. Don't get your fingers dirty.

Compared with the situation in the hinterlands before the reforms, when court presidents would simply call upon the judges and bluntly instruct them on how the case should be decided (He and Ng 2017), this court vice president had become more scrupulous. First, he asked the judge to his office, instead of instructing her by telephone. He not only showed her his notes, but also gave the judge the telephone number of the court president who had called. The notes had been taken not for reporting the interference, but to show that the requests were genuine. He continued, "he is the president of our upper-level court," and "this was the first time he called," to show that he was under pressure. Moreover, he specified that "you just see what you can do," to remind the judge not to overstep her discretion. "Don't get your fingers dirty" was the punch line; any favor, if possible, should be granted within the discretion of the law. On the other hand, this also suggested that should anything occur, the judge had to bear the responsibility herself.

What if an illegitimate request exceeds the scope of the judge's discretion? There are signs that judges have become more resistant to attempts at illegitimate influence. In a rural basic court case, a defendant received a shipment of cement worth 700,000 yuan, but refused to pay (the *Cement Case*) because "the contract was signed by the defendant's project department without the defendant's authorization." The law regards this as "apparent agency" and assumes the defendant's authorization has occurred. Accordingly, the judge was to adjudicate in favor of the plaintiff, requiring the defendant to pay the 700,000 yuan, with added interest. This had been finalized until the municipal secretary of political-legal affairs summoned both the president and the judge to "report the case." Although the secretary had no specific recommendation, it was apparent that he implicitly favored the defendant. After the meeting, the judge took the initiative to settle the case, and the court president issued an official case report to show the court's position, subsequently delivering it to the secretary in person. However, the defendant refused to make any payments beyond 200,000 yuan, far below the plaintiff's expectation.

That refusal left the court president and the judge torn. The law was clear: Anyone with legal training is able to understand apparent agency and its consequences. At that point in time, the impacts of the reforms had kicked in, and the judge would have had to rule against the defendant. To protect themselves, the court president first turned to the judge and requested, "[w]hy don't you delay the decision? Maybe the secretary will leave his post soon." This turned out to be a gross miscalculation—several months then passed while the secretary continued to sit comfortably in his position. Since Chinese courts are strict on meeting the deadlines to close cases, the court ultimately had to announce a decision. Eventually, instead of asking the parties to fetch the judgment from the delivery office, which was considered routine, the judge made a formal announcement in person; he added a special session to address the parties' concerns, explained the legal stipulations and the decision in detail, and encouraged the defendant to appeal.

Each of these cases indicates some degree of resistance by judges when pressured by illegitimate influences. In the *Wage Case*, the judge halved the compensation from 10,000 to 5,000 yuan but did not dismiss the plaintiff's claims, as she would have done in the pre-reform period. Reducing the compensation was within her discretion. In the *Son's Case*, the judge defied the special member. Likewise, in the *Cement Case*, both the judge and his president had orchestrated overtures to settle, a typical means of defusing extralegal influence. However, when they soon realized that their advice to settle had been unsuccessful, they ruled against the defendant, defying the wishes of their direct supervisor, the secretary of political-legal affairs.

Of course, not all judges are willing to risk offending their political bosses, and indeed the *Cement Case* might be an exception. It turned out that the neighboring court had received a similar case and faced the same form of interference by the same secretary, to which that court had bowed. A year later, the municipal secretary of political-legal affairs came under investigation because of unrelated reports of unruly behavior, and the supervisory commission soon uncovered his interference in those cases. The judge in the *Cement Case* had "dodged a bullet" (unlike the judge in the *Son's Case*, neither he nor his president were criticized for not recording the attempted interference!), while the neighboring court was reprimanded for bowing to the pressure. Accommodating illegitimate interference has proven to be riskier since the reforms, and that might be why such occurrences have declined.

Legitimate Influences

What about legitimate influences? Legitimate influences can be classified into influences that are internal, occurring within individual courts, and influences that are external and come from either upper-level courts or other powerful actors.

Internal Influences

Administrative influences within individual courts have dropped, and the previous requirement for court officials to approve case decisions, which once characterized the bureaucratic nature of the courts, has been abolished. The responsible judge and her/his collegial panelists now have the final say in most cases.

Nevertheless, this does not suggest that administrative influences in individual courts have vanished. Court officials still exert influence through both formal and informal channels. The SPC Opinion (2015, Art. 21) lists several categories of cases for which court officials can demand briefings. Another form of control of the judge is exercised through the case management system. Despite the SPC's abolition of all "unscientific criteria" for assessing judges' performance and ranking the courts, it still holds that the closing rate, appeals rate, and remands rate—indications of the percentage of cases closed against cases filed (SPC 2015a, Art. 21), of court decisions being appealed, and of cases that the appeals court returns for retrial, respectively—are commonly compared against those of other courts. As one official said: "With only a few courts within the region, one does not need to officially rank their performance to know which court is doing better. And how do we define 'unscientific criteria'? How can the court officials mobilize the rank-and-file judges without concrete numbers?" (Kinkel and Hurst 2015). One basic-level judge complained to me that, "the case-closing rate continues to be the primary measure to gauge our performance. Our court president only cares about the outcome, whatever means we have to take." As a result, many judges report having told litigants to withdraw their petitions before the stipulated deadline for the court to submit annual statistics, and then promising to take them up again later. This long-entrenched practice has survived the reforms.

Indeed, court officials are now concerned that judges enjoy too much power. Several court officials and lawyers who I have interviewed asserted that the judges' expanded powers, especially at the appellate level, have spun out of control. In some courts, the legal standards followed by two judges sharing an office are inconsistent. As a response, some courts have set up specialized judges' committees to determine cases in which the collegial members' opinions are split. Others have adopted more subtle and informal means. According to a vice president of an intermediate court in a hinterland area, the quality of judges' decisions had declined, partly due to the judges' expanded powers, and the revision and remand rates had doubled—from less than 10 percent to 20 percent. Alarmed by this change and the potential of hurting the court's performance, the vice president now requires briefings for all cases with dissenting opinions. She either makes suggestions or recommendations for cases to be heard by the adjudication committee, even when she has not signed off on any documents. All of her suggestions have been followed thus far (SPC 2017b).[1] As Selznick (1966) suggests, informal mechanisms may be more effective within the confines of an institution.

---

[1] The SPC (2017b) states, "the presidents and division heads cannot approve the cases in the form of oral instructions, sitting on the discussion of the collegial panel, and reviewing documents." Due to pressure to reduce the remand rates, however, this court has nonetheless adopted an approach circumventing the SPC requirement.

External Influences

Meanwhile, the "legitimate" influences emanating from upper-level courts and the government and Party organs have only been strengthened. Inside the judiciary, the higher-level courts now have a greater say on both the appointment of senior court officials and the recruitment of judges from lower-level courts. All told, there are greater vertical controls over the lower-level courts. Many of the decisions on judiciary staffing and budgeting have been elevated to the provincial level. Moreover, the role of adjudicatory supervision has become more prominent and is now a major force for uncovering wrongfully decided cases (Minzner 2009).

Nonetheless, many basic-level courts have been eager to liaise with local Party and government entities, especially because the local government and Party organs still hold major influence over the appointment of court presidents. Moreover, the courts still need these entities' support in securing infrastructure and support staff. "Informally, their interaction might have been reinforced" (Zhang 2019, 104).

Significant and sensitive cases are now defined as those affecting social stability, the general public, and the image of the state. In handling these cases, co-ordination between the courts, the Party, and government entities has been strengthened. The key phrase for the mechanisms of handling these cases is "the three synchronizations": to process cases according to the law, to guide the media, and to control society (*Legal Daily* 2016). This protocol is equivalent to the long-standing slogan hailing "the combination of legal and social effects" (Liebman 2011). Controversial cases should be reported to the upper-level leaders, both inside and outside the courts, as part of efforts to synchronize with the public responses.

Examples abound. When an underage girl was allegedly raped, a court had already formed a Special Case Group before the procuratorate transferred the case to that court, because the potentially sensational case had drawn the attention of the provincial Party chief. A judge in a major metropolitan area's intermediate court commented that intellectual property cases involving foreign parties have always been reported to the SPC, both before and since the judicial reforms. Such cases are "sensitive" because they may affect the image that China is projecting internationally. For court cases regarding mass protests that threaten social stability, co-ordination between various government agencies and the court has been indispensable (Chen and Xu 2012; Su and He 2011). A court vice president said to me that he had co-ordinated with Party leaders and the government for almost a decade regarding cases of auctioning pieces of land held by a state-owned enterprise, because of local concerns and general opposition to such auctions. Another court president said that she had liaised with the local Party and government on an eminent domain case. In that case, the compensation for the villagers had been set a decade earlier at 2,000 yuan per square meter, but the decision had never been enforced. With subsequent housing prices surging to 30,000 yuan a square meter (a 15-fold increase), the prospect of a forced eviction without extra compensation had become unjustifiable. When the land purchaser sued for compulsory eviction, the court needed the help of government organs to secure higher compensation. And in particular, criminal cases involving high-ranking officials have been processed using the same pattern both before and after the 2014 reforms. For example, the trial of Zhou Yongkang, in June 2015, entailed a high degree of "legitimate" intervention by the top Party leadership, as occurred in the trial of Bo Xilai in 2013 (BBC 2015).

Reassigning the budgets and staffing decisions to the provincial level has reduced some of the leverage held by local government organs and the Party at the same level to control the courts. However, the political stature of the courts has hardly changed, and the mutual reliance between political actors and the courts continues. After all, the courts are still under Party leadership, and court officials and government officials are both Party cadres. Despite the slogan, "to place adjudication at center stage" (CCP 2014), mutual cooperation, instead of mutual restraint, dominates the relationship between the Party and the legal apparatuses.

From Hierarchical to Panoptic Control

Whereas direct, level-by-level, hierarchical supervision has been eliminated and the judges' decision-making power seems to have been expanded, a series of sophisticated mechanisms of control have also been put in place.

Prioritized Issues

Under the earlier, procedurally hierarchical system, most court decisions needed supervisory approval, and the cases were undifferentiated. Now, with a truncated system of hierarchy, the state differentiates at least some of the politically sensitive cases from the mundane ones, thus demonstrating a chronic problem that many authoritarian states have to face: "They cannot afford not to control the former, while they lack the capacity to scrutinize the latter" (He 2021b, 70). Franco's Spain had notoriously fashioned two separate systems that existed in parallel to each other (Toharia 1975, 475). However, China does not have two separate systems. Thus, the authorities must seek a way to differentiate the sensitive cases from the ordinary ones, in a process which legal scholars have labeled "dualism" (Fu 2019, 3; Fraenkel 1941).

How do Chinese judges single out cases that are significant and sensitive? Formally, and in contrast to the Spanish system under Franco, there have never been two parallel systems. Indeed, the guidelines specified by the SPC, as well as those of individual courts, are vague and vary across time and regions. A routine divorce petition can escalate into homicidal or suicidal cases, and seemingly mundane quarrels between judges may be blown out of proportion on the Internet. In Xinjiang, the ethnic tensions between the Uyghurs and the Han majority can result in a local workplace disturbance being regarded as a serious incident, while in Guangdong mass incidents over delayed wages are frequent and draw little public attention.

The reforms have addressed this concern. First, the prioritized issues are identified through official documents. The progress of "four types of cases" —social stability-threatening, difficult and influential, conflicting with higher-ranked courts, and relating to misbehavior of the adjudicating judge—shall be reported to court officials (SPC 2015b, Art. 6). Second, there are classified documents that provide keywords and guidelines. A vice president of an intermediate level court in Guangdong told me:

> The SPC and various political-legal organizations have routinely issued classified documents to help judges determine the nature of cases. Not only are sensitive issues specified, but keywords are listed to alert the judges. For example, are there any lawsuits against the Communist Party or state leaders? Any lawsuits over how the government has handled a terrorist attack, or more recently, over mismanagement of the coronavirus? Any suits related to lawyers advocating for human rights?

Ideological Indoctrination

Loyalty to the Party has been stressed since the quota reforms. Although ideological indoctrination in Chinese courts has never been abandoned (Ahl 2018), there were instances of occasional subsidence before the reform. The judges, especially those who were legally trained, had tilted more toward legal analysis and had become increasingly pragmatic (Fu and Cullen 2011a). Nowadays, however, Chinese judges have been intensely drilled on political principles and education, and loyalty to the Party has become an explicit requirement of their behavior. Sessions on political education, which had not been held since the turbulent years of the Cultural Revolution, have been revived. In 2021, the political education session lasted for ten months. One judge described to me that, during that period:

> [W]e heard cases during the daytime and studied the Party Constitution and the disciplinary rules of the supervision commission during the evening. For most judges, three thick volumes of notebooks were filled with handwritten reports of self-criticism. In addition, each judge had to submit 12 pieces of reaction papers on the disciplinary rules, 2,000–3,000 words each, handwritten too. The problems must be genuine. If one does not self-report the problems, others will find

out for him or her. One shall be sweating, face flushed. No weekends, nor exact time to get off work.

Another judge told me that, "if one cannot recite the rules, he or she would immediately face disciplinary actions." The judges are repeatedly educated and reminded through various forms that they must know and support their major duty: to help the Communist Party preserve its monopoly on political power. Originally, judges relied on personal loyalty to their supervisors for promotion and other benefits; now, they must demonstrate institutional loyalty to the Party.

Judges may be punished for being disloyal toward or dishonest with the Party, and of course they are subject to various forms of discipline regulated by the Judges Law. Article 46 of the Judges Law stipulates 10 circumstances that lead to penalties, even though none of those circumstances is explicitly political. The Judges Law also provides procedural protections for occasions when the judges are to be subject to these disciplinary inquiries. However, Chinese judges are also civil servants. The Law on Administrative Sanctions for Civil Servants (2020) applies to them as well, and under that law, political offences are paramount. Judges who publish articles, speeches, declarations, or announcements opposing the Constitution, the Party's leadership, or the socialist system are to be dismissed (Art. 28). In addition to loyalty to the Party, another consideration is virtue. Any behavior by a judge that violates social morality or order, such as participating in gambling or "superstitious" activities, or committing domestic violence, will also lead to disciplinary action. The law provides few procedural safeguards for those under investigation, but instead requires them to provide "factual information" (Art. 42).

External Controls

Before the reforms, control over the courts was primarily internal and relied heavily on direction from the judges' supervisors and the Adjudication Committees of individual courts. Following the reforms, with the case approval system eliminated and the adjudication committees' scope of review narrowed, internal control has been loosened and the judges' decision-making powers have been expanded from their original "constrained" status. The emphases are now placed primarily on external mechanisms. The general public has also been mobilized to monitor the judges' behavior and decision-making, which is why judicial transparency has been stressed. The current system kills two birds with one stone: it exposes court cases to the general public, so as to enhance the state's legitimacy, and also allows the state to control the rank-and-file judges via the users of the judicial process—the litigants and the general public.

Originally, judges were not very exposed to disciplinary actions, due to the multilayered supervisory process and the patron–clientele relationship between supervisors and supervisees (Walder 1986). However, judges are now directly exposed to such actions: The Party's disciplinary departments can take action simply on the basis of litigants' complaints. Judges are also now held responsible for any inappropriate behavior on their part and are afforded significantly less protection by their supervisors.

The strengthening of external controls over the courts can be exemplified by the power of the Supervision Commission, which has played a more prominent role in asserting control over the judges. With the Supervision Law enacted in 2018, the Party's control of the courts through the Supervisory Commission has become formidable. Whereas the Commission sits at the same rank as the courts constitutionally, in actuality it enjoys more power and resources than the courts do (Li and Wang 2019, 967). The Party's hierarchy places its head supervisory authority one or two levels above the court president at the same administrative level. That head authority acts on official inspections and litigants' complaints, including legal and procedural flaws, inappropriate behavior, and even rudeness. Complaints have been lodged against judges for interrupting the litigants' presentations, for typographical errors in judgments, for inaccurately recording statements, and for immoral or corrupt behavior. The rule is that any complaint from a verified whistle-blower must receive an official reply. In this system, "[t]he due process requirements of China's criminal justice and administrative legal systems do not apply to the supervision authorities; they have broad investigatory, detention, sanctioning and confiscatory powers. The accused has no right to remain silent. Persons detained ... have no right to counsel" (Finder 2021, 87).

The Supervisory Commission is now required to find a certain number of problematic judges. A judge from a hinterland court told me that:

> [T]the rate of judges which would face disciplinary actions was artificially set at 20 percent. When it [the court] cannot fulfill the set quota, they [the Commission] would nevertheless try to find problems by scrutinizing closed cases. A judge in his early 30s was reported by a disgruntled litigant for taking a 300-yuan shopping card. He denied the claim and the complainant conveniently did not have evidence. But the investigation was extended across a period of more than two years, and the judge was eventually disciplined for taking a free ride of the litigant.

As a result of the sheer anxieties of facing discipline, that judge's hair had turned gray during the process. Another judge in the case-filing division, who had been investigated for her decision against accepting a case, said: "We are no more than caged chicken[s]. They can pick any of us, at any moment, and do whatever they want." Her decision not to accept the case was reversed by the appeals court, but she insisted that she had done nothing wrong, and that the decision had just been her interpretation of the law. Even so, both the court president and her division head persuaded her to acknowledge the "mistake," out of fear that the Party's disciplinary department would attempt to scrutinize all of the cases she had handled over her two decades as a judge. Few judges expressed confidence that no mistakes could be found in these old cases, especially when examined against the current and more stringent standards. According to one of my informants, a basic-level court president in Jilin Province openly warned his judges, "while you are granted the power to make decisions, it would be naïve to believe that you can do whatever you want."

The Supervisory Commission may also penalize judges through the internal Party disciplinary division within the courts. The court's Party disciplinary department is to "conduct investigation promptly, verify possible legal violations and deal with them in light of the circumstances" (Finder 2021, 92). Now that political ideology and the court's role to "serve the general public" have been stressed, the turnover of judicial malpractice dossiers handled by the disciplinary and political departments has been brisk.

During Xi Jinping's era, investigations by anticorruption and political offices, and the application of the so-called eight-point austerity regulations, which stress moral behavior and loyalty to the Party, have increased "significantly" (Li 2019). According to the Annual Work Report of the SPC, each year 200 to 1,000 court staff have been found to have violated the eight-point austerity regulations, and approximately 500 to 3,300 to have violated disciplinary rules or law. As documented by Finder (2021, 100–02), some judges have been found to have favored litigants after accepting gifts or taking shopping cards. Some have resisted the Party's investigations, insulted the Party on social media, or have been found to have been dishonest to the Party. Such judges have been "shamed," "warned," "demoted," and "removed" from adjudicating posts, or even "jailed" (Finder 2021, 101–02).

Ex Post Control

The original hierarchical mechanism was *ex ante*, with court decisions being composed and controlled before they were announced. However, the reforms have strengthened *ex post* control. In the judge's "responsibility system," which is another pillar of the reforms, the thrust is to "let the adjudicator judge, but hold those who adjudicate responsible." These *ex post* measures have thus tightened the party-state's grip over the judges, as the scope of responsibility has been broadened and simultaneously changed from "moderate" to the far more severe and daunting "lifelong."

Specifically, Article 25 of the SPC (2017e) document "Several Opinions to Perfect Judicial Responsibilities" stipulates that a judge is held responsible for life for the quality of the cases she or he has handled. This responsibility covers not only issues of corruption, factual mistakes, and inappropriate legal applications, but also procedural and paperwork flaws that "cause serious consequences," whether those flaws are intentional or grossly negligent. These stipulations leave much space for interpretation—for example, what constitutes "serious" consequences? Inside the court, mistakes can be traced in cases reversed on appeal or remanded for retrial by superior courts, and through internal case checks, and what are called letters-and-visits complaints (Wang 2016). With any appearance of political sluggishness, the most insignificant issue can trigger a serious investigation. A judge complained to me that: "Originally the political department belonged to the support staff; now it has become the frontline."

According to judges in previous interviews (Xu and Wang 2017, quoted from Finder 2021, 93), the current standards for responsibility are "broad" and "uncertain." A retired judge who went through the investigative process for an alleged bribery claim told me that the most dreadful thing was that "they never told you whether your case was closed or not." Half of the judges surveyed are of the opinion that the responsibility system is "unfair" (Finder 2021, 105). Scholars similarly find that it lacks clarity; there are no provisions exempting judges from responsibility (Hu 2019, quoted from Finder 2021, 93).

To further complicate the situation, the judges are also required to bear the responsibility for the mistakes of their support staff. Since the reforms, each judge is supposed to have an assistant and a clerk (the 1+1+1 model). The assistant and the clerk are to liaise with litigants and lay assessors, establish schedules, deliver subpoenas, transcribe court hearings, and prepare draft judgments. However, some of the judges that I interviewed mentioned that the 1+1+1 model has not fully materialized. For example, sometimes two judges have no choice but to share one assistant, and in some instances the assistants are simply unreliable and fall below standard. Many of the support staff enter the court system as fresh graduates, often without a law degree, and some of them have little incentive to take their roles seriously because they regard the job as a springboard to other opportunities.

In addition to the current system of required lifelong responsibility, the SPC has installed regulations that place special restrictions on judges. For instance, judges must withdraw from the judge's track if both their spouse and their children are living overseas. That requirement was originally imposed on high-ranking officials, but has now been extended to ordinary judges. The SPC further stipulated in 2018 that "judges, upon leaving the judiciary, may not practice as a lawyer for two years, and must never practice as lawyers in the court(s) in which they have worked."

Panoptic Control

Under the terrorizing gaze of all of the post-reform judicial system's responsibilities, mechanisms, and punishments, frontline judges' decisions are subject to vigorous monitoring by the Party. The new form of control has evolved from a

Table 2.2 Control Over Chinese Judges before and after the Reforms

Forms of Control	Before the Reforms	After the Reforms
Judges' Decision-making Power	Constrained	Expanded
Ex Ante Review	Undifferentiated	Differentiated
Ex Post Responsibilities	Moderate	Broadened and Lifelong
Internal Control	Rigid	Truncated
External Control	Moderate	Diffused
Loyalty	Personal Loyalty to Supervisors	Institutional Loyalty to the Party
Ideological Control	Mild	Intensified
Discipline	Less Exposed to Party Discipline	Exposed to Party Discipline
Overall	Hierarchical	Panoptic

narrow, procedural, technical level to a broadened, *ex post*, and ideological level (See Table 2.2). Gone are the rigid, hierarchical authorities between frontline judges and their supervisors inside the courts—the control is now more external-ized than internalized, more indirect than direct, and more diffused than concrete. The new information technology, and especially the computerized case manage-ment system, allows upper-level officials to review the handling process of every case. One judge said to me: "All blind spots are eliminated; the SPC president can review a case in a basic-level court in a remote area of the country."

In the words of Xu Jiaxin, the head of the SPC's political department (2018), control is asserted over the entire corps of the adjudicating judges and remains prominent throughout the whole judicial process. He explains:

A micro supervisory mechanism focused on approving individual cases and signing off on adjudicatory documents has been replaced by the scrutinization of the whole process and of all the judges. In practice, the power of the heads and presidents is delineated by how they have reformed the mechanisms for control-ling the key junctions, as well as the quality and efficiency [of judges]. Moreover, we rely on smart courts and information technology to improve internet-processing, thus recording, tracing, and controlling all key junctions of the case-handling process.

Thus, as Xu Jiaxin (2018) illustrated, all key case-handling junctions are now exposed and controlled. He summarized this process as "releasing power, but not responsibilities." Originally, the senior court officials did not dare to release the decision-making power, for fear of the possibility of mistakes made by the frontline judge. Now, equipped with all of these mechanisms and technologies, the state has found an efficient and convenient way to detect all mistakes. The control has thus become "panoptic."

Xu's statement highlights the issue of responsibilities. Article 25 of the SPC document "Several Opinions on Judicial Responsibilities" stipulates that a judge is to be held responsible for the quality of cases she or he has handled, for life (SPC 2015b, Art. 25). As discussed earlier, this covers not only issues of corruption, factual errors, and inappropriate legal applications, but also procedural and paperwork flaws, whether intentional or grossly negligent, that "cause serious consequences" (SPC 2015b, Art. 26.5).. It holds judges accountable to their superiors in the judicial hierarchy, upper-level government, and Party entities. The additional room allowed for judges to make decisions now comes at the cost of more severe and comprehensive responsibilities for those judges.

Conclusions

A key question in the study of Chinese judges is, are they the agents of the central authorities or of the local governments? Because they are being tasked to implement the laws and policies of the central government, the judges are expected to be agents of the central government. However, for a long period in their history, the local courts were the local governments' courts. Under that scenario, the judges chose primarily to promote the policy agenda of the local governments, and were sometimes motivated by personal gains, thus often leaving the central governments' laws and policies circumvented. In reality, at that time the judges' roles were more akin to serving as agents of the local governments.

It is in this context that one can understand why and when President Xi launched the recent judicial reforms. The judges' quota reforms established a profession that is both capable and also loyal to the central Party. Soon, faced with dramatically exploding numbers of cases in the court dockets, a reduced number of capable judges, an eroded legitimacy of the judiciary, and mounting grievances among the general public, the hierarchical procedures between the frontline judges and their superiors became less effective under those changed contexts. After the 2014 inauguration of the judges' quota reforms, the previous level-by-level hierarchical control was truncated and judges were afforded more latitude in making decisions, especially in routine cases.

At the same time, however, the judges' expanded autonomy has been balanced by a greater emphasis on their responsibilities, by external and *ex post* controls, and by ideological indoctrination. Loosened hierarchical control is now compensated for by intensified control in other aspects, with the original hierarchical control being replaced by a panoptic control that monitors every stage of the case-handling process and the subsequent consequences. The truncated hierarchy within the court system allows the courts to handle cases more efficiently in response to the ever-increasing caseloads, and even more importantly, to be exposed to greater control by the Party. The reforms have certainly not transformed the judges' status into that of social elites. As agents of the Party, they are still tightly controlled by the Party, and are not free to make their own decisions. In addition, extralegal influences, and legitimate influences in particular, remain undefeated.

Arguably, the new format has been quite effective. Such a mechanism of control allows the courts to achieve their two goals: policy implementation and legitimacy enhancement. Professional yet party-loyal judges are indispensable in carrying out the Party's policy agendas. The current judges excel in legal analysis, but are also politically capable of steering away from malicious outcomes. They can handle a large number of cases effectively and efficiently. Such a group is crucial for the perception of justice and, by extension, the legitimacy of the state.

By and large, the state still relies on "bureaucratic accountability, instead of professional accountability", which focuses on the judges' legal knowledge in writing opinions and their skillful management of trials (Solomon 2012). Quantitative indicators dominate their performance evaluations. The way that Chinese judges are controlled is closely related to the policy-implementing nature of the courts. Chinese judges are being regarded primarily as bureaucrats rather than neutral arbitrators adjudicating cases solely by interpreting laws. They are trained as lawyers, but have been shaped to behave like bureaucrats. They are required less to adjudicate cases through interpreting the laws than they are to implement policies. "To rectify the mistake of a *judge*, one appeals his or her decision. But to rectify the mistake of a *bureaucrat*, one asks that person to bear lifelong responsibility" (Ng 2019, 815).

Due to the eternal tensions that exist between policy implementation and legitimacy enhancement, the judges are kept under tremendous pressure. Their decisions are required to be accountable to the law, but even more importantly, they must meet the expectations of the state and the Party. Compared with the pre-reform period, the judges have been offered only an insignificant pay raise, while at the same time they now have to bear significantly more responsibility. It is not surprising, then, that an exodus of judges has occurred. Some court officials have even expressed a desire to leave their influential positions—positions that most judges would have strived hard to achieve in the past.

Ms. Feng was exhausted. She knew that, sooner or later, negative incidents would occur, but it was never made clear when that would take place, and there was no way to prevent such events from occurring. As the court president, she also bore the heavy burden of taking leadership responsibility for any such incidents.

Living in a perpetual state of stress and anxiety, she suffered from insomnia. She wanted to quit but was not sure whether such a request would raise eyebrows and invite corruption inquiries. She recently shared a piece of good news with me: She was being rotated back to the intermediate court as a vice president. Although it was not a promotion, it would bring a significant reduction in responsibility. She was filled with relief.

3

People's Assessors

One may have the impression that the people's assessors in China are crucial in judicial decision-making, either because of the law or the number of cases in which they have participated. The Law of People's Assessors (LPA, Arts. 21, 22) stipulates that the people's assessors are vested with powers that are largely identical to those of judges; indeed, people's assessors have recently participated in more than 70 percent of cases processed under the Ordinary Procedure, which is conducted by a collegial panel consisting of at least three judges or assessors. Indeed, in some courts the rate has been as high as 98.42 percent or even 100 percent (Gao 2021, 343–344).

Still, most legal scholars would agree that the institution is merely decorative. According to my own investigations (He 2016), the assessors usually had not read the case profile prior to the hearing, many never deliberated the cases, and some did not even have a chance to see the judgments. The people's assessors have long been derided as no more than "the ears of the deaf" in the courtroom (Landsman and Zhang 2008, 211–212; Zeng and Wang 2007; Yue 2001, 52). In the Chinese word for lay participation (陪审), only the first character, 陪 (accompanying), is implemented, whereas the second component, 审 (adjudication), is ignored. Some people's assessors have borne the title only and have simply been drivers or errand clerks who have thus not participated in any court hearings (Gao et al. 2009, 145–149). Some have been garage mechanics or grocery managers who rented the extra offices in the courts (Ding 2014, 85). According to Liao and Liu (2014), many assessors have been administered by the courts in a manner akin to that of court staff.

The people's assessors' marginal role in judicial decision-making stands in stark contrast to their seemingly significant role as specified in the law. Why does the state need such an institution? It has been reinvigorated in recent years as an antidote to the legitimacy crisis facing the judiciary. Zhou Qiang, the Supreme People's Court (SPC) president (2013–23), in his 2017 "Explanations on the LPA," stated, "[t]he institution of the people's assessors, as an important component of the socialist democracy, has played a significant role in materializing judicial democracy, facilitating judicial transparency, safeguarding judicial fairness, and enhancing judicial confidence." The institution is thus being used specifically to address the legitimacy of the courts and the state. Despite the tremendous costs associated with its management, the state is determined to establish and strengthen this institution.

This chapter begins with the recent revival of the institution of the people's assessors. It then describes the major changes in the 2018 Law of People's Assessors,

The Judicial System of China. Xin He, Oxford University Press. © Xin He 2025. DOI: 10.1093/9780198927815.003.0004

evaluating the implementation of the new law and focusing on whether it has truly turned the people's assessors into meaningful decision-makers. Although some progress has been made, their role in the judiciary continues to be marginal. The chapter concludes by exploring the reasons for their minimal progress, in light of the governance model.

The Recent Revival

The fate of China's institution of people's assessors has been closely related to the process of judicial reforms. A lay-participation institution had already been in operation in the revolutionary bases before the Communists took power, but despite its long history, that institution had been sidelined during the first three decades of the People's Republic. When Deng Xiaoping launched the legal reforms in the late 1970s, little attention was paid to the institution of the people's assessors (Landsman and Zhang 2008). Later, when legal education, legal professionalism, and institution building were stressed in the 1980s and 1990s, the institution underwent a further decline, and it suffered a notable turning point with its removal from the Constitution in 1982. In the 1979 Organic Law of the People's Courts, which was amended in 1983, the people's assessors were downgraded from a compulsory arrangement to an optional choice. Over the following two decades, the assessors' role in the judiciary was, at best, negligible.

In the early 2000s, however, when the reputation of the courts was tarnished by judicial corruption, limited access to justice, and growing popular discontent, the idea of a *people*'s judiciary had become appealing. The state perceived a people's judiciary as an institution that would be in tune with grass roots realities, and which might thus serve to narrow the divergence between the populace and the elitist orientation of the judiciary by particularly representing the concerns of the less-educated and socially marginalized communities. Echoing the return to a populist form of justice, an independent statute on the institution of people's assessors was promulgated in 2004 (NPC Standing Committee 2004). Extending participation in the administration of justice to the citizenry was intended to expose the masses to the elaborate concepts of the law, and to develop public confidence in the judiciary and the legal system (Peng 2011; Yu and Wang 2022; Landsman and Zhang 2008). However, the institution's optional status was not reversed, and it remained a convenient instrument and "decorative vase" for the courts.

A watershed moment occurred in 2014, when the decision (CPC 2014) passed by the Fourth Plenary Session of the 18th Central Committee of the Chinese Communist Party (CCP) included a paragraph on lay participation in the justice system, with more than half of the passage emphasizing a strengthening of the institution of people's assessors. The decision stated that such strengthening was necessary,

To perfect the people's assessor institution, protect the rights of citizens participating in judicial decision-making, expand the scope where the people's assessors will participate in the decision, perfect the random selection of assessors, and enhance public confidence on the institution of people's assessors. It calls for the gradual implementation of a system whereby assessors will decide only issues of fact and not issues of law.

In 2015, one year after the decision, 50 courts across the country were summoned to conduct a two-year pilot reform program. In April 2018, the LPA was promulgated and took effect immediately. Subsequently, the Ministry of Justice (MOJ) (2018) issued the Measures on the Selection of People's Assessors, and this was followed by an interpretation issued by the SPC (2019a) on the implementation of the LPA.

These advances, and especially the promulgations of new laws, were part of wider efforts to respond to the duality of problems that had plagued the institution of people's assessors—that many people's assessors were not randomly selected, and that they did not meaningfully participate in the decision-making processes.

Major Changes in the New Law

To enhance representation and participation in this process of "democratic" politics, the LPA stipulates that people's assessors must be selected from the general public, under the criteria of the catchphrase "one increase and one decrease." According to "one increase," the minimum age has been increased from 23 to 28 (LPA, Art. 5), to ensure that those with experience and practical knowledge are selected to represent public opinion; the complexities of legal affairs can only be understood upon reaching a certain level of maturity. "One decrease" denotes a lowered educational requirement, specifying just a high school diploma, which is significantly lower than the previous requirement of a college degree (LPA, Art. 5). This change seeks to break down the stereotype that people's assessors are part of an elite group.

The LPA also clarifies the types of cases that require participation by assessors. Whereas assessors can participate in almost all cases that fall under the Ordinary Procedure, the underlying crux of the matter is their participation's potential impact on society. After all, the institution is intended to boost the legitimacy of the courts and the state. Incorporating laypeople into the trials of controversial first-instance cases that could bring about significant social impacts serves to boost governance. Such cases can be categorized as follows: cases involving mass or public interests; cases with major social impacts or the potential to attract widespread attention; and cases with complicated facts or other situations (LPA, Art. 15). In order to dispel any concerns about judicial corruption and unfairness, the LPA states that the litigants have a right to request assessor participation (Art. 17).

To address the chronic issue of using *professional* people's assessors—a small group of assessors who attend most of the trials—the LPA states that the selection of candidates for people's assessors shall be kept "random." First, most assessors are to be *randomly* selected from the pool of habitual residents in a given jurisdiction (Art. 9), and the number of individuals selected for consideration is to be more than five times the number of actual assessors recruited. Second, the authorities must then *randomly* appoint the assessors, from those who are recognized to have passed the qualification requirements, and who have given their consent to serving (Art. 10). While the people's assessors can be appointed from other channels, such as through personal applications or the recommendations of social groups, such collection of applicants must form less than one-fifth of the total number of people's assessors (Art. 11). Third, and most importantly, the courts must also randomly select the people's assessors who have been appointed. To prevent scenarios wherein certain people's assessors participate in a disproportionate number of cases, the SPC interpretation (SPC 2019a, Art. 17) states that, in the absence of special permission, one assessor can attend a maximum of 30 cases per year. The interpretation further stipulates that the people's assessors can serve only one term, which is equivalent to five years. In other words, all of the assessors on the list must be afforded *even* chances for participation.

To avoid a lack of meaningful participation, the LPA reiterates that the assessors are to enjoy the same rights as judges. However, it provides one exception: on grand panels of three judges and four assessors, who are to hear complicated and influential cases, the role of the assessors is confined solely to determining the facts, thus leaving legal issues in the hands of the judges. The SPC and the MOJ have also provided guidelines to distinguish the boundaries between legal and factual questions (SPC and MOJ Reply 2020, 13). Creating this distinction utilizes the assessors' unique insights into the perspectives of the average citizen effectively. At the same time, legal issues may exceed their capabilities, so there is simply no need to seek their legal opinions.

In several other respects, the laws have also sought to boost the participation of the people's assessors. The courts are required to randomly determine the assessors seven days before a trial and grant them access to the case files (SPC 2019a, Arts. 3, 8). The assessors have the right to raise questions in the hearing process, and the chief adjudicator will direct them to challenge disputed issues (Art. 11). During the deliberations, the assessors are to express opinions before the judge does (SPC 2019a, Art. 12). The judge in charge must provide guidance and reminders on factual recognition, evidentiary rules, and legal stipulations, but refrain from interfering with the independent judgment of the assessors (LPA, Art. 20). The case is to be decided according to the majority rule. In the event that significant controversies are at stake, it falls within the discretion of the court president to decide whether the case should be presented to the adjudication committee for the final decision (LPA, Art. 23). In grand panels of seven persons, a list of factual and legal issues must be provided for the assessors to consider (SPC 2019a, Art. 9).

Before these reforms, assessors were selected, managed, trained, evaluated, and paid solely by the courts, meaning that, naturally, the courts were able to assert full control over them. The assessors were in positions that were completely subservient to the judges and the courts (He 2016; Zeng and Wang 2007). The LPA now provides that both the bureau of justice and the basic-level courts are to come together to select, train, assess, punish, and award assessors (LPA Arts. 9, 10, 25), and the courts are still required to cover their renumeration and other fees (LPA, Art. 30). The SPC has also clarified that only adjudicatory tasks can be assigned to assessors (SPC 2019a, Art. 18).

Most revisions in the law books make sense. But how are the revisions implemented? Have they changed from their originally decorative nature? Specifically, how are the people's assessors appointed? How are cases assigned to them? Do they have the opportunity to review case dossiers in advance? What consequences do they face if their opinions differ from those of the judge? How do judges view the assessors, and vice versa? Are the people's assessors held accountable for the decisions in which they participate? Or do the people's assessors serve as a check and balance on the judges?

Because the LPA has only been in effect since 2018, few empirical studies are available on its implementation. However, there are studies that have focused on the transition period, and these may help illustrate the operational mechanism of the institution.

Controlled Randomness

The new rules on appointing people's assessors have brought significant impacts. Originally, some courts had experienced difficulties in recruiting appropriate candidates for people's assessors, and many resorted to court connections for their recruitment (Zeng and Wang 2007), but this is no longer the case. According to the Notice on the Situation after the LPA had been Implemented for Two Years (SPC and MOJ Notice 2020), the number of assessors had reached 336,000 in 2020, which was a 58.1 percent increase from two years before. According to the official statistics published in 2021 (People's Daily 2021), the number of randomly selected assessors at that time totaled 219,000. However, while the number of randomly selected assessors is impressive, the reality is that it does not meet the new law's requirement—this figure should not fall below four-fifths of the total number of actual recruits (LPA, Art. 11). Despite this shortfall, the assessors had participated in 6.59 million cases from 2018 to 2020. In particular, the grand seven-person panel had made appearances in 12,000 influential cases.

The Notice also reported a notable increase in the extent of assessor participation and representation. As with other socialist states, the pre-reform institution of assessors could be considered to have been largely dominated by women (Machura 2003, 133). A study by the present author (He 2016) found that women made up 76 percent of China's assessors at the time. After the implementation of the process of random selection, 54.6 percent were reported to be men (SPC and MOJ Notice 2020). Originally, the majority of assessors were from the ranks of retirees or the unemployed (He 2016), but now the average age is 45. Presumably most of them are employed.

Still, the randomness is controlled. According to Miao's study (2021a, 446) within three pilot courts that had implemented most of the new rules on random selection, Party members continued to be "over-represented," with their percentage ranging from "a third" to "73 percent," despite their forming only "6.4 percent" of the population. In Liao and Jiang's study (2018, 68), Party members formed 36 percent of the assessors. Furthermore, according to Miao's study, the largest two groups by profession were "government employees" and "pensioners," comprising 29.6 percent and 17.3 percent of the total number, respectively (Miao 2021a, 446), which was similar to the situation before the 2014 reforms. On the other hand, peasants represented only 4.1 percent, despite constituting 48.3 percent of the total population. Liao and Jiang's study (2018, 68) did find that, in some areas, the issues surrounding representation had seen noticeable improvements after the reform. The number of government employees decreased by half, from 24 percent to 12 percent.

Previously, the level of formal education among assessors was high. My study (He 2016) showed that most of the pre-reform people's assessors held college degree qualifications at the very least. According to the Notice (SPC and MOJ Notice 2020), however, after the reforms this rate dropped to 87.4 percent. The situation has shown a slight change—those with higher education are still afforded more representation, especially in light of the statistic that only 7 to 15 percent of residents have such degrees. It is clear that the courts do not want to work with the poorly educated, such as peasants, as assessors.

In regard to the second level of random selection—the point at which assessors are randomly assigned to individual cases—some problems have, nevertheless, persisted. Before the reforms, a fundamental reason for *disproportionate* participation by some assessors was the mutual reliance between the assessors and the courts. Some assessors were preoccupied with work and family commitments and, therefore, had a tendency to avoid service, whereas other assessors were retired, approaching retirement, or unemployed. Unsurprisingly, however, the feelings of enthusiasm about the honorarium were shared, especially among those who could not find a better pastime. In the words of a retired assessor, "[y]ou sit back and relax on the bench for roughly two hours, and the honorarium is enough for food and fruit. Why not?" (He 2016, 743)

For the courts, the assessors' availability was always a primary concern. If the courts were to have selected the assessors randomly, some hearings would likely have needed to be postponed. This delay would have caused significant inconvenience for both the judges and other litigation participants, so it made sense that the judges often chose to rely on the lay assessors who were consistently available.

A judge told Tongfei Gao (Gao 2021, 225–226):

Our courts have a database of people's assessors, but only for information. We never use the database for random selection, nor is it allowed by the system. No judge would want to have random selection. It is infeasible, in addition to the extra workload. Some assessors have migrated to other cities. Can they come? How would they come? Who would pay for the trip? Moreover, can we postpone our case processing when an assessor is not available? With such heavy caseloads and demanding deadlines, where does the time and energy come from? Our colleagues all have their own assessors, who are always available.

Disproportionate participation has thus persisted. According to Yu and Wang (2022), one assessor attended 3,165 cases in 2015, participating in an average of more than ten cases per work day. Apparently, he was not randomly selected—how could this level of participation be explained if he was not always "on the spot" to "make up" the numbers? Another assessor attended 1,244 cases from 2014 to 2016, covering civil, criminal, and administrative cases that concerned issues such as "theft, traffic violations, and private lending," "family disputes," "intellectual property," and another "110 separate causes of action." During this time, he served more than "40 judges" (Yu and Wang 2022, 192). According to Lusheng Wang's (2020) study on 30 million criminal cases from 2013 to 2017, 20 percent of the assessors attended 80 percent of the cases (144). Eight percent of assessors attended more than 30 cases each year, exceeding the bar set by the SPC (SPC 2019a, Art. 17). In one court (Liu and Liao 2016, 56), four out of sixty assessors were primarily brought forward to take responsibility for all cases; three were retirees, and one was in a position without substantial duty. Of the 60 assessors, 35 never attended a single case. Although the court's internal computerized system did not show any assessor attending more than 20 cases per year, one assessor attended more than 10 cases per month. She even received a full-time salary for this job, despite her undocumented status in the system.

Under the new rules, the attraction of the remuneration associated with the role may not seem as appealing to the randomly selected assessors, or they may have other priorities. Some selected assessors may refuse to come, or they may fail to make an appearance after promising to do so. Because selection is random, the job title carries little symbolic political prestige. Despite the honorarium for each case having quadrupled over the last decade, some assessors have continued to gravitate toward avoiding service altogether. How do the courts deal with such practical difficulties?

As mentioned, the SPC requires both the selections of the assessors and extra assessors to be random (SPC 2019a Art. 3). However, some courts have adopted a slightly different approach—they ask the assessors to list their availability first, and then use that information to make their "random" selection of available assessors (*People's Daily* 2019). The courts have also resorted to selecting extra available assessors as a backup in the event that the originally selected assessors fail to show up. One model assessor admitted, "some assessors are reluctant to serve; some employers are not supportive." There is not much the courts can do about it.

To be fair, the phenomenon of disproportionate participation has been somewhat alleviated since 2018, but even so, the selection is far from random. Many courts have been resistant to the changes, and many judges are dismayed by "the wasted resources and the delayed proceedings because of the assessors' incompetence and lack of commitment" (Miao 2021, 450). When selecting the assessors, the courts state their preferences: availability, low maintenance, and efficiency. Apparently, some courts have "limited the scope" of their random selection (Liao and Jiang 2018, 68). Some individuals are chosen because they are "more available, and enthusiastic to public affairs." Moreover, no candidates are allowed to damage the reputation of the assessors' institution and the courts—they must be mindful of their behavior and words and cooperate with authorities.

Active Participation?

Before the LPA's implementation, the assessors were normally unaware of the facts of the cases and were not granted access to the case dossiers in advance (He 2016; Liu and Liao 2016; Zhang 2015). They were given insufficient time to study the cases, and often had to resort to deciphering elements while simultaneously listening to testimonies and dialogs during the trial. Unlike the situation in an American or English trial, the presentations were tailored to facilitate ease of understanding for a layperson without knowledge of the investigative file. It was common for the assessor to be unable to identify the issues of the cases (He 2016). Assessors rarely raised questions (*China Youth Daily* 2014), and "[m]ost judges behaved as if the assessors were non-existent" (He 2016, 741).

To what extent has the situation changed, then, since the LPA? The official propaganda (*People's Daily* 2019) may paint a sanguine picture, but the reality is another matter. According to Miao's survey (2021, 448), the new rules were "too idealistic to implement," and there have been too many "practical concerns." Due to the heavy caseloads, to arrange a pretrial meeting for each case is simply impossible. Concerns about efficiency mean that some meetings only last "a few minutes to half an hour", and only review the main issues. Few assessors have the time or interest to read files with hundreds of pages. Some cases are too technical and subtle to be grasped immediately. Only "70.4% of the surveyed PAs indicated that they attended such meetings and others said they didn't" (Miao 2021, 449). Most courts "failed to live up to the expectation" of the SPC (Miao 2021, 448).

The recent initiative to distinguish between legal and factual issues was intended to make a clear division of labor between judges and assessors, and was expected to increase the participation of assessors. However, this attempt at reform has only left some assessors feeling more bewildered (Miao 2021, 449). The surveyed courts often fail to create a distinction between factual and legal issues. Perhaps unsurprisingly, most assessors find it difficult to disentangle the two types of issues during a hearing. Upon being asked about the advice that has been provided, most assessors focus on the sentencings instead of the types of crimes (Liao and Jiang 2018, 70).

With neither a strong understanding of the basic facts and issues nor an ability to grasp the difference between legal and factual issues in advance, some assessors have struggled to comprehend the issues at stake in the cases as they sit through trials. In similarities between the present situation and the previous circumstances (Miao 2021, 440–450), the assessors have remained taciturn. Their impaired level of understanding often prevents them from exploring alternatives to the questions raised by the presiding judge (cf., Machura 2001, 459–460). At the same time, the dire shortage of information about the cases has forced them to listen carefully in order to gain a firm understanding, and thinking of useful questions has proven to be difficult when they are preoccupied with the task of simply trying to understand what is going on. The assessors have also reported being afraid of making mistakes (Liu 2016). Many of them believe that the hearing process brings with it an air of solemnity, and that any mistake might disturb it.

Meaningful Deliberation?

Before the LPA, the deliberation process was acknowledged to be largely fictional or nominal (He 2016; *China Youth Daily* 2014; Zhang and Yu 2009). The minutes were prepared by court clerks, and some statements were attributed to the people's assessors, which would be conveniently verified by the assessor with the single word, "agreed." Sometimes, the assessors were asked to do "the makeup signing"—to sign the minutes after the judgment had already been announced and all of the files had been bound. Occasionally, signing on behalf of other assessors, also known as "vicarious signing," was allowed.

The reforms in the new law have, at best, led to incremental improvements. Formal deliberation has taken hold, as explicitly required by the LPA. Still, Liao and Jiang (2018, 70) have reported that some courts stray away from the exact wordings of the law that require "face-to-face" deliberation conferences, and instead hold "back-to-back" conferences wherein the assessors do nothing more than fill out a factual questionnaire and list their main points on the issues at stake.

These points would provide references for the judges' use in making decisions. Such a practice has been adopted to facilitate the process, and has "avoided the direct communication and confrontation" between the assessors and judges. Some assessors are even under the impression that a face-to-face deliberation with the judges is a waste of time and serves only to add unnecessary burdens on the judges. In Miao's survey (2021, 449), 69.4 percent of the assessors believed that their positions had little to no significant impact on the cases' results. Approximately 60 percent of them never uttered a word during either the hearing or the deliberation processes, and 32 percent of them admitted to aimlessly signing deliberation minutes without participating in the deliberation or discussion. Those who refrained from speaking often did so out of a sheer lack of understanding of the facts or, sometimes, they doubted whether their input would truly bring any impact. In other cases, they were simply not given the opportunity.

Indeed, whether the assessor speaks may not be important, because the judges' continued dominance in the decision-making process is the key. A judge interviewed by Miao (2021, 451) said, "I haven't seen any assessors who disagree with me significantly so far. We are able to persuade people's assessors to change their mind (even if they do so). If an assessor repeatedly refuses to cooperate, we will not use him again." The courts certainly have discretion over the removal of a recalcitrant assessor. On the grand panels that require assessors to express opinions on factual issues, the judges are able to enjoy exclusive authority over sentencing, sharing their views on legal issues with the assessors (Miao 2021, 449). In Zheng and Li's survey (2016, 82), 42.5 percent of the assessors believed that they had eventually followed the judges' opinions when their opinions initially differed significantly from those of the judges.

Some empirical studies have found differences in case outcomes between the collegial panels with assessors and those decided solely by judges, or between panels with some assessors and those consisting only of judges. However, those differences may not represent the assessors' true impact. Rather, it seems far more likely that the judges had predecided the outcomes and changed the procedural arrangements. For example, upon finding that a divorce case was laden with complications and a denial of divorce could bring about confrontations stemming from the resisting party, the judge would conveniently exercise her/his discretion and switch from the Simplified Procedure to the Ordinary Procedure, which would then entail one or two assessors (He 2021a, 79).

From "Professional" to Unprofessional Assessors

Before the LPA, the courts relied on those assessors who were always available to fulfill the procedural requirements. In courts without enough judicial staff to serve documents and enforce judgments, the people's assessors often performed the tasks of judicial clerks (Liu 2007). Some worked as quasi-staff members of the courts and were "professional" or, more accurately, full-time assessors.

The assessors' reliance on the courts for the stability of their jobs had meant that most of them were submissive to the judges and were intimidated by the judges' power and expertise. Many feared being ostracized and not sought after, should they earn a reputation for uncooperativeness. While some judges were open to considering the assessors' opinions, even when those opinions occasionally contrasted with their own, they were much less tolerant when assessors openly challenged their authority. Fortunately, such incidents rarely occurred.

Now, with the current implementation of randomly selected assessors, the assessors' jobs no longer rely on the judges. Likewise, the assessors presumably do not have to be submissive to the judges. What, then, is the new situation?

Without a vested interest in the monetary gains from attendance at trials, the randomly selected assessors may indeed have dropped their previously submissive habits. That said, the new arrangement has also brought a new set of problems. Judges often complain of post-reform assessors being of low *suzhi*, or poor character. According to judges interviewed by Miao (2021, 444, 450), assessors are "recalcitrant," "incompetent," "lacking in commitment," "illiterate," and "bad-mannered and ill-disciplined": "They may change their schedule at the last minute." One judge reported that, "[a] peasant woman suddenly stood up in the middle of a trial, walking away while declaring 'I need to go home now and cook lunch for my granddaughter.'" Another recalled,

> [s]ome assessors answer phone calls and play games on their mobiles during deliberations, despite our warnings. I would say that about fewer than 10% of the assessors take their duty seriously . . . In the post-trial deliberation phase . . . only 30–40% of the assessors could even articulate their opinions. Some refused to speak no matter what . . . Others could not logically organize their thoughts.

According to Zheng and Li (2016, 83), attending trials appeared, for assessors, to be comparable to "going shopping," and being late for trials or loitering around trial venues minutes before the trial was set to commence was common. In short, the assessors are *unprofessional*.

The participation of unprofessional assessors undoubtedly lowers the quality of the trials and causes unnecessary delays. Poorly educated assessors find it difficult to understand both the substantial laws and the procedural rules, despite intensive training and repeated explanations, and some refuse to cooperate with judges. Instead of facilitating the trials, their participation has only proven to be a cumbersome addition to the process.

A vice president of a basic-level court in Guangdong said to me:

Involving people's assessors is not an issue of money; yet we cannot afford the energy. Assessors would find all sorts of excuses to avoid service. They would meticulously calculate how many times they came and how much they shall be paid. Even if we pre-arrange back-up assessors when the originally picked one does not show up, we would have to go through the procedures again—at least notifying both sides of the litigation. They are not genuinely participating in the trials—why bother?

In the grand panel trials, deliberation has become a rather stagnant process (Su and Jiang 2017, 39). For administrative cases, a judge commented bluntly (Liao and Jiang 2018, 69): "The randomly selected are always farmers in these suburban areas. They are not good at administrative cases. With them, more time will be wasted." What was conveyed by the judge was not confined to the assessor's participation being a waste of time; he also stressed that "more" time would be wasted.

All of this stands in direct contradiction with the judges' concerns for efficiency. As was shown in Chapter 2, the looming concerns regarding accountability and efficiency have cornered judges and brewed resentment among them. It has become time-consuming to offer opportunities for assessors to read files in advance, explain the issues to them beforehand, guide their questioning in the hearings, and listen to their opinions carefully during the deliberations. The institution of lay assessors also causes insurmountable administrative inconvenience, and judges have gradually begun to lose their patience. One judge interviewed by Miao (2021, 458) explained:

To be honest, not many people's assessors are granted pre-trial access to case dossiers. I know the reform encourages us to do so. But it wastes too much of our time. I close more than 200 cases per year. I have no time for this. In fact, I have never seen other colleagues welcoming the reform. Most people put on a show to convene a grand panel when demanded by the court leader. Assessors won't be able to play any substantial role without the support of judges, right? They enjoy no such support.

Another judge said, "No one has the time to put on the democracy show" (Miao 2021, 458). To many judges, the concept of including three judges and four assessors on a grand panel is ridiculous. Indeed, for some judges, having three judges sitting on the bench is already perceived as a huge waste of time and resources (Su and Jiang 2017, 39), and it is perceived as a further waste of time to hold a deliberation with four more assessors. Some courts have thus limited the use of the grand panels—in Beijing's second intermediate court, the grand panel has handled only 1 percent of the total caseload (Su and Jiang 2017, 39). In the interests of satisfying the procedural requirements and ensuring the smooth operation of court trials, according to the vice president in a Guangdong court, "[e]very court must have enough assessors who are always available. In our court, the maximum number of cases that one assessor can attend has been increased from 30 to 70."

The Dominance of the Judge

One crucial characteristic of the institution of people's assessors is that judges and assessors deliberate decisions together. This state of affairs has been reinforced (SPC and MOJ Reply 2020). In other systems with mixed deliberations, the participation of lay assessors is minimal, and professional judges tend to dominate the entire process (Hans 2008; Ivković 2007; Rennig 2001). As Kutnjak Ivković (2007) argued, assuming equal influence between professional judges and lay assessors in a mixed tribunal is unrealistic; decisions must be made in accordance with existing legal rules, with the possibility of being appealed by the litigating parties. This situation, alongside their existing expertise, inevitably places judges in positions of greater influence.

Similar patterns exist in China. When the judges are outvoted, they can always find ways to make the final decisions conform to their own will (He 2016). It comes as no surprise that the manipulation of procedural rules has persisted following the new law. As has been mentioned, the judge can first choose whether to adopt the Simplified Procedure or the Ordinary Procedure, which also leaves in the hands of the judge the question of whether to exclude or invite people's assessors (He 2021a, 79). Even if the assessors are to come forward to express their opinions first, as is stated by the new rules, the judges in some courts will ask one assessor to express their opinions before the judge does. If the assessor's opinion stands in contrast with the judge's, the judge will immediately intervene to influence the second assessor with their own opinions.

The law also permits judges to have discretion over which assessors are chosen and when they are needed. According to my own interviews with judges (He 2016), a Guangdong court deliberately invited two or more assessors for cases involving difficult litigants. The victims of medical malpractice cases, for example, are always skeptical of being put before a panel of biased judges; any unfavorable judgment from the courts could trigger protest. In one case related to a man who became comatose during hospital treatment, four assessors and one judge determined the compensation. In another case, in which a man in his seventies sued his daughter for a maintenance allowance, despite having left her three decades previously, the court set up a panel consisting of four assessors. During the hearing, the four assessors interrogated the man heavily on why he had abandoned his daughter. Morally humiliated by the assessors, the man caved in for a settlement. The president of the Guangdong court shared her tactics with me with a grin on her face—allowing lay assessors some authority to make decisions had the effect of pacifying these difficult litigants.

To evade the potential for protests is only one of many functions for which the judges are likely to employ assessors. Likewise, they rely on assessors who are experts for cases with technicalities, so as to avoid mistakes. Yu and Wang (2022) reported that a retired headmaster from a local high school participated in numerous cases concerning minors. Having more knowledge about minors than the judges did, he claimed that he "had steered trial proceedings in the correct direction", and frequently preached on behalf of the defendants. An employee of an insurance company had also "actively participated in insurance-related cases." A court invited a law professor to participate in a case, so as to provide theoretical justifications for "equal protection." The professor was pleased to have been chosen, because his operational experience in trials had facilitated his work. In Beijing, an intermediate court reported its reliance on assessors with backgrounds in accounting to discern the facts in bankruptcy cases; similarly, assessors with medical knowledge had instructed the court on professional standards for injuries in criminal cases (Su and Jiang 2017, 40; see also Zhao 2016, 116–122). In that court, assessors for specialist cases were narrowly selected from a pool of experts (Su and Jiang 2017, 40). The problem for many courts, however, is the difficulty in finding enough experts in certain fields, such as intellectual property cases, maritime cases, and securities cases. In spite of such needs, expert assessors constitute only a tiny proportion of people's assessors.

According to the LPA (Art. 16), assessors are required to participate in politically sensitive or influential cases, although the data show that they are mainly used in routine cases, and that their participation in politically sensitive cases has been conspicuously lower. For example, only 40 to 60 percent of murder cases have included the involvement of assessors, while their average rate of overall participation was 80 percent (Yu and Wang 2022, 185). Insolvency cases have also seen very low levels of assessor participation, perhaps due to their susceptibility to protests. Other types of sensitive cases include dereliction of duty and corruption cases. Wang (2020, 148) reported that, for sentences shorter than three years, the rate of lay participation was 80.4 percent, but the rate for sentences exceeding 10 years was only 3.1 percent. Apparently, local courts do not want "outsiders" to be involved in politically sensitive cases.

Some statistical analysis on a large amount of court decisions suggests that lay assessors' participation has made a difference to case outcomes. For example, Xiang Wang and Xiaohong Yu (2023, 38, 40) report that, in criminal cases with lay participation, the sentence was reduced by 13 months, or 15.3 percent, in comparison to cases without lay participation. They also claim that the more assessors there are, the more lenient the outcome. Yet, their analysis may not have adequately dealt with the selection bias: the judge has all the power to determine how many and which assessors to participate. In other words, the judge already had a rough idea of the outcome, if not having determined it already, before asking assessors to participate. Since plea leniency (see Chapter 8) has swept the process of criminal justice, the impact of people's assessors has only been weakened further: the decision is primarily made by the procuratorate, long before the court hearing or the participation of people's assessors.

In short, both the informal and formal rules serve as justifications for the judges to determine the outcomes. In cases of genuine divergences, the judges can utilize their positions to explain to the assessors that a decision has been altered by the adjudication committee. These arrangements reveal a hierarchical relationship of power between judges and the people's assessors, with the judges possessing a monopoly on the final decision-making power.

Control by the State

The gap in legal knowledge and status between professional judges and people's assessors forms only part of the explanation for the unfortunate plight of people's assessors in Chinese courts. This situation must also be understood through a consideration of how the state reins in judges who, in turn, control the people's assessors (Z. Liu 2008). The authoritarian nature of the Chinese state has determined that people's assessors cannot have real independent power, however rarely they might attempt to exercise it.

The jury system functions well in democracies partly because jurors work to shield judges from politics, and judges cannot be held responsible for jurors' decisions (Lempert 2007). In contrast, people's assessors in China cannot shield judges from taking responsibility for decisions made in court. Indeed, it is a daunting task to explain all of the laws and informal rules to the assessors, especially because the many subtleties are hard to communicate. The institutional arrangement between judges and people's assessors means that there is no way for the assessors to be entrusted with independent powers in the decision-making process.

Only in these contexts, then, can we understand the full extent of the ironclad control that courts and judges have over assessors. Assessors might be given the chance to express their views, but the judges and the courts continue to have a tight grip on the final say. The judges may, from time to time, explain their rationale, or without any elaboration they may send cases to the adjudication committee for the final decision. The dissenting opinions of the people's assessors might be recorded in the minutes, or be voiced to the court officials, but they are usually muted by the overriding power of the courts.

At the system's core, the judges are nonetheless held responsible for the decisions made, and thus it is no wonder that they are unwilling to share their decision-making power with the people's assessors. One judge said to me (He 2016, 755):

We have to be accountable for the decisions—we might be punished for wrongfully decided cases, and our performance is assessed against other criteria, such as the appeal rate and the remand rate. How can we give up the dominant role in decision-making to the people's assessors who cannot even understand the issues?

Indeed, deferring authority and responsibility for decision-making to the people's assessors is akin to the dramatic act of the judges giving away control over their own fate. We should note that judges now face the threatening prospect of lifelong judicial responsibility for erroneous decisions! A court official told Miao (2021, 451) that:

> They won't give the lay assessors the opportunity to speak and deliberate because they fear they might make mistakes and could slow down the process. They can accept lay assessors as mere accessories and assistants but no more ... The truth is, overtired and overworked judges don't want troublemakers.

The role of the institution of lay assessors in China should be understood through the assessors' relationships with the judges and, ultimately, the relationship between the state and the judges. Even though judges and lay assessors take equal positions under the law, a clear imbalance of powers prevails. Moreover, unlike the situation in the former Soviet bloc, where people's assessors had some control over the professional judges whose bourgeois judgment was prone to a false conscience, such control in China, if any exists, is offset by the dominant position of the judges.

The LPA also establishes a safety valve over the construction of the institution of lay assessors. The LPA requires the courts and the Bureau of Justice to select the assessors, after which they are appointed by the local congresses (LPA, Art. 10). In other words, they are scrutinized and appointed by the state. Furthermore, after enduring rounds of mandatory training, the assessors become well-versed in the dos and don'ts associated with their role. During the process, they may have experienced a forceful sacrifice of their beliefs and identities in order to live up to the state's expectations. When there are significant divergences on a decision, either the assessors or the judges can take the cases to the adjudication committee, which is the final decision-making body and is composed solely of senior court officials (LPA, Art. 23). After all, the people's assessors only operate in the first-instance trials, beyond which there are *de novo* appellate procedures. To date, there have been no reports of case outcomes determined by people's assessors that have been overturned by appellate courts in China, although such instances have been reported in Russia (Thaman 1999). Nevertheless, the possibility of such an occurrence in China is low, especially when considering the extremely marginal role of the people's assessors.

Conclusions

The impact of lay participation is thus rather limited. It suffers from what the present author has called a "double whammy" (He 2016). The lay assessors deliberate together with the judges, and thus are heavily influenced by them; more importantly, the state tightly controls the courts' decision-making process, further minimizing lay assessors' impact. This distinguishes China from many continental jurisdictions such as Germany, Japan, Taiwan, or South Korea. The juries or lay assessors there may not have a significant voice, but it is not as marginal as those in China.

China's institution of people's assessors is thus more symbolic than substantial. It has been deliberately established by the state as a tool to represent popular justice. The recent reforms have attempted to utilize the institution as an effective check on the exercise of judicial power, while it acts as the mouthpiece of civic opinions on judicial affairs. In fairness, these efforts have indeed strengthened the credibility of the lay-participation institution and have eliminated many laughable practices. Still, its decorative nature remains unchanged, and obtaining the meaningful participation of assessors in millions of cases seems unrealistic. The institution's current structure even decreases the function of assessors in mediating cases (Liao and Jiang 2018, 71). Some judges have proposed calling upon the grand panel of seven only in exceptional cases (Su and Jiang 2017, 41). At the end of the day, a supposedly democratic institution cannot bear fruit on undemocratic soil.

The futilities of the institution of people's assessors also reflect the existing tensions between the judges and the assessors. The judges are agents of the state and are subject to various forms of control, whereas the state cannot exercise similar levels of control over the people's assessors. That tension exists especially with regard to the system of responsibility, which the party-state has relied upon heavily in its efforts to control its cadres, including the judges (Liao and Liu 2018, 70, 86, 102). As a result, the requirements specified in the law—including the newly promulgated LPA—are destined to be sidelined.

Therefore, the question remains: Is this state vessel truly effective in improving the legitimacy of either the state or the judiciary? Liao and Liu's (2018, 16, 109, 215) sporadic surveys of dozens of litigants, judges, lawyers, and prosecutors have consistently found that whether people's assessors were present or not made little difference. Yet a recent study based on an online survey found that the general public hold a more positive view of cases decided with lay participation (An and Fan 2024). In this study, only 6.9 percent of those being surveyed claimed that they were "very familiar" with the institution. This indicates that, despite being malfunctioning, the institution could still be deceptive to the general public, who have little understanding of its real operation.

Despite the institution's overall incompetence and the widespread resistance from the judges, the state is determined to strengthen the role of lay assessors—a goal that only exemplifies the contradictions among the many goals that the judiciary is required to achieve. As the judiciary faces a crisis of legitimacy, the state hopes to employ people's assessors to provide relief, and to salvage the judiciary from its lack of democratic participation. At the same time, the assessors also serve as a force that is expected to meet the goal of dispute resolution, wherein efficiency becomes vital. As a result, a clash arises between the implementation of the institution and the judiciary's goals of efficiency. For many judges, the institution is "infeasible" and "troublesome." Such a contradiction is hard to avoid, when the state wants the courts to pursue the ultimate goal of governance.

4

Lawyers

Lawyers are prominent players in common law courts and legal systems. However, their role is far more limited in China's courts. As in other jurisdictions, lawyers take on a series of roles in China, ranging from litigation representation to law enforcement, dispute resolution, and even political change. Because this is a book about the Chinese courts, not the overall Chinese legal system, the discussion will be limited to lawyers' roles in the courtroom.

China's legal profession was eliminated during the Cultural Revolution, when the legal system was dismantled. Later, in the wake of Deng Xiaoping's reforms, the state realized that lawyers could serve the market economy. On August 26, 1980, the National People's Congress (NPC) issued the Provincial Statute on Lawyers (effective in 1982), legitimizing the profession.

In this statute, lawyers were defined as the *state's* legal workers, and they were expected to provide legal assistance to the government, businesses, and citizens. Lawyers did not work in law firms, but in legal consulting offices, or in work units under the justice bureaus or other state institutions. Fifteen years later, in the first Lawyers Law, which took effect in 1997, lawyers were redefined as the legal service providers for *society*. The nature of the profession was switched from public service to private practice. It took another decade (with the 2007 amendment of the Lawyers Law) for lawyers to be redefined as legal service providers for *clients*. Even after that change had been codified, Zhou Yongkang, then the political-legal tsar, still defined lawyers as "socialist legal workers with Chinese characteristics." Their role was to "support the Party's leadership and socialism" (Renhelaw 2008), and that mandate has since been incorporated into the oath used for swearing-in newly licensed lawyers (MOJ 2012).

The business organizations of lawyers have also undergone fundamental changes. In the 2000s, *partnership* law firms became the dominant format for licensed lawyers, although this private form of organization had only been allowed since 1988, when the Ministry of Justice (MOJ) permitted it as an experiment (Li 2014, 209). This organizational milestone was a watershed moment for privatization. In the 2007 amended Lawyers Law, *individual* law firms were allowed. The market share of state-funded law firms plummeted from 70 percent in 1997 to 11 percent in 2009 (Li 2014, 210), while partnership law firms have mushroomed since their legitimization in 1988. Today, the most prestigious law firms are private and are headquartered in the booming megacities of Beijing, Shanghai, Guangzhou, and Shenzhen. Roughly 150 Chinese law firms have merged with

The Judicial System of China. Xin He, Oxford University Press. © Xin He 2025. DOI: 10.1093/9780198927815.003.0005

international law firms and established offices in Hong Kong, London, Frankfurt, and New York. In 2020, the percentage of state-backed law firms' number further shrank to 2.56 percent, while that of the partnership firms increased to 60.59 percent (MOJ 2021). Moreover, the number of licensed lawyers increased from 8,330 in 1984 to 522,510 in 2020, or 62.7-fold (MOJ 2021).

Nowadays, formal licensed lawyers are the major providers of litigation services, but before the 2010s there was a shortfall, and the profession was unable to meet the market demand. The resumption of legal education in the 1980s initially yielded only a few law graduates. To complicate matters, even fewer of those graduates wanted to pursue a career in the profession (Li 2014, 208)—most still preferred to become civil servants or to work for state-owned enterprises, because those jobs were considered more stable and decent. Most entry-level lawyers were earning little more than the minimum wage (Yi 2013, 13). Another important consideration has been that law firms usually cannot arrange for the often sought-after household registrations (for more on this complicated system, see Chan and Buckingham 2008) in big cities, such as Beijing and Shanghai (Liu 2016, 423, fn. 49).

On the other hand, the need for legal representation skyrocketed. In the 1980s, Chinese society was awakening from the Cultural Revolution and was growing so quickly that it was bursting at the seams. Although previously the demand for legal services had been "anemic and scattered" (Komaiko and Que 2009, 135), the economy was gathering speed and thereby generating numerous disputes and lawsuits. The state had a slogan: "Use the law as your weapon!"—but there were too few lawyers to meet the demands for legal representation. At the same time, regional distribution was uneven. It might not have been difficult to find lawyers in big cities, but it was hard to find a licensed lawyer in the vast hinterland areas. Even as late as 2013, 164 counties did not have a single lawyer (Liu 2016, 423). According to Komaiko and Que (2009, 137), 16 percent of China's lawyers were concentrated in Beijing and Shanghai, which held only 3 percent of the national population. The big three metropolitan clusters—Beijing, the Yangzi Delta, and the Pearl Delta—had one-quarter of all of the lawyers in China, and they shared about half of the revenue (Liu 2016, 423).

As was mentioned in Chapter 1, legal education programs in China have proliferated since the late 1980s. With more than 600 law schools and 300,000 registered law students, the 62.7-fold increase has caused another problem—law has been ranked as the university major with the lowest employment rate, and the market has been inundated with lawyers who are poorly trained and inexperienced (Minzner 2013, 351). Some lawyers literally "wait on the steps of the courthouse to solicit clients" (Givens 2014, 747; Yi 2013, 201). A Supreme People's Court (SPC) death penalty judge told one of my informants that a lawyer had been soliciting clients outside the SPC's death penalty division, promising "not to charge any fee if the penalty were not lightened."

Legal Workers

To understand the work and life of the legal profession, we must start from a special category: legal workers. The threshold for licensing lawyers was low in the 1980s: no formal legal training or exams were required. Those involved in economic and/or technological businesses were qualified, as long as they were familiar with the relevant laws and statutes and had "legal training" (Provincial Statutes for Lawyers 1982, Art. 8.3). Only beginning with the 1997 Lawyers Law have licensed lawyers been required to pass the bar examination, which was first held in 1986.

For most people who aspire to become lawyers, those loose requirements have nonetheless been too high, and this has led to the rise of the profession of legal workers (Fu 2006, 46). Originally, many of these workers had not received higher education, and they certainly had no formal legal education. Many also lacked the capability to pass the examination required for the bar. Some had experience in legal procedures, some had sporadic legal knowledge, and others simply had experience in business transactions or the world beyond their villages or towns. Some were experts, such as former judges, prosecutors, or policemen, who could not obtain a formal license for various reasons. In any case, the threshold was practically nonexistent until 2018, when it was increased to a bachelor's law degree (MOJ 2017). Notably, according to this new regulation, an associate's law degree or a nonlaw bachelor's degree still qualifies in remote areas.

How do these unlicensed legal workers survive, and what do they provide for their clients in litigation? The following three portraits are informative.

Ms. Ping

After junior high school, Ms. Ping was selling tickets for a local theater. In 1997, the local court rented the theater building and took over the theater's personnel to work either as clerks or enforcement staff. Eight years later, realizing the pathetic salary level of the court staff, she quit her clerking job and opened her own office as a legal worker. With a sweet smile and easygoing personality, she was close to most of the judges. She played cards, had dinners and lunches, shopped, and traveled with them. Two years after she had set up her office, she still managed to keep a telephone number within the court, so that she could dial the four-digit internal line and thus save on telephone fees! She was particularly close to a female head in the civil division. Once, she ordered a pair of boots online, but found that they were too big, so the female division head wore them. They shared cosmetics, and the division head enjoyed the discount from Ms. Ping's VIP account for luxury brands. Ms. Ping had even paid for the fuel for court vehicles when needed. When the division head was rotated to lead a dispatched tribunal—a court division stationed in rural areas for local litigants' easy access—Ms. Ping's cases followed her.

Whenever Ms. Ping had a hearing at the tribunal, she would order roasted chicken, beef, and cuts of tripe from the most popular restaurant in town, lighting up the tribunal's lunch table. Ms. Ping walked in and out of the judges' offices at will, calling the judges "Sister Wang" or "Brother Li," even though they were not related. Most judges interacted with Ms. Ping on a regular basis.

For a time, Ms. Ping monopolized the cases of the "married-out" women in one dispatched tribunal. These women had married outside their natal villages but had claimed compensation for land requisition within those villages (He 2007; Chan 2019). In rural areas, it is common for litigants to be illiterate and to find it difficult to accurately articulate their needs. Providing a written legal petition would naturally be even more difficult for them. Many courtrooms are crammed with married-out women seeking proper compensation, each with a plethora of questions that the judges cannot answer. After litigants attempt to explain several times and are still unable to get their point across, judges often suggest that they find a legal representative, to which the litigants respond, "you shall find one for me!" It was usually in such instances that the women would be referred to Ms. Ping, thanks to her close ties with the judges.

These cases shared a pattern: The amount in dispute was small, often less than 10,000 yuan. Licensed lawyers had little interest in taking them. The legal issues were not complex. The courts often processed these cases with the same legal rationale and standards. Thus, legal workers were ideal for this situation, because they would patiently talk to the women separately and then file the lawsuits on their behalf. The legal workers earned their fees, and the judges increased their overall number of disposed cases—an important performance metric. When the legal workers were puzzled by technical legal questions, the judges were happy to clarify them, especially in light of the workers' cordial demeanor. Thus, their relationships were mutually beneficial and reciprocal—after all, it was easier for the judges to explain issues to the legal workers than to the masses of semiliterate litigants! In providing representation in all sorts of civil cases, Ms. Ping did nothing more than fill out a standardized form for her clients: When did they get married? Where were their household registrations located? Did they receive benefits from other sources? Ironically, at times her income was higher than that of licensed lawyers.

As an added benefit, Ms. Ping spoke a language that was more understandable for the rural, uneducated population, such as the married-out women. Most of her clients had no conception of the law or what a lawyer was. In their eyes, Ms. Ping was a "lawyer" anyway (see Fu 2006, 21). Their discourse was—to use Conley and O'Barr's term (1991)—relationship-oriented: Their relationship or status in the context was more important than the legal rules were. Most disputes were related to land compensation, bride prices in divorce cases, stolen domestic animals, or the right to use a co-owned buffalo. Explaining the situations with a pragmatic approach, Ms. Ping fit the expectations of the local clients. She understood their relationships in that context better than most formally trained lawyers did.

Mr. Fei

Mr. Fei's mother was a legal worker. Under her influence, Mr. Fei, with his sister, opened his own office of legal workers. With only a high school diploma, Mr. Fei might not have fully understood the legal issues or the court processes, but he would convince his potential clients that he would win their cases. When he did lose, he blamed it on the judges' mistakes. Due to his poor legal knowledge and Janus-faced personality, many judges looked down upon him. When a judge scolded him for improper behavior or provided him with advice, Mr. Fei would frequently just nod. A judge told me that Mr. Fei might not even understand the instructions, because, in most cases, he could not respond appropriately.

In a case of sudden occupational death, for example, Mr. Fei was unsure about whether he should add the insurance company as the third party. Like other untrained legal workers, he may have made legally incorrect claims (He 2021a, 189–190). Indeed, extravagant or hyperbolic claims, which only incurred higher fees for his clients, were common. In another case, he represented a married-out woman seeking land compensation. The court found that the woman had received benefits from a state-owned enterprise, and according to the law, one cannot receive double compensation. Mr. Fei had nevertheless persuaded the woman's father-in-law to file a lawsuit on her behalf. Of course, the case was dismissed.

Mr. Fei also struggled to locate evidence. One of his cases concerned a tour company's denial of any employment relationship with a man who had died of a heart attack during a bus trip. Mr. Fei could not provide anything to the court other than receipts for the man's medical treatment. The judge had to make efforts to reach the bus driver and the tour guide, in order to understand whether the man had indeed provided services to the tour company.

Nonetheless, for a time Mr. Fei represented nearly half of the plaintiffs in a dispatched tribunal. Mr. Fei consistently managed to maintain a close relationship with the judges, especially the mid-ranking officials. In addition, he often sent gifts to each judge and clerk during festivals—items ranging from a box of fresh vegetables or fruit to the occasional case of mooncakes, worth about 200 yuan. In a tribunal head's words, the gifts were "nothing special and we did not favor him for this."

If these insignificant benefits did not change Judge Zhang's impression of Mr. Fei, Fei's condolences when the judge's mother passed away definitely made a difference. According to the local custom, Judge Zhang's relatives, close friends, and colleagues were to attend the funeral, offering their condolences. On the afternoon of the day before the burial ceremony, the busiest time for the event, Mr. Fei and his client managed to greet the judge, who was surrounded by a sea of people. Mr. Fei also sent a red packet—a gift of money for special occasions—of 200 yuan. The money itself meant little, but it was touching that Fei had traveled 150 miles over bumpy mountainous roads to reach the judge's remote hometown. The judge decided to accept the 200 yuan, which was the going rate among colleagues. Officially, Judge Zhang had accepted Mr. Fei as a colleague. From that point on, instead of calling the judge "Judge Zhang," Mr. Fei called her "Elder Sister Zhang," and of course he insisted that many of his cases be allocated to Judge Zhang.

Ms. Qing

Ms. Qing represents another genre of legal workers. A graduate of a prestigious law school, she was a capable judge and had been promoted to division head, but a judge's salary was too low for her, and she chose to take early retirement after 30 years of work. The early retirement scheme allowed retired judges to enjoy most of the benefits of the working staff. Before the recent judicial reforms, Ms. Qing could have become a "black lawyer," meaning someone who has no formal license and is not affiliated with any formal business organization. Black lawyers survived because of their legal expertise and/or connections. In the absence of an office, they often resorted to meeting clients in the cafeterias of luxury hotels (Liu 2017, 85).

However, that gilded period was gone. The amended Judges Law prohibits retired judges from practicing as formally licensed lawyers during their first two years of retirement, and for life at the court where they had worked. As a result, Ms. Qing only worked as a legal worker. Nominally, her clients were represented by other colleagues in her office, but Ms. Qing pulled the strings. She often sat in on court hearings, typing instant messages to guide the colleague who was officially representing the client on how to respond to the judges' questions.

Ms. Qing understood the laws and court procedures inside out, but that was not the key to her business. The key was her web of connections within the judicial system and the government: the judges, government officials, and village heads, all of whom referred most of her clients to her. In one case, the judge had been her former supervisee. In another, she had managed to freeze the defendant's property within one working day, when the normal procedure would have taken two weeks (a speedy freezing was often crucial in debt-collection cases). Ms. Qing could ask the judges to schedule her cases earlier, another advantage when the court docket was heavy. With her rock-solid *guanxi* with the judges, Ms. Qing may also have wielded the power to influence their decision-making.

Guanxi (see this chapter's section on *guanxi*) with judges and geographic proximity are crucial for legal workers in their quests to obtain clients. When a hinterland court, located far away from an urban center, decided to open its case-filing division in the city in order to become more accessible to the general public, the exact location became a piece of priceless information for legal workers. Geographically, whoever was closest to the case-filing division had an upper hand in the market competition. Taking advantage of having close ties to the court, Ms. Ping ended up renting the second floor, right above the future offices of the case-filing division. Even today, almost any basic-level court is surrounded by stalls with plaques such as "legal service center," "legal consulting company," "investigation company," or "legal services firm" (See Liu 2017, 75). None of these are formal law firms, but potential litigants, many of whom are first-timers in court, have little concept of the difference.

Compensating for their lack of legal knowledge is legal workers' special way with potential litigants, judges, and officials. Mr. Fei and Ms. Ping are not exceptional. A judge told me that one disabled legal worker, in his fifties, often had a female client pushing his wheelchair and, in exchange for his legal services, she was providing *other* services. When the judge asked questions that he could not answer, the legal worker would raise his voice to show his confidence and his courage to challenge the judge. Another female legal worker became the mistress of a court clerk, who had special ways of mediating cases. Although a clerk is not officially allowed to handle cases independently, the judges with whom he worked often allowed him to *mediate* cases. Needless to say, most of the litigants whose cases he handled were represented by his mistress. Many legal workers often exaggerate their *guanxi* with the judges and claim to have won most of the cases in which they had provided representation. One legal worker often boasted that all his clients in criminal proceedings had been let off without being sentenced. That earned him a nickname—the "non-guilty lawyer."

As these portraits illustrate, legal workers coexist and compete with formal, licensed lawyers (Fu 2006, 13, 21). They focus on areas in which formal lawyers are less interested. For example, few lawyers are willing to go to the grass-roots level and take cases such as divorce, inheritance, and land compensations. For them, married-out women's cases are not profitable and the clients often have a lower educational background. In a sense, the licensed lawyers have given up this territory to their unlicensed colleagues (Liu 2017, 91; Fu 2006, 22). Another core reason for legal workers' competitiveness is their fees. When formal lawyers choose to take those cases, they can charge over three times as much as legal workers do (Fu 2006, 32).

There are no data to indicate whether licensed lawyers or legal workers are more successful at winning cases (Fu 2006, 20). After all, the two professions attract different pools of clients and cases. In any event, as will be discussed below, the litigation lawyer's role in case outcomes is simply insignificant. Nonetheless, legal workers provide services to a different layer of clients. As the saying goes, "formal lawyers hunted whales while legal workers got sardines" (Fu 2006, 20). One legal worker put it this way: "[T]here are different types of restaurants, hair salons, and even telephone network providers. A lot of consumers cannot afford the best of them" (Liu 2017, 92). For this very reason, the state has not eliminated legal workers from the market.

Lawyers in Civil Trials

Let us now turn to the lawyers in civil trials. In many cases, parties are not represented; in others, parties are represented by friends and relatives; while in still others only one party is legally represented. In our 2013 study (He and Su 2013), Yang Su and I found that the majority of individual litigants did not have professional attorneys. In almost 3,000 cases in Shanghai, the percentage of cases in which the plaintiff had an attorney ranged between 24.62 and 40.79 percent across various types of cases; the corresponding figure for defendants was below 20 percent, and may have been as low as 9 percent. The newest official statistics show that 5.3 million civil litigation cases were represented by attorneys in 2020—approximately 30 percent of the civil dockets.

Even for cases in which parties are represented by lawyers, the role of the lawyers remains more advisory than adversarial. Despite the newfound emphasis on in-trial proof-taking, the primary role of a Chinese lawyer is to act as a spokesperson and advisor for the clients they represent. This undoubtedly has something to do with the lack of legal professionalism, but it is also related to the judges' dominant role. In China, civil proceedings remain largely inquisitorial. Although lawyers conduct a limited form of cross-examination that is aimed at obtaining oral testimonies, the judges rely more on their own questioning. In this process, the lawyers' role remains marginal (Wang and Fu 2015, 216).

In an Anglo-American adversarial trial, the counsel call and question witnesses, whereas in China the judges dominate the process of proof-taking. The judge will often limit the number of questions a lawyer can ask an opposing witness, and the drawn-out process of cross-examination is unheard of in the Chinese context. Experienced lawyers know they can ask only a few questions, and that it is important for them to be succinct. Indeed, it may be misleading even to compare the questions Chinese lawyers raise with those from cross-examinations conducted by Anglo-American advocates. First, Chinese lawyers do not take evidence from witnesses. It remains the job of the judge to take evidence from witnesses—to ask what happened and to raise questions when ambiguities arise. An opposing lawyer only becomes involved toward the end of the process. Second, cross-examination in Anglo-American trials presents an opportunity for a lawyer to confront an opposing witness's account with the account of their own client, in a confrontation that is performed through a series of questions intended to expose inconsistencies in the witness's story. In the Chinese context of very strict time limits, it is arguably an even harder task for a lawyer to undermine a witness's account, and the lawyer needs a focused plan of attack.

Kwai Hang Ng and I (2013a) sat in on a case in which a security guard had sued his employer for wrongfully dismissing him on the grounds that he had picked fights with his colleagues. The guard's attorney put up one of the best perform-ances we observed during our fieldwork. The judge allowed him to ask no more than three questions of each witness. Individually, he asked each of them on which part of the body his client had punched the alleged victim. The alleged victim said he was punched in the face, whereas a chef who had witnessed the alleged attack implied that the guard had thrown punches at different parts of the alleged victim's body. A dish cleaner said it had been in the abdomen. The attorney then submitted to the judge that the three witnesses had failed to give a consistent account of the fight for one simple reason—the guard did not hit the alleged victim; instead, it was the other way around.

The plaintiff's attorney's powerful questioning completely exposed the wit-nesses' inconsistencies. However, that evidence was given little weight in the judge's decision: The judge simply inferred that because the security guard had rushed into the kitchen, he must have been the one who had initiated the fight. At best, Chinese lawyers' questioning is given secondary importance to a judge's reasoning process. Most judges today still see proof-taking, whether it is behind the scenes or in trial, as lying firmly within the scope of their work. Furthermore, the attorney's above-described performance was an exception among the cases we observed—most of the questions the lawyers raised in court were generic and for-mulaic, and were more akin to comments than to probing questions. As a general example, lawyers often challenge a witness's neutrality—whether the witness is an employee, friend, or relative of the party for whom she or he is testifying; by defin-ition, whatever such a person says cannot be trusted.

Furthermore, cases that feature oral testimonies from witnesses constitute only a minor part of all civil cases. The vast majority of trials are conducted on the basis of written evidence, and only the judge is able to raise detailed questions regarding the contents of the written documents submitted. In those cases, a lawyer's job is even further removed from the role of an advocate, with the typical responsibility of lawyers at trial being to examine documentary evidence submitted by opposing parties on behalf of their respective clients. A lawyer will raise questions if, in ac-cordance with Chinese evidence laws, they are dissatisfied with the identity, au-thenticity, or relevancy of a document submitted by another party. In the trials we observed, it was on the point of relevancy that lawyers were most likely to raise objections. For example, a lawyer would, often rightly, suggest that certain docu-ments (e.g., a personal letter in a divorce trial or a certificate of recognition in a labor-dispute trial) were irrelevant and should be excluded from consideration. Notably, this practice contrasts with that of legal workers, who often deny every piece of unfavorable evidence. Even for official state documents, legal workers still deny the documents' identity and relevance, without giving a reason. The purpose of denial is to show their clients that they have discredited every point raised by their opponent. Of course, the questions raised by lawyers, or the legal workers' denials, may still have little impact: It remains within the judge's discretion to decide how much weight should be given to a piece of documentary evidence.

The more important role of lawyers in civil trials is to answer questions raised by the judges, on behalf of their clients. Skilled lawyers frame their answers in the best interests of their clients, and know what (and what not) to tell the court. Judges are, nonetheless, ambivalent about lawyers' presence. On the one hand, lawyers help explain the trial process to the litigants. Some unrepresented litigants are difficult for judges to deal with, and in those scenarios a lawyer can act as an intermediary in the cases. Lawyers' advisory role is most apparent, and most welcomed by judges, in dealing with technical matters, such as the calculation of compensation payments (labor disputes) or child support (divorce proceedings). On the other hand, lawyers may complicate the process of truth-finding by putting forth excuses for their clients, thus thwarting the judge's ability to determine what actually happened. In one study, while applauding the latest reforms, which assigned more responsibility to the litigants, the younger judges also indicated that one obvious "adverse" effect of the change was the more important role assumed by lawyers. Some judges simply suggested that lawyers would, under the new system, have more opportunities to influence their clients into giving false evidence (Wu 2007, 194).

Due to their dominant role in the hearing stage, judges may become offended when challenged by a lawyer attempting to doubt their opinions on the law. For example, in the following excerpt, a lawyer wonders whether a judge's calculation of child support is correct, when the judge pressures the two sides to agree to a sum of 600 yuan (He and Ng 2013b):

> [Plaintiff's Lawyer:] … But according to the legal rules, child support only amounts to 20 to 30 percent of a person's income (the plaintiff says his income is 2,000 yuan).
> [Judge:] So, how much is it then, if it is 30 percent of his income?
> [Plaintiff's Lawyer:] But according to the rules, you don't necessarily have to use the upper limit of the range for your calculation.
> [Judge, louder:] But am I not allowed to use the upper limit in my ruling?
> [Plaintiff's Lawyer:] The calculation should consider the circumstances the plaintiff faces.
> [Judge] That isn't necessarily true. If you want to talk about the law, I'll talk about the law with you. It's 20 to 30 percent.

The judge's tone intensified as she felt the lawyer challenging her authority. After the episode, the lawyer kept silent for much of the rest of the trial. He did not speak again until the judge asked him to respond to other questions.

Despite their repressed role in court, lawyers can facilitate the process of hearings. Because they are familiar with the laws and court procedures, they are in an excellent position to help their clients' narrow issues in disputes. It is also easy for lawyers to communicate with the judges: They know the boundaries of what should and can be done. In insurance cases, in which the insurance company is usually represented by lawyers, the lawyers can focus on a few cases and thus the handling process becomes routinized. Unlike legal workers, who often challenge the evidence provided by the other party, lawyers are more professional. By maintaining the focus, lawyers can prevent hearings from getting off track and wasting time on frivolous issues. In divorce cases, the lawyers may have communicated to their client that a first-time divorce petition is rarely granted (He 2021a)—"This is the routine of the courts!" Some lawyers even let the judge know that they have more or less convinced their clients of this, thus simplifying the judges' job: The judges are relieved from the anxiety of having to face the consequences of denying the petition. They can simply focus on routine issues, and thus shorten the hearing process.

Although, on the trial stage, lawyers appear to have little impact, offstage they can be helpful. As mentioned, due to their training and experience, they often present a better-focused petition on issues. They are also more helpful in locating evidence than the litigants themselves are. In divorce cases, for example, the lawyers can help their clients locate evidence of domestic violence, such as records of police visits, medical reports and receipts, social media records, and sometimes confession letters. In personal injury cases, they can help locate the appraisal letters from the authorities. In debt-collection letters, they can help locate the defendants' addresses, which is often a challenge.

Offstage, lawyers can also coach their clients to behave strategically. In divorce cases, a pattern is well known among lawyers: If one party wants a divorce or child custody, he or she may be willing to sacrifice property rights (He 2021a). Whoever initiates the divorce process will get the short end of the stick: The initiator is usually the more eager party to be divorced. The other party can take advantage of this fact and respond with firm opposition, so as to force the initiator to compromise on other aspects, such as property or child custody. Under their lawyers' influence, defendants may claim that they want child custody, even if they do not really want it. They may also even refuse a divorce, even though they are sure that the marriage has fallen apart. Sometimes, divorce defendants ask for a greater share of matrimonial property, even though they do not deserve it. The reasons behind these exaggerated claims are straightforward: With more claims and more intense resistance to the divorce, they will have a higher stack of bargaining chips, and thus will be in a more advantageous position for negotiating.

Lawyers in Criminal Trials

Rarely are lawyers specialized in criminal defense (Smith, 2020; Liu 2016): "They take any case available" (Liu 2016, 437). Criminal defense cases are considered to be at the low end of the legal service market (Yi 2013, 320), meaning that the lawyers who are more inclined to take criminal cases are often not the cream of the crop. Compared with their peers in other sectors, their incomes are low. Revenue generated in criminal defense in Beijing was roughly 100 million yuan in 2013, while nonlitigation revenues hit 4.2 billion yuan (Liu 2016, 423). Criminal law is also the least desirable area for law graduates when choosing where to work (Liu 2017; Liu 2016, 423). Indeed, most of China's criminal defense lawyers do not conduct research and have little expertise beyond their common sense, so the defenses they provide tend to be generic rather than specific (Liu 2016, 420, 440). Jurisdictional disputes, unlawful evidence, and defendants' mental unsoundness are the top three orders from their menu (Liu 2016, 440). Similar to "the traveling lawyers" in the nineteenth-century United States (Friedman 1998, 269), many criminal defense attorneys focus on eloquence rather than evidence in court discussions. Unlike their US counterparts, however, they have no jury to influence; they know that they cannot influence court decisions and that they are just staging a show for their clients. The existing literature has highlighted the difficulties that the state authorities pose for lawyers, but in reality their biggest challenge is their clients: The lawyers have to convince their clients that they have done something meaningful (Yin 2018; Liu 2016, 439). Shenghua Yi, a senior criminal lawyer, once stated, "[o]ur biggest enemy is our own clients" (Yi 2013, 40). Furthermore, few experienced litigators will pass skills on to their partners or associates (Liu 2016, 426): "Masters would starve to death once their apprentices acquire the craft" (Yi 2013, 51). Even when they are "partners" in partnership firms, rarely do they collaborate with each other (Yi 2013, 200). Senior law firm partners usually keep themselves busy with refining their public images, in an effort to attract more potential clients (Liu 2016, 430–431).

Traditionally, lawyers have struggled to participate in criminal proceedings: The authorities might prevent them from being involved in the defense until it is too late. It was common in the past for criminal defense lawyers to be harassed by surveillance and even violence. Often, the officials of justice bureaus pressured the defense lawyers to withdraw from their work (McConville et al. 2011). Denying lawyers access to the files potentially deprived them of their best means of defense, because whatever they said in the hearing process had little impact on the predetermined decisions. Despite having some adversarial elements, the system remained inquisitorial. The emphasis of the system, as is also true with those in continental countries such as France and Japan, is on the police's investigations and the procuratorate's charges. A defense lawyer, characterizing the criminal hearing process, once said, "[w]hen the judge raised questions, the prosecutor was sleeping, or the other way around" (Liu 2017, 205).

In the past, "three difficulties" for criminal defense lawyers have exemplified the state-imposed challenges to criminal lawyers: meeting with suspects, accessing case files, and collecting evidence (Yu 2002). Meeting with suspects, for example, required the detention centers' approval, and often the majority of requests for meetings were rejected (Yu 2002, 835). Even when lawyers were allowed to meet with the suspects, the police were always present. Moreover, there were limitations on the number and duration of meetings (Yi 2013, 149–168).

The difficulty in collecting evidence in the pretrial stage had been the most dreadful of the three difficulties (Li 2010). According to Article 306 of the Criminal Law, nicknamed the "Big Stick," any defense lawyer who falsified evidence or induced witnesses to change their testimony would be subject to criminal investigation. Although the Article made sense, in practice the police and procuratorate often used it to retaliate against defense lawyers who dared to challenge their evidence and prosecutions. Criminal lawyers regarded the Article as a "sword of Damocles" over their heads (Liu and Halliday 2016, 44; Li 2014). It has been estimated that, since 1997, hundreds of criminal lawyers have been detained, arrested, prosecuted, or jailed for perjury (Liu and Halliday 2016, 45). As a result, lawyers were reluctant to take on cases that "might pit them against the state" (Komaiko and Que 2009, 47).

The situation has recently improved. With the rise of the plea leniency system, a suspect can now admit guilt and accept proposed sentences for a more lenient punishment, and the defendants in most criminal cases are now legally represented (Daum 2018; 2021; see more in Chapter 8). The authorities now require a "full coverage of lawyers" in criminal defense cases. The suspects have the right to a lawyer, even while the criminal investigation is still in progress (amended Criminal Procedure Law (CrPL) 2018), and this has led to a sea change. In an empirical study conducted in the 2000s, McConville et al. (2011) reported that, in 26 percent of the trials, the defendants had had no legal representation, not even by individuals such as family members. In 2020, in contrast, of 1.12 million first-instance criminal cases (SPC 2021 Work Report), 1.04 million featured representation by lawyers (MOJ 2021). On average, a Chinese lawyer now handles two criminal cases per year, twice the number reported in the early 2000s in Beijing (Li 2014, 226). Some law firms now specialize in criminal cases (Li 2014, 224), although many struggle to survive (Liu 2016, 437). The quality of criminal defense has also improved, and criminal defense lawyers' work has led to positive changes in the legal system (Li 2014, 223–224).

Under the plea leniency system, a lawyer is required to be present during the discussions of the guilty confessions, so that the suspect understands the meaning and consequences of a guilty admission. According to recent empirical studies (Li 2022a, 2022b), the authorities are now cooperative in allowing defense lawyers to meet with the suspects and to have access to the case files, which eliminates at least two of the three difficulties described above. Even this may be insufficient for achieving the intended goals, however. The lawyers rarely defend the suspects' rights independently. Instead, they tend to become the "explainers, persuaders" of the law, and even the assistants of the procuratorates. They are there merely to satisfy the procedural formality; to provide protection for the authorities in case any suspects later change their minds. According to Enshen Li (2022b, 93), one lawyer said that he was there to "put up the last piece of the puzzle" and "assist the procuratorate with the pursuit of guilty admission."

Many factors contribute to the marginal role of criminal lawyers: Alongside the vague language of the law in promoting the lawyers' role, it is often the case that political influence, ideological beliefs, and institutional arrangements each work against them (Li 2010). The institutional reason for the lawyers being relegated to a marginal role is that the courts are part of the apparatus that combats crime and criminals. The courts are held responsible if criminals are free and the social order is in danger. In this process, they are neither neutral nor detached. To free a defendant means that the procuratorates have made a mistake. Moreover, the procuratorates enjoy a dual role as both the prosecutors and the superintendents of the court process, and of course, they push for the decisions that they have already made and avoid any challenges that the lawyers impose. The best that the courts can do is to mitigate the recommended sentence. Thus, the defense lawyers are not supposed to intervene with the preset course, and any challenge to the predetermined decision is likely to be regarded as "sabotage."

Ultimately, then, the iron triangle in criminal justice—the police, the procuratorates, and the courts— does not include lawyers. Lawyers are regulated by the Bureau of Justice, but they are not the staff of the Bureau. Although the Lawyers' Association exists, it does not possess a strong official status. Thus, the lawyers are not backed by a state apparatus. Their participation is often unwelcome in the criminal justice system, and they may even be regarded as potential troublemakers. What they tell their clients may not be considered as a source of legitimate defense; sometimes it is regarded by the state authorities as an evil suggestion. If the criminals are considered the enemy of the state and the people, then helping them, regardless of whether that help is in accord with the law, becomes tinged with sin. Once again, rights protection is secondary to crime control, and to solidifying the state's legitimacy.

Weiquan Lawyers

Most lawyers, including legal workers, simply want to eke out a living from the business. They are pragmatists. Some of them feel angry about, and frustrated by, the injustices they witness, but social change is not their goal (Yi 2013, 321). Most "eat what they kill". When possible, they rely on their connections with state officials (Li 2022b; Liu and Halliday 2016; Givens 2014). Politically, they are not liberal, and few get themselves into trouble, as long as "they stay within the bounds of the legal system" (Givens 2014, 116–117).

However, a unique group exists, widely known as *weiquan* lawyers, who advocate for interests larger than those of their individual clients. They push for causes as diverse as women's rights, food safety, labor issues, constitutional matters, and human rights (Teng 2016). For some time, *weiquan* litigation has been the major form of political activism in China, and crackdowns on the *weiquan* lawyers have frequently made headlines (Fu 2018; Pils 2014).

There are a variety of *weiquan* lawyers, such as activist lawyers, public interest lawyers, cause lawyers, and "barefoot" lawyers. They can be moderate, critical, or radical (Fu and Cullen 2011b). Moderate lawyers usually accept the legitimacy of the legal system, and often provide legal aid in individual cases, while critical lawyers and radical lawyers challenge the political system as being the cause of injustice. As local courts, the police, and the procuratorates create barriers for them and often deny their requests, these lawyers have to innovatively escalate their tactics (McAdam 1983), and sometimes they resort to radical measures (Fu and Cullen 2011b). Following a repertoire of contentious politics (Tarrow 2011), they expose the irregularities in the practice of local law enforcement activities and seek help from the international world and the media. They share a common characteristic: They use the courtroom as a site to challenge the state's policies and/or behavior, with the rhetoric of law (Fu and Cullen 2011b).

If politically conservative legal aid lawyers are excluded, the number of *weiquan* lawyers is tiny. Nevertheless, they have received tremendous attention in both the media and scholarship. Many of them have been invited abroad to give talks and interviews. In those settings, they are deemed to be heroes fighting against the authoritarian regime at home, and those invitations and images embolden them. They then take on more politically sensitive cases and become more radical.

For a time, the state was actually ambivalent toward this group. As part of the efforts to establish the rule of law, the privatization of the legal profession has provided some space for the *weiquan* lawyers. At one point, they were regarded as an important force for political development, and it seemed that, at least to an extent, the state tolerated criticism from this unique group. Nonetheless, the state has always been cognizant of the danger that this group poses. Even before Xi Jinping's rise, their space had narrowed.

For example, the barefoot lawyers, who were neither formally educated nor licensed, were at one time the primary focus of both the media and academicians. Zhou Guangli, a self-taught farmer specializing in administrative litigation, was touted by China's official media (Wang 2011, 162). Cheng Guangcheng, the blind farmer who had fought for the rights of the disabled, managed to enter the US embassy in Beijing and flee to the US (*New York Times* 2012). However, this group of barefoot lawyers has largely vanished since the Administrative Litigation Law (ALL) was amended in 2015. The amended law narrowed the scope of citizen representation, and the entire group was wiped out.

Under President Xi Jinping, the previously ambivalent official position toward this group changed to one of hostility. The tipping point came on July 9, 2015 (known as the 709 Crackdown), when more than 100 *weiquan* lawyers were arrested nationwide (Teng 2016). The trigger event was a case that involved police use of deadly force. A police officer had shot a petitioner dead while they were arguing. Was it a legitimate use of force or the murder of a petitioner who had simply insisted on his rights? The official conclusion, based on an edited video, was that it was a lawful use of force. However, this was an issue that sparked a nationwide discussion. Subsequently, organized mobilizations discredited the police, and, allegedly, *weiquan* lawyers were at the heart of those mobilizations. According to the official rhetoric, *weiquan* lawyers "spread rumors" and organized street protests without proper permission. The crimes of which they were accused varied, and included jeopardizing national security, colluding with petitioners, and eliciting drug consumption. Many of these lawyers disappeared. Some were tried and thrown into jail, and most of them were not allowed to go abroad, despite protests from the international community. Whereas previously, fame, connections with the state apparatus, or support from the international community were thought to act as a reliable shield against state oppression (Liu and Halliday 2016), the reality has often been grimmer than expected when the regime reveals its true colors. In this situation, the signal was crystal clear: The regime had stopped tolerating this group. The *Xinhua News*, the state's chief news outlet, commented that, "under the banner of 'rights protection,' the substance of it was a criminal organization attempting to subvert the state" (Quoted from Wang 2020b, 1101). Since then, the authorities have employed a heavy-handed approach toward this group (Palmer 2017), using tactics both legal and illegal (Ong 2018), and administrative and criminal. The means have been multifaceted and technologically smart, and the law enforcement presence has been expanded from domestic to international in nature (Pils 2018; Teng 2016). The impact of the 709 Crackdown has been described as "enormous" (Teng 2016). *Weiquan* lawyers have been left with two choices: acquiescence or imprisonment (Fu 2018). If cause lawyers have played an important role in challenging many authoritarian states, they have also invited severe repression in China.

What has become the status of *weiquan* lawyers since the 709 Crackdown? As a result of the state's attitude shift, many previously effective means of protest are no longer usable, and the situation has reached a nadir. *Weiquan* lawyers, although courageous and spirited, are lone fighters. They cannot form widespread alliances, lest their networks be injured (Y. Wang 2021). Can the state eliminate them all? Unlikely. As long as the state relies on the legal system as an important mode of governance, not even the Party can deny the legitimacy of people's rights and thus the lawyers' use of rights. As Hualing Fu (2018, 567) argues, "conscience-shocking episodes, unfilled legal promise and political intolerance" are the warm bed for *weiquan* lawyering. The reform period has produced generations of *weiquan* lawyers. Fu does not believe that repression is the best tactic for the state, and suggests that the most likely outcome will be co-optation. Since the 709 Crackdown, the state has used both "carrots and sticks," disciplining lawyers, on the one hand, and luring them from the street to the courtroom, on the other (Fu 2018, 566). Carefully casting its net, the state differentiates between those who push the legal limits within the courts (the so-called "diehard lawyers") and those who mobilize outside the courts and target the regime itself. In the state's eyes, the diehard lawyers still recognize the system's legitimacy, and thus they contribute to the rule of law. Adhering to a conciliatory tone, the minister of justice has even congratulated the diehard lawyers for reducing wrongful conviction cases—a goal shared by the Party (*Caixin* 2017; quoted from Fu 2018, 566).

The state's attitude toward lawyers has had profound effects on molding the profession of legal practitioners. "Red lawyering" has become a slogan, such that a Party committee is to be established in every law firm and the red gene is to be planted (MOJ 2022). Recent studies (Liu and Stern 2021; Stern and Liu 2020) report that the state has instilled hope and purpose for ordinary lawyers, who can find purpose in their work by contributing to the state's legal development project. Instead of protesting, lawyers can also "become partners in governance by serving as government advisors, providing public goods through legal aid, and easing communication between officials and the public" (Stern and Liu 2020, 228). Conventional lawyers do not challenge the political systems by using the laws. Instead, they serve as a bridge between the state and the public, and between the state and the legal profession. Many of them are not just tolerated by the state but are hailed as "outstanding lawyers." They are regarded as facilitators of the state's economic transactions and development rather than as saboteurs of governance. Top commercial and transactional lawyers have been awarded honorable positions as members of the NPC, and even its constitutional and legal affairs committee (Beijing Lawyer Association 2019). The mainstream lawyers have followed a long-standing tradition of political consultation, under the auspices of the Party. They gain both reputational and business advantages in this process. As allies of the state, some of them actually manage to change society for the better.

A line emerges from the contrast between these two entities: In terms of political reform, what does the state want the legal profession to be? Although *weiquan* lawyering is acclaimed by the international community and much of the scholarly literature, it is, at best, simply co-opted by the state. *Weiquan* lawyers are praised outside of China primarily because they pursue the ideals of human rights and follow a judicialization path to political change, a phenomenon that legal orientalists regard as self-interested idealization (Ruskola 2002); but challenging the state has turned these lawyers into the state's enemies in the real world. In contrast, state-adjacent lawyering has been preferred and complimented. The state wants better governance, and if changes occur, they must do so under the gaze of the political leadership.

Guanxi

As a defining characteristic of Chinese society, *guanxi*, which refers to the beneficial connections or relationships among people, figures prominently in the work and lives of Chinese lawyers. Givens (2014) reports that *guanxi* with the state, rather than political ideology or motivation, distinguishes administrative litigators in China. Until recently, a civil or criminal litigation lawyer might not have survived without having *guanxi* with the judges. Sida Liu (2008, 240; 2011, 279–280) characterizes this relationship as a "symbiotic exchange" in China's legal services market. Put another way, it is "an interdependent and mutually beneficial relationship." Liu extends this even further and suggests that "power dependence is an underlying theme" of *guanxi* (279–280). The judges have the power to decide cases; they also have the sources of potential cases. Their decision-making power and referrals of cases both have critical consequences for lawyers' livelihoods. Legal services providers exchange their revenue and labor with judges for case referrals and decision-making power.

China's lawyers are subordinate to the judges in a hierarchical, patron–client relationship. The judges have rock-hard power and follow instructions from their leaders, not the law (Li 2012, 862). As the saying goes, when they are in front of judges and other legal officials "the male lawyers behave humbly, while the female lawyers are flirting" (Yi 2013, 89). Judges commonly scold lawyers harshly in front of their clients (Yi 2013, 12; see also He and Ng 2013b). Another saying goes, "when judges are hiring prostitutes, lawyers are to keep watch." Two Nanjing lawyers told Komaiko and Que (2009, 125) that "it is rarely possible to escape an interaction with a judge without offering a bribe." "Several female lawyers" have reported experiences in which "judges demanded sexual favors." This does not suggest that all judges are corrupt, but some lawyers do have judges on their payroll (Liu 2017). A more subtle tactic for lawyers has been "striking ... with emotions" (Liu 2011, 287):

> To maintain these relations, even if [you have] no money and cannot give gifts, [you] still have to accumulate emotions in a piecemeal way, to penetrate step by step. Even if nothing is urgent, make some phone calls for greetings, ask whether he needs help in the family, and keep in touch, when cases come up give it to me, your buddy. Remember his birthday and his child's birthday, because some people may not support their parents, some people may not love their wives, but everybody cares about his children. Send a small cake when the time comes, some emotional credits are established, and let him refer cases to me. These kinds of things are not about the amount of money, because the greediness of human beings could never be filled, but about striking him with emotions. If I give cigarettes to the judge, no matter how many judges are in the office, I always give each person a pack, five packs of cigarettes are only a little more than 100 yuan. Just

like the commercial says, 'Input one drop of water every day, when difficulties come up, you will have the Pacific Ocean.'

Mr. Fei, the legal worker who attended the funeral of Judge Zhang's mother, exemplifies this approach. If the gifts of fruits and vegetables he sent to the judges did not make a difference, his attendance at the funeral definitely did.

On the other hand, judges also need lawyers or legal workers for benefits or convenience. After all, judges are not well paid, compared with lawyers. In the past, some judges needed lawyers or legal workers to bring cases to them in order to generate sufficient litigation fees (Fu 2006, 24). Even in the present day, some legal workers have resorted to cleaning court offices and compiling files. Legal workers deal with the litigants that are considered to be troublesome, such as married-out women. Legal workers take legal aid cases, and they also help judges tour remote jurisdictions. When judges stage legal shows in the villages for educational and propaganda purposes, legal workers act as the "secretaries" to help select which cases are appropriate, where to hold the trials, and what to feed the media. The legal worker profession even provides a channel for judges' early retirement, as demonstrated by the case of Ms. Qing.

Guanxi appears to have subsided since the recent reforms. Judges' behavior has become highly regulated, and any misbehavior can ruin their careers. Many judges are punished for their improper *guanxi* behavior (See Chapter 2). Judges have become cautious in their relationships with lawyers. A vice president of an intermediate court told me that she never added lawyers to her WeChat (a popular Chinese social media app); she maintains a cautious distance from the legal profession. Judges' attendance at banquets held by lawyers, which would have been common a few years ago, has vanished since the so-called eight-point austerity regulations under Xi Jinping. Of the 75 death penalty lawyers that Smith (2020, 92) interviewed, none claimed to have "untoward connections."

Guanxi still works, but now it operates in a less visible way, and is more prevalent in less urbanized places (Feng and Xu 2021). Still, even in the big city of Shanghai, maintaining a sound relationship with the Bureau of Justice, the procuratorates, and the courts is the key to criminal lawyers' survival, as the plea leniency system has swept the landscape (Li 2022a, 2022b). Feng and Xu (2021) argue that, in Chinese courts, the operational pattern of *guanxi* has evolved from overt to covert. In the overt form, *guanxi* is a social norm; it operates openly and abusively. In the covert form, it has become more prudent, devious, and deceptive. The force of *guanxi* operates beneath the formal rules. Behind this change are the pressures of severe political control, the reforms for judicial professionalism, and the competition in the legal services market.

In a way, the current scenario makes sense. Market competition, by providing alternative resources, has mitigated the influence of *guanxi*, both within and outside the courts (He and Ng 2017; Lin 2002). In addition, the pressures exerted by

the political control are not merely a toothless tiger. The judges and legal practitioners have become more cautious. When Ms. Qing, the division head who
chose early retirement to become a legal worker, asked the head of the enforcement
bureau for help in freezing the other party's assets in a litigation involving a client,
she deliberately asked a close friend in the civil division to make the telephone call,
even though she herself was closer to the head. In addition, she reminded her civil
division friend to call the head of the enforcement bureau's landline instead of their
mobile, which would have left a record of the call.

The means of communication for *guanxi* is not key, of course. The point is that
the legal practitioners and the judges are linked, whether via landline or WeChat.
The symbiotic relationship between the two professions seems to have become
less visible, and nothing beyond that. *Guanxi*'s influence might be disguised, but
it remains critical between the two professions. Commenting on the relationship
with legal workers, one judge whom I interviewed said: "We live together, grow together, help together. Legal workers are like colleagues. We simply have a division
of labor. Both groups are a transitional phenomenon in the nascent rule of law."
This symbiosis explains why legal workers survive, even in a time when the rule
of law has been deepened and the judges have become professionalized. Article
46 (14) of Regulations on Grassroots Legal Service Workers (2017) prohibits legal
workers from meeting relevant judicial staff for the purpose of influencing the
outcomes of judicial processes, sending them gifts, or inviting them to banquets.
Given their mutual needs, however, the implementation of that requirement appears to be less sanguine.

Insignificant Contributions to Case Outcomes

Chinese lawyers seem to contribute rather insignificantly to the outcomes of criminal cases. Criminal defense (刑事辩护) has been known as a *formality* defense
(形式辩护)(Yin 2018, 116), which is understandable, given the lawyers' marginal role, narrowed space in which to maneuver, and numerous other difficulties
in the process. After reviewing 239 theft cases two decades ago, Lu and Miethe
(2002, 276) suggested that there was "little indication of the effectiveness of defense
attorneys in China." Instead, the case outcomes were based on "legal and extralegal factors such as seriousness of office, confession, residential status and education." Furthermore, they found that a defense that legitimized the system was
likely to be accepted, but a defense that challenged the system would not be. They
even discovered that a stronger defense could invite harsher punishment (Lu and
Miethe 2002, 271). Notably, the system has seen little change over time. According
to Liebman (2015), the lawyers' and their clients' contestations of guilt have had
little effect. The courts almost always convict defendants of the exact crimes
charged. Apparently, a non-guilty verdict is nearly impossible, thus making it wise

for clients to acknowledge guilt and accept the sentences that are suggested to them for leniency. A survey of defense attorneys, as well as of prosecutors, police, and judges, found that criminal defense lawyers agree with other state officials that "their work bears little substantive impact on the final outcomes of the criminal trials" (Liang et al. 2014, 585).

This is not to say that all criminal defenses are useless. Zuo and Ma (2012, 62) found that 6.1 percent of lawyers' defenses were accepted by the courts, and that this number far exceeded the equivalent figure of 0.6 percent for those defendants who represented themselves. However, the lawyers' primary effect is on reducing sentences. In a system with an acquittal rate below 0.2 percent, legal representation can do little by pleading innocence. Even if the 6.1 percent figure cited above indicates some slight effectiveness, legal representation's overall impact was too low, especially at a time when only approximately 20 to 30 percent of the defendants were legally represented (He 2014, 140; McConville et al. 2011; Lu and Miethe 2002). Zuo and Ma (2012, 72) further found that lawyers meeting their clients and questioning the evidence was rarely impactful. Instead, defense activities beyond the trial—in the forms of research, communication, and written opinions—were more likely to be impactful.

Regarding the defenses in death penalty cases (including suspended death penalty cases), a variety of defenses can be raised, including challenges to prosecutorial evidence, mitigating factors of the crime, and defendants' postcrime good behavior (Xiong and Miao 2017). Mitigating factors and challenges to prosecutorial evidence tended to generate much less success than confession and self-surrender. Because confession and self-surrender had occurred before legal representation intervened, the usefulness and effectiveness of legal representation were questionable (Xiong and Miao 2017, 284–285). Another empirical study based on 6,517 death penalty verdicts reported that "acknowledging guilt for leniency" was accepted by most courts (Wang 2021). Wang (2021) concludes that the effectiveness of legal representation is low, given that the defense lawyers' opinions overlook the aggravating or mitigating circumstances, which are the common bases of court decisions.

It could be argued that lawyers are more effective in capital drug cases than in capital murder cases, because in drug cases they can operate using the standards of drug quantity and purity (Smith 2020, 94; but see also Yi 2013, 261). Even so, those lawyers admit that their influence on case outcomes is "low" (Smith 2020, 88). It is estimated that the SPC affirms nearly 99 percent of its death penalty cases (Smith 2020, 89). An SPC death penalty judge once asserted, "I don't think I ever met a lawyer whose opinion on a case was helpful" (Smith 2020, 75). After all, death penalty lawyers are not specialists; they are usually general practitioners "with little interest, experience or expertise in death penalty defense" (Smith 2020, 75). Most such lawyers have no desire to take the job, since it is dangerous and not well paid (Li 2014, 226). In addition to being charged with falsifying evidence, they may receive complaints from their clients, and may sometimes be punished by the Bureau of Justice (Li 2014, 112–115). They also invest little time in preparation; one legal aid lawyer said that he "only spends 3 to 5 hours prepping a capital case" (Smith 2020, 83). Whereas nowadays legal representation is required for all criminal cases, the presence of representation is different from a truly effective representation (Yin 2018). According to Yin (2018, 117), 70 percent of legal representation is private, while the rest is from legal aid lawyers. It is common for law firms to send young and inexperienced legal aid lawyers for death penalty review cases. On average, legal aid lawyers in Beijing charge approximately 2,000 yuan per case, while privately hired lawyers can charge 1,000 times more (Smith 2020, 83).

A similar pattern exists in administrative cases. Most lawyers also prefer not to take administrative cases—not because the cases are dangerous or impossible (as is sometimes depicted by the media), but because they are "difficult, controversial, time consuming and tend to produce only meager financial returns" (Givens 2014, 127): "A lawyer specializing in administrative law would quickly starve to death" (Givens 2014, 116). Most administrative litigators take the job because of their connection with the state, and thus their challenges to the state are often "diluted" (Givens 2014, 133). Only occasionally do these challenges have an effect beyond individual cases (Givens 2004, 130). One administrative litigator told Givens (2014, 131), "you cannot single-mindedly pursue legal change—that is not your purpose." Furthermore, with the increase in administrative litigation, the ratio of legal representation *has decreased*. Ji Li (2013) suggests that lawyers are unwilling to pursue administrative litigation against powerful state agencies. Apparently, they advise their clients to "lump it", or simply to settle without a lawsuit. According to Li, "professional legal assistance adds little value." Echoing Li's research, Mao and Qiao (2021, 848) found that, in eminent domain cases, "hiring a lawyer does not necessarily increase a plaintiff's probability of winning. Overall, lawyers make an insignificant contribution to the final case outcomes."

The situation in civil cases is more complex. As shown above, even if the parties and their legal representatives cannot produce evidence, the judges have to locate evidence themselves, in order for their decisions to be able to withstand scrutiny. Civil lawyers or legal workers may present a lengthy and enthusiastic speech at the court hearing, but for most judges this is merely a show that wastes everybody's time. Indeed, for cases that have been settled before the hearing, lawyers and legal workers may have done virtually nothing. The present author witnessed one judge tell a litigant: "You should get your money back from the legal worker, because he ain't doing nothing!" Of course, there are variations across the types of lawyers. If the "two hemispheres" of the legal profession (Heinz and Laumann 1982) also existed in China, Beijing lawyers focusing on commercial litigation with large disputed amounts or intellectual property cases with multiple technical issues would undoubtedly have a greater effect on the case outcomes than would the rural legal workers. An empirical study based on 3,016 copyright lawsuits found that the presence of lawyers alone did not affect the case outcomes, but the presence of professional lawyers did (Tian et al. 2021, 173). In other words, the quality of the lawyers, not their mere presence, makes a difference.

Although the lawyers in civil litigation play a weak role in court, they can still contribute to evidence collection and can sometimes coach their clients into behaving strategically. Do these efforts improve the likelihood of winning? Yang Su and I (He and Su 2013) assert that legal representation consistently contributes to a party's chances of winning. We suggest that legal representation may help the litigating parties locate evidence. The professional lawyers may also have expertise in the type of evidence that counts and how to locate it. Because the judges rely on written evidence for their decision-making, the evidence provided may be influential.

However, there is another possible explanation for the increased likelihood of winning with the presence of a lawyer. The parties with more resources, especially those who have *guanxi* with the state and the courts, are better positioned to win. It is likely that the party who can afford to hire lawyers is also more well-connected, and those connections are able to influence the case outcomes more. Yang Su and I should have delved deeper, in an effort to single out the singular effect of lawyering on the civil litigation process. Thus, the effects exerted by the lawyers in civil litigation remain inconclusive.

Wouldn't lawyers with *guanxi* have an impact? This is likely, but it does not prevent the other party from also having lawyers with *guanxi*. An empirical study on contract cases showed that the presence of lawyers did not significantly affect the outcomes, but the presence of *local* lawyers did (Yu and Wei 2017, 95). To influence a case outcome, one needs rock-hard *guanxi*: personal, intimate connections, or strong ties, to use Granovetter's term (1974). Indeed, impactful *guanxi* often carries significant political weight (He and Ng 2017). Lawyers may maintain strong ties with judges, but they do not have a politically superior role over the judges (Li 2012). All of that said, it is relatively easy for lawyers to obtain case referrals from judges—and they are unlikely to be punished for this, as is the case for expediting asset freezing, which is lawful and within the judges' discretion—but it is not so easy to influence the case outcomes. A death penalty lawyer said, bluntly, that in big cities in which the rule of law is well established, "[a] lawyer who says he relies on connections is basically a swindler" (Smith 2020, 92). In administrative lawsuits, "[a] lawyer cannot expect a judge to rule against the State on the basis of connections alone" (Givens 2014, 122). One informant told Givens, aptly, that "connections are probably least important in administrative cases because even if you had good connections with the government, it is the government that you are suing" (Givens 2014, 123). No judge would be "foolhardy enough" to treat the state unfairly (Givens 2014, 123). After all, judges are under scrutiny for their decisions and are held responsible for these for their whole lifetimes. Most would pause before altering a case outcome simply because of *guanxi* with legal practitioners.

A Profession without Professionalism

As early as 2005, Lo and Snape (2005) had already found among lawyers a "well-developed sense of professional identity, based on an enthusiasm for the profession, as well as a sense of professional obligation," and "a growing client orientation ... accountable to their clients before society or the state." For the lawyers surveyed by Lo and Snape, this might have been true, but two decades after their survey, their assertion seems far from being an accurate characterization of the profession.

If competence, loyalty to clients, and independence are the major criteria for legal professionalism, Chinese lawyers sit below the bar. Especially in the past, some have been characterized as "three-no lawyers": in soliciting clients, they say "no problem"; when things are not going well, they say "no worries"; and when the case is decided, they say "no solution" (Yi 2013, 41). Granted, over time their overall competence has increased, with the proportion of legal workers declining and the educational level of lawyers rising. However, even today, lawyers' educational and legal-knowledge backgrounds are still at lower levels than those of judges and prosecutors (Liu 2016, 415). *Guanxi* remains an important factor in their survival. *Weiquan* lawyers try to support a better rule of law, but most are co-opted by the state, and their impact is minuscule. The majority of criminal lawyers serve less as advocates for their clients' interests and more as assistants of judicial officials in repressing their own clients—they actually help prosecutors coerce their own clients into accepting guilty pleas despite the detrimental consequences of those deals. They also help the judges explain the laws, the political concerns, or the routine of the courts. Their job includes facilitating mediations and criminal reconciliations, and some judges even nickname them the people's mediators (Yi 2013, 37). In addition, they help control veteran petitioners, and they participate in legal propaganda campaigns. A criminal lawyer told Enshen Li (2022b, 95):

> We show our 'sincerity' through cooperative work with police, procuratorates and judges. At the end of the day, they are happy to refer some cases in one way or another. You know, finding stable sources of cases is the greatest interest of most defense lawyers in China ... who doesn't want to have a good life?

Lawyers worldwide screen clients, but Chinese lawyers are blunt toward the vulnerable and poor (Michelson 2006). One lawyer said: "Lawyers are not like people think they are. They do not find justice, they do not bring the truth out, and they do not restore the truth of law" (Michelson 2006, 14). Ke Li (2015) found that legal professionals routinely subject women to gender bias and stereotypes; women's attempts at legal mobilization have been blocked or even derailed, and, as a result, women's grievances and rights are often not transformed into formal claims. In one extreme case, when a woman had sought a legal worker's help because she had been domestically raped, the legal worker responded that "what he did was lawful!" (Li 2015). Whereas it is true that marital rape is not considered a criminal offence under the current laws, the legal worker still could have advised the woman to seek civil remedies (Li 2015, 170). Legal workers frequently filter disputes, preventing them from escalating into events that could threaten social stability.

Indeed, the state has never had the goal of sculpting a "professional legal profession." In the Chinese Communist Party (CCP)'s landmark *Decision to Comprehensively Advancing Rule of Law* (CPC 2014), the professionalism of judges, prosecutors, and other members of the rule of law team is stressed, but lawyers do not belong to *the rule of law* team—along with notaries public, grass-roots legal workers, mediators, and volunteers, lawyers belong to the team of *legal service providers*. In the paragraph of the *Decision* on these legal service providers, the first sentence places emphasis on the need to strengthen the thoughts and political indoctrination of lawyers: "Loyalty to the Party and the support of socialist rule of law is a fundamental requirement for lawyers." The *Decision* requires that, in law firms, whether private or public, the Party organization is to play a core political role, and it emphasizes how lawyers are to be regulated. All Party, government, and social organizations and groups are to have government lawyers, while enterprises are to have company lawyers. There is not a single word about the need to protect the safety of criminal defense lawyers and *weiquan* lawyers, or about enhancing lawyers' social or political status.

From the perspective of governance, the development of the Chinese legal profession presents a critical challenge to traditional assumptions about lawyers in Western jurisprudence. It is assumed that China's lawyers, "whether out of idealism or self-interest or some blend thereof, will prove to be a principal force leading the PRC toward the rule of law and a market economy ... and a more liberal polity" (Alford 2007, 287). In the eyes of the state, however, lawyers play, at most, an auxiliary role in governance. Although lawyers may facilitate economic transactions, advise litigants, preserve social harmony, or even help enforce rights, professional and elitist lawyers who prioritize clients' interests over the state are not needed, and the state has little tolerance for the equivalent of the "professional lawyers" that are common in a civil society. Ideologically, Ma Xiwu, who defined the Chinese judicial system during the revolutionary period, stated that "the opinion of the masses is more powerful than the law" (D. He 2021). Indeed, the state is cautious about the potential impact of *weiquan* lawyers. Even during the period when they were tolerated, the senior party leader in charge of political-legal affairs said, "[b]e highly vigilant, closely preventing the sabotage under the banner of *weiquan*" (Renhelaw 2008). In the state's eyes, this type of lawyer may not necessarily help governance;

instead, they may be considered a medium for promoting Western ideology, and therefore a threat to the legitimacy and even the very existence of the state. Why would such a group ever be needed?

Conclusions

The four decades from approximately 1980 to the present have witnessed a surge in the number of lawyers in China. In the early 1980s, the presence of a lawyer in Chinese courts was a rare occurrence, but today, trials without lawyers are far less common. In criminal trials, a lawyer's representation is compulsory, either through a private hiring or state-sponsored legal assistance. Lawyers have also become better trained and more professional. The number of nonlawyer legal workers has declined, and those workers are being further pushed toward underdeveloped areas and service markets that formally licensed lawyers have relinquished.

Lawyers in Chinese courts have limited roles. Similar to many continental jurisdictions, judges hold the power in the litigation process. Lawyers' roles are weaker in this process. Chinese judges are closely monitored by the state, so their self-protection is a priority. They are not willing to give up power or trust lawyers.

Specifically, in civil trials Chinese judges rely largely on themselves to find evidence, and thus marginalize the role of lawyers. Here, the dynamic bears a resemblance to the Russian system (Hendley 2007). In criminal trials, lawyers play only a support role, as the state apparatuses are the leading actors. As this chapter's examples have demonstrated, lawyers' impacts on case outcomes remain insignificant, except in some rather legally technical cases. A fundamental reason for this is that, structurally, the profession does not have a position in the state apparatuses and instead must rely on the symbiotic relationship of *guanxi* with the state's legal personnel—the police, the prosecutors, and the judges. As a partial exception, some criminal lawyers do, in fact, have an impact on case outcomes, exactly because they have backgrounds or connections in the political-legal agencies. Furthermore, in the Xi Jinping era, the state tightly controls or actively persecutes so-called radical *weiquan* lawyers. Great sympathy is generated in the international community for the *weiquan* lawyers, but their domestic impact has been severely maimed. From the perspective of the state, an unregulated legal profession is out of the question. In Xi's era, the state has more forcefully shaped the profession to boost governance. The room once generated by the market reform has been narrowed (Ohnesorge 2023). Overall, Chinese lawyers are a profession without professionalism.

Why would the state not allow a legal profession to flourish? A full treatment of this question is beyond the scope of this book, but a straightforward answer can be obtained by asking the extent to which the legal profession contributes to the state's governance, primarily in terms of the state's two main goals for the profession: policy implementation and legitimacy enhancement. Recent studies have found that lawyers do contribute to the maintenance of stability (Zheng and Hu 2020), but such a role is minor at best. Lawyers may also facilitate economic development and dispute resolution, and help their clients, but even so, judges sometimes complain that the lawyers make things more complicated. Lawyers do help enhance legitimacy: the judicial system looks better and more credible when it operates with lawyers. They also help protect rights for their clients and advance the legal consciousness of society. Indeed, that is exactly why the profession was authorized in the first place. In reality, however, this function is more decorative than substantive. If lawyers are cooperative in facilitating the state's goals, they are tolerated or even welcomed. Some commercial lawyers and "red" lawyers have gained prominent positions, and have been recognized favorably by the state. By contrast, radical *weiquan* lawyers have suffered. The link between cause lawyering and social movements, which is common in liberal democracies (Scheingold and Sarat 2004), remains unrealistic in China.

5

Litigants' Views of the Courts

How the courts are viewed by the general public is far from trivial. If the public's impression of the courts in liberal democracies is comparable to "consumer satisfaction," then authoritarian states, such as China, will be likely to place their focus on "regime satisfaction," because such states rely on the courts for effective governance. According to Gallagher and Wang (2011, 204), "creating positive citizen attitudes toward the legal system is part of a strategy to avoid democracy." Xi Jinping (2015, 1) stressed that "the ultimate yardstick for judicial reforms is whether public trust toward the judiciary has been improved."

President Xi's concern is not misplaced. The juxtaposition of the party-state's reliance on the laws to govern and the general public's mistrust of the laws and the courts creates a constant tension. Adopted by the party-state as an instrument of governance, the laws are imposed upon the population and thus are external to Chinese society. Public mistrust toward the laws and the court systems is widespread. The Chinese people continually have high hopes for two alternative routes to justice. The first is for *guanxi*, or the social network of persons with whom one has connections that can facilitate one's business transactions and other dealings. Popular opinions about *guanxi* include: "[t]o file a lawsuit is to employ *guanxi*" (Komaiko and Que 2009, 48); "[o]nce the litigation is taken, the two sides were busy with locating connections" (Gao et al. 2009, 389); and "[w]ith *guanxi*, everything is fine, whilst nothing can be done without *guanxi*." The second alternative that inspires the public's hope for justice is to petition for help from upper-level officials. Another saying goes, "petitioning is more trustworthy than law."

This chapter begins with a discussion of the public's first belief in legal consciousness—*guanxi*—and its relationship with the law in the courts. The discussion then moves on to the people's second belief—petitioning—which litigants often use when they lose their cases. I will then demonstrate that, unlike the procedural justice in Western societies, procedural justice in China provides little cushioning to help Chinese litigants accept unfavorable outcomes. After describing the dilemma faced by Chinese courts in improving the public's confidence toward the judiciary, this chapter concludes with an insight into the tension that exists when the courts are employed as a mechanism for governance.

The Judicial System of China. Xin He, Oxford University Press. © Xin He 2025. DOI: 10.1093/9780198927815.003.0006

Guanxi as an Entrenched Worldview

Patricia Ewick and Susan Silbey (1998, 47–49) propose a typology of legal consciousness among the general population in the US: before the law, with the law, and against the law. "Before the law" is used to suggest that most Americans, who usually have no experience with law enforcement or the courts, believe in "the appropriateness and justness provided through formal legal procedures" (Ewick and Silbey 1998, 47). Objectiveness and impartiality are the characteristics of the law. Even though Americans may express frustration and powerlessness before the law, they "defer to" the law's authority (Ewick and Silbey 1998, 47).

However, such respect toward the law is uncommon among average Chinese citizens. In Fei Xiaotong's (1992, 63) iconic metaphors, Western society resembles a haystack composed of bundles of straw. Individuals, represented by the pieces of straw, form organizations with clear boundaries. By contrast, Chinese society can be illustrated by the concentric ripples that emerge when a stone is thrown into water. Each individual stands at the center of a unique network of *guanxi*, an egotistical network that has no explicit boundaries and has varying magnitudes of beneficial personal and business relationships consistently infiltrating it. *Guanxi* is regarded as a broad, diffused, and deep-rooted phenomenon of Chinese society. According to Fei, Confucian ethics comprise a form of tiered social ethics: familial relationships, long-term friends, classmates, schoolmates, in-laws, colleagues, business partners, and acquaintances. Society is composed not of discrete individuals and organizations, but of overlapping networks of people linked together through differentially categorized social relationships (Fei 1992, 20).

Once Chinese citizens encounter disputes in which legal authorities are involved, their default response is not necessarily to find a lawyer—instead, it is to turn to *guanxi*: "Do I know someone who can help? Or can my network of *guanxi* help?" In other words, people have little trust in the law; on the contrary, they believe in the person with whom they have *guanxi*.

In one example, an uncle of a retired judge consulted her in relation to a tort lawsuit. He had paid a laborer 4,000 yuan to demolish his house. Unexpectedly, the laborer fell from the roof of the house and was consequently injured, with medical bills that totaled 200,000 yuan. The laborer sued the uncle for 50 percent of the cost, and the uncle said to the retired judge:

[The laborer] fell down due to his negligence. Why am I being held responsible? 50 percent of the cost? I won't pay a cent. Apparently *li* [reason] is on my side. But things have become uncertain after he filed the lawsuit in court. You must find *guanxi* for me; I am willing to pay for the favor.

The uncle had little trust or confidence in the law. After the court had taken the case, he remarked, "[t]hings have become uncertain." He believed that *li* was on his side, but the legal process created uncertainty. Ultimately, he displayed immense trust in *guanxi*, which is why he entreated of the retired judge: "You must find *guanxi* for me."

The judge said:

It depends on whether your relationship with him is *employment* or *contract for work*. If it is the former, you are responsible. You hired the person to demolish the house for you, quite a dangerous undertaking. Yet you did not provide enough safety protection for him. You may be negligent. If it is the latter, you are not responsible.

The uncle exclaimed, "[o]f course it is the latter! He always demolishes houses like this. I paid for his service. Why should I provide safety protection for him?!"

The judge countered, "[y]ou have to provide evidence for this." The uncle then invited a middleman who had helped them form the agreement, to come and recount their "contracting process" in the court hearing. The court nevertheless ruled that the uncle was liable for paying 60,000 yuan, or 30 percent of the worker's medical bills, because the court found that he had hired a worker who lacked a license in housing demolition.

The uncle's mistrust toward the court was apparent: "I have lived for 60 years and I have never heard that a license is needed for demolishing houses! This court decision is just absurd!" He immediately blamed himself:

It was all my fault. An acquaintance in the Industrial and Commercial Bureau said that he knew the court division head. I only begged him to talk to the head. I did not manage to meet the head, nor did I send him any money. I only sent him, through the acquaintance, two bars of cigarettes, worth 1,500 yuan. Obviously, the two bars of cigarettes were not effective. Nowadays, *guanxi* must be obtained beforehand.

His deep trust in *guanxi* had evidently prompted him to blame himself for the unfavorable outcome, which he thought had happened only because he had not worked hard enough on building *guanxi*.

The uncle was so dissatisfied with the judgment that he proceeded to launch an appeal, and this time he found an overwhelmingly powerful *guanxi* in the appeal court. The final decision reduced his responsibility to 20 percent. The uncle grinned:

The *guanxi* said, 'Had I contacted him before the first instance trial, he would have guaranteed that I would not even have to pay a cent!' If only I found this *guanxi* earlier! The effectiveness of the laws that you mentioned, at the end of the day, depends on who is using them.

To the uncle, the person who applies the law is more important than the law itself, which explains the significance of finding the right *guanxi*. His scorn toward the laws is transparent in his choice of words. He did not mention "who is applying the law." Instead, he said it "depends who is *using* the laws." The law is there as an instrument, to be utilized by the judges to achieve whatever purposes. In short, he showed a greater reliance on the person than on the law.

The uncle did indeed have every reason to believe in *guanxi*, and his case outcomes only served to verify his beliefs. Rock-hard *guanxi* makes a clear difference. This may explain why *guanxi* is ubiquitous in the operations of Chinese courts (He and Ng 2017). In one survey, 52 percent of judges said that cases were frequently influenced by *guanxi*, and 61 percent said that as long as that influence from *guanxi* fell within the scope of discretion, they tended to favor the connected parties (Wang 2015, 249, 265). A trial judge said to me: "Everywhere we are embedded in *guanxi*. Indeed, *guanxi* has become part of our lives. We make use of *guanxi*; as a chain of the network, we are also being used by others in *guanxi*" (He and Ng 2017, 841). If, as Rousseau (1762) suggests, "[m]an is born free and everywhere he is in chains," for the Chinese those "chains" are largely manifested in *guanxi*. In some exaggerated accounts, one might even argue that *guanxi* has formed part of the genetic makeup of Chinese people. *Guanxi* is what Chua and Engel (2019, 336) call the element of "worldview" in the legal consciousness of the Chinese people. *Guanxi* is the people's "understanding of their society, their place in it, their positions relative to others, and accordingly, the manner in which they should perform social interactions" (Chua and Engel 2019, 336–337).

As an influential factor that has long dominated the legal consciousness of Chinese people, *guanxi* works against the principle of equal protection which forms the foundation for the contemporary legal system. How the law is used and whether a legal application is fair depend on who is using it. The legal consciousness of litigants is thus a function of *guanxi* between the judges and those litigants. With *guanxi*, the judge becomes one of "those on our side," or *zijiren* (H. Wang 2019), and the law can be bent. This dovetails well with what Qian Liu (2023, 214) refers to as "relational legal consciousness"—that the expectations of "how to respond to law change[...] significantly when we situate ourselves in different types of relationships."

Despite the harsh punishment of *guanxi*-influenced judges since the 2014 judicial reforms, empirical evidence suggests that the impact of *guanxi* persists (Feng and Xu 2021). Recently, a judge of the Hunan High Court was murdered by a former classmate simply because the judge refused to find *guanxi* for the classmate (Xinhua Net 2021). Of course, this hideous crime is worthy of being denounced. That said, the reaction of the classmate—to murder the judge after being rejected— also reflects the extent to which *guanxi* has permeated citizens' beliefs.

Belief in Petitioning instead of in the Law

Dissatisfaction with China's court system has been widespread. Judges are often depicted as officials who "take advantage of the defendant after having taken advantage of the plaintiff." The public has little sense of legitimacy and respect for the courts and the judges.

In addition to their belief in *guanxi*, Chinese people's mistrust toward the courts can also be reflected in the phenomenon of "believing in petitioning instead of law." Complaints to upper-level governments about the courts, also known as petitioning (上访或信访), are persistent. In 2015, the Chinese courts received almost 8 million petition cases, constituting 4.52 percent of the total caseload (SPC Work Report 2016).

Petitioning is an umbrella term to describe "Chinese appeals to justice" (Minzner 2006, 110). Almost all Chinese social management organs have set up petition offices at various levels, including the people's congresses, judiciaries, government apparatuses, and Party committees (Minzner 2006; Cai 2004). Litigation-related petitioners are people who have exhausted the legal procedures but remain dissatisfied with the decisions of the courts. Most have lost not only their cases, but also their faith in the judges (Gao et al. 2009, 228). Some petitioners may have followed routine appeal procedures or may be in the midst of the appeal process, and many see petitioning as their last resort in seeking remedies through the adjudication supervision process. Petitioners normally give up after one or two unsuccessful visits, although a tiny portion of them stay persistent in making repeated claims over their original disputes. In addition, some add to their claims by highlighting the problems they have encountered during the course of their repeated petitioning, which may have lasted for years or even decades.

Why would the litigants believe in petitioning instead of in the law? On one hand, the rhetoric of the Party projects the petition system as a platform from which the voices of the people can be heard. As a result, these petitioners believe that the central committee of the Chinese Communist Party (CCP), or a more abstract idea of "heaven," will bring them justice (Li et al. 2012; Hou 2011). Although many endure the unbearable sufferings of the petition process, such as potentially facing unemployment or experiencing the decline of their mental health, some still flock to Beijing and other provincial political centers to petition for justice. Many choose politically sensitive periods to visit Beijing, such as during the Two Conferences (the National People's Congress Conference and the National Political Consultation Conference), May 1 (Labor Day), or October 1 (National Day) (Feng and He 2018); some even remain in Beijing permanently (Hou 2011, 650). To maintain stability in Beijing, many local governments have illegally detained these petitioners in "black jails" (Hou 2012) and sent them back home, only to find that they reappear in Beijing the next year.

On the other hand, petitioning sometimes works. Until recently, the judiciary was more inclined to buy off the most determined and "disruptive" petitioners, using for those payoffs the budget allocated for stability maintenance. Sometimes, courts were "over-responsive" (Liebman 2011) and petitioners were willing to take the money and drop their cases (at least temporarily), despite being deprived of a more solid legal remedy. As seen in the *Medical Malpractice Case* cited at the beginning of the book, judges in the past compensated diehard petitioners to dissuade them from petitioning, fearing that if petitioners were to escalate and publicize their protest activities, they might put the judges' careers at risk and leave them in the awkward position of using taxpayers' money to bail themselves out (Hou 2011, 658). The stability-maintenance fund, therefore, became a compromise that served as a feasible substitute for legal remedies. In that process, the petition procedure became less pertinent, however, as petitioners turned out to be more concerned with outcomes.

Petitioners often view their litigation and subsequent petitioning experiences as injurious and prefer to blame officials for these. In normal dispute contexts, the type and scale of the disputes depend more on the person's initial perception of injury than on any later decisions (Felstiner et al. 1981; Barton and Mendlovitz 1960). In the case of petitioners, however, the injurious experiences are assessed and accumulated throughout the process of petitioning, with the judges and petition officials often replacing the original target of their complaints and becoming the major source of their grievances. Although petitioners have their own disputes before they turn to the petition offices, most petitioners believe that officials are the ones who cause and aggravate their misfortunes (see He et al. 2013). In their minds, their unsuccessful attempts at litigation and their laborious petition experiences deprive them of the benefits they deserve, and they believe the officials should be held responsible for this.

I was told by a judge that, in one case, Ms. Zhang was clawed by a pet dog, and in court she reached a settlement of 8,000 yuan with the dog owner. Several months later, Ms. Zhang contracted vasculitis and made a claim to the trial court. The judge declined her lawsuit, quoting the *ne bis in idem* principle, which prevents a defendant being tried twice for the same matter. Ms. Zhang then submitted a petition to the intermediate court for a second trial, arguing that the judicial settlement had failed to take her vasculitis into consideration. As a first-instance petitioner, Ms. Zhang, like most litigants, framed her complaint as a tort case, naming her vasculitis as injurious and pointing the finger at the dog owner. Her naming and blaming were based on her understanding of the law: the owner should be held responsible for the harm caused by his pet. Yet a medical examination for Ms. Zhang subsequently revealed no causal relation between her injury from the dog and the vasculitis infection. Ms. Zhang's petition was, therefore, rejected.

Lacking a legitimate cause, Ms. Zhang refrained from petitioning for a while. However, her family could not afford her medical expenses, leaving her with no choice. She then submitted another petition to the intermediate court. After several unsuccessful visits, Ms. Zhang reached a boiling point and obstructed the car of the municipal party secretary in order to win the attention of the official, who had previously expressed concern regarding her case. Under political pressure, the intermediate court granted Ms. Zhang extra compensation. However, Ms. Zhang found this outcome to be unsatisfactory, feeling that it did not adequately acknowledge her devotion, time, and energy. She then began to switch her focus to the intermediate court, blaming them for her misfortune. She condemned the judges for maliciously declining her application for a new trial and treating her arrogantly. Her tactic of naming and blaming thus shifted focus away from the dog owner and onto case mishandling by the judges. The tort case henceforth evolved into a mishandling dispute.

Once judicial mishandling becomes the target of naming and blaming, the judiciary is treated as an opponent rather than a neutral decision-maker, and the original personal disputes are transformed into a nasty feud between the powerless individual and the almighty state. This transformation of disputes results from the petitioners' changed perception of legality. In their original personal disputes, the law enables them to shape their perception of legality, thereby allowing them to voice their complaints on that basis, even if the law may not provide a remedy. In disputes between petitioners and state apparatuses, in contrast, the petitioners find the legal framing unrealistic, and they increasingly resort to other means to draw official attention to their complaints. The extended scope of naming and blaming imposes political pressure on the courts.

The lack of authority and finality of petitioning has turned the petition process into an ineffective yet vicious cycle. Therefore, realizing the gravity of the issue, the Party's politburo has recently sanctioned a new regulation for the petition process (Central Committee of the Party and the State Council 2022), replacing the original one issued by the State Council. The new regulation represents a watershed moment in several respects: First, the highest decision-making body of the Party has usurped the legislative role of the State Council; second, the Party's role is omnipresent in this process. The Chinese character "dang" (the Party) appears 82 times in the regulation and echoes the trend and narrative that "the Party leads all" (DeLisile and Yang 2022). Finally, the new regulation clearly states the finality of the petition process: after being reviewed, the same issue will no longer be further considered (Art. 36). Apparently, the evolving petitioning system will continue to influence the perceptions of justice among Chinese litigants.

Does Procedural Justice Matter?

Thibaut and Walker (1975) argue that the public's perceptions of procedural justice affect their level of satisfaction toward the overall process, regardless of the actual level of fairness of the outcomes obtained. Scholars generally believe that procedural justice can act as a "cushion of support," alleviating the negative emotions elicited by unfavorable outcomes (Lind and Tyler 1988). Of course, no one likes to lose, but one cannot always expect to win when facing conflicts with others. In spite of this, "losing" is more willingly accepted if the loser believes that the court procedures adopted were fair. People view "bad" distributive outcomes more positively and with greater mercy if those outcomes result from a procedure they consider fair. Procedural justice can promote satisfaction, belief in the legitimacy of authority, and willingness to comply and cooperate with the law (Creutzfeldt and Bradford 2016; Tyler 1990). The importance of procedural justice has been demonstrated in various settings throughout North America, Europe, and Asia, and through a wide range of methodologies (MacCoun 2005, 173).

Do Chinese litigants also subscribe to procedural justice? Some studies suggest that distributive justice may be more important (e.g., Su 2014), but these studies are often based on surveys of the general public, in which most of those surveyed had no experience with the real litigation process. Existing studies focusing on litigants who had experienced court proceedings nearly invariably pointed to the decisive role of distributive justice, or outcomes, in shaping Chinese litigants' view of the courts. Feng Li's Shanghai survey (2013, 142) suggests that distributive justice is far more important than procedural justice. My study on debt-collection cases (He 2011, 269) found "a strong correlation between the enforcement result and the impression of the court." Positive impressions would prevail if the court helped to recover the debt, and that would especially be the case if there was a chance for it to be fully recovered. Otherwise, the impression was negative. One plaintiff said:

> We could not recover our debt by ourselves, that's why we resorted to the court. But if the court could not even get its own judgment enforced, how could we have a good impression? We did not have issues with the adjudicating judge, but were skeptical about the court's efforts in enforcement.

A pragmatic user of the courts evidently values substantive justice much more than procedural justice.

Yuqing Feng and Qing Cao (2014) present a dramatic scenario in their demonstration of the importance of substantive justice for litigants in a dispatched tribunal in rural China. For the litigants' own good, the judges imposed their "expected outcomes" on the litigants, regardless of the litigants' intentions. Arguably by ignoring the litigants' own voices and harming their self-dignity, this approach contradictorily enhanced the litigants' recognition of the court's decisions. It showed that, as long as the litigants gained something, their *voices* or *self-dignity* were not important.

These findings are consistent with the statement of a judge who we interviewed (Ng and He 2017a, 76):

Sometimes litigants who lost would say to me: "You must have taken money from the other party." Many of them are elderly. When I had the time, I'd sit down and chat with them. And I'd tell them: "Grandma, we're talking about 3,000 yuan (the disputed claim). You lost and you said I took money from the other party. So, please tell me, how much money did you think the other party paid me to make you lose?"

The litigants who lose almost reflexively blame the judges for being corrupt, even though it is uneconomical to pay off a judge for such a small amount of money in a dispute. In this light, it is evident that the role of procedural justice is minimal.

In a systematic study on the topic, Jing Feng and I interviewed and surveyed 142 litigants who had experienced the courts in southern China (He and Feng 2021). In face-to-face interviews with those who had endured the civil justice system in China, we inquired about their litigation experiences and explored the role of procedural justice in their impressions of the court. Notably, we found that procedural justice played a minimal role. The interviewees' perceptions of justice were overwhelmingly determined by distributive justice, or whether they had obtained a favorable outcome: "Distributive justice alone explained more than 70% of the variation in satisfaction with outcomes" (He and Feng 2021, 122), whereas "[t]he unique contribution by procedural justice was 13%" (120). Furthermore, we observed a high correlation between procedural justice and distributive justice, suggesting that those obtaining less equitable outcomes tended to believe that their trials were procedurally lacking in guaranteeing fairness. When the outcome is unexpected, litigants infer that the process has been unfair.

Sources of Dissatisfaction

What are the sources of litigants' dissatisfaction? Distributive justice draws links to three questions to be asked in judicial decision-making: What constitute the facts? What role will the judge play? And what criteria will the judge apply? (He and Feng 2021). Litigants' subsequent dissatisfaction often stems from tensions between legal facts and their perceptions of the facts, between paternalistic judges and neutral arbitrators, and between moral principles and legal rules. Such tensions are so remarkable in China that they appear to suggest high levels of mistrust between the litigants and the courts, alongside the lack of authority and confidence that the court receives from the public.

Perceived Facts

Litigants often present their perceived facts, or their own interpretations of the disputes, and in their views those facts are straightforward and crystal clear. In a divorce petition documented by Wei Ding (2014, 239–240), the plaintiff claimed that her husband had had an extramarital affair. She lamented to the court staff, "it is a matter known to all villagers. What other evidence do you need?" In another case, the parents of a child believed that the medicine taken by their son would suffice as evidence for their son's capability to recover from a psychiatric disease, thus providing a legal basis for divorce (Ding 2014, 236–238). Any subsequent judgments would only be deemed fair by the litigants if, and only if, those judgments had been based solely on the evidence they provided. However, in scenarios where these litigants realized that the decisions had been based on legal facts—those proven by admitted evidence, rather than what they perceived to be true—they were immediately dissatisfied. In our interviews (He and Feng 2021, 125), Mr. Zhang, a construction worker in his mid-30s who had been injured in a traffic accident, provided a cunning example.

> Q: Were you given adequate opportunity to present evidence and opinions?
> Mr. Zhang [ignoring our question]: The compensation for lost income was rather unfair. I was out of work for 31 days, but the court only awarded me 3,500 yuan. I can earn much more than that, even with my part-time jobs ... I can earn at least 250 yuan per day, sometimes 400 or 500. In fact, I had only asked for 5,500 yuan, which is lower than my monthly income.

Mr. Zhang's disregard for our question on procedural justice provided room for him to focus on the unfairness of the outcome. His perceived facts were that he could earn at least 5,500 yuan per month, and that he was out of work for a whole month due to the traffic accident. Therefore, he deserved 5,500 yuan in compensation for his lost income. However, the judge chose to adjudicate on the basis of the legal facts, namely the facts that had been proven by evidence or directly stipulated by the law. Because Mr. Zhang had failed to present any evidence to prove his monthly wage, the judge had instead relied on the average income of a construction worker as stipulated by law, which was 3,500 yuan. Hence, the legal facts in the case were: (a) Mr. Zhang had been unable to work for one month; but (b) he only earned 3,500 yuan per month, rather than 5,500 yuan. Obviously, there was a gap between Mr. Zhang's perceived facts and the legal facts. Although we explained the court's rationale to him, Mr. Zhang remained unconvinced and angry. The discrepancy between the legal facts and his perceived facts had led to his dissatisfaction.

The Judge as a Parent

Litigants usually consider the judge to be a "parent official (父母官)," a Confucian image that illustrates closeness to the masses, friendliness to the litigants, and patience and proactivity in ensuring and supporting the litigating parties' interests.

In the litigants' views, judges should take the initiative to investigate the facts, summon witnesses, and collect evidence, whereas the litigants themselves should only be required to play a subsidiary role. Litigants are also generally unaware of the fact that the burden of proof is on them, and that the judge merely acts as a neutral and passive arbitrator. Although this misunderstanding has similarly been reported in the US (O'Barr and Conley 1988), in China it is so ingrained that it often leads to disputes and submissions of complaints.

In a divorce case (He and Feng 2021, 122), the defendant, Ms. Lin, criticized the judge for failing to thoroughly investigate the case in order to seek out the "truth." She had insisted that her son had been raised entirely by her, and had accused her husband of infidelity. She failed to prove either of these accusations, however. By contrast, the plaintiff had provided sufficient evidence to prove that the boy had always lived with his grandparents, thereby invalidating Ms. Lin's claim.

Ms. Lin responded:

> The judge did not violate the legal procedure [She paused for a few minutes, calming herself down]. However, I really felt it was unfair, very unfair! ... You [judge] just follow a formalistic procedure. As you just told me, only in criminal cases are the authorities supposed to take the initiative in investigating. However, we are just ordinary citizens, the weak. We need help! ... It is wrong to only care about the cases [she meant the criminal cases] which they think are valuable. (He and Feng 2021: 123)

As to why she believed that judges should be responsible for the investigation process, her reasoning was, "we are ordinary citizens, and we need help." Her perceptions painted the judge as a protector rather than a passive and neutral arbitrator. After her lawyer had explained the appropriateness and legality of the judge's passive position, Ms. Lin remained in denial and refused to accept the judgment. In her eyes, whether a protector or servant, the judge should have taken the initiative to investigate, collect evidence, and offer guidance and expertise. However, in contrast to the traditional role of judges in the inquisitorial system that Chinese litigants are familiar with, the Civil Procedure Law (CiPL) now requires judges to neutrally follow a formal legal procedure and adjudicate with sole reference to admitted evidence. Therefore, there had been a gap between the role of the judge in Ms. Lin's perception and the legal role of the judge, and that gap had contributed to Ms. Lin's disappointment.

Morality as a Criterion

Morality, sentiments, and *li* [reason] have often been used, instead of the law, to evaluate the fairness of a judgment. For example, in the above-mentioned divorce case, Ms. Lin had found it unthinkable that custody of the child could be awarded to her adulterous and alcoholic husband. She had been ignorant of the legal value of her husband's stable occupation and income.

The following case further details this pattern. Mr. Zhong, a young plumber, had accused his wife of immorality, and had fought for the custody of his four-year-old. He claimed that his wife had committed adultery and was, in his view, an immoral woman. In addition to accusing her of stealing, lying, and "illegally" cohabiting with a lover (Chinese law does not regard cohabitation as illegal), he ultimately argued that his wife was not qualified to be a guardian. However, the legal decision was ambivalent to his arguments and moral standards, leaving him very unsatisfied.

With regard to his wife's infidelity, Mr. Zhong had expected the judge to investigate. He said, "I had hoped that the judge would investigate her theft and the immoral cohabitation." Complaining that the judge had paid scant attention to his statements, he said:

> I repeatedly emphasized that she was a liar. Much of her evidence was fabricated ... However, whenever I stated this, the judge interrupted me. I was told that the court did not care about moral rhetoric. I responded, 'If the court does not care about social ethics, why does it still exist?' In essence, the court is a place where ordinary people can argue and resort to ethics ... Actually, if she [his wife] had been an upright person, I would have been happy to transfer my custody to her. Why I strive for custody is not to vent my anger or seek revenge against her, but so that my son can grow up in a healthy environment. Since both she and her mother are morally unqualified, I am really worried about my son.

Morality was thus the dominant criterion in Mr. Zhong's perception of how the case should have been decided. He believed that the court was a site that advocated for the implementation of moral principles and ethics, and in his opinion, being morally sound was crucial for a qualified guardian. This morality was linked to whether a court decision was reasonable.

Many litigants have been under the impression that "the court is the place for *li* or reason," that "I know that I will win because the other party['s claim] is without *li*," and that "I am ignorant of the law, but I know that my claim makes sense. This conforms to human conscience and *li*." To their dismay, once it is revealed that the outcomes of their legal disputes do not conform to their sense of justice, which they have based on their moral beliefs, they feel that the courts have failed to perform in accordance with their expectations.

Therefore, inherent in the tensions surrounding these three sources of dissatisfaction of the civil justice system is the litigants' mistrust of the courts. Litigants believe that the judges are neglecting to gather facts that are important to their accounts. Furthermore, there is a discrepancy between the law and people's perceptions of the facts, and according to those litigants, the process cannot be trusted. Some litigants make their mistrust toward the courts and the judges explicit in their statements.

In summary, litigants often approach the courts with high but erroneous expectations. Most of the litigants reported on here were wrongly under the impression that the judges would take the initiative to investigate the facts, summon witnesses, and collect evidence, with the litigants playing only a supporting role. Misunderstandings and unrealistic expectations abounded. A judge interviewed by Wei Ding said (2014, 241), "[t]he rules of evidence in civil procedures are nothing less than a myth to many peasants."

The Courts' Dilemma

The gap between the court's application of the law and litigants' legal consciousness is not unique to China. In Merry's (1990) noteworthy research on the legal consciousness of the working class in the US, she documented such a gap and the corresponding litigants' frustration about it. O'Barr and Conley's (1988, 137) investigation of litigants' perceptions of justice in the US revealed that, despite their unfamiliarity with and misconceptions about the purely adversarial nature of the proceedings, litigants were still "at least as concerned with issues of process as they are with the substantive questions."

That said, the size of this gap seems far more noticeable in the Chinese context. The American litigants in Merry's (1990) research did not believe that the court could have violated the law, and their frustrations did not present themselves as a challenge to the legitimacy of the legal system. In China, the level of trust in the judges and courts appears to be much lower. Indeed, most litigants in China are new to the legal process, and many believe that being involved in a lawsuit is a harbinger of bad luck. Being sued is synonymous with having done something wrong. The ideal in China's grass-roots society has always been to avoid litigation (Fei 1992). Being served for a civil trial and even being called a "defendant" is often enough to lose face among peer villagers (Gao et al. 2009, 388). Some even refuse to sign court subpoenas, asking, "[h]ow come the court is on the side of the hooligans who initiate the lawsuit?" (Ding 2014, 230). Litigation is usually the grass-roots public's first and last encounter with the courts. Most plaintiffs and defendants are involuntarily dragged into the legal process. They are familiar with neither the law nor court procedures, including the roles of the judge and of themselves as litigants.

The vast gap stemming from lay people's unfamiliarity with the current legal system is consistent with Gallagher's (2006) findings. Her study focused on the labor arbitration, a prejudicial institution that deals with labor disputes; it is not exactly a court, but it is similar. She found that, whereas all disputants had held high expectations of the legal process, their legal knowledge was ambiguous. They had held only a vague, yet positive, sense of the law, and knew little about how it worked. Subsequently, their first legal encounters led to disillusionment and negative perceptions of the system.

The engineering effects of the state-controlled media, to give a positive spin on the judicial system, had given the disputants that Gallagher studied the impression that the legal process was fair and efficient, whereas the reality revealed that it was a time- and energy-consuming process. Furthermore, the sheer technicalities of the legal process also required the disputants to present exact evidence to win an arbitration.

Whereas the state has encouraged its people to use the laws, these efforts do little to sufficiently detail the procedures or explain procedural justice. As a result, most litigants have a limited understanding of the operations of the court and the rules surrounding evidence. Their ignorance toward the opportunities at their disposal can also explain why procedural justice means so little to them. Indeed, even the courts and the judges do not show a full commitment to obeying the procedural requirements (Woo and Wang 2005). Due to the policy-implementing nature of the courts, the outcomes are far more important than procedural niceties. All of these factors have reduced procedural fairness to nothing more than petty even-handedness. The parties with unfavorable outcomes are rarely satisfied with their court experiences, and often conclude that corruption has played a role in their unfavorable judgments.

Strengthening judicial legitimacy and authority is thus vital to the maintenance of China's judicial and legal reforms. Yet, what can the authorities do to increase people's satisfaction with China's judicial system? To promote procedural justice seems an obvious solution, by instilling in the public the values of procedural justice when they are evaluating the performance of the legal system. Research in the US suggests that informed consent, a type of procedural justice, can prevent some lawsuits against medical malpractice (Brodsky et al. 2004). Once litigants possess an improved understanding of the procedures or become more familiar with the system as a whole, they can appreciate the value of procedural justice.

Yet, one should not forget that Chinese courts are mainly there to implement policies; they care more about the outcomes. In so doing, they need to have discretion when applying the laws. Procedural justice would inevitably take away the judges' discretion. As a consequence, it is hard to expect procedural rules to be developed in a sophisticated manner and for judges to take them seriously. Due to this dilemma, Chinese courts have attempted to improve the negative public perceptions of their work on procedural justice *and* on other aspects. For example, a Beijing court has repeatedly required its judges to follow procedural requirements with appropriate manners *and* to explain the rationales of their decisions to the litigants, so as to prevent any misunderstandings (Beijing No. 2 Intermediate Court Research Group 2014). Similarly to Russian judges, they educate the litigants about the substance of the law, with an eye to resolving cases more efficiently. By so doing, they will gain more "respect within the judicial corps, which, in turn, is translated to salary increases and promotions" (Hendley 2007, 266).

More importantly, the courts have made efforts, other than procedural justice, to improve their work toward containing negative views. For example, the courts have sought to ameliorate the chronic problem of enforcing judgments (Chapter 6). They have boosted the institution of the people's assessors (Chapter 3). They have also improved judicial transparency (Chapter 2), set up specific means to communicate with the media, and established mechanisms for dealing with crises. Ensuring a tight grip over the tide of public opinion has come to form part of the guidelines for legal decision-making. Regulations regarding the protocol of the judges when communicating with the litigants have also been enforced. In a Shenzhen court, judges are required to reply to *every* statement raised on their social media app, including making trivial polite expressions such as "thank you" or "bye-bye," following the realization that some mishandled cases and scandals have been the main source of negative assessments of their performance (Beijing No. 2 Intermediate Court Research Group 2014).

The recent technological initiatives, such as making millions of cases available online and using artificial intelligence systems to streamline adjudicatory processes, thereby expanding the public's access to justice, belong to this effort. According to an online survey (Chen and Li 2020, 49–50), 90.8 percent of respondents pointed to the digitization and publication of judicial documents in their explanations of the increased public confidence in the courts. Furthermore, 87.7 percent of respondents suggested that big data and machine learning would enhance the certainty of court decisions. The researchers also found that netizens with prior participation in lawsuits were generally satisfied by the resolutions they had achieved. This is surprisingly high, given that more than 40 percent of participants in their database had "previous litigation experience." The increased professionalism of court staff and the imposition of strict requirements on their conduct, as well as the issuing of measures detailing the ways in which judges would be held accountable for wrongly decided cases, all formed part of the effort. Various internal requirements regulate the work procedures of court staff.

Conclusions

Because adherence to the rule of law is an explicit goal of the Party, *pufa* (普法), or disseminating legal knowledge, has become a major task assigned to the state-backed media. Naturally, the official propaganda often paints the laws and courts in a positive light. According to Mary Gallagher and her coauthors, the media always report on workers' victories in labor cases (Gallagher and Wang 2011), and those reports often depict judges as servants of the people. They are "officials like parents," and thus are competent, caring, and selfless. Such propaganda devices do indeed make impacts: those who are more likely to watch the legal news hold a more positive view of the judiciary (Feng 2024). Zheng Yongliu et al. (1992, 94) highlighted that peasants rely on the state-backed media as the primary source for obtaining legal information. Their miscalculated trust has prompted many peasants to believe that bringing their issues before a panel of judges in a court would provide the most satisfying outcome, even if it was both time-consuming and expensive (Zheng et al. 1992, 98–99).

Still, even though the media may have enticed some people to use the law as a weapon of justice, the Chinese people's world view has hardly changed. Most people still believe in *guanxi* or petitioning. They are most familiar with the importance and reliability of a person, not of the law. The state has adopted the rule of law as a dominant means of governance, yet the citizens do not really believe in it, nor do most of them have a clear understanding of its substance. Most people are indifferent to the *pufa* campaign; they simply find the law irrelevant. When by some misfortune they are dragged into the legal process, they intuitively revert back to the familiar territory of *guanxi*. When some of them lose their cases or receive outcomes that counter their expectations, they immediately accuse the judges of being corrupt or incompetent, or declare that the other party had access to more concrete *guanxi*. As a final resort, they switch to petitioning.

Ironically, *guanxi* and petitioning sometimes work—a fact that further reinforces the undeniable belief and trust that average citizens place in these means, and which thus creates a daunting challenge for the state and the court system. Tremendous efforts have been made to enhance the legitimacy of the court and the state, yet the courts cannot rely on procedural justice, a common solution to the problem. Due to the policy-implementing nature of the courts, they have to rely on other means: substantive justice, efficiency, transparency, communications with the litigants, the judges' protocol, and the reaction of the media.

6

Civil Justice

When one suggests that court caseloads in China have exploded in the past four decades, this refers solely to civil and commercial cases. In 1979, a total of 389,943 civil cases were accepted by first-instance courts, and a decade later that number had increased to 2,511,017. By 1999, it had reached approximately 5 million, and by 2019 it was almost 14 million (*China Law Yearbooks*, various years). In other words, caseloads have increased by a factor of nearly 36 over the last four decades. Overall, civil and commercial cases account for roughly half of all cases in Chinese courts.

Not only has the total number changed, but so has the composition of the cases. Family-related cases amounted to 73.1 percent of all civil cases in 1978, but this had dropped to 13.28 percent by 2019. During that period, contract-related cases proliferated, surpassing family-related cases in 1988, and constituting 66.13 percent of all civil and commercial cases by 2019. More recently, cases related to securities, financing, and intellectual property have also snowballed, increasing more than 50 percent annually (SPC Work Report 2022).

As far as the filing fee is concerned, one could argue that the state channels civil grievances to the courts. Access to civil justice is encouraged, not constrained—most of the fees charged for many categories of cases are nominal: 10 yuan for a labor case, and 50 to 500 yuan for other non-monetary damages (The State Council 2007, Art. 13). For a divorce case involving the division of property worth less than 200,000 yuan, a flat fee of 50 to 300 yuan is charged. If the cases are mediated or withdrawn, the fees are cut by half, and for some other categories of cases the fees are waived. These rates have not been raised since 2007, despite China's rapid economic development and noticeable inflation over the last 15 years. As a result, many minor or even trivial cases have flooded the courts. In 2013, the present author witnessed a judge informally complain about a lawyer who was representing a company that had filed a lawsuit against its former employee for less than 1,000 yuan!

Only against such a backdrop can one understand why efficiency has been a theme throughout the reform period. The Civil Procedure Law (CiPL) stipulates that cases tried by the Ordinary Procedure are to be completed within six months, and that those using the Simplified Procedure must be finished in only three months. Some senior officials managing their own courts even shorten those

The Judicial System of China. Xin He, Oxford University Press. © Xin He 2025. DOI: 10.1093/9780198927815.003.0007

limits to 90 and 20 days, respectively, to allow themselves more room to maneuver (Ng and He 2017a, 57). The case closure rate, which is considered an indication of the effectiveness and efficiency of court operations, appears in every court's annual work report. The statistics suggest that the prescribed deadlines are rarely violated. Of course, for complicated cases, and during specific periods, the judges and courts have to find ways around the deadlines. Notably, by December of each year many courts stop taking new cases so that they can increase their case closure rate for the year, thus suggesting that the courts struggle to meet the deadlines and also showing that, in most cases, they do stick to the prescribed deadlines. Efficient case handling is a basic metric for evaluating a judge's capability, and by that metric, the Chinese system can be considered one of the most efficient judiciaries in the world.

To ensure that the cases are processed and closed in a timely manner, the original inquisitorial system has been overhauled. The courts and judges have forgone the responsibility of collecting evidence for the parties involved. With an explosive docket, evidence collection exceeds their capacities, so an expedited channel has been established for cases with straightforward evidence and issues (SPC 2020). Procedural justice has also been somewhat stressed, in an effort to facilitate efficiency.

On the other hand, for the sake of social stability, the state also wants the case decisions to be accepted by the relevant parties and the general public. This issue is controlled by monitoring the appeals rate, the remands rate, the petitions rate, and the number of malicious incidents, including social protests and deaths. The judiciary trumpets the slogan "to achieve the combination of both legal and social effects." Whereas espousing the goal of legal effects suggests the observation of legal principles and rules, the protection of social effects implies that society must accept the decisions peacefully. Ideally, those two goals would be consistent and mutually reinforcing. When they conflict, however, legal principles and rules have to make way for the social effects, and that is when the law is compromised.

Dispute resolution, in itself, is an important policy for the state—accessible civil justice boosts citizens' support for the legal system in authoritarian states, as do the efficiency and effectiveness of dispute resolution. The state wants the judicial decisions to be enforced; an empty check erodes legitimacy. Judges are expected to ensure that the litigants find the decisions largely acceptable, or at least tolerable.

This chapter demonstrates the unique characteristics and challenges that prevail in the operation of Chinese civil justice. The discussion begins with the operation of the so-called adversarial procedures. It then shows the effectiveness of the courts in handling civil and commercial cases. In these areas, the 2014 judicial reforms have intervened in few of the previous practices, while the heightened responsibilities of judges have only made some patterns more conspicuous. At the same time, since 2014, local protectionism has declined, especially following the budgetary and personnel reforms. Finally, the enforcement of judgments has been tightened.

Adversarial or Inquisitorial?

China's civil justice system has undergone significant reforms since 2000. Until the mid-1980s, mediation was the major mode of dispute resolution, and adjudication was rare. During the 1980s, the judges assumed all of the responsibilities of investigation and were required to seek out the truth (Wang and Fu 2015, 213). More recently, however, as a response to the new market economy and the growing volume of civil disputes arising from increased economic and social activities, civil court procedures have been comprehensively revised to shift the burden of producing evidence onto the individual litigants. The revised CiPL (1991, Art. 64) stipulates that the major task of the courts is to review the evidence presented by the litigating parties, with the courts only collecting evidence by themselves when necessary. The Several Rules Relating to Civil Litigation Evidence, issued by the Supreme People's Court (SPC) in 2001, borrow many elements from the adversarial system. Those rules stipulate that the burden of proof rests on the litigants rather than the judges, making court-involved investigations secondary and exceptional. Chinese legal reforms seem to have moved away from the civil law inquisitorial tradition, and the Chinese courts have now adopted the policy slogan of "litigantism."

Unlike trials under the common law system, in China's civil trials a full-fledged cross-examination is not the key component. In accord with the policy change requiring that civil trials be more formalized, there are four stages in a Chinese court hearing process: court investigation, court discussion, court mediation, and decision announcement (CiPL 2014). By definition, court investigations focus on evidence, while court discussions focus on legal applications. In reality, delineating the two has been difficult, and has often caused great confusion (Zhang 2001). One expert in civil procedures has estimated that court discussions usually take less than 10 percent of the court's hearing time; some even less than 5 percent (W. Zhang 2015). Subsequently, the SPC (via The Interpretations of the CiPL 2014, Art. 230) has allowed the two processes to be combined, subject to the litigating parties' consent.

The laws do not articulate the roles of the adjudicative personnel, but throughout the Stipulations by the SPC on the Reform of Civil and Economic Trial Methods (1998), one can sense their crucial role in the process. The Stipulations state (Art. 17) that, "the adjudicative personnel shall guide the participants to debate on the issues. The adjudicative personnel shall forestall any talks which are irrelevant or repetitive." Before the hearing, it has been common for the judges to contact the litigants to obtain their views, the causes of the dispute, and the evidence. The judges also try to mediate before the trial, if possible (Wang and Fu 2015, 215), but the pressing caseloads have made this practice less common (He 2021b).

Using case files, surveys, and interviews, Woo and Wang (2005, 933) observed that judges still exercise their powers of investigation and evidence collection to "varying degrees, depending on judicial temperament, philosophy, and ability." In a Guangdong court in 2013, Kwai Hang Ng and I zoomed in on the revised role that judges have assumed under the new arrangement of litigant-initiated fact-finding and evidence-gathering (He and Ng 2014). The decline in the out-of-court investigations was evident. As Ding (2014, 239) documented, with a clerk's response to a peasant woman's request to investigate her husband's extramarital affair: "Maybe you can ask, if anyone knows a thing or two about the law, which judges still conduct out-of-court investigations these days? If you want us to investigate, you must file a formal request."

In fact, judges rely on a limited form of cross-examination to obtain oral testimonies that can be used to justify a decision, and this judge-initiated questioning has become an inexpensive substitute for the previously labor-intensive court investigations. In other words, a court investigation stage offers the judges an important opportunity to collect evidence that can form the basis of a later adjudicative decision should a settlement not be reachable. The evidence on which their potential adjudicative decisions are based must be strong enough to safeguard the judges from any potential liability for wrongfully decided cases, so although the judges rarely conduct out-of-trial investigations, they make significant efforts to collect evidence during the trial process.

Active Judging

According to the CiPL, all cases are either decided according to Ordinary Procedure, with a panel usually composed of three persons (at least one judge and two lay assessors), or by the Summary Procedure, with only one adjudicating judge. In practice, there is always a designated responsible judge, while the other judges on the panel, including the chief judge, are largely symbolic. The responsible judge—or the adjudicating judge, when the Summary Procedure is employed—is the one who is actually in charge. He or she presides over the trial and eventually delivers a judgment or steers the case to a settlement.

According to the observations of Kwai Hang Ng and I, the designated responsible judge plays a pivotal role in trials. The judge dominates a trial from beginning to end, coordinating with all participants, raising questions, and controlling the pace. In most situations, other judges or lay assessors rarely speak up. The significance of the interaction with the judge becomes even more apparent in the mediation stage, which is when the judge endeavors to convince a party, or both parties, to accept a deal. The judge can ask one party to leave the courtroom first, so as to caucus with the other party. "As a mediator, the judge's role in the process is controlling and dominating; they can easily reduce, revoke, or cancel the requests of the parties" (Chen 2007, 393). This dominant role produces the situation that Philips (1990) described as having "the judge as the third party"—and probably the most important party—in the trial.

In the first two stages of a hearing, the judge allows the litigating parties to question each other's arguments and evidence. Even in these two stages, however, the judge decides what the major issues are, who gets to speak, what evidence will be questioned, and how many questions each party can ask. He or she is often the person who asks the most questions, and who determines when to dwell on a certain point, when to move on quickly, and when to interrupt. Failure to identify the major issues would lead to a cumbersome and inefficient trial (W. Zhang 2015). The judge often reminds the litigants that they do not need to repeat their points. As long as the judge has located enough evidence to justify his or her later decision, any repetitive debate becomes redundant.

Judges often interrupt the speeches of litigants and their representatives, including lawyers, and this is done for many reasons. In many cases, the litigants are eager to talk, and at times they are too eager to get their message across. They can also easily become emotional when they believe an argument or allegation raised by their opponents is unfair or simply untrue. Many of them fail to wait for their turn to speak. Judges, therefore, interrupt to stop these back-and-forth sparring sequences from escalating into shouting matches. Moreover, many matters that litigants raise are repetitive or irrelevant, and this is especially true when they do not have legal representatives, which is typical. Judges often have to interrupt to prevent the process from falling apart.

That said, other interruptions by judges are more controversial. Judges sometimes interrupt because they are under time pressure. Typically, a Chinese case is expected to be completed in a half-day session, which means at most two to three hours of actual court time. When witnesses are involved, opposing parties and their lawyers may not be allowed to dwell on their evidence for very long.

Although, in most cases, the first three stages of the court hearing are separate, sometimes they are combined. In one divorce case Kwai Hang Ng and I observed, the judge moved quickly to mediation without formally announcing that the investigation and discussion stages had ended. In fact, she did not formally ask the two parties if they would agree to participate in mediation, as most judges would do at the end of the court discussion. She took her unusual stance because the interactions between the two parties had been confrontational, and the court atmosphere was tense; the parties might have refused to participate in mediation had they been formally asked. Avoiding the question and moving directly to the mediation bolstered the likelihood of a successful mediation. In another divorce case, the female plaintiff claimed that her husband had beaten her—allegations that her husband denied. The debate on the issue appeared to have been over, but the judge questioned the husband on this issue again, even though the trial had already moved on to other issues. This time, the husband admitted that he had "choked" his wife a couple of times, which, according to our interview with the judge after the trial, would have been regarded as adequate evidence for domestic violence. Upon the husband finishing his statement, the judge instructed her clerk to insert the confession into the gap in the trial record where the issue had been discussed. According to the judge, the reason for the repeated questioning had been to raise the question when the husband was less prepared. This is a tactic for obtaining important (but self-incriminating) evidence from a party, which is related to proof-taking, the topic of discussion in the next subsection.

Proof-taking

Under the new laws, the emphasis on proof-taking has shifted from the pretrial stage to the trial stage, and from the judges and the courts to the litigants (CiPL 2014). However, notwithstanding the slogan of "litigantism," the judge still plays a significant role in locating evidence, although the proof-taking process is done only through in-trial examination instead of out-of-court investigation. In divorce cases under the old system, the judge usually conducted on-site investigations to locate the reason for the divorce in the first place (Huang 2005). Nowadays, however, the judge has turned their attention to evidence provided by the litigating parties. As another new source of evidence, witnesses are sometimes asked to testify in court, and are examined by the judge during court hearings (Woo 2003, 132; Huang 2010). Judges have many reasons for wanting to avoid out-of-court investigations—the ever-increasing caseloads that the courts receive, the limited human and financial resources, and the pressure to boost efficiency by closing cases within a short time frame.

In civil actions, there are now two crucial components: first, the litigants are required to provide evidence and exchange evidence before the trial; and, second, over the course of the trial, after the plaintiff and defendant have each presented their evidence, the court asks the other side to respond. Huang (2010, 129) believes that "what the court relies on is mainly two methods: one is written documents, and the other is the 'confrontation.'" Furthermore, "if each side insists on his/her version, and there is no written evidence, the courts can only exclude it from consideration as a non-ascertainable fact" (Huang 2010, 131). This protocol seems consistent with the law. In the Several Rules Relating to Civil Litigation Evidence of 2001, the plaintiff bears the consequences in cases in which the courts cannot get the evidence. In reality, though, judges often take a more active role, and the proof-taking process is more complex.

For instance, when domestic violence is alleged, it is the judge who obtains the evidence to validate the claims. A proven domestic violence allegation is consequential for the plaintiff and her family. Not only does it make the victim more likely to receive a favorable divorce settlement and win the battle for child custody, but she will also receive court protection from potential future abuse by the offender. The court that Kwai Hang Ng and I studied can issue a protective order to remove the husband from his home and prevent him from seeing his children, or even from talking to his wife.

Although female plaintiffs often raise the issue of domestic violence during the court investigation stage of a trial, the first problem facing these women is that they do not know how, as it were, to produce evidence and give testimonies in court. Many of them are unrepresented, and even when they are represented, they usually do not have the documents required for the purposes of the law (police report, medical records, or their own written statements made at the time they were abused). Moreover, an allegation of domestic violence is usually denied or refuted by the husband. To collect evidence, the judge will employ various tactics in questioning the husband.

During a trial that we witnessed, the plaintiff, a "rural wife" of low educational background, was emotional. She claimed that her husband had beaten her and their son 600 times over the course of their marriage. She struggled to hold her composure. She testified with a wailing voice, recounting the violence inflicted upon her. However, the husband denied that he had used violence. He described what had happened, in Chinese, as *duida*—meaning "fighting with each other." The judge tried to determine whether there was any police report which might constitute strong evidence against the defendant, but apparently the police had simply made a routine visit on one occasion and left without investigating the incident in detail. Without a police investigation, the focus of the case turned to the evidence the wife produced in her testimony. Apparently, the judge was of the view that the wife's oral testimony alone did not carry enough weight to warrant factoring domestic violence into her decision on the divorce petition. In a bid to draw out more damning details from the husband, the judge launched a series of probing questions to get the defendant to acknowledge the use of violence.

The judge first caught the husband off-guard when she asked him if he had ever choked his wife, to which he admitted that he had done so once. In the interviews with us right after the court trial, the judge said the choking had been serious— it was life-threatening—and once a husband has done this to his wife, he tends to repeat the behavior, often with later incidents of choking, perpetrating even greater violence against the wife. From the judge's perspective, choking, whether admitted or proven, constituted a piece of strong evidence for domestic violence claims. To make the case beyond reproach, the judge then asked the husband how many times he had choked his wife and son. The judge was also meticulous in asking the length of time the man choked his wife and son during these incidents. The judge was doubtful that the man was telling the truth. Upon hearing his testimony, his abused wife became emotional and asked him not to contradict his conscience. The man tried to downplay the severity of these choking incidents—he said that they only happened once or twice, that each time they lasted for just four or five seconds, and that, above all, they happened not as unprovoked violence against his wife, but as self-defense in a fight with his wife, who he claimed had been trying to hit him hard. As the judge told us afterward, the man had, from the perspective of the law, admitted enough to prove domestic violence. Word by word, she instructed her court clerk on what to record on the court records—which would be signed by both litigants—in ways that captured the gravity of the man's testimony. "He admitted he choked her, and he also choked his son." The judge had carefully rephrased the language so that it aligned with the man's testimony, including the relevant facts that constitute the legal definition of domestic violence—which is an important technique, as identified by Mather and Yngvesson (1980–1981).

The judge did not stop there. She further inquired about another incident in which the wife had claimed that the husband had taken her away from work and threatened to tie her up and abuse her. The judge, once again, tried to retrieve the details of the incident by questioning the defendant. In this instance as well, the judge got the defendant to admit that the couple had changed several taxis before they finally got into one on the day he had pulled his wife from her workplace. The judge said that the fact the couple had changed taxis was another good piece of evidence to corroborate the domestic violence claims. In her opinion, it was difficult to explain why the couple had had to change taxis, and had gone back and forth on the trip. The judge argued that this suggested that the wife had been resisting her husband's attempts to carry her away from work, and that physical violence had likely been involved. While the judge did not undertake a full-fledged cross-examination, she sought to build a case through oral testimony within the limited time available in a Chinese civil trial, which normally lasts only half a day.

As a result of the virtual abandonment of out-of-trial investigations by the courts, the in-trial court investigation stage has become more important for judges in their efforts to prove domestic violence. Whether or not a judge wants to "cross-examine" an alleged abuser remains within their discretion, but for those judges who do, in-trial court investigations have become their main tool for proving or disproving allegations of domestic violence.

These examples indicate the proactive role that trial judges assume in collecting, validating, and dismissing the evidence submitted. Admittedly, given the time and resource constraints, proof-taking as an institutional practice continues to rely significantly on individual judges' skills and willingness to collect evidence at trial—a problem that Woo and Wang (2005) point out. In most cases, the role of proof-taking is complementary rather than determining, but judges go beyond the neutral role of collecting written evidence by questioning the parties, who then submit or refute the evidence. Some judges may simply rule, as Huang (2010) suggests, on the narrow but secure ground of written evidence. However, more empirical data demonstrate that, according to the varied responses among judges, this kind of in-trial oral proof-taking has now become an independent source for determining the facts of a case, even in cases where the oral evidence is contested. As is shown in the case just described, the judge's decision depended considerably on where the fighting had taken place, a detail that did not come out until both sides had testified before the judge. Thus, the *in situ* performance of the litigants can swing a judge's decision one way or the other.

Examination of Witnesses

In China, witnesses are "examined" primarily by the judges, who do so with few restrictions. However, the other parties and the lawyers, upon receiving the judge's permission, are also allowed to ask witnesses questions. Because the witnesses take the stand at the request of one side of the litigation, and there is no consequence for a witness who ignores a subpoena, the witnesses generally lack credibility (Huang 2010, 132–133; Xu 2006). Huang (2010, 133) asserts that the witness system "is basically just a hollow frame."

Of the 20 cases we observed in our fieldwork in a Guangdong court, only four featured the examination of witnesses in court. In those cases, the judges played a crucial role in the process of witness examination. All four were labor cases, suggesting that it was difficult to obtain witnesses in family law cases. In one case (hereinafter the *Security Guard Case*), a migrant security guard had sued his employer for wrongful discharge, and the employer presented three witnesses: a chef who had fought with the guard, and two other coworkers who had worked in the dining hall. Both sides agreed that there had been a physical altercation after a quarrel over the quality of the food. However, the issue was whether the guard had initiated the fight. All three witnesses, including the assistant chef who had been in the fight, said that the guard had run into the dining-hall kitchen and hit him. However, there were inconsistencies in the witnesses' statements. Some said that the assistant had been hit in the stomach, while others said that he had been hit on the neck. It was only during the final minutes of the questioning that the judge offered an opportunity for the guard's lawyer to ask questions.

The judge commanded the evidence-taking in the trial. It was he who had decided when to summon the witnesses, what questions to ask, which questions to repeat, when to interrupt, and even how many questions the other litigant could ask (in this case, he said the guard's side could ask only three questions). He also occasionally instructed the clerk on how the questions and answers should be put into the record. Without the presence of a jury, the judge is the only person determining the verdict, which is based on the written evidence submitted and oral testimony given. There are no clear exclusionary rules that disallow the admission of certain types of evidence (e.g., hearsay). Instead, the judge alone decides when to stop taking evidence and move on in a trial. In ways more similar to what we know about trials in civil law jurisdictions, Chinese judges seem to practice the "free-admission principle," which allows for the broad admission of evidence (Damaska 1997).

In our posttrial interview with the judge, he said he believed the guard had hit the chef first. The judge reasoned that, since the fighting had taken place inside the kitchen, the guard probably had rushed in to start the fight. He noted that there were obvious inconsistencies in the accounts of the different witnesses, and as the guard's lawyer pointed out, the witnesses were employed by the defendant (the employer), and therefore the accounts they provided could not be considered neutral. Even so, the judge did not pay much attention to these details.

When gathering evidence from witnesses, Chinese judges do not concern themselves with legal issues such as relevance or admissibility. It is, after all, an inquisitorial system in which judges pay little attention to the evidence rules derived from jury trials. Instead, they use their own common sense to guide their decision-making processes, and their goal is to determine what actually happened in the most expedient manner. As Zhong and Yu (2003, 401) point out, Chinese judges are, traditionally, said to be concerned with objective truth, not legal truth. In other words, it is against their philosophy to exclude a piece of evidence just because that evidence fails to fulfill certain evidential requirements. The theory of objective truth suggests that judges consider everything relevant in order to ascertain the truth. Any rules of evidence or requirements of proof that complicate the ascertaining of what actually happened assume a secondary role. This is similar to the focus on substantive irrationality or substantive rationality described by Weber (1954). Overall, evidence-taking is an eclectic process in which there is much room for judicial discretion.

Contrary to Huang's (2010) claim, formality has not overtaken the trial process; most claims lacking evidence will not be disregarded by judges. Evidence-gathering is based on the judges' personal skills, and is still very much guided by their search for "objective truth" or "substantive justice." It is also clear that judges can choose between gathering evidence proactively and acquiring it passively. Again, the point is that judges are not barred from taking action to gather evidence, and they can choose to be proactive if they wish. However, there is a delicate line: they will only seek to determine the truth as far as the process allows, and will not exceed that limit.

Why Inquisitorialism?

Why do the judges choose not to take advantage of the language of the new rules and simply remain passive? More specifically, why do they not dismiss cases when the parties fail to sustain their burden of proof? One explanation is that the judges' behavior is a continuation of the long-held goal of the Chinese judiciary to determine the objective truth (Zhong and Yu 2003). Still, if that is their goal, one must admit that most Chinese judges are not doing enough to dig out the truth. As has been mentioned, judges have abandoned the practice of conducting investigations for evidence themselves, and they do not exert sufficient effort to explore witnesses' contradictory statements. Instead, they render verdicts against those who bear the burden of proof, even if the truth has yet to be elucidated (Wang and Fu 2015, 215).

This change is attributable primarily to the institutional constraints to which the judges are subject (see Chapter 2). The recent reforms of evidence procedures have created a new institutional framework for the role of adjudication as a process for public dispute resolution, and the institutional constraints created by this framework both enable and constrain the adjudicative work that the judges perform. A combination of the role of the judges, the courts in which they are embedded, and, in particular, how the judges' performance is assessed, suggest that institutional constraints are exerting a force that is shaping the landscape of China's civil trial proceedings.

On one hand, the reforms try to maximize the total number of cases the courts can handle, and to do so with maximum expediency—which is why judges are reluctant to hold a hearing that lasts beyond a single court session. Judges are also incentivized to mediate disputes or persuade plaintiffs to withdraw—before, in the middle of, or even after the trial process. On the other hand, they cannot focus merely on efficiency. As we saw in Chapter 2, the party-state has adopted certain markers, including the appeals rate, reversals rate, remands rate, and complaints rate, to evaluate judges. When a judge receives a complaint or an appeal, especially when the event drawing the complaint is publicized and discussed in the media, that complaint becomes a problem not just for the individual judge concerned, but for the whole court as an institution. Such "troublesome" cases would leave a black mark against judges and court administrators, and can be serious enough to derail their career prospects. Thus, judges are motivated to exhaust all of the means at their disposal to ensure that disgruntled litigants are attended to, in whatever way possible, and mollified. As we have observed, judges are cautious with any decisions that could lead to future complaints and/or appeals.

Consequently, judges work expediently to gather evidence within the relatively brief trial processes allowed for both adjudication and mediation. The evidence they acquire is used for multiple purposes. Obviously, it can form the basis for a subsequent judgment, but it can also be used as a bargaining chip to persuade and cajole parties to accept a proposed settlement. By the same token, only with sufficient evidence (at least according to the judges' own standards) can they justify their adjudicative decisions in the event that a settlement is not reached. Within those bounds, the judges will certainly consider the values of fairness, accessibility to litigants, and legal popularization.

However, it seems to the present author that the judges' primary motivation is self-preservation. For many low-level judges in China, their primary consideration is protecting themselves from possible reversals from the upper-level courts. Equally important is protecting themselves from investigations in response to legal or ethical complaints lodged by external institutions, such as the procuratorates, governments, Party committees, or people's congresses (Yu and Sun 2022), because the formal justice emphasized in the Civil Evidence Rules issued by the SPC is not believed in by the general public or other government entities. If the court decisions are based solely on the evidence admitted in accordance with the formal procedural rules, they can easily lead to absurd decisions that defy popular understandings of justice. Therefore, the judges face challenges not only by the litigants, but also by society at large. There was a well-publicized case in which an elderly couple committed suicide right in front of the courthouse when the claim that they had written an IOU under duress was rejected. The judge had made the decision for procedural reasons because the couple had produced no evidence in support of their claim. The case was reopened because the IOU was invalidated by the police investigation following the suicide. The judge was later prosecuted for negligently conducting his duty (Sohu 2003). Although he was eventually proven innocent, the fact that he was prosecuted speaks volumes about the pressures and risks to which a judge is subject in handling seemingly trivial disputes. Judges are under tremendous pressure from within the judiciary, and from other government branches and the public. Following the Civil Evidence Rules "by the book" is not necessarily a safe policy, as judges can still be criticized for applying them mechanically.

For all of these reasons, judges cannot sit passively on the bench and simply apply the rules, nor can they just wait for the litigants and their representatives to produce evidence. Instead, they must take the initiative to raise questions in order to determine the validity and weight of the evidence submitted. In addition, they intervene during debates in trials, to ensure that the process does not get off track or fall apart. They also rein in lawyers whose goal of getting the most for their clients may undermine the likelihood of a settlement. In rural areas where the litigants know little about law or the importance of evidence, judges taking the initiative to investigate is the rule, while sitting passively is the exception (Gao et al. 2009, 249–258). This is why the trial process remains inquisitorial, despite the new adversarial rules in the books. The term litigantism is a slogan, but a more accurate description would be to say that judges are "adjudication-centered": the judge is dominant in court hearings, and it is his or her duty to determine whether the litigants' claims are valid, to discern the facts, and to apply the law (Zhang 2020).

The Haves versus the Have-nots

To what extent are Chinese courts' decisions fair? This is a difficult empirical question. In an ideal world, a court would adjudicate impartially, but in reality courts often favor the rich and powerful. Rousseau deemed this "the universal spirit of the Law" (Morley 1886, 227). A Chinese saying imparts it as: "The court gate opens as wide as *ba* [the Chinese character 八], but enter not if one possesses only a righteous claim but no money." As revealed in the previous section, the litigants' locality is only one of many factors that determine the case outcomes. Whereas the procedural laws have been designed and reformed to balance both parties, and fairness is routinely a slogan of the judiciary, the case outcomes from civil trials are far from fair. Galanter (1974) proposed that, despite the institutional arrangements in place to guard against particularism, private power, and inequality, the haves still come out ahead of the have-nots in the US court system as well.

Drawing on 2,724 documents from adjudication decisions from Shanghai courts, Yang Su and I tested the Galanter thesis (He and Su 2013), which posits that the stronger party tends to prevail over the weaker party in litigation. We found that the stronger parties not only win more often, but they also do so by a large margin. Overall, institutional litigants fare better than individual litigants. When litigants are classified by their organizational and social status, government-related companies are the biggest winners and enjoy an enormous advantage. Meanwhile, farmers are the most disadvantaged underdogs, with other groups of individuals and companies in between. When we controlled for legal representation, these winning gaps remained significant and sizable. The stronger parties' edge recurs across categories of cases, and in different issue areas of the law.

Our analysis revealed a clear and consistent pattern: the haves edge out the have-nots. The gaps we found were much larger than the repeat players' advantage reported elsewhere (Songer and Sheehan 1992, 243; Wheeler et al. 1987, 422). Indeed, the gaps became extraordinary when we further specified the social financial status of individual litigants and the types of organization litigants. Furthermore, we found that the biggest winners were government agencies or government-owned firms. Such status left their opponents, whether private companies or individuals, with a next to zero chance of winning any cases. Thirdly, we found that firms had the upper hand over individuals, but when they faced government-backed opponents, their chances of winning were minuscule.

In other words, when a party in a case is a government institution or is government related, it leaves little opportunity for the opponent to win. This exceedingly high win rate is difficult to explain without appreciating the fact that Chinese courts operate under the shadow of the government. Haitian Lu et al. (2015) confirm the effect of firms' political connectedness on court outcomes. According to them, there is "robust evidence that Chinese courts favor state firms and private firms with personal political ties." Yongcheng Yu and Jian Wei (2017) found similar results in contract cases. Litigants within the establishment, such as state-owned enterprises (SOEs), had a 26 percent edge over those outside the establishment, such as private enterprises (Yu and Wei 2017, 93). Local litigants were in a much better position than nonlocal litigants, and litigants represented by local lawyers also came out ahead. Local litigants, Yu and Wei (2017) speculate, may have better connections with the judges. Jian Xu (2020) also found that the composition of a firm's board membership is a good predictor of its lawsuit outcomes. A higher percentage of corporate board members with political connections leads to a higher probability of lawsuit success. Political connections are indeed important, Wang argues (2018). A lawyer he interviewed said the government will intervene in court decisions under two circumstances: when a government official is involved, or when the matter threatens social stability.

In a sense, the handling of divorce cases also demonstrates a haves versus have-nots situation. My recent book on divorce cases (He 2021a) demonstrates that, when judges work under the primary concerns of social stability and case-load numbers, men often come out ahead because they are more resourceful and realistic in initiating stability-threatening events. As a result, concerns for gender equality and women's well-being are left by the wayside. In the US, the haves come out ahead because they can game a rule-based system, as the more resourceful party. In China, the haves (mostly husbands) game the system of contested divorces, and not so much the rules.

Unsatisfied with the resource capability theory (Galanter 1974), Yanmei Tian and her coauthors (2021) suggest a theory of litigation capability. They argue that the status of litigants, such as whether they are institutional or individual players, is insufficient to gauge their likelihood of winning. Instead, one needs to understand how much of the litigant's resources that individual is willing to invest in the litigation. Some litigants with plenty of resources may not care about litigation, or may simply use litigation as a strategy or gesture. In contrast, less resourceful litigants may devote every penny they have to litigation. The amount of each party's investment in a litigation, rather than the status of the litigants, is the key to understanding the case outcomes.

Illustrating that point in copyright litigation, Tian et al. (2021) demonstrated that SOEs, with abundant resources, input little effort into litigation. On the other hand, the administrators of copyrights hire professional lawyers and locate powerful evidence. The status of the litigants has only an indirect influence, and the more direct factor is how much a litigant invests (Tian et al. 2021, 173). This is an interesting argument, but Tian and her colleagues used the ratio of what the litigant asks for to what is awarded as a gauge for assessing a party's litigation capability (170). To what extent this measurement makes sense is for statisticians to judge.

In the Philippines, the concern for political stability has improved the have-nots' likelihood of winning (Haynie 1994). Due to China's policy concerns over social stability and the judges' concerns for self-protection, the have-nots may also come out ahead in China. Chunyan Ding (2019, 189) has shown that, in Chinese medical negligence litigation, the patients tend to win in the "vast majority" of cases. In most cases, the judges defer to the medical experts' opinions. This behavior pattern is in line with the judges' own concerns—deference to the expert opinions spares them "the risk of appeal or the risk of being complained about" (Ding 2019, 188). In the medical cases in our data set (He and Su 2013), the partial win rates for plaintiffs were the highest, even though their win rate was low. Medical malpractice victims try to obtain some compensation through the courts, but they are usually unable to pass the burden-of-proof test required to prove the clinics'negligence. Because the clinics control all medical records, and the appraisal institutions are well-connected with the clinics, malpractice victims struggle to prove negligence by doctors or clinics. However, it is in this category that plaintiffs are prone to complaining. The victims, who have usually lost loved ones or a part of their body, tend to be disgruntled because they have suffered throughout the process. At worst, they tend to be suicidal or even homicidal, and at best they are likely to appeal or complain about the verdict. To avoid such appeals and complaints, which could adversely affect the judges' performance appraisals, judges simply identify minor problems with the clinics and offer partial or nominal compensation to the victims. Because clinics often have more resources, they are less likely to complain, even if they are asked for partial compensation. Overall, the judges may have favored the have-nots in some types of cases, but that favoritism cannot alleviate the have-nots' underdog position.

Decline of Local Protectionism

Local protectionism has long been regarded as a key issue in China's civil trials because the local-level Party and the governments together exercise control over the staff and budgets of the courts, which in turn render decisions favoring those who are important to the local governments (Li 2014; Lubman 1999; Clarke 1996). The belief in local protectionism is so entrenched that several measures of the recent reforms are tailor-made to end it. Local courts' budgetary and staffing decisions have been elevated to the provincial level, and the SPC has set up dispatched tribunals that cover jurisdictions across provinces (See Chapter 1). The central government appears to be determined to resolve this problem.

Studies based on anecdotal evidence often paint a grim picture: nonlocal litigants often have little chance of winning, because the courts will do anything to favor their local litigants (Cohen 1997). Empirical studies based on systematic data have shown that local protectionism does exist but is not as rampant as is often portrayed. Bin Ye and Bingyuan Xiong (2018, 28) found that litigants' win rates increased by 10 to 13 percent when their residences were in the same locale as the courts. The differences were significant, but they also found that the outcomes were partially due to the litigants' efforts—the nonlocal litigants might have perceived a lower possibility of winning and thus invested less in the litigation process.

Similarly, when considerable sums are at stake, and when large SOEs are involved, local protectionism remains a problem. On the basis of contracts between publicly traded firms from 1998 to 2013, Wang (2018, 1035) demonstrated that, whereas SOEs were more likely to win in intermediate-level courts, non-SOEs were more likely to win in basic-level courts. This means that, in basic-level courts, local protectionism is declining, but that it remains strong in the intermediate-level courts, where powerful companies' high-volume disputes are handled. According to Yuhua Wang, powerful businesses can still influence court decisions, judges often have to heed "important taxpayers" (Wang 2018, 1034), and large companies are the main source of revenue for provinces and regions. One lawyer told Wang (2018, 1033) that a particular company "has a strong voice in this city. To a large extent, it can influence city policies and demand special treatment, otherwise it can threaten to lay off people or hide revenue." Certainly, money talks—but it has to be big money.

These findings are consistent with certain findings by others documenting that local protectionism is more visible in rural areas where the economy is less developed and the private sector is smaller. In such places, the local government may rely especially on a few SOEs for its revenue (He 2011, 2009b). In addition, rural areas usually do not have robust legal institutions (Lu et al. 2015; He 2012).

In an empirical study of intellectual property cases, Long and Wang (2015) found that local protectionism exists in first-instance cases but the same cannot be said about the appellate courts. At the basic-level courts, they argue, there is relatively more institutional corruption and inappropriate behavior. More corruption may also occur as a result of the connections between the local people and the court staff. However, most of those connections are linked to the lack of professionalism, rather than to local protectionism.

The strength or weakness of local protectionism may also be related to penetration by the central state, including by the SPC (Ip and Kwok 2017). The SPC's efforts to rectify local protectionism, including the publication of guiding cases, seem to have been effective only in the appellate courts (Long and Wang 2015). However, Lu et al. (2015) also found that the new national laws, such as the Property Law, have mitigated the SOEs' advantages, but that this trickle-down effect would not be obvious within a short time frame.

Notably, numerous other studies have shown that local protectionism has declined. Based on debt-collection cases in the Pearl River Delta, a study (He 2009a) by the present author presents a generally positive view of the situation, with only rare instances of local protectionism, and more recent studies have confirmed this trend. Other scholars have reported similar results in Shanghai courts (Pei et al. 2010)—for example, Howson (2010) found that the handling of corporate cases in Shanghai has been fairly professional. In tort cases, Fen Lin and I (He and Lin 2017) found that local protectionism in defamation cases is limited. Belonging to the local media does not always offer an edge (see also Liebman 2006). Instead, the professional working model of the media is more significant in affecting case outcomes. Tian et al. (2021, 173) discovered similar outcomes, having found no traces of local protectionism in copyright cases, because "the amount at issue in copyright cases is rather small, [and] thus unable to activate the mechanism of local protection." A recent study of commercial cases between foreign and Chinese litigants does show that Chinese litigants have an edge, but in-depth interviews with the judges and lawyers revealed that the reason for that advantage has little to do with local protectionism (Xie 2022). Instead, it is primarily due to institutional arrangements and cultural differences. For example, foreign litigants have to hire Chinese lawyers to present their cases in the courts, thus causing numerous communication problems. Furthermore, foreign litigants, which are usually big companies, care more about procedural justice than substantive outcomes. In Xie's (2022) study, the foreign litigants fought less hard for the outcome than the domestic parties did.

Several reasons underlie the decline in local protectionism. First, China's economy has diversified; the SOEs have lost their traditionally dominant role in coastal areas, and in those regions local government income now derives more from taxing the broader private sector than from SOEs and collective enterprises. The overall economy has become more diversified, with the private sector playing a more important role. The fate of any single company is less important than it previously was to the local governments, which now have a broader interest in protecting their areas' reputation as attractive environments for investment. For similar reasons, there is little danger of social instability if SOEs are pushed into bankruptcy. Thus, local governments have become less dependent on SOEs, and have fewer incentives to assist them with their disputes in court. Put differently, local protectionism is only pronounced in areas in which big companies can affect the local government's revenue.

Indeed, because regional economic performance has become the top measure used by local political leaders (Zhou 2017), the local courts have been allowed to adjudicate with greater latitude, in an effort to help boost local economic development. By not having accounted for local development models, economic structures, and ownership changes among enterprises, recent estimates of local protectionism are likely to have been exaggerated (Liu 2019).

Second, the financial reforms of the judiciary have reduced the courts' incentive to engage in local protectionism. Under the reformed financial policy, the courts' budgets are now controlled directly at the provincial level. Thus, the basic- and intermediate-level courts, which handle most of the civil and commercial cases, have no incentive to please the local governments simply to obtain expanded budgets. At the very least, the courts are no longer entirely financially dependent on local enterprises, nor do they need to provide the special protection they previously did for those enterprises in return for funding.

Third, under the reforms intended to improve judicial professionalism, the higher courts in a region, rather than local governments or party officials, have come to play a more determining role in court appointments and promotions. Indeed, the trial court presidents are now rotated regularly, and many were previously court officials of upper-level courts. Although the local governments still play a role in this process, their influence has waned.

In summary, the reforms in the arenas of both personnel and finance have weakened local governments' influence on the courts. Zhong Liu (2016) even asserts that local protectionism was only a phenomenon before the 1990s, when Zheng Tianxiang and Ren Jianxin were the SPC presidents. According to Liu, the financial and staffing reforms enacted since the mid-1990s have eliminated most of the incentives for both local governments and party leaders, as well as court officials, to engage in local favoritism.

Improved Enforcement

In most jurisdictions around the world, either marshals or the police enforce the courts' judgments and orders. In China, the courts are responsible for enforcement, but until recently it has been notoriously difficult to succeed in having court judgments enforced, regardless of whether personal rights or monetary rights are involved. Some have estimated that 50 percent of judgments and awards remain unenforced (*Zhejiang Daily* 2019). In turn, enforcement difficulties have affected how the courts have taken up and adjudicated cases. For example, some courts have refused to take up disputes that have been deemed difficult to enforce (He 2007). Limited by their available resources and a lack of legitimacy, the courts have also tried various tactics to enforce judgments, such as reconciliations (Chen 2018), campaigns (Hou and Chen 2020; Yu 2020, 116), and even offering rewards for providing clues on the whereabouts of the property at issue (Gao et al. 2009, 343). Many enforcement efforts have been discounted in terms of their enforcement time, amount, type, and means, in order to pacify stability-threatening protests (Li 2012).

However, this stereotypical picture has not gone unchallenged. From 2000 to 2009, the closure rate for enforcement cases increased from 85 percent to 89.42 percent nationwide (Li 2012, 53). Working from case files and interviews with litigants in a Pearl River Delta court, the present author showed that "more than half of the non-payment petitions [were] fully enforced, [with] 76 percent of the creditors recovering some monies, and 61 percent of them recovering more than half the demanded amount" (He 2009a, 448). In hinterland Shaanxi, although I did not find the result to be as good as that in the Pearl River Delta, enforcement has, generally speaking, been reasonable, and in 78 percent of the total enforcement cases the plaintiffs recovered something (He 2011, 260). Approximately 30 percent of the civil cases entered the compulsory enforcement stage, in which court intervention was needed, and of those cases, 50 percent recovered something.

Moreover, the main reason for nonenforcement in the past was that the defendants were judgment-proof—they were either insolvent or their assets were encumbered. No blood can be squeezed from stone, and no legal system is able to enforce judgments in such circumstances. Comparisons between countries can be misleading, but the enforcement numbers in China may actually be less problematic than in other jurisdictions, such as the US (Clarke 1996), the UK (Baldwin 1997), or Russia (Hendley 2004). In fact, data provided by the World Bank on enforcing contracts places China at number five, well above most developed countries (*China Justice Observer* 2020), and with the improvement in enforcement having accelerated since the 2010s. The state has long held that enforcement difficulties erode the state's legitimacy and authority, and top the list of problems that provoke the general public's dissatisfaction. The state regards enforcing judgments as a crucial component of implementing the law, maintaining the lawful interests of the general public, and realizing societal fairness. A staff writer of the *China Justice Observer*, an English language e-journal of the SPC, points out that, with effective enforcements of court judgments, the courts improve their "credibility and authority", and thus are "respected by the public" (Du 2018).

Thus, the state is determined to tackle this chronic problem. The Decision to Comprehensively Advancing Rule of Law (CPC 2014) states the following objectives: "To fully resolve the enforcement difficulty, legislate compulsory enforcement law, standardize the judicial procedures in seizing, confiscating, freezing and disposing of litigation-related properties. To accelerate the legal systems with supervision, deter and punish dishonest debtors." The goal of the SPC, in its 2016 work program (SPC 2016b), was to resolve the difficulty of enforcement within two to three years. The CPC's Central Committee (CPC 2019) further issued a special opinion addressing the difficulty of enforcement, and shortly thereafter the SPC also issued an outline for strengthening judgment enforcements. At the time of writing, the draft of the Civil Compulsory Enforcement Law (SPC 2022a) is still under review.

Enforcing judgments has since become a top priority of the courts themselves, and many severe measures have been implemented (*People's Daily* 2020). For individuals, penalty restrictions have been imposed on anyone who defaults on court orders, preventing them from traveling, and from applying for loans and credit cards. The SPC has also cooperated with airlines and railway companies to bar those who default on judgments from purchasing tickets, based on identity card information and their passports. Moreover, restrictions are imposed when the defaulters are being considered for promotions at work, or are acquiring real property, investing in stocks or other financial instruments, or bidding on merchandise. The police can detain defaulters, even if they are unable to pay. If debtors or other obligors are capable of fulfilling the obligations specified by the court decisions but refuse to fulfill them, they can face criminal charges (Criminal Law, Art. 313), and can also be detained by the courts for up to six months, as well as being subject to monetary penalties. Commonly denigrated as deadbeats (老赖), such individuals' personal information, including their name, photograph, sex, age, ID number, and address, will be publicized on official platforms (Pan and Niu 2021, 179).

Li and Gao (2021) have documented the courts' "innovative" tactics against debtors, such as placing restrictions on their ability to drive non-business-operating vehicles, adding restrictions on their use of telephones, and pinpointing their locations. Shaming has also been common, since it has proven highly effective (see Friedman 2016, 159–170). By cooperating with telecom companies, some courts have created tailor-made ringtones for deadbeats. One court showed dishonest debtors' information on the screen before playing movies in theaters, with each segment including headshots of 110 deadbeats along with related personal information, lasting 33 seconds and broadcast almost 4,000 times per month. Enforcement staff may also assault the debtors during holidays and in the middle of the night or early in the morning. Another court resorted to seizing the property of the debtor's spouse (Yu 2020, 117, fn. 64). A judge in a hinterland area told me that her court was even more creative: the information about the deadbeats was put on the walls of schools where their sons and daughters studied (although these practices have prompted concerns for human rights protections) (Li and Gao 2021; Pan and Niu 2021, 179). Regarding property, in 2014 the SPC established an information-monitoring network with various government branches, banks, and financial institutions, allowing any court to locate savings, securities, or any other major forms of property. Furthermore, lawyers and other individuals or organizations related to the debtors are obligated to provide clues to the courts regarding debtors' personal and property information (draft of the Civil Compulsory Enforcement Law).

In the SPC's 2020 Work Report, SPC president Zhou Qiang declared that the enforcement challenge has, by and large, been resolved. The courts were at that time handling more than 10 million enforcement cases. In several indexes on the enforcement capabilities, a greater than 10 percent increase over the previous three years' average was recorded. Whether enforcement is still difficult remains a topic for scholarly debates (Zuo 2022). Nonetheless, in Zhou Qiang's 2021 and 2022 Work Reports, enforcement was no longer mentioned.

Conclusions

In many respects, the developments in China's civil justice system are stunning. Just look at the sheer number of cases that the courts have handled, and how efficiently they were processed! The incredibly low threshold for cases allows average citizens, including many who are underprivileged, to file their often minor or even trivial complaints. This is no small feat, as the majority of such disputes in other parts of the world end up without any recourse at all, as the dispute pyramid implies (Felstiner et al. 1980–1981). China's courts are being shaped in the context of the overarching concern for social stability, which is a daunting challenge for governance. The courts are expected to deliver a solution while simultaneously offering some comforts for otherwise grieving complainants. The judges have handled most cases delicately, preventing routine disputes from escalating into large troubles. The decline of local favoritism and the improved enforcement of judgments are far from unimpressive. No matter whether the difficulties in judgment enforcement or local prejudice had been exaggerated, the Chinese courts have nonetheless made strides, when compared not only with the nation's past, but also with the situations in most other developed economies.

As a major component in Chinese justice, civil justice perhaps best exemplifies the policy-implementing characteristics in the governance framework: efficiency and effectiveness in dispute resolution, and a supreme concern for maintaining social stability. Equally prominent in this area are intensive efforts toward enhancing legitimacy. That said, the tensions among those goals are also palpable, and achieving one goal often means sacrificing another. The impressive improvements in enforcement of judgments are laudable, but they come at the expense of fundamental rights. The process of civil justice is by no means fair, as pronounced inequalities are documented in adjudicated cases.

7

The Courts' Role in Alternative Dispute Resolution

Civil justice reform worldwide is abuzz with alternative dispute resolution (ADR) (Resnick 1995). One trend is to merge informal justice with state-run litigation. The US, for instance, encourages pretrial settlement conferences (Galanter 1986), which have had a remarkable impact. Some even argue that formal trials are disappearing (Galanter 2004; Kritzer 2004).

China seems to follow the trend of integrating informal justice into state-run litigation. But there are two fundamental differences: First, Chinese courts and judges actively mediate before and during formal legal proceedings; second, unlike the West, China has other policy objectives for ADR. In judicial mediation, China aims for social stability maintenance and judicial legitimacy enhancement. Due to heavy caseloads, judges also prioritize court efficiency, resolving disputes quickly while ensuring litigants accept outcomes. Judges often face role conflicts in judicial mediations, leading to inequality.

In contrast to judicial mediation's goals of stability, efficiency, and legitimacy, arbitration serves a different purpose. Foreign and foreign-related arbitrations aim to boost foreign investor confidence in China, a crucial element in the nation's economic development. Therefore, the policy goal of arbitration is to portray an arbitration-friendly image to outsiders, with Chinese courts aiming to display professionalism in line with international best practices. Nonetheless, courts remain a tool for state governance.

This chapter begins by discussing pretrial mediation, which is used in an effort to control the sources of litigation. Next, it reviews the evolution of policy toward judicial mediation, and this is followed by a microanalysis of judges' mediation tactics. Whereas dispute resolution can be effective in judicial mediation, litigants may not receive a fair resolution. The chapter ends with an analysis of the courts' role in enforcing arbitration awards.

Pretrial Mediation

The situation of "more cases and fewer judges" constitutes a constant challenge for Chinese courts. The authorities soon realized that it is unrealistic to rely solely on the courts to handle all disputes. This has been especially true since the judge

The Judicial System of China. Xin He, Oxford University Press. © Xin He 2025. DOI: 10.1093/9780198927815.003.0008

quota reform in 2014, which froze the number of judges (see Chapter 2). In response, the Central Party Committee (CPC 2021) launched "the management of the sources of litigation" (诉源治理) in 2021, which was aimed at nipping disputes in the bud. This management program stresses that disputes are to be contained at the grass-roots level, and that various mechanisms are to be established to prevent them from escalating. This is to echo Xi Jinping's call for the "Fengqiao experience (枫桥经验) in a new era." Fengqiao was a town in which, during the Mao era, the Party controls all aspects of everyone's daily life that no trouble can even arise (Wang 2024).

Soon after those reforms, the Supreme People's Court (SPC) issued a series of documents to promote pretrial mediation (SPC 2021b), in part requiring that basic-level courts provide mediation platforms in villages and communities, and play a major role in the grid of the social control system. In addition, the courts are to provide a one-stop mechanism for mediating disputes before they are converted into formal litigation. Pretrial mediation centers have now been established across the country.

The procedure is as follows: Once disputants decide to file a lawsuit, they are channeled to the pretrial mediation center. Different types of cases are allocated to mediators with the appropriate specialized expertise. Labor disputes, for example, can be mediated by an official who has just retired from the labor bureau. Divorce disputes may be handled by a retired judge who had previously processed thousands of divorce cases. A former village head may deal with property disputes brought by neighbors.

Of course, the mediators encourage and facilitate settlement of the disputes. Indeed, the income of the mediators is closely related to their number of mediated disputes. The mediators may also refer the disputes to other government branches or arbitration centers. Only when the mediation and channeling efforts fail can the disputes be filed as litigation.

This system looks very similar to the community or professional mediations that are conducted in the US (Merry and Milner 1993). A crucial difference, however, is the role of the state. In community mediations in the US, the state has retreated. Mediators resort to expert knowledge or legal authority to establish their authority (Silbey and Merry 1986, 12). Indeed, due to the lack of state authority, several neighborhood justice forums failed (Abel 1982).

In China's pretrial mediations, however, the state plays a prominent role. The settlement deal, once it has been verified by the courts, has the same legal effect as a final court judgment does. The disputants are not supposed to negate or appeal a verified settlement, otherwise the court can enforce the deal compulsorily. Although the pretrial mediators are neither judges nor court staff, most of the local mediation centers are located inside the case-filing lobbies of courts. In many courts, the phones of the offices of the mediators are part of the same phone system as the courts. The mediators join other court staff to eat lunch at the dining hall;

some go to work using court buses. In other words, the mediators are camouflaged as court staff, which offers them extra leverage in facilitating settlements.

With the courts' support, pretrial mediation has been quite effective. In 2021, such mediations resolved more than 8 million disputes, about one-third of the formal caseloads (SPC 2022b).

Judicial Mediation

One of the most striking phenomena in China's legal landscape is the stubborn plateau of judicial mediations. As shown in Figure 7.1, the combined rates of withdrawals and mediations have remained between 50 and 60 percent throughout most of the judicial reform period. In accordance with the shifting political winds detailed in Chapter 1, judicial mediation has alternately either been stressed as one of the criteria to assess the performance of the courts and judges (Li et al. 2018; Minzner 2011) or sidelined as a backward trend in the process of judicial professionalism (Fu and Cullen 2011a). The most recent high point for mediation was in 2012, the final year of Wang Shengjun's SPC presidency. After Xi Jinping took power, the SPC's emphasis became more "precautious" and "nuanced" (Gu 2021, 159). According to Fu and Palmer (2015, 4), the appointment of Zhou Qiang, the first SPC president trained in law, was "a clear indication that mediation would no longer receive the same priority that it once did." Nonetheless, the Civil Procedure Law (CiPL) (Art. 9) stipulates that the courts, when appropriate, are to first mediate all civil disputes filed, unless the litigating parties refuse to mediate. In other words, mediation is practically mandatory for civil cases. In reality, therefore, mediation and case withdrawals combined still account for 51.02 percent of family cases (*China Law Yearbook* 2018).

In a judicial system that has become more formalized and professionalized, mediation has not proceeded without resistance. Minzner (2011) dubs the resurgence of mediation a "turn against law," which in the long run undermines the legal spirit. Moreover, Li (2016) suggests that court-annexed mediation in China acts as a "barrier to justice" instead of providing "access to justice." Some judges, especially those with professional legal training, are unwilling to conduct mediations, because they believe doing so contradicts the rules-based image of a typical judge (Fu and Cullen 2011a). Indeed, Kwai Hang Ng and I (Ng and He 2014) argue that there are internal contradictions in judicial mediation. It is difficult to achieve mediation within the formalized legal procedures: the judges' authority is challenged, they cannot easily manipulate the legal process to meet their ends, the issues are difficult to expand, and the norms of harmony have little currency among confrontational litigants. Li et al. (2018) documented that, in order to bolster the mediation rate, the courts "strategically produce" the number of mediations performed, by expanding the definition of mediation, or by incorporating the "mediated" cases

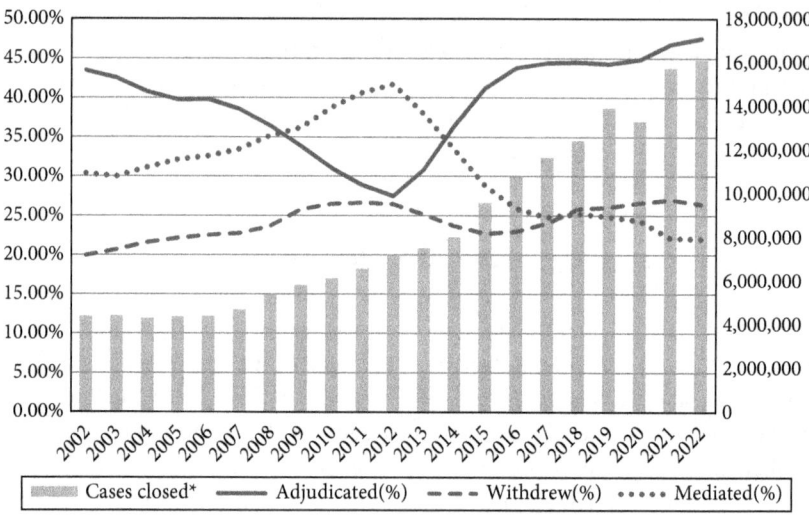

Figure 7.1   The Courts' Handling of First-instance Civil Cases (2002–22)
Source: China Law Yearbooks, 2002–22.

of out-of-court mediations, such as those in the labor arbitration center, into their own dockets. One judge said to them: "What if disputants in a litigation process do not want to mediate? We cannot force them to sign the in-trial mediation agreement" (Li et al. 2018, 72).

Notably, in most common law jurisdictions throughout the world, institutional arrangements are established to prevent some forms of inequality from being perpetuated in judicial mediations. For example, both parties are represented by lawyers throughout the process. In an open hearing, those parties' positions are competitively argued by their lawyers. Moreover, most judges in the US who participate in mediations are less involved in the process than their Chinese counterparts are. According to a comprehensive survey of US trial judges reported by Galanter (1985), the majority of the respondents surveyed believed that they had made themselves available for conferences with counsel, and had given suggestions when asked—actions that tend to reduce the likelihood of judges using their legal knowledge to legitimize power. Moreover, in a typical common law system, judges cannot simultaneously be the adjudicator and the mediator; they cannot use their adjudicatory power to coerce the litigating parties to settle. In a mediation session, private caucusing occurs, but it is done in the presence of a lawyer—which is why, when inequalities have been documented, they have often occurred in places where the claimants are rarely represented by a lawyer. Notable examples include the courts in Tokugawa Japan (Henderson 1965, 178), mediation centers in New England (Silbey and Merry 1986), and clerk screenings of the initial filings in a Massachusetts court (Yngvesson 1988).

In China, there are no such institutional firewalls. In China's civil law judicial format for mediation, lawyers are often excluded. In addition, when judges conduct mediations, role conflicts are common. Echoing earlier studies that indicated that judicial mediation in China is often nonvoluntary, coercive, and manipulative (Huang 2010; Cloke 1987), scholars have also lambasted the nation's tendency toward involuntary impositions of settlement (Chen 2015; Xian 2015). Judges serve as both mediator and adjudicator. They can credibly threaten a party with severe consequences if the party does not comply with the proposed settlement. In addition, Chinese judges have tremendous power in the hearings processes. They can prevent lawyers from participating in the mediation sessions, and can repress the lawyers' presentations in the hearings—which may be why repression is frequently employed in divorce cases, with most of the plaintiffs lacking legal knowledge. In fact, in many civil cases in China the litigants are not represented, let alone represented by lawyers! These institutional arrangements provide judges with massive leeway in imposing their preferences in settlements.

Scholars have long called for separation between mediation and adjudication in China. Ji (1989) pointed out the paradoxes between mediation and the legal system. H. Li (2013) famously argued: "Let mediation be mediation, let adjudication be adjudication." Tang and Qi (2012) argue that the best solution is to separate adjudication from mediation. Wang (1999; quoted from Li 2019) even suggested transplanting Taiwan's Americanized pretrial mediation institution into China.

Apparently, for reasons mentioned above, these calls have so far had limited effects toward any policy change. The SPC (2016a: Art. 30) stated that "to push for suitable separation between mediation and adjudication ... In principle, the judge responsible for mediation in case filing shall not adjudicate the same case. But the adjudicating judge can still mediate." In reality, it is hard to define "suitable." Practices vary between courts, but there is always one commonality: a thorough separation between mediation and adjudication has run counter to the fundamental goal of efficiency (X. Li 2019, 146–147). As one judge commented to Li, only when mediation and adjudication are combined can both the quality and efficiency of settling a dispute be materialized (X. Li 2019, 147).

All of that said, some judges still prefer to mediate many cases, even though their mediation rate has ceased to serve as a criterion in assessments of the judge's or the court's performance. Several benefits from settling a case still apply, however, even after the recent reforms. First, in mediation the decision is reached by an apparent consensus of the parties, so that they are unlikely to appeal or complain. Judges today receive little protection from their supervisors, and thus have to take more seriously the cases that may initiate threats, and favor those cases. As the saying goes, the squeaky wheel gets the grease. Judges commonly satisfy the needs of those who are prone to complaining about court decisions first.

Second, with mediations there is complete resolution of the disputes, whereas adjudication can only cover issues on the basis of evidence (Li 2014, 153). Thus, a

mediated case will not result in a wrongfully decided case, and the judges are forever exempt from the lifelong responsibility that comes with a wrongful decision.
Because of the voluntariness of the parties, enforcing the settlement is usually not
a problem. Mediation is especially suited to family disputes, in which social harmony and privacy are preferred. In addition, withdrawal of the cases before their
hearings will save the inconvenience of hearing and writing the judgments.

Finally, as others have argued, judicial mediation helps maintain social relationships and reduces judicial costs (Xiong 2015; Wang 2009). In that light, mediation
allegedly contributes to the maintenance of social harmony and stability.

Judges' Tactics in Judicial Mediations

How do judges conduct mediations? What tactics do they employ? Various mediation tactics are well documented, such as the use of timing, setting, patience, emotion, manner, and device. Examples include putting oneself in the other's shoes,
playing the emotional card, mediating in a harmonious environment, "striking
when the iron is hot," and back-to-back negotiating (Xin 2014, 190–192). Some
descriptions are vivid, such as in private caucusing, delaying, power borrowing,
pressuring, and face-saving (Gao et al. 2009, 288–300).

In my research (He 2022), I have focused on how claims are negotiated, and
my findings show that Chinese judges "expand" and "narrow" claims (Mather and
Yngvesson 1980–1981). In addition, included in the judges' repertoire are "repression," "conversion," and "facilitation." The judges not only badger plaintiffs to drop
their claims (Li et al. 2018), but also to convert or facilitate them.

For example, claims sought for divorce and domestic violence compensation
are frequently repressed. As far as the law is concerned, the issues of divorce, property division, and child custody are considered independently of one another, with
each issue having its own governing principles and rules. Divorce is determined by
whether mutual affection has broken down, while child custody is determined by
the children's best interests. According to the law, the decision on one issue should
not affect the others, but in reality these three issues are inextricably linked, especially in mediation. The judge has to weigh all of these elements in a mediation.
Whether a person agrees to be divorced, for example, may depend on how the
other two issues are negotiated—for a judge, these are the three bargaining chips
for mediation. When the issue of divorce is contested, the other two bargaining
chips become useful. If one party is steadfast on child custody, for instance, the
claims for divorce or property rights have to be repressed. This dynamic means
that many women—who make up approximately 70 percent of the plaintiffs in
Chinese divorce litigation—have to trade their child custody or property in exchange for obtaining a divorce (He 2021a).

In the *Disabled Team Leader* case (He 2022, 1189), the plaintiff, a disabled team leader of migrant workers, sued a labor company for unsettled wages. According to the contract, the unsettled wages were roughly 15,000 yuan. However, the plaintiff claimed that, with the contract price, he would have been unable to recruit workers for the job—a point that the defendant admitted. When the defendant resisted the judge's pressure for more compensation, citing his lawyer's interpretation of the contract, the judge repressed those claims about the contract with the following justifications:

> The court of course follows the law, but it also follows *li* (理). A disabled man, relying on neither government nor society, was supporting himself with his woodcraft. However, the job your company offered only made him worse off. Is the contract fair? Our judgment should materialize not only legal effects, but also social effects. I have to make sure the plaintiff will not petition to the district party chief, nor will he be waiting to see the court president. He will not intercept me in the street and I could walk past him comfortably. We are to resolve the dispute, not add another dispute or petition. One of our responsibilities is to maintain social stability.

In this mediation, the judge invoked *li* and political considerations to justify her decision. Challenged by the defendant's lawyer, she stressed that it was not the law which had dictated the decision; *li*, or "reason," had also had a role. Under *li*, the contract offered to the disabled man had been unfair. Furthermore, she stressed that maintaining social stability was the responsibility of the judge. She did not want to make a decision that would elicit a petition, complaint, or even threats to the judge (He 2017; Liebman 2011). Put differently, whether she chose to follow the law, or *li*, or social effects, the decision was subjected to the varying contexts of individual cases—and in this case, the fact that the plaintiff was disabled made the difference. The contract that should have prevailed under the law had to make way for *li*—that is, for political considerations. The defendant, with a lawyer behind him, thought that the law was on his side. However, the judge relied on another set of rules.

Judges also narrow claims, truncating parts of broad claims that were originally initiated by litigants, thereby making it is easier to focus on, and settle, those claims. Whereas judges in other nations' jurisdictions may also narrow claims for other purposes (Merry 1990; Yngvesson 1988; Mather and Yngvesson 1980–1981), Chinese judges are expected to "dispose of the cases" (see O'Barr 1994, 371). When a direct settlement cannot be reached, narrowing the claims paves the way for the final decision to be accepted.

In the *Father-in-Law* case (He 2022, 1180–1181), the father-in-law had been hit by the defendant, who had gone to the father-in-law's home to request his wife's (the plaintiff father-in-law's daughter's) return. The father-in-law's claims had totaled 35,000 yuan, including his medical expenses, lost wages, broken locks, and "damages to mental health." The defendant had already been detained by police for ten days, and had been fined 200 yuan. The judge's first attempt was to repress the claims: "Technically you are the defendant's father-in-law. Is it really worth a fight in court? Why don't you just settle?" Still, the father-in-law was determined to go through with the court proceedings: "No way! I am not settling. I do not care how much the court asks him to pay. But he has to pay. He beat me and he said he would not pay a cent."

Realizing the emotional aspect of the claims, the judge changed her strategy. She scanned the file page by page and said: "You also asked for lost wages, transportation fees, personal care fees, medical fees, and lock repair fees. Where is the evidence?" After the plaintiff shook his head, the judge continued: "A lawsuit is all about evidence. You only have evidence of medical expenses. Without other evidence, how can I believe that you suffered those losses? How do I know you are a taxi driver or how much your income is? Does the medical record state you missed work for 50 days?" She challenged his job status, his income, and other claims. In other words, the original claims were narrowed down to the medical expenses only. This strategy, once again, served to suggest that it was not worthwhile going through with the hearing with such a small stake, and therefore the plaintiff had no logical choice but to settle.

When the father-in-law still refused to settle, the judge narrowed his claims even further: "Usually, we only recognize lost wages for the period of hospitalization. And you asked for 10,000 yuan for spiritual damage. But the spiritual damage is only granted for serious injuries." To ensure that the narrowing strategy worked, the judge confronted the emotional issue: "I know that you just want to save face by taking your son-in-law to court, because he hit you. But in the hearing, I need you to show evidence for every item. If you cannot produce it, I will blame you for unpreparedness. Your son-in-law might laugh at you and you will lose face instead." She stated that the court would only recognize the hospitalized period for lost wages. She also hinted that the spiritual damage would not be upheld. By this point, the claims had been narrowed from the original 35,000 yuan to 2,535 yuan for the medical expenses. Understanding that the plaintiff was suing primarily to vent his grievances, the judge suggested that the plaintiff would lose face precisely because he could not produce evidence. Emotional issues should not cloud the legal issues. His goal of venting grievances would prove to be unsuccessful. Without evidence, the emotional claims would have to be truncated as well.

After talking with the plaintiff, the judge approached the defendant: "You beat him so hard, causing two broken bones. You have to pay the damages." Stoically, the defendant said, "I have no money. What can he do to me?" The judge said: "Should your father-in-law seek judicial appraisal, the injuries would definitely constitute light injury in the criminal sense, and you would have to do time. Given how angry he has been, he would surely send you to jail. You'd better just pay, whether or not you have money. Otherwise, the police and the prosecutor will handle this case." The judge had evidently already noticed the broken bones when she was reviewing the files. She knew that it would constitute "light injury." As mentioned, her strategy was to narrow the claims, not to instigate new ones. In the posttrial interview, she told me: "I am not his lawyer. My job is to dispose of the case." She had saved this point for the defendant because it was a powerful bargaining chip for coercing him to settle.

Sometimes the judge facilitates claims. Unlike repressing and narrowing, in which claims are truncated and muddled, facilitating can strengthen the claims by placing one party in a legally advantageous position in order to settle the case. As argued by Mnookin and Kornhauser (1979), when a court decision can be predicted, bargaining outside the courtroom transpires. A pragmatic judge depicted in He and Ng (2013b) facilitated a husband's claims for divorce by urging the wife to accept a divorce settlement earlier; otherwise, the wife would have further jeopardized her financial situation. In another study, the claims of a husband in resisting divorce were facilitated by the appeal-level judge in the judicial mediation, who cited that their mutual affection had not truly broken down (He 2021a, 131). In mediating labor disputes, the strategy of facilitating claims is more often employed by judges in Guangdong Province than elsewhere in China (Chen and Xu 2012).

In the *Businessman* case (He 2022, 1185–1187), a businessman had sued a female doctor, who owned a midsized hospital that could accommodate 200 patients, for a personal debt of 100,000 yuan. Due to her clerk's negligence, the judge was not notified about the case until 20 days before the closure deadline (three months, under the Simplified Procedure), which caused her to process the case in a rush. However, when the petition, the subpoenas, and other relevant documents were mailed to the defendant, the package was returned because "the addressee does not exist," and nobody answered the telephone. Due to the approaching deadline, the judge asked if the plaintiff could withdraw the case and then file it again after the new year, a common maneuver used to improve the case closure rate. The plaintiff rejected the request, but the judge responded with threats to reject the claim on the grounds that the plaintiff could not provide a valid address for the defendant. The plaintiff said:

> When I filed the lawsuit, the defendant was right at her hospital. Now she has disappeared because of the court's delay. About the same time, I had another case filed in the neighboring court, which has already granted me the judgment. If you cannot offer me a reasonable explanation for this delay, I will have two mud diggers in front of the courthouse, blocking your entrance!

Apparently, the plaintiff was a difficult character. Shrewd and cunning, he seemed to be a master of court operations. To block the courthouse entrance with two diggers was the last thing the judge wanted. From her interaction with him and knowledge of his thuggish background, she felt that his threats were realistic. If diggers actually blocked the court's entrance, the court leaders would not be able to remove them because of illegal parking, and instead they would first question whether the judge had taken any bribes or other unlawful transactions. Then they would go through the case files to look for any inappropriate procedures (Finder 2021). In addition, the media's reaction to such a scene would be that "the court and the judge must have done something egregious that the litigating parties have to protest in this way!" (see *Xinhua Net* 2017). Neither the court leaders nor the Party's disciplinary division would be likely to account for the fact that the judge had been overburdened by heavy caseloads—instead, they would punish the judge for any oversight, in order to ensure that the incident was under control.

Fearing such an outcome and acknowledging the previous suboptimal efforts made in handling the case—considering that the subpoena had not been served in enough time, even though it was still within the time limit—the judge took the initiative to look for the defendant. With a luxury car provided by the plaintiff, they visited the defendant's clinic. During the journey, the judge learned that the plaintiff and the defendant had engaged in numerous loan transactions. The plaintiff had also boasted that they had had a sexual relationship. Although they did not find the doctor at the clinic, the judge and the plaintiff served the doctor an absentee notice, which was deemed to have been delivered legally. While examining the evidence, the judge found another discrepancy: although the evidence of payment had been signed by the defendant, the money had been transferred from the plaintiff's wife to an unrelated third party, instead of the defendant. Because it was hard to convince witnesses to appear at the court hearing (He and Ng 2013a), the judge took another trip with the plaintiff to find the unrelated third party, who verified the transaction. At that point, with all of the evidence collected, the hearing was merely a show. The defendant did not appear, but her legal representative accepted all of the claims. Her representative simply asked for more time to pay, which the plaintiff instantly granted.

In this case, the judge could have repressed the claims. Under the Simplified Procedure, the judge and the court are under no obligation to serve a notice—the rules are that the plaintiff must provide an accurate address. Otherwise, the court can dismiss the claims after verification that there has been an unsuccessful attempt to serve the notice. At the very least, the judge was not supposed to take any trips with the plaintiff to locate the witness, because whoever makes the claim must bear the burden of proof. As a result of her heavy caseload and the strict deadlines to close cases, there was no way the judge could have made such efforts for all of her cases. Moreover, the plaintiff's sexual relationship with the defendant would have blurred the line between a loan and a gift. Indeed, when the plaintiff boasted of his sexual relationship with another woman, he confessed that he could not recoup his loan because of that relationship. The judge could have pressured the plaintiff to forgive the debt, given her shrewdness on social norms. Nonetheless, she did not take this route. Instead, she chose to facilitate the claims by making herself available for the investigation, and for serving the notice. Thus, she ensured that all of the evidence was secured for an inevitable settlement.

It is true that, since the recent judicial reforms, judges have become better trained in the law and are more professional. It is also true that novice judges may have difficulty in mediating cases (He et al. 2017). Given the institutional and political incentives, however, today's well-trained judges have little difficulty acquiring and deploying such tactics as repression, conversion, and facilitation. This suite of approaches has commonly been used by judges who are experienced, who have a fundamental grasp of law and politics, and who are capable of deploying everything in their arsenals. Similar approaches have been detected in the provinces of Guangdong (He 2021a; Li et al. 2018; Ng and He 2014; Chen and Xu 2012), Henan, Zhejiang (Michelson 2022), Hubei (Su 2000), Gansu (Erie 2016), Sichuan (Li 2015), and Yunnan (Xiong 2015). Some are even found in appellate courts (He 2021a, 131–132). In addition, case withdrawals remain a major outcome of China's judicial mediations (Figure 7.1), and many of those are withdrawn as a result of repression.

Unlike with adjudication, in which empirical studies can assess the win rates between the plaintiffs and defendants, mediation does not have a loser. Both parties agree to the settlements. Conventional wisdom suggests that power is exercised unequally along the parameters of gender, class, and social status (Yngvesson 1988). In China, however, a judge can be a socialist for a disabled worker in one case, but a coward when facing a nasty businessman. Walking on a tightrope, she has to do a great deal of balancing. Influenced by various political concerns, judicial power is not necessarily based on gender, class, or status. Somewhat formless and baseless, such power is intertwined instead with concerns for maintaining social stability. The connection between power and the judge's proposed settlements only makes sense in light of the underlying political goal. In such a negotiating process, the judge often convinces or coerces litigants who are financially vulnerable, inexperienced in the courtroom, legally bewildered, or timid toward the judge's authority in the settlement. Furthermore, the mediation process occurs behind closed doors, leaving no paper trail, and thus judges are practically exempt from any lifelong liability for wrongfully deciding cases (Li 2022, 204). Thus, inequalities are generated, reproduced, and reinforced.

Enforcing Arbitration Awards

Chinese courts have extensive powers in reviewing and enforcing arbitration awards. The Arbitration Law (Art. 58) specifies the conditions under which the courts can invalidate an arbitral award. The laws and conditions are more or less in line with international practices, but doubts abound. Would the courts go beyond the procedural review and also conduct substantive reviews? Are the courts in economically backward areas competent in reviewing awards? The SPC has responded with tight controls: it has issued judicial opinions to regulate the practice of arbitration. For example, all arbitration cases must be reviewed by a collegiate committee, which must meet with the applicants (SPC 2017d, Art. 11).

More serious concerns lie with the enforcement of awards. For a long time, Chinese courts were notorious for not enforcing international arbitration awards, and the reasons cited were familiar: a high degree of local protectionism, a low level of judicial competence, and the institutional weakness of the courts. However, is this impression supported by empirical evidence?

Peerenboom (2001) fired the first shot. He collected empirical data from arbitration cases and surveys from foreign companies and their counsels, as well as information from official arbitrational organizations, and found that the situation was much better than had been portrayed in the media. Local protectionism did not significantly affect the likelihood of enforcement of court decisions. He also found that only rarely did Party members intervene in specific cases. Peerenboom concluded that the Party had retreated from involvement in the day-to-day governance of commercial and legal activities. Still, many scholars took Peerenboom's research with a grain of salt. After all, anecdotal evidence suggested that, in some instances, the courts had not played by the rules. Even so, two decades later, based on 98 publicly available SPC decisions in which local courts had refused to enforce foreign or foreign-related arbitral awards, Shen and Shang (2020, 164) further verified that local protectionism is not a hindering barrier, since "no single non-enforcement decision" was derived from "clear local protectionism." This finding was further verified by subsequent studies (Gu 2021, 191; Liu and Wang 2018).

To account for this positive outcome, all of these authors point to a "pre-reporting system," which was launched after 1995. According to that system, before a Chinese court refuses to enforce a foreign or foreign-related arbitration award, it must first report to and obtain approval from the SPC. Gu (2021, 191) found that the SPC consistently overrules the majority (from 52.73 to 58.82 percent between 2009 and 2018) of the reported cases. Specifically, while public policy is widely regarded as a safety valve to deny enforcement under the New York Convention, rarely has the SPC invoked public policy as the basis for deciding not to enforce an award. In one exceptional case in which the SPC did cite "judicial sovereignty," and thus refused to enforce an award, there were no signs indicating that the SPC had bluntly violated the norms of international law (He 2013). It is fair to say, then, that due to the pre-reporting system, Chinese courts have been extremely prudent in dealing with international arbitration awards.

As effective as the pre-reporting system is, however, it has also been criticized for being discriminatory: it has only been applied to nondomestic arbitral awards.

In 2017, in line with the efforts to enforce civil judgments, the SPC (2017c) finally extended the system's application to domestic arbitral awards. The SPC further specified that the courts are usually to make their decision within two months. It is expected that these changes will further strengthen enforcement.

All of these efforts, clearly, are intended to boost the confidence of investors. As Gu (2021, 209) argues, the positive change is motivated by "economic factors." To dispel investors' doubts about the impartiality of Chinese courts, China has vowed to establish a pro-arbitration jurisdiction. The courts have fully embraced the policy—they are there to support the national policy on economic development. For example, to support the Belt and Road Initiative (BRI) (see Chapter 1), the SPC established two international commercial courts and, as part of their one-stop service, those courts were empowered to directly enforce the arbitral awards issued by their accredited arbitration institutions.

The Chinese courts' efforts to create an arbitration-friendly jurisdiction are understandable, given the importance of foreign investment and trade. While Chinese courts officially reject the notion of judicial independence as a Western ideology, they are still required to follow the rules, although extralegal influences persist. Creating an arbitration-friendly environment is a crucial factor in re-assuring foreign investors. As a result, Chinese courts provide unwavering support for this process. However, with the Party reasserting control over the courts, it may be challenging to convince foreign investors to use Chinese courts for international business dispute resolution. Therefore, arbitration, and particularly international arbitration, may be seen as an extra track for resolving international business disputes.

Conclusions

The role of Chinese courts in ADR sets them apart from most courts worldwide. Chinese courts actively participate in both pretrial and in-trial mediation, particularly since managing litigation sources has become an explicit Party policy. The objective is clear: mediation aligns with the courts' concerns for efficiency, social stability, and legitimacy. Despite fluctuations in relevant policies, mediation remains a significant aspect of civil trials at various stages. Regardless of issues related to due process and equality, mediation has been permitted, promoted, and even preferred.

The involvement of courts in arbitrations presents an interesting contrast. Chinese arbitrations conform closely to international best practices, and China has carefully adhered to its obligations under the New York Convention. However, this compliance does not indicate that Chinese courts are free from the influence of the Party; on the contrary, highlighting arbitrations is an expected outcome of the party-state. The state aims to create an arbitration-friendly jurisdiction that is crucial for enhancing legitimacy and, more directly, for economic development. A credible arbitration system is essential for attracting inbound investors to China. Similarly, China's outbound investors in projects such as the BRI need an alternative to litigation for dispute resolution. The courts' various practices in ADR further confirm the policy-implementing nature of the courts.

8

Criminal Justice

China's criminal policy has been oscillating between two goals. The first goal is crime control, which is related to the state's safety and social stability. Traditionally, the approach of the criminal justice system has been to deal with one of Mao's two contradictions: the "enemies of the people." During Deng Xiaoping's period, with economic development replacing class struggle as the theme, the definition of enemies began changing and their scope narrowed. The line remains flexible, however. Indeed, Biddulph et al. (2017, 101) argue that "[f]lexibility—the flexible determination and style of criminal procedure and flexible criminal punishment, from conviction to trial and beyond—is central in criminal justice system operations." On one hand, Xi Jinping personally repeats a Maoist expression that political-legal apparatuses are the dagger handle of the Party (Xinhua 2014). Robbery, murders, drug crimes, corruption, terrorism, territory separation, dissent, and black and evil forces have been punished severely. On the other hand, excessively harsh punishment threatens social harmony, and a more lenient approach is now adopted, especially for minor crimes (Li 2018, ch. 4; Biddulph et al. 2017, 102–103).

The other goal of China's criminal policy is to enhance the state's legitimacy. The state wants the criminal justice system to maintain social order and deliver social justice. Thus, the general public's opinions become crucial. Does the state gain the desired recognition? While the influence of popular views has gradually declined since the 2000s (Wu and Liu 2023; Li 2018, 58), it sways the decisions of the most sensitive cases.

Overall, the last two decades have witnessed a trend from harsh punishments to lighter ones. Since the 2000s, the policy of "swift and severe" has been replaced by a policy of "the combination of leniency and severity." The signature policy on crime control, the Strike Hard Campaign, began in 1983, and was removed in the late 2010s (Trevaskes 2010a). The scope and number of death penalty sentences has decreased. Crimes against the state, and incidents of sex taboos, have been treated leniently. The state has realized that harsh punishments can backfire by delegitimizing legal authorities and the efforts put into building a harmonious society. The judicial system now also pays more attention to international norms and rights protections, as China has become an economic superpower and aspires to improve its international standing (Li 2018, 62). The state has become more confident that crime control can be achieved with lighter punishments.

The Judicial System of China. Xin He, Oxford University Press. © Xin He 2025. DOI: 10.1093/9780198927815.003.0009

This chapter first introduces the relationships among the three apparatuses in the criminal justice system—the procuratorate, the courts, and the police—and then describes the transition from "investigation-centeredness" to "prosecution-centeredness" following the rise of the plea leniency system. The discussion demonstrates how the procuratorate, under the banner of efficiency and stability maintenance, has, since 2014, gained an upper hand in the competition among the three apparatuses. After assessing the implications of the situation with the procuratorate, the chapter discusses the death penalty and wrongful convictions, both of which are significant in terms of crime control and legitimacy enhancement. Finally, the chapter describes a trend toward leniency, which has characterized China's criminal justice system for the last four decades.

The Mutual Constraints between the Procuratorate and the Courts

In the Anglo-American system, criminal trials are "the most dramatic and familiar ways of deciding innocence or guilt" (Friedman 1998, 191). The prosecution and the defense lawyers operate like the two sides of a duel, cross-examining witnesses and questioning their opponent's evidence. Under the legal guidance of the judge, the jury decides whether the defendant is guilty. In this process, the judge and the courts play a prominent role.

In many respects, Chinese criminal trials are the opposite of the Anglo-American system. Never are the courts an independent institution in fact-finding or decision-making, rarely do witnesses appear in the trials, and the lawyers assume only a marginal role. There are two reasons for this difference: one, the Chinese system shares many characteristics of the continental system, and has also been influenced by the former Soviet Union; and, two, the system operates according to its own institutional logics and ideological principles.

Criminal justice in China is conducted by three state apparatuses: the police, the procuratorate, and the courts. The judicial process is sequential and can be depicted as a relay race or conveyor belt that turns criminal suspects into convicted prisoners (Miao 2021b, 246; Chen 2006). The Criminal Procedure Law (CrPL) defines the relationship between the apparatuses as a "division of responsibility, mutual coordination, [and] mutual constraint." Nicknamed the "iron triangle," coordination, more than constraint, underlies their relationship. Rather than forming a triangular framework of checks and balances, the three apparatuses collaborate to ensure criminal conviction. Few mechanisms enable them to check one another.

According to some surveys (McConville 2011, 355), China's conviction rate for all charges ranges from 92.3 percent to 99 percent. If partial convictions are included, the conviction rate is close to 100 percent. The ratio has hardly changed over decades, even after the recent judicial reforms that stress trial-centeredness.

In 2020, the official statistics state that, of 1.116 million criminal cases completed, in only slightly more than 1,000 cases was the defendant declared innocent (SPC Work Report 2021). Of those cases, 384, or almost 40 percent, were privately prosecuted cases, which involve minor crimes that do not need the involvement of the procuratorate. In other words, after being charged by the procuratorate, it is extremely rare, if ever, that a defendant will walk away. A judge may not have a single acquittal for years. By contrast, US juries acquitted 16 percent to one-third of defendants during a comparable period (Friedman 1998, 192).

Although high conviction rates have been common in some continental jurisdictions, such as Japan (Ramseyer and Rasmusen 2001) and Taiwan (Ye and Xiong 2018, 134) (in the latter case, approximately 90 percent), the extremely high rate in China has its unique reasons. The pro-conviction ideology is crucial, of course, but the institutional constraints are the most direct and immediate variable. In China, the three judicial apparatuses comprise a family in combating criminal activities. The courts and the procuratorate are expected to mutually coordinate and supervise each other. On the surface, the procuratorate initiates public prosecutions on behalf of the state, similar to the actions of a district attorney in the US. However, that role differs from the work of a US district attorney in that the office of the procuratorate also serves as the state organ for legal supervision. The office thus holds broad power to supervise trials and other aspects of the court operations.

If that is just an abstract principle, at the institutional level the detailed appraisal system ensures that both the procuratorate and the court take each other's concerns seriously. The appraisal system that assesses the performance of judges, prosecutors, and police has influenced their decisions immensely. For example, "[l]ife-taken cases must be 100 percent resolved; for theft, robbery, and fraud cases, 20 percent shall be resolved" (Yin 2021, 145). As a result, the police try their best to arrest suspects, and not uncommonly, the principle of due process is not observed. Similarly, the Supreme People's Procuratorate (SPP) has required that, nationwide, the non-guilty charge rates cannot exceed 0.2 percent (Miao 2021, fn 41). Any prosecutor failing to meet the threshold can be disqualified from obtaining honorary titles and be subject to disciplinary actions. A single case acquittal may deprive the prosecutor of their bonus for the year, and even their promotion prospects. As a result, the presumption of innocence has been eroded.

Furthermore, these assessment criteria affect the relationship between the procuratorate and the courts. On paper, the court has the final say on the case outcomes. Identifying problems in the prosecution, either with regard to evidence or procedure, will not adversely affect the performance of the judge—indeed, judges will be awarded for locating such problems. Why can they not just make an independent evaluation of the evidence, however? This has to be understood via the terms of the procuratorate's power and concerns. Under the principle of mutual supervision or constraint, the procuratorate has the power to oversee the court operations, making sure that court decisions are legally made. Regarding potential mistakes, the procuratorate has the power to "protest" a decision at the appellate court. If a mistake is confirmed, the judge responsible for handling the case will be subject to disciplinary sanctions.

Under such institutional arrangements, the two judicial apparatuses—the courts and the procuratorates—have to live with each other's shortcomings and find a way to avoid undesirable outcomes. Resistance, negotiations, bargains, and trade-offs occur when the courts disagree with the charges. It would be inaccurate to say that the courts function simply as a "yes-man". Indeed, the procuratorates do not care whether the courts convict on all of the charges, or whether the convicted crime is the one that was charged. The outcome is acceptable as long as it is a conviction, no matter whether it is a partial, light conviction or is for a different crime. An acquittal is unacceptable, however, because it suggests a prosecutorial blunder. As a result, when a judge is about to issue an acquittal, the procuratorate will approach the court official and propose a trade-off, such as dropping potential protests (Mou 2020, 183). Nonetheless, such trade-offs are not the normal solution between the two judicial apparatuses. Neither acquittals nor protests are supposed to be used—they are what Ayres and Braithwaite (1992) call the "benign big gun," and are used only when the relationship is ruptured.

Under a "healthy" relationship, when the court finds a weak case, the judge is expected to assist the procuratorate in avoiding a potential acquittal. The procuratorate, in return, is to also avoid any protest of an erroneous judgment. As a result, if a case is weak, the court will not drop the charges or exonerate the defendants—instead, the court will ask the procuratorate to fix the defects. This is called "the reversal of procedures" (Chen Ruihua 2017a, 12, fn 1). If an acquittal is likely, the court will ask the procuratorate to withdraw the case, or, in extreme cases, "to secretly replace the case with a different one prior to the court hearing" (Mou 2020, 181). For controversial cases, the judge and the prosecutor often meet in order to reach a common understanding. As game theory shows, for two repeat players, cooperation is the best strategy. In a repeated game, the last outcome that the two wrestlers want is to harm each other. Albert Alschular (1975, 1210) calls this "bureaucratic symbiosis." To maintain the best interests of both judicial apparatuses, the relationship between them needs to be harmonious instead of confrontational.

In this overall process, the courts are thus under tremendous pressures to cooperate and always render conviction decisions. After the 2014 reforms, some so-called "unscientific" or "unreasonable" performance measurements have been dropped. However, the performance evaluation has never been completely eliminated. The position of the reforms is ambivalent—after all, these performance requirements are fundamental for the proper functioning of the criminal justice agencies (Miao 2021), which, once again, are in essence bureaucratic institutions implementing policies.

The cooperative relationship between the judges and prosecutors is manifested during and beyond the trial. During the trial, the judges never treat the prosecutors as a party in the litigation—they are an authority, and a significant amount of unprofessional behavior on the part of the prosecutors is tolerated (Li 2014, 104–107). A judge told me that criminal judges often form a more intimate relationship with the prosecutors than with other court colleagues. They have lunch more often with the prosecutors than with their own colleagues. Each year, the criminal judges and prosecutors have dinners, parties, outings, and other celebrations together. "Decisions of the criminal cases were often made based upon ... casual telephone conversations, in which chit-chat, negotiations and compromises were blended" (Mou 2020, 186). Consequently, the mutually supervisory relationship has degenerated into mere communication (Mou 2020, 182). In recent years, due to heightened concerns for the security of judges, the courts have established security lines that prevent outsiders from gaining access to judges' offices. Even so, the prosecutors are often offered free access to judges' offices (Mou 2020, 186). The social ecology and spatial arrangements reveal that prosecutors and judges are more akin to "comrades" than to professionals working for different entities.

Substantiated Hearings?

As is also true with many continental systems, the authority in China's criminal trials was extremely hierarchical in the past. The top echelon had the ultimate power, supervising the detailed handling of matters for the lower ranks and requiring a strong sense of uniformity and loyalty in decision-making. The criminal policies and reform measures were all schematized at the top level and were implemented throughout the lower layers. The discretion engaged in at the bottom was to be kept to a minimum. In most cases, the trials themselves were nothing more than a show.

The 2014 judicial reforms, however, have tried to promote trial-centeredness (CCP 2014). The question is, however, whether the new policy has been implemented. If substantiated hearings mean confrontation between the prosecution and the defense, then the policy change has achieved very little. According to a recent empirical study on the judgments in which evidence was challenged, Hou and Xing (2019, 126) found that 9.72 percent of challenged testimony was excluded. The most common reason for exclusion (approximately 21 percent of that excluded) was that an investigator inquired of different witnesses at the same time, which apparently reflected a procedural defect. Only 7.2 percent of the testimony was excluded because of violence, threats, or imprisonment—in fact, violence occurred in only one case out of more than 100 judgments (Hou and Xing 2019, 127).

Most of the evidence challenges in that study were raised by defense lawyers (89 percent), while 47 percent were brought by defendants (the two may have overlapped). Only in 1 percent of the challenges did the judges initiate such inquiries, thus indicating their lack of incentives to do so, and showing that the defense lawyers are not totally useless. In rare cases, they even provided new evidence. For example, in one case, the defense lawyer provided a picture of the beaten face and medical records of the witness (Hou and Xing 2019, 127–128). Still, that is not the general pattern, and most only raised questions on prosecutorial evidence.

Due to the tightly cooperative relationship between the courts and the procuratorate, the judges often assume that the evidence provided is reliable. Once the evidence has been challenged, the judges do assess it critically, usually asking the police or the prosecutor to provide explanations. Only when the explanations are unconvincing do the judges strike down that evidence. Indeed, the Regulations on the Exclusion of Illegal Evidence (2017) remain ambiguous on many key concepts, such as the use of torture to obtain evidence. In addition, the procedures are not clearly defined—the procedural requirements are regarded as fairly complex, and the standards for proof are set too high (Wang 2015, quoted from Biddulph et al. 2017, 107). No clear remedial actions have been established for situations in which a judge refuses to exclude evidence. In most cases, only part of the evidence is excluded, which is consistent with the exceedingly high conviction rate.

The hearings allow the trial judges to observe the demeanor of the defendants and evaluate the weight of the evidence, but these factors remain secondary in the decision-making process, and function mainly to verify the evidence contained in the dossier. Most hearings are simply a prearranged show. In a southern court in which the present author conducted a fieldwork investigation, the hearing, following a punctual schedule, pinpointed the time needed for a given case and thus transferred the defendant from the detention center and back. On average, single cases lasted roughly 20 minutes (Zuo 2017, quoted in McConville 2011, 351). The trials were dominated by the judge and the prosecutor, and other people rarely spoke. The defendants often said yes when asked something by the judges (see Li 2014, 105–107). Some were so terrified that they could not speak clearly. Some cried. Most lawyers' defense statements were perfunctory and simply pled for lighter sentences.

Whereas the judicial system's hierarchy has been truncated since the 2014 reforms, the case dossier's role remains crucial. Any appeal, petition, or supervision request needs to review the dossier. Thus, it is natural to have a dossier that "incorporates all traces of official activities and materials used for decision-making" (Mou 2020, 177). All of the materials and the evidence, including the courts' internal minutes, are assembled in a manner that makes them suitable for future audits. The dossiers provide the basis on which the decisions are made, and in fact, Chen Ruihua, a prominent professor in China's criminal procedure law, contends that dossier-centeredness is the key for understanding China's criminal justice system. A judge interviewed by Mou (2020, 175) said that "judges in China are responsible for the truth that is embodied by the dossier ... Do we dare to make a judgment just by hearing the witnesses' testimony in the court? No. No judge has the courage to do this in China." The files are transferred from the police (or sometimes the procuratorate) to the courts. The court decisions are also subject to review, *de jure* and *de facto*, by upper-level courts or the Party committees. They thus have to justify their decisions by written evidence that is entered into the dossier.

Witnesses are rarely seen in the trials, under the traditional explanation that they fear reprisals. However, most witnesses provide written evidence with their identities disclosed. If they are afraid of reprisals, why would they give written evidence in the first place? An empirical study even found that most of the witnesses who were studied were willing to offer oral testimony at court (Zuo and Ma 2012).

The real reason, argue McConville et al. (2011, 246), is that the court and the procuratorate are reluctant to include witnesses in court hearings—they just want witness statements, which are settled and have been scrutinized before the trial. Zhiyuan Guo (2021, 194–196) also found that both the prosecutors and the judges lack an incentive to have witnesses in person at the hearings. Judges prefer written statements over witnesses in person because it is time-consuming to determine conflicting oral testimonies. Some judges, apparently inexperienced in handling witnesses and cross-examinations, have no idea what to do when witnesses present accounts that differ from their pretrial depositions. The memories of witnesses are fluid and malleable, whereas the witness statements are settled. There may be different interpretations of oral testimonies, verbal exchanges, and the demeanors of witnesses, and witnesses may not be able to corroborate the evidence prepared by the police or the prosecution, thus creating problems when the case is reviewed. It is no wonder, then, that the judges try to preclude witnesses from being cross-examined in the hearings.

In a nutshell, state officials still have a substantial monopoly over the framing of events and the presentation of evidence. The evidence is mostly provided by the officials, and the courts rarely dismiss it. Rarely is evidence provided by the lawyers, who often exist as a formality and sometimes urge defendants to confess. At best, the lawyers challenge the existing prosecutorial evidence according to the Regulations on Excluding Illegal Evidence (2017) and the amended CrPL.

The Plea Leniency System

Hearings become further hollowed out when plea leniency enters the picture. Since trial-centeredness would have diminished the procuratorate's influence in the criminal justice process, the SPP has tried to maintain their status (Yu 2021). Therefore, the plea leniency system, although only mentioned in passing in the Party's 2014 plenum decision, has been adopted as a major vehicle. Of course, efficiency, social stability, and overcrowded detention centers, which cannot detain minor offenders for very long, are the formal arguments.

With the plea leniency system, if a defendant acknowledges guilt and accepts the proposed sentence (either a specific sentence or a sentencing range), he or she receives leniency. Acknowledging guilt means that the defendant/suspect confesses offenses honestly and does not dispute the charges. Accepting a sentence means that the defendant feels contrition and is willing to accept the requisite penalty. The litmus tests are the defendants' attitudes and behavior—whether they offer sincere apologies and adequate compensation to victims (Arts. 6–7 of the Guiding Opinion 2019).

The plea leniency system originated in the expedited procedure that is used in minor criminal cases. The expedited procedure applies in cases in which the defendants are subject to less than three years of imprisonment, and the court investigation and debate have been curtailed, preserving only the announcement of judgment (CrPL, Art. 224). Apparently, the plea leniency system addresses the efficiency concern. The SPP argues that, given China's increasing criminal caseloads, complicated cases will be channeled into a different procedure from those for straightforward cases. Only through expediently processing minor cases can more resources be allocated to the serious and complicated ones. This argument was endorsed by Meng Jianzhu, then the head of the Central Political and Legal Committee: "Leniency in substance and simplification in procedure will better allocate resources, and provide both leniency and rights protection. It reduces confrontation and facilitates the confessions of both the suspects and defendants, making them cooperate with the judicial apparatuses in lawfully handling the cases" (Xing 2016). In 2016, a pilot scheme for plea leniency was implemented in 18 cities (NPC Standing Committee 2016).

Is the concern for efficiency in criminal cases real and pressing? While the overall caseloads in the courts have increased, the criminal caseload has remained at a plateau of approximately 1 million annually since the late 2010s (SPC Work Reports, various years). In addition, as Weimin Zuo (2017) points out, the handling of criminal cases, due to the launch of the expedited procedure, is already efficient. There is little room for further truncation. According to him, under the expedited procedure in 2017, an average court trial lasted only 5 minutes, 90 percent were shorter than ten minutes, and it took just 6.4 days for the court to process a case (Zuo 2017, 168).

Other scholars have questioned whether plea leniency can protect human rights (Chen 2017b). Some have also been concerned about whether plea leniency is compatible with trial-centeredness (Gu and Xiao 2017).

All of these concerns have been ignored, however. On the eve of the 2018 amendment of the CrPL, the SPP, in an interim report, stated that the pilot scheme had achieved "stunning" success.

Until October 2018, about 50 percent of the criminal cases had adopted the scheme in the pilot cities. The prosecution duration had been shortened to 26 days. 70 percent of them were processed in the expedited procedure, in which 95 percent of the court decisions were handed out instantly after the trial. (Zheng 2020)

Backed with these numbers, the plea leniency scheme was officially incorporated into the CrPL (2018). However, it is not merely an alternative channel; now listed as one of the general provisions, it has become a fundamental principle of criminal proceedings (CrPL, Art. 15). It is to be applied throughout all phases of the criminal process and covers all kinds of crimes. In 2019, the two Supremes (the SPP and Supreme People's Court (SPC)) and three ministries jointly issued detailed regulations on its implementation (Guiding Opinions 2019).

Traditionally, China has had a primary policy in criminal justice—"leniency for those who confess; severity for those who resist." However, this vague policy may not induce suspects to confess—people often do not trust that the authorities will materialize their leniency promises. In many cases, the policy has been regarded as a hoax to entice confessions and self-incrimination. A cynical saying goes, "one stays imprisoned forever once they confess." An empirical study (Fang and Liang 2019) of more than 6,000 judgments on intentional injuries showed that confessions following the policy did not lead to lenient punishments, because "confession is the duty." Therefore, the introduction of the plea leniency system was meant to overcome this mistrust (Zuo 2017). Under the system, the type and amount of sentencing are usually specified in the confession affidavit. In addition, the Guiding Opinions (2019) stipulate that, under the plea leniency system, one who confesses receives more leniency than one who only admits guilt. In practice, the leniency scope is approximately 10 to 30 percent of the length of the original sentence (Daum 2018). The promises of the prosecutor, with specific sentencing terms written into the confession affidavit and witnessed by defense lawyers, are more credible than the policy "leniency for those who confess."

To address concerns over rights protection, China has made it mandatory to have either a professional lawyer or a legal aid lawyer assist every defendant (the lawyer-for-all scheme) (SPC and MOJ 2018). For suspects and defendants who do not hire a lawyer, authorities must assign a duty lawyer to stand by at detention centers. When prosecutors process the cases, they must consult the lawyers. The CrPL also clarifies that, *inter alia*, the authorities must allow the lawyers to review the dossiers and meet with the suspects or defendants (Art. 173, CrPL), to ensure that when they accept a plea leniency sentence, they understand its nature, processes, and consequences (Guiding Opinions 2019, Part 4).

Under the goal of efficiency, plea leniency has been implemented at breakneck speed. Less than two years after a 2016 pilot program, it was enacted into the CrPL in October 2018. As an overarching principle of the "mini-constitution," it has since gripped the entire criminal process. Plea leniency is applicable for an array of crimes, from minor personal injury, to property damage, to drug trafficking, to rape, and even murder. Moreover, it is applied at all phases of the process, from the police investigation, to the public prosecution, to the court trial. In January 2019, the system was applied in only 20.9 percent of all criminal cases. By 2020, the rate had skyrocketed to 86.8 percent, and from January 2020 to November 2021, 85 percent of criminal cases followed this route. By 2021, the courts were confirming 96.85 percent of the sentences the procuratorates had proposed (*Guangzhou Daily* 2021). The appeal rate for these cases was 3.5 percent, which was 20.51 percent lower than the rate before the system was implemented. The system was touted by Zhang Jun, then the SPP President, as a "modernized governance approach to control crime with Chinese characteristics" (Zheng 2020).

From Investigation-centeredness to Prosecution-centeredness

Until recently, China's criminal proceedings were known to be "investigation-centered" (Miao 2021; Mou 2020; Chen 2017a; McConville et al. 2011; Trevaskes 2010a), and traditionally, of the "iron triangle," the police have played the dominant role. Although they have been responsible only for the preliminary investigations, the police have gained ascendency over the entire criminal justice institutions. Indeed, the police have had enormous formal and informal power to deprive suspects of personal liberty for a significant amount of time, and to dispose of the property connected with the alleged offences (Chen 2017a). A popular saying captures the relationship until recently among the three criminal apparatuses: the police cook the rice, the prosecutors deliver the rice, and the judges eat the rice (Fu 2003). In that sequential yet collective process, the cooks—the police—take center stage. Once the rice is cooked, the judges will eat all of it.

In this traditional mode, the procuratorates, acting with their supervisory power as the middleman between the police and the courts, already had considerable power over those two branches. Now, the plea leniency system allows the procuratorates to assert even more power over both the police and the courts: a change that can be observed in their relationships with all participants in the criminal justice system—the police, courts, defendants, defense lawyers, and victims.

Overshadowing the Police

Plea leniency boosts the procuratorates' status over the police. Although plea leniency is a process covering all three phases of criminal justice, leniency promises can only be granted in the prosecutorial phase, which means that some of the police's teeth have been removed. The police can invoke plea leniency or educate suspects on how to plead, but the Guiding Opinions (2019, 23) expressly prohibit them from granting leniency and recommending sentences. If the suspects do plead, the police are only to record the pleas in the dossiers and transfer them to the procuratorates, and only after the procuratorates step in can leniency promises be made.

In addition, plea leniency allows prosecutors to constrain the police's investigatory power. In the traditional mode, prosecutors intervened only after the police had finished their investigation, interrogation, and evidence collection; the rice had already been cooked. Plea leniency offers the prosecutors another reason to determine whether to grant arrests (CrPL, Art. 81.2). Moreover, the prosecutors intervene earlier, usually following the subject's arrest or detention (Lu 2021, 61–62). Once the prosecutors step in, "the police no longer need to do further work gathering substantial evidence" (Lu 2021, 62). From that point onward, collecting evidence is the prosecutors' job: they are not just one of the cooks—they become the head chef. A vice president of the SPP said that the procuratorates have assumed part of the investigatory responsibility (Zheng 2020).

Although the police remain dominant in the investigation period, the plea leniency system allows the procuratorates to have more of a voice: "During the arrest granting period or on influential cases, the police shall carefully listen to the opinions and suggestions of the procuratorate with regard to plea leniency and conduct relevant work accordingly" (Guiding Opinions 2019, Art. 24.3). This is the opposite of the traditional mode, in which the procuratorates followed the requests of the police and helped fix any defects. Now, they share with the police the power to interrogate defendants/suspects.

In terms of the post-investigatory period, the procuratorate has power and enormous discretion that the police can only envy: the procuratorate rephrase, redact, and frame the elements of the crime, and they communicate with the judges, defense lawyers, and victims. The procuratorate has the power to initiate charges, determine detention periods and conditions, and, more importantly, to decide whether there is culpability. They determine whether to charge or to spare charges (Guiding Opinions 2019, 8.2). They recommend sentences. If the police have remained the initiators of the criminal justice process, the procuratorates have become the terminator. The police, although dominant in the investigation period, have almost no say in the charge initiations or adjudication outcomes. According to Zhaohua Yan (2020, 42), the police's power to initiate the process or withdraw cases is under regulatory scrutiny: "They cannot determine the case's trajectory and outcome under plea leniency." However, the procuratorate's power, in granting leniency, is more flexible. The prosecutors seem to have transformed from being the middleman between the police and the courts to assuming the role of a dominant actor.

Since 2019, the SPP President has officially stated that the procuratorates shoulder "the dominant responsibility" in the criminal process (J. Zhang 2019, 9–10; SPP Work Report 2019). Obviously, "responsibility" is a polite way to suggest the dominant role. The plea leniency system has been cited as the leading evidence for the change (J. Zhang 2019, 9).

Why have the police given up so much power? For one thing, the goal of reducing wrongful convictions requires a more regulated police power. Xi Jinping has tried to transform wrongful convictions into a battleground, in order to consolidate full control of the justice agencies (Nesossi 2017). For another thing, the police are now relieved from collecting evidence once the procuratorate step in, which also reduces their chance of making mistakes. Arguably, wrongful convictions become rare under plea leniency. After all, the defendants have voluntarily admitted their guilt and accepted punishment.

Marginalizing the Courts

The procuratorates are never shy in asserting dominance over the courts. The SPP openly states that the procuratorates have replaced the courts in assuming "much" of the judicial responsibility (Zheng 2020). Under the traditional mode, the procuratorates brought the charges. Under plea leniency, they determine whether there is culpability, what the type of crime is, and the exact sentence. Thus, prosecutors have become *de facto* judges.

The courts, too, have been further marginalized. Under the traditional mode, the courts reserved the power to make the final decisions, whereas under plea leniency, the judge only verifies the voluntariness, authenticity, and legality of the plea: is there violence or duress involved? Is the defendant mentally healthy? Is there effective communication between the defendant and the procuratorate? (Guiding Opinions 2019, 39). Yet the procuratorates have already answered all these questions. The CrPL stipulates that, with the exception of five situations, the courts must confirm the procuratorates' recommendations (Art. 201), and all of those exceptions are difficult to establish. For example, one exception is that the defendants have confessed involuntarily. However, it is hard to prove voluntariness under the threat of greater sentences. Even according to the US Supreme Court, as long as one understands the pros and cons of one's choices, an action is generally regarded as voluntary (*Brady v. The United States*, 1970). According to Sun and Tian's (2021) empirical study, in China the trial is little more than a formality. They found that, although only 23.73 percent of judges regarded the recommended sentences as accurate, 95 percent still followed the recommendations (Sun and Tian 2021, 11), primarily to maintain a good relationship with the prosecutors and to avoid protests or appeals. Moreover, Li found that lawyers did not even appear in almost two-thirds of the trials studied (Li 2022a, 89).

The most crucial component of a trial is the evidence. Originally, few witnesses were likely to appear in court trials (Guo 2021, 194–196; Mou 2020, 193; McConville et al. 2011, 246). Now, however, under plea leniency, there are even fewer witnesses. Because in a completed plea arrangement the prosecutors have reached an agreement with the defendants and their lawyers, any negotiation between the lawyers and witnesses has already been incorporated into the confession affidavit. What is the point, then, of calling more witnesses to the stand? The prosecutors' burden of proof is exempted (Sun 2018, 181). All other evidence has been sifted, scrutinized, arranged, or rephrased by the prosecutors. Is there any need or incentive to challenge the prosecutorial recommendations?

With the procuratorates thus encroaching upon the courts' power, one might expect a turf war or resistance from the courts, but that is not occurring. Indeed, the courts quickly found that plea leniency conforms with, and perhaps even maximizes, their institutional interests: plea leniency lowers both the appeal rates from the defendants and the protest rates from the procuratorates; the trials' durations have been shortened; most decisions can now be handed out immediately after the trial—a goal long yearned for by the courts; some plea agreements even lay out the means of implementation; and the number of closed cases for individual judges has tripled or even quadrupled.

Although the criminal caseloads have remained stable, the civil and enforcement dockets have exploded. The average caseload per judge has been climbing since the 2014 judicial reforms, when the judges' quota reforms nearly halved the number of judges (Chapter 1). Thus, plea leniency does not merely deliver marvelously efficient relief from a suffocating workload, but also sets aside for separate processing the most complicated and organized crimes, in which some of the defendants refuse to plead guilty through the regular trial channel.

Furthermore, plea leniency spares judges from the risk of appeals. In fact, because plea agreements erase the possibility of factual and legal errors in the proceedings, the judges are rendered exempt from the lifelong responsibility of any errors that are later found in their plea agreement cases (Lu 2021, 61). Thus, although, since 2014, judges have been held accountable for their professional mistakes for life, plea leniency agreements provide an ideal rescue from that liability. In addition, plea leniency appears to promote the legitimacy of the system as a whole. Consequently, the courts are happy to cooperate with the procuratorates in implementing the practice. Indeed, empirical studies have shown that judges even urge defendants to confess and plead for leniency (Chen 2017b). As long as neither the victims nor their families complain, both the judges and the prosecutors are happy. In this situation, those two apparatuses both win.

In most cases, the courts merely rubber-stamp whatever the procuratorates have presented—they eat all of the rice that the procuratorates have cooked. The courts have no reason to conduct a full-fledged cross-examination of witnesses or do any serious questioning of the evidence. Excluding illegally or improperly obtained evidence and altering suggested sentences has become increasingly rare. In the traditional mode, the trial time had been short, but with plea leniency, trials have become even shorter; the judges simply check the boxes. The trials have become more administrative than judicial, and the judges' judicial power has been stripped, or usurped, by the procuratorates.

Overwhelming the Defendants

With plea leniency as a target, it is natural that the procuratorates pressure defendants to plead (Lu 2021, 63). The capability imbalance between defendants and prosecutors epitomizes the contrast between "repeat players" and "one-shotters" (Galanter 1974). Following Galanter's analysis, the prosecutors are repeat players, with repeated involvement in similar cases, and most defendants/suspects are one-shotters who are first-timers in the process. The defendants simply have no way to compete against the prosecutors in terms of knowledge and resources.

Armed with their ability to use their discretion in offering leniency, the procuratorates exert immense pressure on defendants. This discretion is a versatile tool. In addition to the 10 to 30 percent discretion allowed in setting sentences, the prosecutors can grant probation, bail, or even withdraw the charges; they can increase or shorten the duration of detention; and they can schedule an earlier or later trial date. Non-guilty-pleading defendants will likely be stuck waiting in custody at the detention centers (Li 2022b), and will also have no idea how long the process will take. Pleading defendants, in contrast, are likely to receive bail or be tried within a few days. The defendants' attitudes, including any hesitation, reluctance, or eagerness to admit guilt, make a difference. The pressure on the defendants to plead leniency is staggering, and most defendants can do little to resist.

The procuratorates can also withdraw any leniency that has been granted. If defendants later have regrets and reverse their original confessions in their trials, the confession affidavits will be revoked and the cases will follow the regular route. Thus, most defendants are reluctant to make reversals themselves—after all, guilt is not really the issue. When reversing a confession, there is little to gain, but much to lose.

In a guiding case issued by the SPP (no. 82), the suspect was found to have committed the offenses of breaking, entering, and stealing. He had pled and accepted the proposed sentence of 25 months in jail, but had then appealed, citing that the penalty was too heavy. This sparked a protest from the local procuratorate, stating that

> any defendant who provides neither new evidence, nor new facts reneges his commitment to the confession and the proposed sentence. The appeal is solely based on the fact that 'the sentence was grave,' without proper legal basis. This move wastes the state's resources and the original condition of leniency has vanished.

Under pressure from that protest, the appeal court remanded the case to the original basic-level court, revoked the original 25-month sentence, and handed out a new sentence of 31 months.

Controlling Defense Lawyers

Even with defense lawyers supporting the defendants, the imbalances between the defense and the prosecution persist. First, the skills of the lawyers—especially those of the public defenders—pale in comparison with those of the prosecutors. Duty or legal aid lawyers are usually not the cream of the profession. Many of them are neophytes. They are selected and salaried by local justice bureaus (Li 2022a, 87; SPC and MOJ 2018). Privately hired lawyers might not be specialized in the crimes for which the defendant is charged. The prosecutors, who regularly deal with criminal charges, understand the law inside out, while the defense lawyers may be unfamiliar with the particular sections of the criminal law and process.

Second, and even more fatal, is the lawyers' lack of independence and professionalism. Privately hired lawyers rely on state officials for case referrals and favorable decisions, as do duty and legal aid lawyers. There might be a tiny group of rights-advocating lawyers, but most attorneys are pragmatic deal-brokers. Originally, the judges were in a better position to control the lawyers because the judges monopolized the decision-making power and controlled the case sources. Under plea leniency, however, the prosecutors control the case sources and make decisions that are nearly impossible to refute. In addition, the lawyers have to rely on the prosecutors to make a living, meaning that any belligerent, confrontational, or uncooperative behavior will only harm the lawyers' interests, and could even sabotage their careers. On the contrary, by treating the prosecutors with cooperation and kindness, the lawyers can earn extra discounts on the charges and sentences for their clients (Li 2022b).

The tendency of lawyers to defer to prosecutors is also illustrated by the SPP's guiding cases, which the procuratorates across the country are required to follow in similar cases. These cases are intended to exemplify plea leniency's superiority in terms of fairness and rights protection. However, of the four guiding cases (nos. 81–84), one does not even mention the presence of lawyers, and perhaps did not even have any (no. 84). In another, the lawyer's role was limited to that of a notary public witnessing the hearing (no. 81). In a third, the lawyer helped convince the defendant to accept the deal which the procuratorates had proposed (no. 83).

Only in one case (no. 82) did the defense lawyer play a role, albeit minimal. The defendant had injured his friend, leading to the friend's death, and the prosecutors had consulted the defense lawyer on whether the defendant had turned himself in (自首), whether there had been self-defense, and whether the victim's family had forgiven the defendant. The defense lawyer suggested that the injury had been the consequence of the defendant's act of self-defense. In response, the procuratorate explained that the evidence showed that the defendant, after being hit on his head with a wine glass, had taken a knife from the kitchen to stab the victim: "This is an instigated response, instead of self-defense."

The legal analysis in the guiding case no. 82 is not problematic. The point, instead, is that the procuratorates had dominated the lawyer throughout the process. They had physically controlled the evidence; the defense lawyer had nothing new to add. The guiding case also showed that the lawyer had immediately accepted the procuratorate's narrative, which stated, "after communicating with, and seeking the opinion of the lawyer on duty, the prosecutor, under the presence of the lawyer on duty, explicated the detailed elements and the legal basis of the sentences." The lawyer cast no doubt on whether any evidence should have been excluded, or whether there had been any alternative interpretation, nor did he suggest any alternative opinion on the proposed sentences.

Traditionally, there have been "three difficulties" for criminal lawyers, but in plea leniency, two of these are alleviated—the difficulties in accessing case files, and in meeting with suspects/defendants. However, the so-called symbiotic relationship has changed little. Indeed, the two difficulties are the facade. The root of the system is that the cases are controlled by the procuratorates. When the procuratorates have only a few weeks to complete a plea leniency case, they in turn pressure the defense lawyers. One study found that, while lawyers may access the dossiers or meet with the suspects, they are often reminded to be expedient and notified that the defendants have already been informed about their rights (Li 2022b). In many cases, the confession affidavit is prepared before the lawyers have even been notified. Many lawyers help the procuratorate convince or urge the defendants to plead. Thus, instead of defending their clients, the lawyers have primarily become "explainers," "persuaders," or "observers" (Li 2022b). According to another survey, 89 percent of lawyers admitted that their role was confined to seeking "lenient sentencing outcomes" (Hu 2019, 115, quoted from Li 2022a, 89). Enshen Li (2022a, 89–90) found that, in 99.67 percent of the cases he surveyed, the lawyers raised no objection to the prosecution's case. Some were there only to witness the "signing ceremony," thus allowing themselves to be downgraded to the role of a notary public. Their presence is, therefore, the best evidence that plea leniency has been "voluntary." In most situations, their presence is ceremonial and symbolic, simply serving the purpose of fulfilling the procedural requirement. They work more for the procuratorate than for the defendants.

In this scenario, does the legal representation in plea leniency cases have any effect on the case outcomes? According to Yuhao Wu's (2020b) empirical study, after lawyers' representation for defendants in plea leniency cases increased from less than 10 percent to nearly 50 percent, the overall case outcomes did not change. The positive effect from court-appointed lawyers even disappeared after the lawyers-for-all program was implemented.

Pacifying the Victims

Granting leniency to defendants can, of course, breed discontent among victims, who not only want to see the murderers, rapists, thieves, and burglars duly punished by the law, but also often want financial compensation. This is similar to criminal reconciliation, in which the defendant may get leniency if they financially compensate the victim and are forgiven. Usually, more leniency is justified when there is more compensation. Thus, pacifying the victims has become part of the procuratorates' job.

Under the plea leniency system, the prosecutors are equipped with additional resources. The prosecutorial relief fund, a scheme to help victims who cannot obtain proper compensation from defendants, tripled between 2018 and 2021 (*China News* 2022), the period during which plea leniency was introduced.

In case no. 82, the prosecutor had learned that the compensation the defendant had provided to the victim's family was still insufficient to cover the family's losses. The prosecutor then paid several visits to the family, offering not just condolences, but also judicial remedies. The family promised that they would not take their hatred any further.

In this case, the prosecutor not only demonstrated that he cared, but also provided funds. By showering goodwill and/or material benefits on the victim's family, he had effectively ended the dispute. Ensuring that the defendant will not appeal is one matter; ensuring that the victim's family will not complain or petition is another. Thus, under the plea leniency system, the judicial relief fund further empowers the procuratorates.

Consequences

The rise of plea leniency is likely to have an immense impact on the operation of China's criminal justice system. According to the official rhetoric, both social stability and judicial efficiency have been achieved with the shortened case durations and diminished appeal rates. However, there are consequences beyond the official rhetoric. Efficient it may be; fair it is not. The increased efficiency has been at the expense of the defendants' rights.

Now that the procuratorates have become the crux of the three apparatuses, they enjoy enormous and almost unconstrained discretion. Under the current arrangement, the courts have lost any meaningful supervision over them. If, in plea bargaining in the common law world, the prosecutor's constrained discretion may have become a source of unfairness (Hessick 2021, ch. 3), in plea leniency the procuratorates' unleashed discretion can only be worse. The procuratorates can easily strike an agreement with the defendants by manipulating the evidence. For example, they need only disclose unfavorable evidence, to urge the defendants to confess and accept the suggested sentence. Neither the CrPL nor the Guiding Opinions stipulate mechanisms that guarantee full disclosure, let alone any penalty, should the procuratorates fail to fully disclose the evidence. The procuratorates can intentionally conceal or subconsciously impair any evidence that is favorable for the defendants, and can manipulate the timing of its disclosure, with the favorable evidence coming only after the striking of a plea deal (Liang and He 2014). On the other hand, the procuratorates can also drop charges, in part or in full, due to the suspects' "meritorious service," which is by and large subject to the procuratorates' interpretation (Part III of the Guiding Opinions 2019). Such a decision can terminate the criminal process even before the courts have become involved.

Plea leniency also creates incentives for overconfessions, forced by the threat of being labeled unwilling to plead guilty. As Biddulph et al. (2017, 110) highlighted, there are no mechanisms to verify whether the acknowledgment of guilt is accurate or reliable in cases in which the defendant has confessed; defendants can shoulder the responsibility for others. Due to information asymmetry and the inhospitable conditions of detention and interrogation, a defendant's acknowledgment of guilt may not be the product of judicial deliberation about the strength of the evidence.

While lawyers have become ineffective since the rise of plea leniency, the courts can be even less useful in countervailing police or prosecutorial defects. In the traditional mode, if the evidence had defects, the courts would ask the procuratorates to fix them. Similarly, the procuratorates also required the police to rectify defects. The mutual supervisory relationship among the three—even though it was tilted, as I have already shown—provided a certain balance of power that offered defendants some protection from the abuse of power by officials. However, under plea leniency, proposed charges are rarely rejected, and the incentives for further investigation have declined. As long as the defendant acknowledges guilt and accepts the proposed sentence, why bother with anything further? Now, the system simply relies more on confessions than on any other type of evidence. After all, it is the confession that determines the case outcome. In this scenario, both the police and the procuratorates will only become more unscrupulous—both entities spend less time gathering evidence (Lu 2021, 61–62), with the result that both evidence and witnesses are marginalized.

Furthermore, without a fully developed factual record, it is hard to determine specifically what has gone wrong when an innocent person has been wrongfully convicted. Neither police, prosecutors, judges, defense lawyers, nor anyone else in the criminal justice system will admit responsibility. Instead, they will all blame the defendant who "voluntarily" confessed.

Indeed, plea leniency has sharply reduced appeals. In guiding case no. 82, the defendant was burdened with six extra months' imprisonment because he appealed his sentence after taking a plea leniency agreement, causing his jail time to increase by 24 percent. An entrenched legal principle in CrPL is "no added penalty for appeal"—a principle that exists to safeguard the defendant's right to appeal—but under plea leniency, that principle has been eroded. Arguably, the practice may still be compatible with the principle: the original sentence is a result of lenient treatment, so no penalty is added when the consideration of leniency vanishes. However, in reality, the leniency agreement is a threat for any defendants who have confessed—for them, the first-instance trial becomes the final one. When a conviction is imminent in China's criminal process, few defendants appeal. For that reason, across the country the appeal rate has fallen to a low of 2.3 percent. In Lu's (2021) study of 388 plea leniency cases, only four were appealed, and none of those decisions were changed on appeal. Thus, the legal principle and the defendants' rights have taken a back seat to concerns for efficiency and stability. Indeed, as long as confession remains a core value of the system, appeals may not be regarded as indispensable.

The developments of plea bargaining and plea leniency are strikingly similar. Plea bargaining means that, through negotiation between the prosecution and the defendant, usually via their lawyers, the prosecutors may "drop some charges or accept a plea to a lesser crime" if the defendant admits to other charges (Hessick 2021, 23; see also Fisher 2000, 864). This bargaining facilitates the criminal trial process—once a deal has been made, a jury or judicial trial is unnecessary. Thus, the plea bargain has contributed to the vanishing of the trial in many jurisdictions. In the federal courts of the US, for example, the plea bargaining rate was more than 97 percent in 2018 (Hessick 2021, 32).

That said, plea leniency, in the way it is worded, already clarifies its difference from plea bargaining. Dominated by the procuratorates, plea leniency is not *bargaining*; it is a "plea for leniency." The defendant is to earn leniency by acknowledging guilt, showing contrition, and providing clues for cracking cases (Zheng 2020). The officials may or may not show mercy. Yuhao Wu's (2020a) empirical study shows that, in felonies, there is no leniency, regardless of whether plea leniency is taken; it is one-sided pleading instead of two-way bargaining. The procuratorates are not negotiators; they are arbitrators—or, to put it bluntly, "judges." They grant leniency according to their discretion, as set by the law. The confession affidavit with sentencing recommendations is not a contract, but a pending judgment for punishment. Whereas justice is negotiated in plea bargaining (Baldwin and McConville 1978), justice is imposed and coerced in plea leniency. Sun and Tian (2021, 5) found that the prosecutors' recommended sentences are a Hobson's choice. No "negotiation" time spent by the duty lawyers has ever exceeded 10 minutes in their surveyed cases (Sun and Tian 2021, 9). In essence, plea leniency gives discounted sentences for an early guilty plea. Unlike plea bargaining, plea leniency does not usually involve the dropping or changing of charges. Therefore, despite the Chinese Communist Party (CCP) having tried to reduce the role of confessions in the criminal process (Biddulph et al. 2017, 99), the rise of plea leniency suggests that confessions remain a gene of the system (Belkin 2013).

Criminal Reconciliation

With plea leniency as one type of reconciliation—between the state and the defendants—criminal reconciliation represents another type of reconciliation, which is, according to the law, between the defendants and the victims (and their families). The practice allows some defendants to substitute money for jail time. Although it was not officially recognized until the 2012 CrPL, criminal reconciliation has permeated China's criminal justice system since the early 1990s. Through private negotiations among parties, offenders can have their sentences reduced or even suspended by offering economic compensation to their victims in exchange for forgiveness. This phenomenon looks similar to the "restorative justice" found in other jurisdictions throughout the world (Braithwaite 2002), but in substance it does not fit with any existing model of restorative justice. It thus offers another vantage point from which to understand China's criminal justice system and the operation of Chinese courts.

According to the law, criminal reconciliation must be limited to intentional crimes in which three years of imprisonment or less are to be imposed, or negligent crimes with sentences of seven years or less (CrPL, Art. 288). By most scholarly accounts, traffic-related crimes and minor physical assaults are the two main types of crimes in which criminal reconciliation is practiced. In reality, however, it has spread to all kinds of crimes, including felonies in which the death penalty is to be applied. In the *Medical Malpractice Case* cited at the beginning of this book, the defendant's original sentence of 14 years in jail for negligent manslaughter was cut by four years, as a result of forgiveness by the victim's father.

Criminal reconciliation also permeates all three criminal justice apparatuses (Song et al. 2008). For a long time, roughly a third of the criminal cases in courts were reconciled (Cheng 2012). A study found that, in some regions, almost half of the minor injury cases filed at the police office were reconciled and thereby dropped (Ge 2008, 340).

Criminal reconciliation has the effect of using money to offset what is supposedly "just" punishment. As a critic points out: "If you have money, you will get a lenient sentence; if you are poor, you will go to prison" (Li 2006, 13). Many scholars argue that the practice violates the principle of equal protection of defendants' rights. Yet, as I argue throughout this book, the state and the courts are concerned more with governance than with rights protection. Unsurprisingly, the rights-focused approach cannot offer an explanation of the widespread use of the practice. Instead, under the governance model, one can see that the political logic behind its widespread application is to pacify the complaints of the victims and thus maintain social stability (Ng and He 2017a).

As the state's agents, judges see their primary goal as the preservation of social stability. Judges dread having their judgments appealed or petitioned, and owing to their weak position in the state bureaucracy, a winner-takes-all adjudicative decision runs the risk of challenges by the losing party. Chinese judges are thus eager to dissociate themselves from situations in which they must commit to decisions that may be reversed on appeal or petition. Criminal reconciliation means that litigants and their lawyers must agree, and as part of the bigger trend of the civilianization of criminal offenses, it is an act of self-preservation for judges.

In addition to removing the potential threat of petitions from disgruntled litigants, reconciliation gives the judiciary leeway to resolve cases in its own way, without defying the authority of its stronger sister bureaucracies—the police and the procuratorates. Some judges have said that they are uncomfortable convicting defendants in cases that have flimsy evidence provided by the police and the prosecutors. Indeed, China's state bureaucracies coexist in a highly complex system of interdependency and competition (Lampton 1992), and open disagreement among the state bureaucracies is avoided at all costs. By suspending the sentences of defendants who reconcile with victims, criminal reconciliation helps judges avoid defying the procuratorates' recommendations.

Exactly due to the judges' concerns about maintaining social stability and avoiding conflicts among the state's political-legal apparatuses, the judges play a crucial role in the practice of criminal reconciliation. It is rare for a victim and a defendant in a criminal case to reconcile on their own—residual hatred and emotions linger. Indeed, there have been cases in which reconciliation at first seemed impossible, but a deal was eventually struck after the extra efforts put in by the courts. In high-profile cases with broad political repercussions, sometimes the entire judiciary will rally to push through an agreement. The *Medical Malpractice Case* with which this book begins is just one of them.

An SPC judge who worked in a death-penalty ratification division said:

At the beginning, the judge was asked to persuade the victim's family to reconcile (in order to get the side to agree to a suspended death sentence). When it didn't work, the chief judge was asked to do work. When it didn't work, the vice division head was asked to do work. Finally, the division head was sent to talk to the family too. These people were all senior judicial officials. But they were instructed to visit the victim's family again and again. They were sometimes humiliated by the victim's family. The victim's side made claims that these judges had taken bribes because they worked so hard to facilitate a deal. It was crazy!

Judges often present themselves as offering impartial analyses to defendants and victims, but, needless to say, judges are far from being disinterested third parties.

Judges often act as intermediaries between the defendants and victims during the process of reconciliation. In fact, what judges do in criminal reconciliation is not far removed from what they do in civil mediation—they broker agreements by caucusing and meeting with the two sides separately. They hear the demands of both sides. They facilitate a negotiation by framing what one side says to the other in the best possible light, usually by accentuating what one party is willing to concede while downplaying any remaining disagreements. Convincing both sides to agree to reconcile provides a guaranteed way for judges to protect themselves. Still, they spin the "what-if" narrative to the litigants as a form of objective analysis, much as US judges do when facilitating plea bargains.

Often judges use the soft power of moral suasion to influence litigants. They play a pivotal role, sometimes in the shadow of the law and other times out of the reach of the law. In addition to appealing to the law, Chinese judges often fall back on cultural notions of remorse, repentance, or simply a positive attitude, to persuade litigants. The net result is that criminal reconciliation in China has become an eclectic procedure that is partly pragmatic and calculating but also partly moralistic and evaluative. Judicial officials are known to lecture parties on their "legal responsibilities," even though such responsibilities are in fact conventional moral views.

As an example, in a criminal case that was privately initiated (as opposed to being initiated by the procuratorates), relating to personal injury and property loss arising from a fight between two middle-aged women, the plaintiff requested 800 yuan for medical expenses for her injury and 14,000 yuan for an earring lost during a fight in the defendant's furniture shop (Ng and He 2017b, 1117). The plaintiff also insisted that the defendant be sentenced to jail. According to the defendant's version, the plaintiff had harassed her, and had taken her computer and two chairs from her shop. However, the judge was dissatisfied with the evidence. Did the plaintiff actually wear the earring on the day of the fight? Was the earring really lost during the fight? Why did the fight start? Who started it? How was the injury to the plaintiff inflicted? Although the laws stipulate that the court may return cases to the procuratorate or the police for further investigation, gathering fresh evidence late in the trial stage is considered impractical by most Chinese judges. In practice, reconciliation is the best option for the presiding judge.

In the case of the women's fight, the judge first told the defendant that "this might involve up to three years of imprisonment." A few minutes later, after the defendant had been asked to leave the courtroom, the judge turned to the plaintiff and her legal representative and said:

> Fighting is usually mutual. How can you claim that the responsibilities are all borne by the other party in a fight occurring in her shop? How can you prove you were really wearing the earrings that day? Why did you wear such expensive earrings when you knew your dispute might escalate into fighting? And you have taken away a computer and two chairs.

The plaintiff, after talking privately to her attorney, immediately proposed dropping the criminal charges and asked for just 3,000 yuan, which the defendant quickly agreed to pay.

Once a deal has been reached, the court will ask the victim's family to write a letter of forgiveness. In some cases, a victim will agree only to partial forgiveness, which means that they will not insist on the maximum sentence, and may even agree to a light sentence, but will oppose total suspension of the sentence. It is common for a judge to inform the victim that "lighter sentencing" includes the possibility of a suspended sentence, to see whether there would be any objection to this. The judge ensures that both sides agree on the details of the reconciliation agreement, thus protecting him or her from future appeals or petitions—the victim's side cannot accept the money and then complain about the lenient punishment given out by the court.

The Death Penalty

Perhaps no other type of case has drawn more attention than death penalty cases. The Chinese criminal law provides two types of death sentences: immediate execution, and a suspended death sentence with a two-year reprieve *(sihuan)*. In a situation of immediate execution, the execution is carried out within a week, once approval has been granted by the SPC. In the situation of a suspended sentence, the death sentence is automatically commuted to a life sentence after a two-year period, unless new crimes have been committed during this period. Indeed, to downgrade most death penalty cases to *sihuan* has also been a pattern adopted by the authorities to reduce the number of executions. Thus, for the vast majority of offenders, the suspended death sentence is a death sentence in name only (Trevaskes 2013). The focus here will, therefore, be on the immediate execution sentence.

Reportedly, China executes more people than the rest of the world combined (Amnesty International 2016; *The Economist* 2013; Bakken 2011), and China's execution rate has become the number one target of the abolitionist movement. China is one of only three countries (the other two are Belarus and Vietnam) that classify the number of death sentences as a state secret (Amnesty International 2017, 4), so the exact number of executions is unknown. Scholars have made tremendous efforts to crack the black box (Johnson and Zimring 2009; Lu and Miethe 2007). The data are incomplete—it is hard to know, for example, exactly how many have been killed because of convictions for committing terrorism in Xinjiang. Some estimates are subjective and hard to verify, but they put together a rough picture. It is estimated that China's annual number of executions declined from approximately 8,000 in 2006 (some estimates were 15,000 before that; Johnson and Zimring 2009; Yardley 2007) to roughly 2,000 in 2018 (Dui Hua Foundation 2019). Few scholars would dispute that the number is in the low thousands.

In the Mao era, the death penalty served as a means of eliminating political opposition. People might be executed for a statement that differed from the political ideology, or a curse against political leaders. In the Deng Xiaoping and Jiang Zemin periods, the death penalty operated mainly as a tool for crime control, thereby safeguarding the social order. For those leaders, the criminal hooligan had been defined as the enemy. The widespread use of the death penalty during that period is also well noted. In the late 1980s, a man was executed for stealing goods worth only a few thousand dollars, in the Shanghai General Consulate of the US. A young woman who had had sex with a dozen men was sentenced to death. In 1995, an accountant was executed for helping her boyfriend to embezzle 160,000 yuan (Chen 2005). From anecdotes and judges' memoirs, it can be gleaned that a typical basic-level court normally executed more than 20 persons per year in the 1980s and 1990s. Curious readers can do the math.

More recently, since the Hu Jingtao era, "killing fewer, killing cautiously" has become China's death penalty policy. Substantively, the penalty is reserved for the most hideous crimes, such as murder and drug-related cases. Overall, the number of death penalty offenses decreased from 68 in 2010 to 46 in 2015 (Biddulph et al. 2017, 97; the Criminal Law, 2011 and 2015 amendments). Smuggling, tomb-robbing, and stealing prehistoric fossils have been removed from the list of death sentence crimes, for example. The method of execution has changed from firing squad to lethal injection (*The Economist* 2013). Of course, reducing the types of crimes punishable by death will not automatically affect the number of prisoners on the death rolls; it is only a good start toward gradually limiting the penalty's application.

Today, China has also largely eliminated the death penalty for economic or non-violent crimes, although embezzlement and bribery are still subject to it, if an extremely large amount of money is involved. The threshold for "extremely large" was set at 3 million yuan in 2016, which serves only to give the authorities flexibility in making decisions, since nowadays the amounts of money involved in such economic crimes have become sky-high, making the threshold almost meaningless. When Lai Xiaomin, a high-ranking financial official, was executed in 2021, the verdict stated that he had embezzled 1.788 billion yuan (*New York Times* 2021).

Changes in death sentence procedures have also been remarkable. Before 2007, for almost three decades the provincial high courts had had the final say in paving the way for killings. Then, under the helm of Xiao Yang, the SPC reversed the National People's Congress (NPC)'s Strike Hard Policy and regained the exclusive authority for every death penalty case. Now, the SPC can apply the cautious killings policy more consistently and rigorously, and the number has declined sharply (*The Economist* 2013). More importantly, as Smith (2020) argues, the ratification of the death penalty allows the central authorities to regulate the behavior of the local agents—the lower-level courts as well as the adjacent political-legal apparatuses involved in the decision-making. Corrupt judges, sloppy police, negligent prosecutors, and biased party chiefs are the targets. Through control mechanisms such as "example-setting," "investigation," and "case remands" (Smith 2020, 69–73; see also *The Economist* 2013), the SPC has streamlined the practice of the death penalty. At the beginning of the SPC's reconcentration of power, approximately 15 percent of death penalty verdicts as a whole had been overturned (China Against Death Penalty 2012, quoted from Li 2018, 54). Since then, the overturned rate has declined steadily, and has now dropped to slightly more than 1 percent (Amnesty International 2017, 26).

In addition, several procedural measures have been adopted to ensure that defendants can have their voices heard by the collegial panel in the review process. The authorities have greatly improved defense lawyers' access to the defendants and the case files (Biddulph et al. 2017, 99). The practice of capital punishment has become more "careful" and "civilized" (Li 2018, 54). Still, as Smith (2020, 65, 67) contends, the shift to a focus on the review was not to protect the rights of the condemned; it was to examine whether the evidence was adequate or whether there were alternative explanations. The state is primarily concerned with regulating the local agents and is keen on avoiding wrongful executions—legitimacy and governance are the top concerns. In that light, one can also understand why the lawyers' impact on the decisions continues to be negligible (see Chapter 4).

According to Xiong et al. (2017), violent crimes and drug trafficking are the two most common types of crimes that currently give rise to the death penalty. A history of multiple violent crimes, and the weight of narcotics (in drug crimes), are two significant factors leading to the defendants being executed. Confession, self-surrender, and having a principal offender as codefendant are factors that can help one avoid being executed immediately. In her study of 6,517 death penalty cases from 2013 to 2020, Yanling Wang (2021, 136) identified that 66.21 percent were murder cases. Yunnan has been regarded as the province with the most death penalty cases, followed by Sichuan and Zhejiang. Apparently, the regional variation is influenced by the number of drug crimes.

The data studied in Xiong et al. (2017) and Wang (2021) did not allow them to examine one important factor: the media's influence. Most cases in their data were routine cases and were not sensational enough to catch the media's attention. That said, the courts have been required to consider public opinion and social impact in rendering decisions (Belkin 2011). Although Enshen Li (2018, ch. 3) argues that the state has managed to limit the influences on sentencing, public demand has swayed many decisions.

Long ago, in the 1990s, Zhang Jingzhu, a high-ranking police official in Henan Province, was sentenced to death for his involvement in a fatal car accident. It is widely believed that he would have been exempted had the incident not been reported. In 2012, guilty of illegal fund-raising and fraud for a large amount, Wu Ying, a rich young lady, was spared because the public opinion showed tremendous sympathy, and rumors of corruption among officials were widespread.

Li Changkui, a man who had raped and murdered his former fiancée and her younger brother, was immediately executed because of the overwhelming public opinion, manipulated by the victim's lawyer. The Yunnan High Court succumbed to public opinion, despite the policy that murders resulting from feuds between family, friends, and neighbors should not result in the death penalty. In 2010, Yao Jiaxin, a 21-year-old college student, after causing a traffic accident, stepped out of his car to fatally stab the already-injured victim eight times. To justify his offensive crime, Yao's explanation was that the victim, who looked like a migrant worker, was likely to request unreasonably high compensation. Despite a possibility of criminal reconciliation, or money for clemency (Bing 2012), the court sentenced Yao to death, apparently under tremendous pressure to avoid risking public outrage. Most recently, Tang Lu, the former husband of Lamu, a Tibetan Internet celebrity, poured gasoline on her and set her ablaze while she was conducting a live broadcast. The horrible scene caused an uproar on the Internet. She later died of serious injuries. Tang was quickly executed (*Mingpao News* 2022).

In summary, public opinion still affects decisions of life and death. Listening to the feelings of the people, which in China is done out of a concern for the judiciary's legitimacy, has been a policy for Chinese courts in their decision-making. Former SPC president Wang Shengjun stated so explicitly (see Chapter 1). What he did not make explicit, however, is the fact that the public emotion is not neutral—it can be manipulated, or influenced by the viciousness of the criminal act or the perceived social status of the defendant and/or the victim (Belkin 2011, 223). It can also be triggered by a perception that the judicial system is corrupt, or that there is social inequality (Li 2018, 58). It can even be manipulated or orchestrated by the government, which controls a massive propaganda machine (Li 2018, 65).

As a result, the public's opinion does not have an effect in all cases—it does so only when it aligns with the state's concerns. Notably, when state personnel are murdered, regardless of whether or not they have been carrying out their duties in an appropriate manner, public sympathy does not count for much. In 2009, Xia Junfeng, a street vendor, stabbed two urban management staffers *("chengguan")* to death. In general, the *chengguan* are notorious for their abusive behavior toward street vendors, but nonetheless Mr. Xia was executed, in spite of an outpouring of calls from the public for leniency. The public may have regarded the offense as a legitimate challenge to the corrupt legal system and privileged ruling elite, but SPC president Zhou Qiang regarded it as a direct challenge to the state's authority, and thus "very dangerous." In another case, in 2008, Yang Jia, a 28-year-old from Beijing who had accused the police of insulting him and beating him during six hours of interrogation for a petty offense, detonated several small bombs outside the police station in Zhabei district, Shanghai, and charged into the station, stabbing six police officers to death and injuring several more. The case was resolved with a speedy arrest, indictment, trial, and execution (*China News* 2008). No psychological examination of Mr. Yang was ever ordered or conducted, despite pleas from his first defense counsel. All of the proceedings, from the incident to Yang's execution, were completed within 144 days. One key factor was that policemen were murdered in the police station. Finally, in a very recent case, a judge in Hunan was brutally murdered by her former classmate whom she had refused to help in a case. The murderer was executed despite the long-term friendship between the two.

China is unlikely to abolish the death penalty in the near future, nor will it make the practice transparent. Flexibility allows political leaders to deal with unexpected events. As argued by Miao (2013b), China's capital punishment regime has become resilient, acting as a buffer between citizens and state authorities, and vindicating the authority of the state by providing a safety net for social conflicts. In Western academia, discussions on the death penalty have revolved around the issue of deterrence; in China, the main death penalty issues revolve around the state's security and whether the death penalty can defuse the hatred felt toward the perpetuators of hideous crimes (Liu 2021). In summary, the state's concerns about social stability and legitimacy help explain the death penalty decisions in Chinese courts.

Wrongful Convictions

In many scenarios, crime control and enhancing the state's and the justice system's legitimacy are consistent and complementary. Control of crimes enhances legitimacy, and vice versa. However, the two goals can also contradict each other, as is typified in wrongfully convicted cases. To control crime, the state apparatuses collaborate and work together. In quelling the so-called "enemies", wrongful convictions or even wrongful executions can result. When the actual murderer emerges years after a legally determined "murderer" has been executed, or the "murdered" victim returns from the grave, that is a slap in the face for the criminal justice system and the state. Such miscarriages of justice fuel discontent among the general public and heighten concerns about corruption, incompetence, and partiality in the criminal justice system. The state's legitimacy is damaged tremendously.

Miscarriages of justice are not new in China, nor in any other jurisdiction in the world. However, the scale of the convictions whose wrongfulness that has been revealed in the last two decades still comes as a surprise. According to the SPC, 94 wrongful convictions for serious crimes (involving 64 cases) were discovered and ratified between 2013 and February 2019 (SPC 2019b).

Of the numerous reasons identified (J. He 2016), investigation-centeredness was widely regarded as a leading cause (Biddulph et al. 2017). The police overwhelmed the process, and the courts did not enjoy the minimum autonomy needed to assess the police evidence impartially (Mou 2020). In an empirical analysis of 141 such cases, Zhong and Dai (2019) found that the top three reasons for wrongful convictions were all related to the police, with torture standing out as the primary one. Police torture and false/forced confessions were explicitly reported in 86.5 percent of the cases in their database, and in the rest, torture could not be ruled out. Fearing torture, some defendants did not dare to appeal. Witnesses and family members were also tortured into giving false testimonies. In addition, the police negligently collected or manipulated evidence.

Why would the police commit these blatant atrocities? This phenomenon shows a dilemma of the state in controlling one of its most powerful agents—the police. The state needs the police to control crime, and it also relies heavily on quantitative measurements to monitor their performance. For a long time, excessive political zeal for "fighting crime" has dominated the minds of the police. Evidence has, therefore, been constructed to fit the convictions. Most crucially, police performance evaluations have been directly linked to the apparatus's budget and individual officials' benefits and promotions (Miao 2021). Driven by all of these incentives, some police officers not only actively sought to convict suspects, but also pressured the courts to accept their stories at the time of the original conviction. Due to repetitive trials, innocent prisoners facing capital proceedings were imprisoned, on average, for 3,161.3 days (Xiong and Miao 2018)!

Xi Jinping has tried to transform wrongful convictions into a battleground to reestablish the legitimacy of the judicial system, and to consolidate full control of the political-legal apparatuses (Nesossi 2017). He has said, "[a] government that doesn't uphold fairness and justice needn't bother existing . . . in the broad daylight of democracy and the rule of law, we must deal with corruption and overturn miscarriages of justice" (Xi 2014; quoted from Nesossi 2017, 154). In a way, such a move kills two birds with one stone: first, by reducing wrongful convictions the state strengthens its legitimacy, and on top of that, the central authorities consolidate their control over the local agents.

The central political-legal committee issued rules prohibiting extracting confessions through torture during the investigation stage of the criminal trial (MPS 2012). Evidence obtained through torture or other illegal means must be excluded (MPS 2012, Item 3). Evidence must be strictly examined and cross-examined in court as the basis for conviction (Item 6). For the first time, the rules specify that instances of torture or forgery should be punished. Judges, prosecutors, and police will be held accountable for life for negligent or wrongful acts that result in wrongful convictions. The rules establish clear standards for cases of miscarriage of justice and procedures for correcting judicial errors. The reform measures are impressive. Even Jerry Cohen, a long-term critic of China's criminal justice system, called the rules "stunning in scope" (Nesossi 2017, 157).

How effectively these regulations have been implemented is not yet known. Some judges have suggested that, "in death related cases, almost no evidence was from torture; the police have made great strides in law enforcement" (Yin 2018, 119). Wrongful cases reported so far have mostly been from the period before the reforms. Of course, in a country with draconianly regulated media, the state could have controlled whether or not these cases were reported, and if so, how many were reported. Commentators also have pointed out some technical problems, such as a lack of full audiovisual recordings of suspects being interrogated, and a lack of access to lawyers during interrogations (Biddulph et al. 2017, 100). With plea leniency taking hold and prosecution-centeredness replacing investigation-centeredness, wrongful convictions remain hard to detect. Under plea leniency, the pursuit of "objective truth" has become the pursuit of "consented truth"—as long as the procuratorates and the defendants reach a consensus, the process is deemed to be over. This ideological change will affect how China defines "wrongful convictions," because the highly pursued consensuses obtained may hide miscarriages of justice. When confession's role has only been strengthened, the roots of miscarriages of justice have not yet been eradicated.

A Trend toward Leniency

"Balancing severity and leniency" refers to treating the few heinous crimes with severity while treating the high number of less impactful crimes with leniency. Over time, leniency has been a trend. There are exceptions, of course—after all, there is no single golden measurement for harshness (Smith 2019). For example, the amended Criminal Law (2011) increased the severity of punishment by introducing a 25-year minimum sentence and life sentences without parole. Some speculate that millions of Uighurs might have been incarcerated without having gone through the criminal process (Nebehay 2018), and that some may have just disappeared (Yanan Wang 2018). Crimes against state interests—crimes by rights lawyers, terrorists, and separatists—still receive long and severe sentences, although even for these cases, the punishments have been lighter. Indeed, for those "enemies," the punishment was much harsher in the 1980s. The sharp decline of death penalty sentences, in terms of both number and scope, is one of the most obvious indications of the trend toward lighter sentences. When the campaign to "sweep away black and evil forces" was launched in 2018, scholars and the public may have wondered if the Strike Hard Campaign had been brought back, but the SPC has clearly limited its application. A recent study also found that, although politics has permeated the process, and intrusive tactics have been used in investigations, "certain local courts had held their baseline and refused to ascertain the black or evil nature of the crimes prosecuted (Yin and Mou 2023, 379). Enshen Li (2018, 77) states that, "[a]lthough harsh punishment has remained visible, leniency, forgiveness and rehabilitation have become the overriding themes in China's Criminal justice and penal system." The new policy stresses "decriminalization, de-incarceration, and moderation of punishment" (Li 2018, 76).

Although crime control has always been important, it needs to be balanced with a concern for legitimacy. The balanced emphasis on the two explains why the criminal justice system has become less severe. Leaders have gradually realized that the hard-line approach has been counterproductive to social stability, and has even adversely affected the policing of crime (Li 2018, 71). The goals of building a "socialist harmonious society" and the "Chinese Dream" hint at softer governance (Li 2018, 68, 91). With a less harsh punishment system, the state achieves both social control and legitimacy enhancement. In a society that has become more open and mobile, and which is characterized by information pouring in, the state has increased its tolerance toward behaviors that may differ from the so-called core values (Durkheim 1993). When socioeconomic development is the theme, and when the state feels more confident, leniency is a natural option.

To illustrate this evolution, sex-related crimes were, back in the 1980s, punished severely. The family was perceived as the fundamental building block of social stability (Li and Friedman 2016). Regulation of people's sexual lives was *politically* important. For decades, only sexual relations that occurred within the confines of the heterosexual marital unit were accepted as legitimate and proper; other sexual activities were deemed immoral and even criminal (Ruan 1991). Under the label of hooliganism (流氓罪), premarital, extramarital, homosexual, and group sex were punished so severely that some received the death penalty (Worth et al. 2019).

Hooliganism was dropped in the 1997 Criminal Law. Picking quarrels and provoking trouble (寻衅滋事) and group licentiousness were added, but with punishments of less than five years in jail. A university professor who organized a sex party with 72 participants, in 2009, was sentenced to only three and a half years in prison (*Sina News* 2010).

Similarly, a person publishing or distributing pornography would have been sentenced to death in the 1980s. In the 2010s, a woman in Beijing uploaded seven "sex novels" online. After 80,000 hits on her novels, she received only six months in criminal detention. For organizing prostitution, a bathhouse owner would have been sentenced to death before 1997. Now, the most severe punishment for organized prostitution is for the business to be shut down (Li 2015).

Even crimes against the core state interests—the financial order—have been treated leniently. In 2008, Xu Ting, a young internal migrant from a rural area who was working as a security guard in Guangzhou, got into trouble, in part due to the error of an ATM, for overwithdrawing 175,000 yuan. The Chinese court first sentenced him to life imprisonment for "disrupting the financial order of the state." However, after waves of debates on the Internet, in the media, and in academia, the final decision was five years in jail, which still was a harsh decision given his almost innocent intentions and the mild damage he caused to the ATM.

A decision by a basic-level court in Huiyang Municipality, Guangdong Province, stirred a heated debate on the Internet in 2015. The case was about another migrant worker's bad luck with a windfall. When he tried to deposit 300 yuan to his own card in an ATM, his account indicated that the money had been deposited, but the machine returned the money. Realizing the machine's error, he received 90,000 yuan from the machine after making 17 "deposits" with money he had withdrawn from another ATM. Approximately one month later, when caught by the police, he had barely spent any of the windfall. He returned most of it to the bank.

Under the principle of consistency, one would have expected results for him that were similar to those in the *Xu Ting* case. What happened, however, was dramatic—the Huiyang Court rendered a suspended sentence to the defendant, setting him free immediately from the detention center. The decision was, therefore, drastically lighter than that in the *Xu Ting* case. Apparently, the judge was going against the prevailing practice. To protect himself, the judge made lengthy explanations in the judgment of why he did not believe that the defendant should go to jail: "My conscience told me that he was not a criminal at that level." The decision was powerful, convincing, and well argued, comparable to many famous decisions in common law jurisdictions. It attracted significant media attention. Once published on the Internet, it was touted as *the* greatest criminal decision ever made in the history of the People's Republic. Millions of netizens applauded. The procuratorate initially protested the decision, but withdrew after the appellate court hinted that it would side with the Huiyang Court.

Under Mao's famous dichotomy approach toward social contradictions, Xu Ting and other ATM victims might have been treated as class enemies. As society has become more open, however, the state is exploring new ways to cope with that openness. In the Huiyang Court's judgment, the defendant was gently referred as a "boy," a term once unthinkable for criminals. He was guilty of stealing, but that was all. The judge did not believe that he needed to be jailed or that he posed a threat to society. During a span of seven years, the punishment for the same behavior had decreased from life imprisonment in the *Xu Ting* case to a suspended sentence in the Huiyang Court's case. Of course, when the judge announced the decision, the state was watching, and when it found that the decision improved the image of the courts and its own legitimacy, the state endorsed the judge's decision.

Moreover, the trend toward judicial leniency has been vindicated not just in substantive laws, but also in criminal procedures. The ban against torture means that minor offenders are less subject to power abuse by local authorities (Smith 2019). Plea leniency marks a further form of leniency in China's criminal justice policy and now covers nearly 90 percent of all criminal cases. The Guiding Opinions on the Implementation of the Plea Leniency System (2019) stipulate "additional" reductions beyond what is covered under the "confession for leniency policy." Indeed, with plea leniency joining forces with criminal reconciliation, the trend has become systemic. Although criminal reconciliation has been driven partially by private forces, plea leniency derives solely from the might of state power. Community corrections, forgiveness, mercy, and rehabilitation have replaced the punitive ethos that dominated the Mao and Deng eras. In contrast to the old "swift and severe" policy, one may even argue that, today, China's criminal justice policy has evolved into a policy of being "swift and lenient." The trend of leniency allows the state to dispose of cases efficiently. Whether rights are protected in these processes, however, is another matter.

Conclusions

The outlook of Chinese criminal justice, even compared with the situation a decade ago, has witnessed remarkable changes. The rise of plea leniency is perhaps the most conspicuous change, and has reshuffled the power relationships within the iron triangle. The procuratorate has taken over from the police as the leading agency in the field of criminal justice, and the courts have been further marginalized. Together with other changes in criminal procedures, such as the widespread use of criminal reconciliation, and the centralized ratification of the death penalty, a trend toward leniency has taken shape. Wrongful convictions have become less visible.

All of these changes, however, have not improved the protection of individuals' rights. The role of the state is staggeringly strong, and rights protection is rather weak. The balance between state power and human rights is heavily tilted toward the state, compared with that in Western countries. As is abundantly demonstrated in the process of plea leniency, most lawyers become the assistants of the prosecution instead of the guardians of their clients' rights. Individuals have few choices other than to confess and accept the proposed "deal." Appeals have been sharply declined. In the SPC's review of death penalty cases, the focus has been on disciplining the unruly behaviors of local courts or police rather than on protecting the rights of the condemned. If Packer's (1964) two models of criminal justice—crime control and due process—also exist in China, crime control often overshadows due process. Rights protection has always been subordinate to the state's interests (Keith et al. 2014, 148), and today it is more a decoration for enhancing legitimacy than for safeguarding the people.

Arguably, in fact, these changes have actually strengthened the state's governance. "Strike less hard" (*The Economist* 2013) helps improve the state's image and thus its legitimacy, both internationally and domestically. The state's legitimacy has been further raised with the reduction in reports of wrongful convictions. As the official statistics show, criminal caseloads have been constant over the last decade. Overall, crime is under control, while the state's legitimacy has been enhanced.

9

Administrative Justice

China's judicial system sidelines administrative justice. The number of administrative litigations handled by the courts constitutes less than 0.9 percent of their
dockets. Essentially, administrative litigation is just one tool for the central authorities to regulate unruly local state agencies. Other tools include administrative reconsideration, administrative supervision, Party disciplining, and petitioning.

Because Chinese courts are merely an agent of the state (see Introduction), administrative litigation is nothing more than the constraint by one agent over other
agents. In a time of dramatic social and economic transformation, executive efficiency is preferred. Deng Xiaoping (1984, 238) once stated:

> The greatest advantage of the socialist system is that when the central leadership
> makes a decision, it is promptly implemented without interference from any
> other quarters. ... We don't have to go through a lot of discussion and consult-
> ation, with one branch of government holding up another and decisions being
> made but not carried out. From this point of view, our system is very efficient.

The state permits courts to impose constraints on administrative power, but
excessive constraints would undermine state incentives. The central authorities
support "administration in accordance with law," but their endorsement of administrative litigation is lukewarm. The 2014 Chinese Communist Party (CCP)
plenum did not give administrative litigation a pivotal role, but addressed problems
in filing suits, adjudicating cases, and enforcing judgments. The Administrative
Litigation Law (ALL), passed in 1989 and amended in 2014, relies on the elite in
the Supreme People's Court (SPC) and National People's Congress (NPC) and
may not receive full support from government officials (Cui et al. 2019).

To further complicate matters, the courts remain largely under the control of
the local governments (Chapter 1). The 2014 judicial reforms elevated the courts'
political status slightly, making them more of an agent of the central authorities.
However, their stature in the political hierarchy remains weak. As members of
the local party-state coalition, the courts struggle to execute central authorities'
law. This "central-local duality" (Ng and He 2017a, 191) is key to understanding
Chinese administrative justice. As the political underdog, the courts find it challenging to vigorously exercise judicial reviews. Their primary concern is self-
preservation and avoiding conflict with more powerful political actors. A judgment
in favor of a plaintiff could lead to an influx of lawsuits, which judges want to avoid

The Judicial System of China. Xin He, Oxford University Press. © Xin He 2025. DOI: 10.1093/9780198927815.003.0010

(Shapiro 2008, 334). To avoid colliding with more powerful political actors, the courts compromise and compete with other local government agencies. This dynamic prevails in administrative justice.

The dynamic in administrative justice shows that rights in China are "conditioned privileges" (Damaska 1986, 83). Whether these privileges can be realized depends on their weight relative to other state concerns. Challenges to state-agency behavior that enhance governance and legitimacy are encouraged, while those perceived to endanger the state are eliminated. Protection of individuals' rights is only considered if it contributes to state governance.

This chapter introduces the changes brought by the 2014 amendment of the ALL. It examines the interactions between administrative litigation and administrative reconsideration, revealing the limited role of the former. The discussion explores the competition and compromise between the courts and other state agencies. It also examines caseload patterns and the probability of winning a case. Despite limitations, administrative justice has had a remarkable impact. The chapter concludes with an analysis of administrative litigation's trajectory and its role in China's governance.

The 2014 Amendment to the ALL

The passage of the ALL, in 1989, was historic. The law allowed citizens to sue the government for the first time in China's history. Since the 1990s, most basic-level courts have established a specialized local division to accommodate administrative litigation. Nonetheless, the 1989 ALL had only 75 articles. The so-called "three difficulties" had been notorious: the difficulties in getting cases accepted, in adjudicating cases, and, ultimately, in enforcing the decisions (Jiang 2005, 9–10; see also *China News* 2013 and Wang 2007, 522–530). Until 2014, the ALL remained untouched and unamended for a quarter of a century—the longest period for any of the major laws. After prolonged outcries for the law's revision, however, amendment was finally executed, and was expected to answer a series of tough questions: Can the abstract acts—the general stipulations in laws and legislative regulations—be challenged by administrative litigation? Can the Party be sued for its acts? What can the courts do if a government agency refuses to enforce a judgment? Will *weiquan* lawyers be allowed to operate as before?

Case Filing

In response to the difficulties with filing cases, a case registration system was introduced. Previously, the courts would accept cases only after a substantive review of the documents filed, and many filings were rejected for being too complicated. In a notorious example, the Guangxi High Court once outrightly rejected 13 categories of cases, many of which were administrative (*Sina News* 2004). Now, however, under the new case registration system, all filings must be accepted without any need for a substantive review, as long as they satisfy the formal requirements. For filings that are not accepted or are not issued a receipt, the decisions are then deemed challengeable. Any court staff member who fails to comply with this stipulation will be penalized.

The 2014 amendment of the ALL also expanded concrete acts slightly, from the original 8 items to the current 12, and it specifically covers areas such as land requisition, rescission of government-franchised agreements, and restriction of individuals' physical freedoms, all of which are frequently associated with social resentment and unrest (ALL 2014, Art. 12). Apparently, this expansion was intended to address the government's concerns about social stability.

Although it is outside the jurisdiction of the courts to review laws or formal legislative regulations, they can now review *informal* policy documents, if they are complained about together with a concrete administrative act (ALL, Art. 53). If these documents are found to be unlawful, the courts can transfer the cases to the relevant authorities for handling, and will choose not to endorse those specific acts for future reference, although they are barred from directly annulling them. This is a nice compromise, learned from the (in)famous *Seed Case*, in which a judge invalidated an obviously outdated local regulation issued by the People's Congress of Henan Province. That judge was subsequently removed from the adjudicative post (Yardley 2005). Under the amended law, since the courts still lack the power to invalidate regulations mandated by a powerful legislature, they can only seek solutions from more authoritative organizations, which they hope will address contested issues. In reality, the courts have been extremely cautious. In some instances, even though they believed that an administrative act derived from an informal policy document was illegal, they still refused to revoke the act, citing "public interest" as their basis (Wang 2021, 362). Once again, this is related to the policy-implementing nature of the courts. They are to see that the policy generates its expected effects, not to invalidate it with rigid legal analysis.

The actions of the Party and its subsidiaries are still immune from judicial review, even if the nature of the decision of the Party is aligned with that of the government. For example, deemed a "criminal," Chen Jia'neng had held an urban household registration and was declared innocent in 1980, but the Party's organic department in Sichuan permanently relocated his existing urban household registration, including his grain and oil rationing registrations, to the remote area in which he was sent to be "labor reformed." Due to the vast urban–rural disparity, Mr. Chen lost access to many valuable benefits. A reply of the SPC confirms that the Party's organic department is not an administrative organ and thus lacks the standing of a defendant in administrative litigation (H. He 2022, 121). The SPC also clarified that the legality of a document *jointly* issued by the Party and government cannot be challenged, nor can it be subject to the rules of information transparency (H. He 2022, 121).

Case Adjudication

To overcome the difficulties in adjudicating cases, the courts have been empowered slightly. Originally, the courts were only permitted to question the legality of specific acts, and were not allowed to challenge their appropriateness. The amendment now allows the courts to strike down acts that are deemed "obviously inappropriate." Previously, the courts were unwilling to adjudicate against the local governments, because of those governments' firm grip on the courts' financial budgets and major staffing decisions (see Chapter 1). Now, cases against the county government are allowed to be brought before an intermediate court, which is of a higher administrative level than a basic-level court. Furthermore, the SPC and provincial high courts can directly appoint a basic-level court to handle a case from another jurisdiction, as part of their efforts to prevent the local governments from meddling in the litigation process (ALL 2014, Art. 15).

One of the more eye-catching amendments to the ALL is the requirement that, in principle, the agency leader of the accused government entity is required to appear in the court hearing; or, at the very least, an employee should make an appearance. It is believed that such a practice enhances the legal consciousness of government agencies, and is a form of showing respect to the courts. It also makes the enforcement of judgments easier (He 2013). Although this signals a move to elevate the relative position of the courts to the level of other state agencies, scholars raise their eyebrows and question whether it erodes the due process of law, and whether facing a high-ranking cadre in the courtroom is one of many mounting pressures that judges must bear (Wang 2021; Yang 2014). In 2014, it was recorded that government officials had attended only 6 percent of administrative trials, but by the end of 2020, this percentage had increased to roughly 50 percent nationwide (Zhang and Liu 2024).

Judgment Enforcement

To alleviate the problems with enforcing judgments against administrative defendants, the courts can now directly deduct fines or monetary compensations from the bank accounts of government agencies. In addition, the courts can impose monetary penalties and even detain or jail agency leaders (ALL 2014, Art. 59). In other words, the courts can hold administrative defendants *personally* accountable for failing to comply with court judgments, and can prevent any open resistance from administrative agencies. This arrangement, as drastic as it sounds, is all but a paper tiger, however—experts doubt that any court will ever take it seriously (Legal Daily 2014). As mentioned, much of the ALL is a reflection of the wishes of the elites in China's top legislature. Whether these wishes will be realized is entirely another question.

As has happened with the efforts to combat local protectionism in civil cases (see Chapter 6), the courts have also launched specific reforms to address the same issue within administrative litigation, thus providing another example of the importance of the relationship between the courts and the state agencies. The 2014 amendment of the ALL allows the courts to publicly shame government agencies that refuse to enforce court judgments or mediations (see Chapter 6). The SPC has established circuit tribunals to adjudicate cross-jurisdictional cases. The provincial high courts can, subject to the approval of the SPC, assign a court to adjudicate cases from other regions (ALL 2014, Art. 18.2). Cross-regional courts have been introduced to target the adjudication of the cases most susceptible to local interference, such as environmental and bankruptcy cases. Intermediate courts are encouraged to take on first-instance cases. Basic-level courts are allowed to swap jurisdictions (Cui et al. 2019, 38). The railway courts, which were not controlled by local governments, have now been converted to be able to handle administrative cases (Ma et al. 2021).

Still, these revisions have, overall, fallen far short of meeting the expectations of the general public and scholars. Indeed, the development of the ALL further truncates the already narrowed scope of sensitive political rights. The 2014 amendment to the ALL provides that a person subjected to, or *with an interest* in, an administrative action can file a complaint (Article 25, italics added). "With an interest" has been interpreted to cover only personal or property rights (SPC 2018, Art. 12). Political rights, such as the right to strike, the freedom of association and assembly, the right to free speech, and the freedom of the press, are excluded. The term has also been narrowly construed to prevent interest groups or individuals from acting as "private attorneys general," thereby prohibiting them from using the law to challenge the government (SPC 2018). The self-taught barefoot lawyers and other *weiquan* lawyers, who had previously drawn mass international attention (*New York Times* 2017), have since vanished (see Chapter 4).

Interactions between Administrative Litigation and Administrative Reconsideration

China allows most of the affected parties to initiate an administrative litigation without the requirement of first having exhausted all administrative remedies. Thus, disputants have the option of filing an administrative litigation before or after going through an administrative reconsideration. First launched in 1991, just over a year after the promulgation of the ALL, the administrative reconsideration process was designed as a mechanism that competes against administrative litigation. Figure 9.1 indicates that, over the last two decades, the two have followed a similar trajectory. The State Council, the head of the Chinese state agencies, further revised the regulations to encourage the process's wider use, and eventually had them upgraded and codified into law—the Administrative Reconsideration Law (ARL). A goal of this law is to prevent disputes from escaping the control of the state agencies. Early on, as long as the disputes were channeled into an administrative reconsideration, the original decisions were often sustained—so often, in fact, that the reconsideration agency was nicknamed "the sustaining agency."

The filtering effects of administrative reconsiderations are unmistakable (He 2014a). Many of the applicants rejected in administrative reconsiderations had chosen not to file a lawsuit. In Zhejiang Province, the filing rate was as low as 17.47 percent in 2020, and in 60 percent of counties, none of the plaintiffs in the reconsidered cases won in subsequent litigations (quoted from Ma 2022, 63). The reasons are intriguing. There is speculation regarding retaliation from agencies, and the weakened courts. However, it could also be the case that the disputes were genuinely resolved in the reconsideration process. By and large, administrative reconsideration has succeeded in preventing many disputes from entering the courtrooms.

The interactions between administrative reconsideration and administrative litigation offer a vantage point from which to understand how administrative litigation gains its status as the perceived outcast. As a process, administrative reconsideration has a number of advantages over administrative litigation. First, administrative reconsideration is free. Second, administrative reconsideration can be used to assess both the legality and the appropriateness of the administrative act. Third, the affected parties can challenge not only the specific act, but also, in some cases, the abstract act on which the specific act is based (ARL 2023, Art. 13).

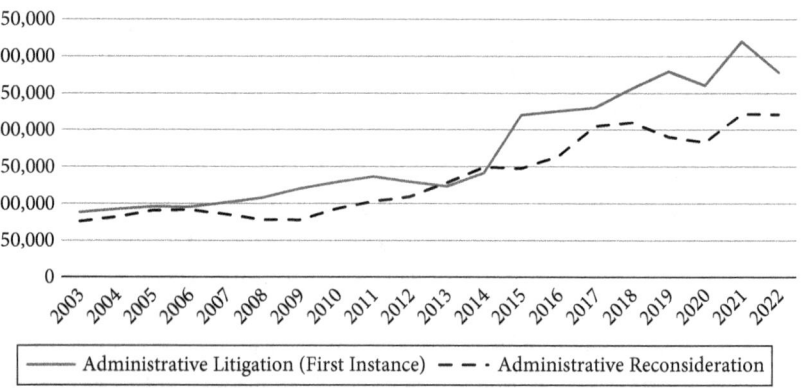

Figure 9.1 The Number of Administrative Litigation (First Instance) and Administrative Reconsideration (2003–22)

To an extent, the 2014-amended ALL signaled a victory for the NPC and SPC against the State Council. In a dramatic move, the reconsideration agency was designated as the defendant when sued, meaning that it matters not whether the reconsideration agency revises the original decision or sustains it—either way, the agency will be regarded as the defendant if the reconsidered decision is sued in an administrative litigation. That change removed the previous arrangement whereby the reconsideration agency was considered the defendant only if it revised the original decision. As a result, decisions to sustain the original administrative action have visibly declined. Decisions favoring the applicants have, in turn, stopped declining, and actually attained 16.8 percent in 2016, the highest over the course of a decade (Ma 2022).

That said, state agencies have responded quickly to this change. To avoid being sued, many agencies have changed the nature of their behavior through the enactment of legislation (Geng 2016b, 230). For example, the police have downgraded their decisions on responsibilities for traffic accidents and relabeled them as "appraisals," thus avoiding judicial review. The Patent Administration, Hygiene Administration, and Land Resources Administration all have taken similar approaches (Geng 2016b, 230–231), and consequently many disputes have flooded to the courts under the guise of civil disputes, thereby potentially hindering the affected parties' access to proper remedies. Some people ridicule that "the rule of law" has been degraded into "the rule of the courts." With the number of disputes on the rise, social stability is being jeopardized (Geng 2016b, 232).

The state agencies are undoubtedly in a better position than the other entities to handle many categories of disputes. For example, the police specialize in traffic disputes. Realizing the indispensable role of administrative reconsiderations, the central authorities have recalibrated them as the "main channel" for settling administrative disputes (ARL 2023, Art. 1). Administrative reconsideration may be further strengthened in the coming years, possibly through the establishment of the uniform reconsideration centers at the county level and above.

Mediation in Administrative Litigation

Mediation in administrative litigation epitomizes the governance coalition between the courts and other local state agencies. The original 1989 ALL (Art. 50) stated that mediation was not to be used in administrative litigation. The rationale for this was straightforward: administrative conduct is either unlawful or lawful, so there is no middle ground for reconciliation.

However, that line of thought has proven to be considered simplistic. Despite the ban on mediation, it has become increasingly common for judges to put themselves forward as mediators. Some have conducted "pretrial mediations" before formally registering lawsuits. Many have "coordinated" during the pretrial period, after the cases have been filed. In an interesting turn of events, "coordination" has been adopted as a disguise and even touted as a new model. Inspired by mediation in civil trials, some courts also have conducted "round-table trials," wherein the litigating parties and the judge are seated at one table to negotiate a resolution (He 2018, 150).

Another way to circumvent the ban on mediation has been for many cases to end up being withdrawn by the plaintiffs. Before 2014, the withdrawal rate was consistently higher than 40 percent in the first-instance administrative cases (Gu 2021). Some withdrew out of the sheer realization of the legality and righteousness of the state act. Others did so because the state agency had conveniently changed its conduct in light of the lawsuit. There have also been cases where the courts openly denounced the inappropriate conduct of the state agency (Palmer 2014, 112), which would then lead to an "exchange" of opinions with the state agency, in the interest of maintaining cordial relations or to ensure that the state agency was not at risk of losing. The agency would adjust or withdraw its conduct accordingly, in exchange for the plaintiff's withdrawal. That last scenario, in both its format and substance, is almost identical to mediation in civil lawsuits. Although the cases have been withdrawn without formal mediation, in actuality what has occurred is clearly an indication of mediation. Sometimes, the written agreement is "notarized" (Palmer 2014, 112).

There have also been cases in which plaintiffs have been coerced to withdraw. In 2002, Yu Shantao, a district court judge, filed an administrative lawsuit challenging the legality of an informal policy document of Harbin Municipality, the capital of the northernmost province of Heilongjiang, that required the owners of every private vehicle in the city to pay an annual toll of 1,100 yuan for the use of the Second Ring Road. The document contradicted a State Council document "forbidding spreading tolls among all vehicles." Indeed, not all vehicles would even use the tolled road. Because the case had attracted the attention of the public as they awaited a court decision, the judge plaintiff eventually withdrew the case. However, the toll requirement was not formally abolished until 12 years later (H. He 2022, 55). Yu's withdrawal was, nevertheless, highly unlikely to have been voluntary.

Realizing the undeniable presence of judicial mediation in administrative litigation, the 2014 amendment of the ALL officially approved this state of affairs, and allowed judicial mediation in administrative litigation. Its application is limited to cases within the discretion of the administrative organizations, and those related to administrative compensation or remedies. Prior to the amendment, judges could only persuade the plaintiff to *withdraw*, whereas the amended version now allows courts to conclude cases with *mediation* agreements.

Mediation has thus been increasingly tolerated and, indeed, is even stressed as the preferred form of decision-making. In practice, the courts recommend and even mandate mediation in the shadow of a trial. A recent SPC Opinion (2021c, Arts. 4, 5) stipulates that the courts shall facilitate *reconciliation* between the two parties or conduct a pretrial *mediation*. In reality, most mediated cases end with the defendants revising their original decisions; in areas that allow discretion by the agency, more than 80 percent of revised decisions offered some reductions of penalty (Gu 2021, 167). According to the law on the books, the scope and discretion of mediation is not supposed to exceed its "limited" capacity, but in reality it is very much "unlimited" (Gu 2021, 171). In 2015, first-instance administrative cases were recorded to have hit almost 200,000, yet reportedly only 278 cases were mediated. However, this statistic should be considered with skepticism, because the number of mediated cases was untrustworthy (Gu 2021, 164–165). Little oversight existed, and a rather low percentage of mediation documents were released. Mediation has, therefore, become the "accomplice" of evading judicial review (Gu 2021, 170).

Many arguments can be presented to support this trend toward mediation. One is that the relationship between the government and the general public has ceased to be "confrontational" or "antagonistic" (Palmer 2014, 114). Another argument is that the lines between the public and the private are blurred (Zhang 2018, 220; Yu 2013, 7). More fundamental, however, is the fact that, while tensions are brewing between the courts and the local state agencies, they share a mutual concern for social stability. In processing administrative litigation, the courts often face a dilemma: they are required to exercise judicial review according to the national law issued by the central government, but must also avoid colliding with local political actors more powerful than they are. It is not surprising, then, that the courts often mediate and contain social conflicts. In addition, mediation is more likely to be accepted than a clear-cut judgment is. The parties in administrative remedies, for example, can negotiate the amount, form, and timing of the remedies. Some even claim that "the worst mediation is better than the best adjudication" (H. He 2022, 547). During this process, coercion is inevitable. Palmer (2014, 123) asserted that the ALL has become more of "an instrument for controlling the citizen than the state." As is true with the inequitable consequences associated with civil mediation (see Chapter 7), the downtrodden are "considerably disadvantaged" (Palmer 2014, 123). Mediation also generates negative externalities for the third party and, more fundamentally, the rule of law (Yu 2013, 11). The persistence of mediation demonstrates that, in essence, administrative litigation in China is "selectively enforced, swinging between law and policy, substantive justice and procedural justice, and maintenance of the government's authority versus the protection of citizens' rights" (Wang 2007, 513).

Case Outcomes

The number of first-instance lawsuits against government agencies has more than doubled, from 130,000 in 2013 to 298,000 in 2021 (SPC Work Reports, various years). This is remarkable, given that the statistic had plateaued over the decade before 2010. Indeed, in 2015, a year after the amendment of the ALL, the number of such first-instance lawsuits had increased by 55 to 60 percent (He 2018, 178; Geng 2016a, 6)—a much higher increase than that of civil or criminal cases.

While basic-level courts take 85 percent of civil cases, intermediate-level courts take almost 50 percent of administrative cases. A reverse pyramid exists in administrative cases: "The higher the court level, the more cases are taken" (Geng 2016a, 10). Indeed, the SPC also receives thousands of administrative litigation cases annually. Several ministries of the State Council have faced hundreds of cases per year, leaving their internal council members with no choice but to fly across the country to testify (He 2018, 179). The Ministry of Land Resources was sued in 11 provinces in 2015 (Geng 2016a, 10). The "three don'ts" phenomena—"don't accept filed cases, don't take case materials, and don't make decisions"— have been reduced markedly (Geng 2016a, 8–9), and the difficulties of filing lawsuits have been "greatly alleviated" (He 2018, 178; Geng 2016a, 6). Most of the cases have been related to "land and housing" or "pension benefits, compensation for work injuries and traffic tickets" (*The Economist* 2017). The State Council stated that, by the end of 2017, county-level government institutions must have hired lawyers to engage with lawsuits and other legal matters (*The Economist* 2017). Because the scope of judicial review has not experienced a significant expansion, the increase is likely to be attributed to the case registration system.

Taking advantage of the case registration system and the inexpensive costs of litigation, some citizens even file "trivial, repetitive, and practically meaningless" litigation. For instance, in the interests of maximizing compensation for a house demolition, an evacuee filed hundreds of complaints on information disclosure, forcing the government to engage in a negotiation (Zhang and Wang 2022, 47; He 2018, 182; Geng and Zhou 2016). Shortly after that altercation, the SPC issued an opinion to regulate such behavior. The Zhengzhou Intermediate Court in Henan Province has even blacklisted litigants and legal representatives who have "abused" their right to litigation (*The Paper* 2021).

As cases have continued to pour in, the courts have been forced to face the vital question of how to handle them. The general withdrawal rate, a disconcerting sign of a plaintiff's failure, decreased from 50 percent in 2012 to 20.16 percent in 2015 (Geng 2016a, 10). Indeed, the rate of plaintiffs' withdrawals after an administrative decision has been modified by the defendants' agency, a move commonly regarded as a victory for the plaintiff, has seen only a slight increase (He 2018). Both of these trends suggest that the courts have become more competent.

In line with these trends, the win rate of the plaintiffs for first-instance decisions has increased, from 33.2 percent in 2014 to 42.2 percent in 2020 (Zhang and Liu 2024). One of the most telling changes is that the central governments have lost 33.5 percent of cases (Geng 2016a, 9). One study found that the cross-jurisdictional arrangement has increased the plaintiffs' win rate (Chang et al. 2020). Similarly, another study has shown that the appeal courts are in better positions than the first instance courts to resist influences from local governments, especially given that the plaintiffs' chances of winning are higher in cases against county-level governments than those at township level (Chang and Liu 2018). In addition, the cross-jurisdictional arrangement can also increase plaintiffs' probability of winning cases related to illegal housing demolitions (Xiang and Fan 2021). Despite some declines in efficiency, the cross-jurisdictional arrangement has proven to be effective in deflecting the influence of the local governments.

However, other empirical studies do not provide such an optimistic outlook. A study on administrative judicial documents has revealed that judges are showing an increased reliance on procedural reasons to rule against government defendants (Zhang and Liu 2024). Between 2014 and 2020, use of the justification of "violating statutory procedures" increased by 12.6 percent in rulings against defendants. By blaming procedural issues, judges can avoid any potential conflict with government defendants, because procedural issues are generally recognized to be less critical than substantive ones (Zhang and Liu, 2024). On the issue of eminent domain, for example, the courts have focused more on procedural issues (Mao and Qiao 2021; see also Geng 2016a, 9), and judgments have rarely been made based on substantial issues, such as those related to just compensation or the public interest. Moreover, the cases have been disproportionately distributed—few cases have been brought in the fields of taxes, traffic, environmental protection, quality supervision, and urban management, which are again closely related to the citizens' rights and interests (Huang 2013, 83).

Furthermore, the development of administrative justice is also dependent on the interface between the courts and other local state agencies. For example, plaintiffs are less likely to win an administrative litigation case when confronted with the police (a powerful agency in China) or another higher-ranking agency. Ji Li's (2014) study on administrative litigation against tax agencies drew similar conclusions. The volume of cases against tax collectors has been low. Very few Chinese taxpayers have litigated against tax agencies (e.g., there were a total of 405 such cases nationwide in 2011), especially when compared with the high volume of such cases in the US and Taiwan. Most of those who do sue eventually settle, despite the low formal litigation costs. Li attributes the puzzling reluctance to bring such suits to the judicial favoring of government officials and to agency retaliations. Wei Cui (2016, 990) offers a contrasting explanation. He makes the argument that potential litigants are reluctant to sue because of their "ongoing, physically proximal, and frequent interactive relationship" with the tax officials and the discretionary benefits that are associated with their affiliation. The tax agencies are able to use this to their advantage, and they can choose not to retaliate; they can simply withdraw the benefits. The taxpayers are thus willing to settle, even if they initiated the lawsuit. According to Cui, "the heart of the story" lies in "the regulatory environment" (Cui 2016, 986). Thieves, tax evaders, and polluters are unlikely to sue the police, tax agencies, and environmental protection agencies. Whether it is retaliation or symbiosis, the overwhelmingly lower rate nonetheless suggests that the power of the defendant affects the case volume and outcome (He and Su 2013).

Unsurprisingly, the authorities who tend to appear on the list of losing agencies are the township governments, construction departments, and labor and social welfare departments. Some of these entities do not have much leverage against the courts, and their lack of impact is most obvious in cases against the township and village governments, which are the lowest rung of the Chinese government. For instance, married-out women, who keep their original household registrations after marrying into another village, have won at least 66 percent of cases brought on issues of land compensation (Chan 2019, 65). In this battle, the opponents of the courts are, again, the politically weak township governments. Zhang et al. (2010) found that the environmental agencies, also relatively weak agencies in China's bureaucratic structure, often choose to follow court suggestions closely.

Power also speaks loudly in public interest lawsuits initiated by the procuratorates. According to a 2021 work report of the Supreme People's Procuratorate (SPP), of 5,976 cases that ended with an adjudication decision, 5,935 were supported by the courts. The SPP had sent out 118,000 prosecutorial suggestions before litigation, 99.4 percent of which received a positive response. As a result, a resolution was reached in the pretrial stages of most of the issues (80–90 percent) raised by the procuratorates (Ding and Xiao 2021, 48–49). According to some estimates, the reform allowing the procuratorates to file administrative lawsuits related to environmental matters has reduced water pollution by 11 percent (Chen et al. 2020). With the procuratorates as the plaintiffs, this type of administrative litigation is no longer reminiscent of the stereotypical case of a feud between citizens and mandarins—instead, ironically, it is solely between mandarins. The reason behind the exceptional win rate of the plaintiffs is straightforward—the procuratorate is not just part of the governance coalition, but it also has the power to supervise the law enforcement of other local state agencies, as well as of the courts. They enjoy a "political insider status." (Wang and Xia 2024, 465) In contrast, when similar environmental lawsuits were filed by individuals, they faced tremendous resistance (Wang 2007; Lora-Wainwright 2012 et al.).

Still, whereas some patterns are discernible, one should also be cautious when drawing conclusions from these numbers. The caseloads have seen a very clear increase, which may be the result of social anomie, as Durkheim (1952) famously suggested. Other possible reasons include structural changes in the litigation process, such as the creation of the case registration system, social changes that have taken shape as a result of the regulatory environment, and the growing sense of legal consciousness among the public. Similarly, the past decade has witnessed a relatively high win rate for plaintiffs. Although that statistic provides a good basis for showing that the courts are more powerful, it may also reveal that the agencies have not been following the rules. Indeed, plaintiffs' win rates in rural hinterland areas are higher than those in developed coastal or urban areas (see Mao and Qiao 2021), yet it would be absurd to suggest that courts in Shanghai are more penetrable than those in Gansu Province, western China. A more convincing argument would be that the agencies in Shanghai are better equipped to enforce the administration of law. Moreover, Qihui Huang (2013, 83) found that one-third of cases are related to registration or rights recognition, and in those cases, although the governments were, on the surface, listed as the defendants, in reality the issues were between citizens. Thus, the courts were not hesitant to rule against the so-called government "defendants." Therefore, it is evident that neither the increase in the numbers of the administrative cases nor the overwhelmingly high plaintiff win rates indicate the neutrality of the courts.

The Impacts

How much "progress" has the ALL truly brought, then, especially under the circumstances whereby progress is defined as "the acceptance of first-instance administrative lawsuits" and "the plaintiff's winning rate"? (He 2018, 137) The number of administrative trials constitutes only approximately 2 percent of the overall caseload in China's courts (Geng 2016a, 9). The increase in administrative trials is much lower than that of civil trials. Indeed, for many, it is puzzling that the number of administrative cases has not seen a notable increase under the popularizing narrative of rights consciousness and the strengthening of the rule of law.

Still, it is baseless to assume that the caseloads would increase exponentially—numerous forces drive the changes in caseloads (He 2009a; McIntosh 1981). Indeed, according to Cui et al. (2019), the per capita volume of administrative litigation in China has already surpassed that of Taiwan, and of many countries with established democratic accountability and judicial independence. Moreover, although China's scope of judicial review may be narrower than that of the US, it remains considerably broader than that of many other major civil law jurisdictions. For a long time, the plaintiffs' win rate in Chinese administrative trials was not considered low when compared with either the US or Taiwan (Peerenboom 2002, 400).

As always, the contexts are crucial. Some legally developed countries may not even have administrative litigation or judicial review. "There was no such thing as judicial review in England, any more than there was in Spain or in Germany" (Friedman 1998, 229). Administrative litigation in China is a means of governance for the Party. The development of China's administrative justice is heavily dependent upon competition and compromise between the courts and the other local state agencies.

Despite the numerous limitations of administrative litigation, such cases have, nevertheless, brought enormous impacts. Wei Cui, a former head of the administrative division of the Nantong Intermediate Court in Jiangsu Province, documented fascinating cases in his book titled *A Long March in Administrative Litigation* (2012). In 1996, his court was the first throughout China's long history to permit criminals to sue the prison authorities for inappropriate administrative activities (Cui 2012, 225–231). A move that once would have been considered unthinkable in a country with such staggering administrative power, and in which criminals have long been regarded as the enemy of the regime, has ushered in a new age of administrative litigation, at least against the prison authorities. Needless to say, the prison authorities have thereafter been hugely "inconvenienced." In another administrative litigation case, the police lost a lawsuit for the rough handling of the dead body of a mentally ill person killed in a traffic accident. Without proper investigations or abiding by due process, the police had rushed to announce that the dead body was derelict, and subsequently they ordered it to be cremated. However, they were sued by a relative who lived tens of miles away and claimed that the mentally ill person was his family member. The police's declaration that the body was ownerless had, therefore, deprived the relative of any access to proper compensation for the traffic accident. One issue for the court to decide, then, was why a piece of pelvic floor was overworked (Cui 2012, 231–237). Because the body had been cremated, the court had no choice but to base its decision solely on an analysis of the evidence presented by both parties. The judge ultimately concluded that, due to insomnia, the mentally ill man had resorted to walking excessively, which provided a reasonable explanation for why the traffic accident had occurred tens of miles from his home. Coincidentally, his habit of walking also accounted for the overworked pelvic floor. The decision was audacious yet sensible. This became a wake-up call for the police, warning them to make similar decisions with greater care.

Likewise, the police also lost a case after chasing an illegally parked minivan on rural roads, because the court reiterated that rural roads did not fall under the scope of a "road" as defined in the Law of Road Traffic. Chasing a vehicle on an unofficial road for illegal parking therefore constituted *ultra vires* (Cui 2012, 258–262). In another lawsuit, the labor bureau lost a case related to a retirement decision because of a failure to prove the plaintiff's date of birth. The plaintiff's decision to retire hinged on when he was born, but since he omitted to present proof of this, the bureau had simply rejected the application. However, the bureau was unaware that there is a reverse burden of proof in administrative litigation—the burden always lies with themselves (Cui 2012, 263–266). The court was also bold enough to serve a subpoena on the mayor of the Nantong Municipality—a move generally regarded as inappropriate, if not outrageous, in China's official culture (Cui 2012, 272).

Such changes have not been limited to Nantong, let alone to Jiangsu Province. In 1997, government agencies in Baokan County, Hebei Province, dramatically lost all 81 administrative cases filed that year. This, naturally, rattled the local Party and government leaders and instilled an air of concern. In response, the Party and government leaders began to train government officials, strengthen internal supervision, and punish officials who displayed an indifference toward administrative laws and procedures. Just five years later, in 2002, government agencies ended up winning 82 percent of all administrative cases (Li 2014). In another example, university decisions, such as disciplinary actions against students and revocations of degrees, were kept outside the purview of the courts for decades, and only after several landmark administrative cases has it been widely normalized and acknowledged that university decisions must be legal, appropriate, and in line with the principle of due process. In addition, management and distribution decisions by village collectives now fall under the purview of the courts. Alongside all these changes, administrative litigation has also changed the landscape of employment rules, reducing and breaking down preexisting discriminatory practices based on gender, height, and noncontagious diseases (Li 2014). Furthermore, administrative litigation breaks the professional monopoly over certain businesses, such as trademark registrations (H. He 2022, 59, 141), grants greater access to more government compensation, and pushes for improved transparency of government information (Zhang 2022).

In addition, changes at the national and local levels have occurred in the contentious area of housing demolitions. Since the 2000s, China has made immense efforts toward the conversion of agricultural and forest land for more profitable uses, as part of the wider process of urbanization and the development of industrial projects. In that process, scholars of Chinese law have reached the consensus that the property rights of the land's original owners have largely been disrespected (Upham 2009; He 2009a; Erie 2007; Pils 2006). Therefore, under pressure from the courts, many housing demolition authorities have streamlined their procedures and increased the accountability of their decision-making processes. Some courts have refrained from approving compulsory eviction permits if the demolition authorities have been unable to reach mutual compensation agreements with the urban residents or if the hearing process on the negotiation of the compensation price lacked transparency. Some local governments further announced that they condemned and forbade forceful demolition before the residents had vacated the premises or before all of the required documentation had been completed. The local governments have also prohibited any disproportionately harsh behavior, such as cutting off access to gas, running water, or electricity, to force residents to move. Other local governments, after being urged by the courts to do so, have been working on an annual standard for housing compensation, so as to fill the legal vacuum.

All of these changes have impacted the interactions between the local governments and the landowners and residents. A dramatic picture of a lone house in Taizhou, Zhejiang Province, standing in the middle of a highway, once swept Chinese media outlets (*Sina News* 2012). The homeowner was a 75-year-old grandmother, for whom intense paranoia over the potential actions of the government had prompted the installation of more than ten security cameras in her house. It was reported that, after signing the demolition agreement several years previously, she had eventually changed her mind.

In summary, Shavell's (2004) opinion on administrative litigation in liberal democracies is germane to the situation in China: administrative litigation is a public good, with positive externalities to the society and to governance. According to a survey of 1,047 administrative judges (Lin and Song 2013, 51), 54.3 percent believed that administrative litigation has facilitated "administration in accordance of law." That said, 59.4 percent believed that administrative litigation was "limited" in the pursuit of protecting citizens' rights. Interestingly, 36.4 percent believed otherwise, asserting that it did indeed serve to protect citizens' rights.

Conclusions

In China, administrative litigation is closely tied to the Party's policy goals. The state relies heavily on administrative power to facilitate economic and social change, and administrative trials could hinder that power (He 2009c). A strong system of judicial review would contradict the state's economic development policy, thus slowing down the development of administrative litigation. However, as social stability and environmental protection have gained importance over economic development, it has become necessary to support administrative litigation that resolves social conflicts.

There are notable regional variations in administrative justice in China. It is more developed in economically advanced regions, but less so in hinterland areas. In some Xinjiang counties, there have been no administrative litigations filed in a particular year, and there is "pronounced political resistance" to public interest litigation (Wang 2024). Local procuratorates must follow the local Party's order to maintain social stability, and any administrative litigation is seen as "antagonizing" the local Party committee. Wang's research also shows marked variations in Hubei and Yunnan Provinces.

Administrative justice's generally positive development can be reversed depending on the Party's policy priorities. During the COVID-19 pandemic, containing the virus's spread was a top priority, and local leaders did not want their measures challenged in court. Despite citizens' rights being infringed upon, not a single COVID-related case was taken up by the courts, despite the stringent lockdowns being a clear restriction of individual physical freedom under the ALL (Art. 12.2) (Shen 2021). Similarly, local parties have shown little incentive to support the courts in cases related to fundamental modes of social regulation that have not escalated to collective resistance, where there is no threat to stability (He 2012).

While housing demolition cases demonstrate support of the local party-state for social and legal change in the courts, the same cannot be said for other cases.

Over time, administrative litigation has brought about a sea change. While isolated regulatory failures still occur, the dramatic incidents that were common in the 2000s and early 2010s have become rare. Cases such as tainted milk formula poisoning babies, miners getting trapped in unauthorized mines, and homeowners committing suicide during forced evacuations were widespread back then. Today, arbitrary penalties and rent-seeking behaviors by administrative agencies have decreased significantly. Administrative justice has played an undeniable role in controlling the behavior of other agents. The courts' closer relationship with the central authorities, rather than local governments, has helped drive the development of administrative justice forward.

Administrative justice in China protects the rights of individuals and social entities to some extent, but its role should not be exaggerated. Its primary goal is to boost governance by exerting greater control over local agencies. The Party's 2014 plenum communique does not mention administrative litigation in the section on human rights protection, but in the section on optimizing judicial functions. The courts prioritize their relationship with other state agencies over promoting rights protection when applying the law (i.e., the commands of the central authorities). While administrative litigation has gained attention from "rightful resistance" enthusiasts (O'Brien and Li 2006), rights protection is not the central focus of administrative litigation. In contrast to other authoritarian states, where "the law versus the state" dynamic operates widely, it takes a back seat, at best, on China's list of priorities (Moustafa 2007, 9).

Conclusion

This book proposes a governance model to understand how the Chinese court system operates. The model recognizes the crucial role the courts play in supporting the state's goals of policy implementation and legitimacy enhancement. It also acknowledges that the policies assigned to the courts to implement, and the approaches used to enhance their legitimacy, have significantly shaped the court system's evolution. Unlike the judicial independence and rights approaches, which focus on specific aspects of the court system, the governance model provides a comprehensive view of the system and reveals the underlying rationales driving changes over time.

After the Cultural Revolution, China's courts underwent a complete reconstruction. In the 1980s, the focus was on rebuilding manpower and infrastructure. Social stability was addressed through the anticrime Strike Hard Campaign, mainly targeting criminals. In the 1990s, as court caseloads increased, there was a push for judicial professionalism, formalism, and trial-mode reforms. This period also saw social stability being seen as under threat, making it a top policy concern. By the late 1990s, there was a shift in judicial reforms. Trial independence and formalism were discarded because the Party believed they contributed to issues like the surge in the number of petitions, and the lack of public trust. In contrast, mediation, previously seen as incompatible with trial independence and formalism, was revived. The Party believed mediation offered a better approach to address concerns like dispute resolution, social stability, and legitimacy enhancement.

The 2014 judicial reforms reshaped the power dynamics between central authorities and local governments. Prior to the reforms, local courts were seen as tools of local governments at the same administrative level, and were known as "local governments' courts." However, after the reforms, the courts became more centralized and aligned with centralized laws, Party policies, and directives from Beijing. The new system elevated personnel and budgetary decisions for courts to the provincial level, making local courts, in many ways, agents of the central authorities. Consequently, local judges now have a closer relationship with the central authorities in the principal–agent dynamic. They also have a role in overseeing other local agents, including local governments, police, and procuratorates.

Despite the reforms, Chinese courts and judges have not gained as prominent position as those in the common law jurisdictions, and their political status remains highly marginal. The President of the Supreme People's Court (SPC) is still not a member of the politburo, the most powerful political decision-making body

The Judicial System of China. Xin He, Oxford University Press. © Xin He 2025. DOI: 10.1093/9780198927815.003.0011

in China, which usually consists of 20 members. Furthermore, after the 2014 reforms, the Party's control over the courts has been tightened, and loyalty to the Party is strongly emphasized. In this sense, the Chinese court system also differs significantly from the judicial systems of many other authoritarian states, where courts and judges are widely respected.

Since the 2014 judicial reforms, China's court system has undergone remarkable changes. Two of these have been the decline of local favoritism and the improved enforcement of court judgments in civil cases. In fact, compared to the court systems in many developed economies, China's courts are performing quite well, particularly in their enforcement of foreign or foreign-related arbitration awards. The Party's policy goals of creating a uniform national market and a pro-arbitration environment are crucial for economic development, and the improved enforcement of court judgments further enhances the legitimacy of both the judiciary and the state.

The role of administrative litigation in China has gained more prominence in recent years due to changing priorities in the country. As China shifts its focus from solely prioritizing economic concerns to addressing social stability and environmental protection, administrative litigation has gained attention and support as a means to alleviate social conflicts and hold government authorities accountable. By promoting administrative litigation, the Party aims to address social issues in a more orderly and legal manner, enhancing the legitimacy and effectiveness of the administrative apparatus.

Over the past decade, China's legal landscape has seen a complex phenomenon whereby some rights, or "conditional privileges" (see Introduction), have been better protected, while others are ignored or eroded. For example, enforcing court judgments may provide remedies for winning parties but may infringe upon the losing parties' basic rights. In contrast, administrative litigation offers a more feasible solution for affected parties, but the once powerful "barefoot lawyers" who played a critical role in this type of litigation have been eradicated. Plea leniency is another example whereby defendants may receive leniency, but it does not guarantee better rights protection. Defendants must confess and accept the proposed "deal," leading to a situation where most lawyers have become mere assistants or even notaries public for the prosecution, rather than serving as guardians of their clients' rights.

One should not mistake rights protection as the genuine goal of the state in China. The governance model sheds light on the contradictions that exist. Enforcing court judgments helps improve the image of the courts and, in turn, the state. While the prohibition of torture is a fundamental human right, its effective enforcement in China has only occurred since the Party discovered that police torture was the leading cause of wrongful convictions. Wrongfully convicted cases can damage the legitimacy of the state, making the prohibition of torture urgent in containing wrongful convictions and maintaining the legitimacy of the political-legal apparatus and the state. The goal of prohibiting torture is less about protecting the rights of defendants and more about controlling unruly police behavior. Similarly, the meticulous process of the SPC in ratifying death penalty cases arose not from the state caring about the rights of the condemned, but from embarrassment about the misconduct of local police, judges, and officials. If the legal system in China is not designed for the delivery of justice, as Clarke (2022) rightly points out, this book's analysis suggests that its real purpose is the governance of the state.

Despite the 2014 judicial reforms, regional variations across the courts remain pronounced. A majority of judges in Tibet have not yet passed the uniform judicial exam, for example. The whole autonomous region has about 300 licensed lawyers, and most of them reside in Lhasa, the capital city (W. Zhang 2022, 93–94). Indeed, unlicensed legal workers continue to provide services in the vast hinterland areas, though their presence in coastal areas has been reduced. Public interest litigation is openly resisted in Xinjiang, and great variations have been documented across the country (Wang 2024). When discussing right-infringing tactics in enforcing judgments (Chapter 6) with a court president in Shanghai, he told me that these tactics "definitely do not occur in Shanghai."

It is expected that these regional variations will gradually narrow. Thanks to budgetary reforms, many courts in hinterland areas are now less dependent on their local governments for operating costs. Additionally, many courts in poor areas can recruit legally trained graduates as quota judges with slightly higher salaries. Technology has also seen increased use in Chinese courts, and this trend is likely to continue, easing workloads, increasing efficiency, reducing complaints from litigants, and, most importantly, asserting central oversight over judges. One of the many tools that technology brings is its support of judges by giving them access to information on all similar court judgments. This information can promote consistency in applying laws, helping to create a fairer and more transparent judicial process. As a result, the state's legitimacy is sustained.

Predicting the future of the Chinese court system is challenging, but it is unlikely that the courts will embrace the ideal of the rule of law or become an independent branch of the government. The primary goal of the 2014 judicial reforms was to sanction any influences that threatened policies originating from Beijing. While judicial autonomy and professionalism may increase to some extent, it is highly unlikely that the Party will seek a Western-style judiciary that independently interprets the law and checks the behavior of other governmental branches. The Party allows for a division of labor, but not of power. Chinese judges are unlikely to make decisions free from the "legitimate influences" of the Party and government (He 2021a). Coordination among the political-legal apparatuses under the Party's leadership is likely to remain the dominant ideology, rather than judicial independence.

At the beginning of the book, it was argued that dualism does not neatly fit the Chinese court system. The line between following legal rules in mundane cases and allowing extralegal influences in politically sensitive cases often shifts due to ad hoc policy concerns. Chinese courts remain an integral part of the local governance coalition, and political influences from local governments are frequent and inevitable. Despite efforts to centralize local courts, immediate concerns on the ground shape the work of grass-roots courts. As agents of the state in governance, courts are expected to deal with problems, which can vary significantly, that bubble up from different parts of the country. Policies from multiple authorities can conflict with each other, leading to courts and judges interpreting policies differently from one another. The process of handling cases depends on the nature of the initial complaint and how it evolves, including the reaction of the media, including social media, which can play a prominent role. Neither the complainant nor the judge can definitively predict whether a case will, ultimately, be politically sensitive.

Due to the shifting policy considerations, Chinese courts do not need to establish a structurally separate track for politically sensitive cases. Unlike the system in Franco's Spain (Toharia 1975), for example, the Chinese courts are essentially unitary. Additionally, with the help of a sophisticated system and the Party's remarkable capacity to control judges and mobilize resources, the Chinese court system is able to differentiate politically sensitive cases from those that are not.

Will the courts and the legal system become rules-based? Some believe that the Singaporean model may be the future of Chinese courts (Ang and Wang 2019). Singapore is an authoritarian state in which the rules matter (Silverstein 2008), yet it also represents a specific type of dualism. In civil and commercial cases, the laws are professionally practiced, as is done in many of the world's common law jurisdictions. In political and constitutional matters, however, a high value is placed on "social order" and "state stability." "With less attention given to civil liberties," the "state institutions" are strengthened, and "rights protections" are marginalized (Thio 2004, 209).

I am skeptical of the view that China will one day adopt Singapore's model. Despite the Chinese courts' evolution towards greater professionalization and more sophisticated legal analysis, having more laws or advanced legal analysis does not necessarily make a system rules-based. Comparing the two countries is challenging due to differences in size, judges' status, litigants' legal consciousness, lay participation, and lawyers' professionalism. Furthermore, the policy-implementing nature of the Chinese court system makes it almost futile to differentiate between civil and constitutional matters. Substantive legal rules are applied flexibly, and extralegal concerns can trump them, rendering procedural rules underdeveloped and discretion plentiful.

Over time, China's judiciary may gain more horizontal strength compared to other government agencies. However, it will still be dominated by policy implementation and legitimacy enhancement. These policies can sometimes be vernacular. Judges are never solely focused on legal analysis of cases on the bench.

In certain situations, the courts have to resort to extralegal means, as seen in their practices during the COVID-19 pandemic, and in Xinjiang.

It is very likely that, for some time, the courts will still be doing what they are doing now, "muddling through with a series of piecemeal, *ad hoc* and eclectic policies that demand the Chinese judicial system to be many things at once" (Ng and He 2017a, 201). The Party requires the courts and judges to be more accountable to the people, and ultimately to the Party itself. When the two are in conflict, however, the job is tough. So far, it seems that judicial accountability without judicial independence is effectively the system that is practiced, and that is exactly why so many contradictions have unfolded. In this light, I expect that the Chinese court system will continue to evolve along with its two guiding characteristics—policy implementation and legitimacy enhancement—in fulfilling its instrumental functions of boosting governance for the state.

Quick Guide

Table 1 Country Characteristics

Respect for rule of law	A public commitment to rule the country in accordance with law, but not to the idea of the rule of law commonly used in the West. Law is used primarily as an instrument to bolster the party-state's governance. In certain dimensions, such as access to justice, efficiency, and enforcement of judgments, China arguably has a stronger track record than many legally developed countries (Chapters 1, 6).
Respect for human rights	Variable and often deficient in practice. A commitment to human rights is enshrined in the written laws, but their actual observance varies with the particular right and the underlying context. Human rights are often weighed against the needs of the state in governance (Chapters 1, 8).
Level of judicial independence	Low for the judiciary as a whole; fair for individual judges, whose prospects for promotion depend upon evaluations by their supervisors in their courts, their ability to manage their courts efficiently, and maintaining a low reversal rate. Judges are subject to various influences from officials. They are also subject to extralegal influences from society (Chapter 2).
Level of corruption	Considerable in public life in general, and in the courts. Bribery in the courts declined after Xi Jinping tightened control over state officials, including judges (Chapter 2).
Level of democracy	Very low. China has an authoritarian polity. The courts promote judicial democracy by strengthening the people's assessors institution, but that institution does not have a meaningful impact on case outcomes (Chapter 3).

Table 2 Apex Courts

	The Supreme People's Court of the People's Republic of China
Year established	1949
Jurisdiction	Handles only appeals in cases that were tried by the high courts at first instance (Chapter 1).
Supervisory, administrative, and other nonadjudicative powers (e.g., election oversight; regulation of political parties; judicial discipline; legislative powers; *sua sponte* orders and opinions)	Manages judicial system. Supervises all lower courts' adjudicatory work. Issues interpretations of existing laws.
Docket (for 2021)	Cases received: 33,602. Judicial interpretations: 24. Guiding cases: 31.
Likelihood of hearing and/or decision on the merits	High. The Court is strictly bound by procedural rules in various statutes on whether to hear appeals (CiPL, CrPL, ALL).
Case screening mechanisms	Arguably no screening mechanisms. It handles appeals from cases which were tried by the higher courts at first instance.
Use of ADR mechanisms	Mediation is widely used
DIVISION OF LABOR	
Use of merits panels: are all decisions on the merits rendered by the full court sitting *en banc* (sometimes called a "grand bench")? Are some rendered by a subset or panel of judges (known in some countries as a "petty bench", or in the US federal appeals courts as a "merits panel" as opposed to a "screening panel")?	The panel is constituted as in lower courts (see below).
Division of labor by (a) subject matter? (b) geography?	Subject matter: Two international commercial courts established since 2018. Geography: six circuit tribunals established since 2014. (Chapter 1)
Panel size: how many judges make up a panel? Do panels differ in size, and if so, when and why?	Usually three judges. No difference between panels.
Panel membership: Fixed? Rotating? Randomly drawn?	Relatively stable but can be changed or rotated by court officials when they deem appropriate.
Case allocation: On what basis are cases allocated (a) between the full court and panels? (b) between different panels? (E.g., subject matter? Importance?)	Assigned by the division heads.

(*continued*)

Table 2 Continued

	The Supreme People's Court of the People's Republic of China
Resolution of conflicts among panels and internal binding effect: What binding or precedential effect do panel decisions have (a) on the full court? (b) on other panels? What mechanisms, if any, exist for resolving disagreements among panels?	Not applicable.
JUDGES	
Number	367 quota judges (judge track) as of 2017 (Chapter 2).
Term	Nominally appointed by the standing committee of the NPC, but can be removed or reassigned at any time by the Party.
Appointment	By SPC's internal selection committee.
Eligibility	The same as lower court judges.
Pre-appointment evaluation and quality control	Various tests and interviews (Chapter 2).
Post-appointment evaluation and quality control	Numerous quantitative metrics and qualitative reviews by supervisors and court officials.
Professional background	Career judges: all. Academics on court: none, though some may hold advanced degrees and teach on the side.
Educational background	Undergraduate law degrees are mandatory; the majority hold more advanced degrees.
Demographics	Age: data not available. Gender: data not available. Nationality: Chinese. Race/ethnicity: data not available. Geographical background: data not available.
COURT STAFF	
Number	Most of the nonquota judges (around 70% of the 1,000 employees of the Court) work in adjudicatory divisions, administrative, political, and logistics departments.
Number assigned to each judge/justice	Usually two.
Number shared by all judges/justices	Data not available.
Background	Many hold academic degrees and used to be judges in the SPC before the 2014 judges' quota reform (Chapter 2).

Table 2 Continued

	The Supreme People's Court of the People's Republic of China
Experience and tenure	All legal staff hold permanent positions with administrative ranks. There are no law clerks working temporarily.
Specialization by expertise or subject matter	Staff who work directly with judges may or may not have specialized knowledge. The roughly 20 staff who work in the research department typically have subject-matter expertise.
Functions and role in deciding cases	Case management; organization of statistics, research, public relations, and some drafting of judgments and sentences (judicial assistants only).
COURT PROCEDURES	
Mechanisms for receiving evidence	Receipt of the case file and witnesses.
Oral hearings	Procedural rules require oral hearings in most cases.
Third-party participation (e.g., *amici curiae*)	As long as the procedure laws allow.
Remedial powers	Only through the adjudication supervision procedure.
CHARACTERISTICS OF DECISIONS	
Types of decisions rendered	Written only.
Is author of opinion identified?	The panel members' names are shown in decisions, but the author is usually not identifiable. Also, the decision may not in reality have been made by the panel members.
How is authorship of opinions determined? (E.g., seniority? Rotation? Assignment by senior member? Subject-matter expertise?)	Assigned by the division head.
Are separate (concurring and/or dissenting) opinions allowed? If so, how common are they?	Not allowed.
Length of opinions	Usually 3–20 pages.
Types of authorities cited	Often includes citations to the laws and occasionally to policies.
Reliance on precedent	No.

(*continued*)

Table 2 Continued

	The Supreme People's Court of the People's Republic of China
External binding effect: What binding effect do the court's decisions have on other courts?	Not binding.
Distribution and availability of decisions (e.g., published? Online? Free? Translated?)	Only select cases are available electronically (either through legal databases or free from court's website). Rarely are decisions officially translated.
TRANSNATIONAL INFLUENCES	
Interaction with foreign courts and judges	Frequent under the Belt and Road Initiative (Chapter 1).
Dedicated mechanism(s) for foreign legal research	None.
Foreign-trained judges	None.
Foreign law usage by parties and/or lawyers	None.
Foreign-trained clerks	None.
Foreign-trained constitutional scholars at elite law schools	Very few.
Foreign law citation	None.
Foreign law research	Rare.
Acceptance of foreign law citation and/or usage	None.
Constitutional/legal provision(s) addressing judicial usage of foreign and/or international law	None.
Courts/jurisdictions most frequently considered	None.

Table 3 Lower Courts

Structure of judiciary and division of labor among courts (e.g., unitary v. federal; hierarchical v. coordinate; division of responsibility over legal and factual questions)	Hierarchical; unitary; responsible for both factual and legal questions.
How many levels of appellate and trial courts?	The local courts have three levels: basic (county-level), intermediate (prefectural-level), and high (provincial-level), each of which can potentially serve as a court of first instance depending on the case. Above the three levels of local courts is the SPC.
Courts specialized by region	Local courts are primarily organized by geography, corresponding to the administrative level and jurisdiction.
Courts specialized by subject matter (e.g., labor courts, commercial courts; administrative courts)	There are specialized courts, such as financial courts and intellectual property courts. All other disputes are resolved by the courts of general jurisdiction.
Caseloads and breakdown of types of cases	In 2021, the courts heard 33.5 million cases, of which 47% were civil and commercial, 28% enforcement, 3.7% criminal, and 0.9% administrative, with the remainder divided among various types of cases.
Duration of typical cases	The procedural code establishes deadlines by which cases must be resolved. Judges respect these deadlines, which are typically several months from filing.
What are the paradigmatic cases found in the trial courts? (E.g., criminal cases? Business litigation?)	Family, contract, housing, and tort disputes are the most common types of civil cases.
What other government organs, if any, decide disputes (e.g., administrative agencies)? What disputes are decided by these organs?	Any government agency (e.g., labor bureau) may resolve disputes related to its activities administratively. The administrative decisions may be reviewed via the administrative reconsideration procedure. The reconsideration decisions are subject to judicial review (Chapter 9).
CHARACTERISTICS OF JUDGES	
Appointment of judges	Candidates are appointed by a committee at the provincial high courts (Chapter 2).
Qualifications of judges	All judges must have an undergraduate degree and at least five years of legal experience.

(*continued*)

Table 3 Continued

Use of panels: How many judges hear a case? How are panel members selected?	Under Ordinary Procedure, trials are conducted by a panel of three or more judges and assessors. Under Simplified Procedure, they are conducted by single judges. Appeals are heard by a panel composed of three or more judges.
Role of court staff in deciding cases	Judicial assistants help draft judgments.
How are cases assigned to judges?	Most courts divide judges by specialty. Formally, cases are assigned randomly, but the division heads often intervene to make assignments.
Role of politics and partisanship in judicial appointment	Party affiliation plays little role in entry-level positions. For administrative positions (court officials), politics has a significant role (Chapter 2).
Role of politics and partisanship in decisions	Extralegal influences are common in cases that the party-state regards as important (see Chapter 2).
COURT PROCEDURES	
Procedures: Adversarial, inquisitorial, or hybrid?	Criminal: hybrid but largely inquisitorial, and the prosecutors play an important role (Chapter 8).Civil: hybrid. The procedural codes mandate adversarialism. In practice, however, judges continue to control the proceedings (Chapter 6).
Evidence and testimony: Preference for written, oral, or both? Is cross-examination permitted?	The parties are allowed to present evidence and arguments. But questioning by judges is more important. Parties desiring to introduce witnesses must petition the court for permission. Judges prefer to rely on documentary evidence. Cross-examination is permitted.
Advocates in court: Is there a divide between elite and nonelite advocates? What characterizes the divide?	There is no formal dividing line between elite and nonelite advocates. Financially secure accused persons may hire elite lawyers. Most accused depend upon duty lawyers assigned by, or legal aid lawyers appointed by, the Bureau of Justice (Chapter 8).Financially secure litigants in civil or business cases may hire their own lawyers, though they need not be advocates.

Table 3 Continued

Role of laypeople: When and to what extent do court proceedings incorporate jurors, lay judges, etc.? How are responsibilities divided between professional judges and lay decision-makers?	Since 2018, the use of people's assessors has been required for certain types of cases—usually politically sensitive cases—in the first-instance trial. People's assessors deliberate together with professional judges. For certain types of cases, the assessors in the grand panel (three judges plus four assessors) are only responsible for factual questions. Overall, the assessors have little impact on decision-making (Chapter 3).
Role of experts in court proceedings	Judges have the right to call on experts when such expertise is deemed essential.
Role of government attorneys (e.g., public prosecutors; procuracy) in court proceedings	Prosecutors play a major role in criminal cases and public interest litigation. They also supervise the operation of the courts.
Administrative procedures and their role	Court administration is handled by court staff and officials. There is no separate branch handling it.
Are there possibilities for forum shopping?	Forum shopping is legally restricted. Petitions to upper-level governments are common (Chapter 5).
CHARACTERISTICS OF DECISIONS	
How common are written decisions? When are written decisions required?	All judgments must be written.
Is the author of the decision identified?	The author of the decision may not be identified. The decision is signed by a single judge in the Simplified Procedure, and by the panel members in the Ordinary Procedure. For influential cases, the case may be decided by the adjudication committee or the upper-level officials.
How is authorship determined when multiple judges decide a case?	Authorship is not clearly identified, but usually the judgment is authored by the responsible judge.
Are separate (concurring/dissenting) opinions allowed?	Separate opinions are not allowed.

Table 4 The Legal Profession

ORGANIZATION OF THE LEGAL PROFESSION	
Prevalence of solo practitioners and small firms	Partnership law firms are the most common type.
Prevalence and size of medium to large firms	Larger firms are more likely to be found in Beijing, Shanghai, Shenzhen and Guangzhou.
Divided bar (division between courtroom advocates and other attorneys)	No clear line between courtroom advocates and other attorneys. Legal workers are still allowed in some regions (Chapter 4).
Division of labor between attorneys and nonattorneys (e.g., clerks, scriveners)	Litigants can ask nonlawyers to represent their interests in court in civil cases.
WORK HANDLED	
Type of legal work typically handled by solo practitioners/small firms	Small firms and solo practitioners tend to have a general practice. Few lawyers are specialized in criminal or administrative cases (Chapters 4).
Type of legal work typically handled by large firms	Large firms are most prevalent in big cities. They specialize in corporate work but take on other tasks when requested by valued clients.
CHARACTERISTICS OF LAWYERS	
Access to legal services (e.g., supply and affordability of lawyers)	Lawyers are plentiful in large cities. Their fees vary widely. Finding a lawyer is more difficult in small towns and rural areas.
Minimum licensing requirements for lawyers	A university-level degree is required for formal licensed lawyers. For legal workers in remote areas, an associate's law degree or a nonlaw bachelor's degree is typical (Chapter 4).
Career path and educational credentials of typical solo practitioner or small-firm lawyer	Lawyers must complete a one-year internship and pass an exam before being licensed.
Career path and educational credentials of typical large-firm lawyer	Large firms tend to recruit only from the most prestigious Chinese law schools. Associates usually attended law school on a full-time basis.
Prevalence of foreign-trained and/or English-speaking attorneys	Foreign-trained lawyers, mostly with LLM degrees, are concentrated in large law firms. English language skills are likely to be stronger at large law firms in big cities.

Table 5 Litigants

CHARACTERISTICS OF LITIGANTS	
To what extent do businesses rely on courts or instead on other dispute resolution mechanisms?	Businesses turn to courts when efforts at negotiation prove futile. They may also opt for arbitration. The courts conduct mediation throughout the whole process (Chapter 7).
Public interest litigation: How prevalent is it? How much do NGOs use the judicial system to pursue their agendas?	The procuratorate are the major initiators for public interest litigation. A small number of NGO/public interest law firms also pursue litigation. Typically, they are less successful than the procuratorate (Chapter 9).
Class actions: Do they exist? Are they common?	Possible in civil claims. Statistics as to the number of class actions are not maintained.
How prevalent is litigation brought by public litigants (state actors)? Who uses courts more, public litigants or private litigants?	Litigation by public litigants concentrates on criminal cases and public interest litigation (prosecutors) (Chapter 9). Litigation in the courts is dominated by private actors.

References

Abe, Masaki. 1995. "The Internal Control of a Bureaucratic Judiciary: The Case of Japan." *International Journal of the Sociology of Law* 23(4): 303–320.

Abel, Richard L. 1982. "The Contradictions of Informal Justice." *The Politics of Informal Justice* 1: 267–320.

Ahl, Björn. 2016. "China's New Global Presence and Its Position Towards Public International Law: Obeying, Using or Shaping?" in *Legal Dimensions of China's Belt and Road Initiative*, edited by Lutz-Christian Wolff and Chao Xi, 481–505. Hong Kong: Wolters Kluwer.

Ahl, Björn, and Daniel Sprick. 2018. "Towards Judicial Transparency in China: The New Public Access Database for Court Decisions." *China Information* 32(1): 3–22.

Ai, Jiahui. 2021. "The Micro-Incentive Basis of the Judicial Compensation and Selection in Transitional China [转型中国法官薪酬与遴选制度的微观激励基础]." *Law and Social Development* [法制与社会发展] 6: 68–87.

Alford, William P. 2007. "Of Lawyers Lost and Found, Searching for Legal Professionalism in the People's Republic of China" in *Raising the Bar: The Emerging Legal Profession in East Asia*, edited by William P. Alford, et al. Cambridge: East Asian Legal Studies, Harvard Law School.

Alschuler, Albert W. 1975. "The Defense Attorney's Role in Plea Bargaining." *The Yale Law Journal* 84(6): 1179–1314.

Amnesty International. 2016. "Amnesty International Report 2016/17," https://www.amnesty.org/en/wp-content/uploads/2021/05/POL1048002017ENGLISH.pdf.

———. 2017. "China's Deadly Secrets," https://www.amnistia.pt/wp-content/uploads/2017/06/AIreport_DP2016_Chinas_Deadly_Secrets.pdf.

An, Yutian, and Yingjie Fan. 2024. "Beyond the Verdict: The Impact of Juries on Judicial Support." Paper presented at Clarke East Asia Lay Participation Roundtable at Cornell Law School, May 2024.

Ang, Lance, and Jiangyu Wang. 2019. "Judicial Independence in Dominant Party States: Singapore's Possibilities for China." *Asian Journal of Comparative Law* 14(2): 337–371.

Ayres, Ian, and John Braithwaite. 1992. *Responsive Regulation: Transcending the Deregulation Debate.* Oxford: OUP.

Bakken, Børge. 2011. "China, a Punitive Society?" *Asian Journal of Criminology* 6: 33–50.

Baldwin, John. 1997. *Small Claims in the County Courts in England and Wales: The Bargain Basement of Civil Justice?* Oxford: OUP.

Baldwin, John, and Michael McConville. 1978. "Plea Bargaining and Plea Negotiation in England." *Law & Society Review* 13(2): 287–307.

Barton, Allen, and Saul Mendlovitz. 1960. "The Experience of Injustice as a Research Problem." *Journal of Legal Education* 13(1): 24–39.

BBC. 2015. "China Corruption: Life Term for Ex-security Chief Zhou," https://www.bbc.com/news/world-asia-china-33095453.

Beijing Lawyer Association. 2019. "Wang Junfeng: Keep in Mind the Mission and Uphold the Fairness and Justice of the Rule of Law [王俊峰:牢记使命 维护法治的公平正义]," https://www.beijinglawyers.org.cn/cac/1573802821555.htm.

Beijing Second Intermediate People's Court Research Group [北京市第二中级人民法院课题组]. 2014. "Research on the Way and Realization of Enhancing Judicial Credibility[提高司法公信力的路径和实现方式研究]." *Journal of Law Application[法律适用]* 8: 108–113.

Belkin, Ira. 2011. "Reforming China's Criminal Procedure: China's Tortuous Path Toward Ending Torture in Criminal Investigations." *Columbia Journal of Asian Law* 24: 273–301.

———. 2013. "China's Tortuous Path Towards Ending Torture in Criminal Investigations" in *Comparative Perspectives on Criminal Justice in China*, edited by Michael McConville and Eva Pils, 91–117. Cheltenham: Edward Elgar.

———. 2018. "Justice in the PRC: How the Chinese Communist Party has Struggled with Managing Public Opinion and the Administration of Criminal Justice in the Internet Age" in *Justice: The China Experience*, edited by Flora Sapio, Susan Trevaskes, Sarah Biddulph, and Elisa Nesossi, 195–228. Cambridge: CUP.

Biddulph, Sarah. 2010. "Legal Education in the People's Republic of China: The Ongoing Story of Politics and Law" in *Legal Education in Asia: Globalization, Change and Contexts*, edited by Stacey Steele and Kathryn Taylor. Oxon: Routledge.

Biddulph, Sarah, Elisa Nesossi, and Susan Trevaskes. 2017. "Criminal Justice Reform in the Xi Jinping Era." *China Law and Society Review* 2(1): 63–128.

Bing, Pu. 2012. "Zhang Miao's Family and Zhang Xian Claimed 200 Thousand Yuan Compensation Fees from Yao's Family. The Situation There was out of Control (张妙家人及张显到药家索要20万元赔款 现场失控)." *Ifeng* (凤凰网), http://news.xiancn.com/content/2012-02/08/content_2563778_4.htm.

Braithwaite, John. 2002. *Restorative Justice & Responsive Regulation*. Oxford: OUP.

Brodsky, Stanley L., Carroll M. Brodsky, and Sarah H. Wolking. 2004. "Why People Don't Sue: A Conceptual and Applied Exploration of Decisions Not to Pursue Litigation." *The Journal of Psychiatry & Law* 32(3): 273–295.

Cai, Congyan and Yifei Wang. 2021. "Transnational Judicial Dialogue in the Rise of China: How the Chinese Judiciary Enhances the Belt and Road Initiative." *Asia Pacific Law Review* 29(1): 149–166.

Cai, Wei and Andrew Godwin. 2019. "Challenges and Opportunities for the China International Commercial Court." *International and Comparative Law Quarterly* 68(4): 869–902.

Cai, Yongshun. 2004. Managed Participation in China. *Political Science Quarterly* 119(3): 425–451.

Caijing. 2008. "SPC President's Comment on the Grounds of Death Penalty Caused Controversy [最高法院院长谈死刑依据引发争议]." *Caijing [财经]*, https://china.caixin.com/2008-04-11/100058781.html.

Caixin. 2017. "Fully Respecting Lawyers' Opinions Can Avoid Wrongful Convictions [充分尊重律师意见能避免冤案]," http://m.china.caixin. com/m/2017-04-27/101083751.html.

CCP. 2014. "Communique of the Fourth Plenary Session of the 18th Central Committee of the Communist Party of China[中国共产党第十八届中央委员会第四次全体会议公报]," http://cpc.people.com.cn/GB/http:/cpc.people.com.cn/n/2014/1023/c64094-25896724.html.

The Central People's Government of the People's Republic of China. 2013. "The Number of Judges in China Reached Around 200 Thousand, which Will Become the Focus of the Classification Management Reform [我国法官人数已近20万人 将成分类管理改革重点]," August 3, 2013. http://www.gov.cn/jrzg/2013-07/25/content_2455484.htm.

Chan, Kam Wing, and Will Buckingham. "Is China Abolishing the Hukou System?" *China Quarterly* 195: 582–606.

Chan, Peter C.H. 2019. "Do the 'Haves' Come out Ahead in Chinese Grassroots Courts? Rural Land Disputes Between Married-out Women and Village Collectives." *Hastings Law Journal* 71: 1–78.

Chang, Yanlong, and Yiming Liu. 2018. "Administrative Ranks of the Government, Judicial Intervenor's Ability and Court Verdicts: Evidence from Court Documents of the Administrative Litigation [政府行政级别、司法干预能力和法院判决——来自行政案件判决书的证据]." *Journal of Guangdong University of Finance & Economics [广东财经大学学报]* 33(2): 99–111.

Chang, Yanlong, Xiaoning Long, and Lei Meng. 2020. "Off-Site Trial, Judicial Independence and Judges' Verdicts—Empirical Research Based on the Judicial System Reform of Jiangmen [异地审理、司法独立性与法官裁决——基于广东省江门市司法制度改革的实证研究]." *Guangdong Province China Economic Quarterly [经济学(季刊)]* 19(1): 101–120.

Cheesman, Nick. 2015. *Opposing the Rule of Law: How Myanmar's Courts Make Law and Order*. Cambridge: CUP.

Chen, Albert Hung-yee. 2016. "China's Long March towards Rule of Law or China's Turn against Law?" *The Chinese Journal of Comparative Law* 4(1): 1–35.

_____. 2018. *An Introduction to the Legal System of the People's Republic of China (Fifth Edition)*. Hong Kong: LexisNexis.

Chen, Benjamin Minhao, and Zhiyu Li. 2020. "How Will Technology Change the Face of Chinese Justice?" *Columbia Journal of Asian Law*. 34(1): 1–58.

Chen, Feng, and Xin Xu. 2012. "'Active Judiciary': Judicial Dismantling of Workers' Collective Action in China." *China Journal* 67(1): 87–108.

Chen, Guoqing, and Ying Zhou. 2016. "'Making the Trial Central to the Process' and Prosecution Work ['以审判为中心'与检察工作]" in *Symposium of the Eleventh National Forum for Senior Prosecutors: Trial as the Center and Trial Work Development*, Conference Papers, edited by the Beijing National Prosecutors College, 557–569.

Chen, Hangping. 2018. "On the System of Civil Execution and Reconciliation: From the Perspective of Simplifying Complexity Simplification [论民事"执行和解"制度 以"复杂性"化简为视角]." *Peking University Law Journal [中外法学]* 30(5): 1222–1236.

Chen, Ruihua. 2006. "File-Transcript Centralism: The Reinspection of Chinese Criminal Trial [案卷笔录中心主义——对中国刑事审判方式的重新考察]." *Chinese Journal of Law* 4: 63–79.

———. 2017a. "The Investigation Centralism [论侦查中心主义]." *Tribune of Political Science and Law* 35(2): 3–19.

———. 2017b. "Several Issues on the System of Leniency on Admission of Guilty and Acceptance of Punishment [认罪认罚从宽制度的若干争议问题]." *China Legal Science* 1: 35–52.

Chen, Tianhao, Jianshu Shao, and Xuechun Wang. 2020. "Study for Effects and Improvement Path of Administrative Public Interest Litigation Filed by the Procuratorate an Empirical Study based on Difference-in-Differences Method [检察行政公益诉讼制度的效果检验与完善路径 基于双重差分法的实证分析]." *Peking University Law Journal* [中外法学] 32(5) 1328–1352.

Chen, Weidong. 2016. "Making the Trial Central to the Process: Interpretation, Realization, and Development [以审判为中心:解读、实现与展望]." *Contemporary Legal Studies* 30(4): 14–21.

Chen, Xingliang. 2005. "Correspondence Concerning Death Penalty [关于死刑的通信]". *Peking University Law Review[北大法律评论]* 1: 341–359.

Chen, Xuefei. 2007. "Gender Preference in Judges' Discourse during the Trial of Divorce Cases [离婚案件审理中的法官的性别偏向]." *Peking University of Law Review* 8: 384–411.

Chen, Yongsheng and Bai Bing. 2016. "Limitation of the System Reform of the Specified Number of Judicial Personnel [法官、检察官员额制改革的限度]." *Journal of Comparative Law [比较法研究]* 2: 21–48.

Chen, Yongzhu. 2015. "The Judge as Mediator in China and its Alternatives: A Problem in Chinese Civil Justice." *Journal of Comparative Law* 10(2): 106–125.

Cheng, Jianjun. 2012. "Civil Mediation in Criminal Reconciliation[刑事和视野下的附带民事调解]," http://www.fk.gov.cn/10171/10171/10000/2012/122605.htm.

China Court [中国法院网]. 2016. "693 Courts Adopt the Comprehensive Reform of the Judicial System. More than 20 Thousand of Judges Registered under the Personnel Quota System, of which 85 Percent are Front Line Judges [693家法院全面推开司法责任制改革 2万多名法官进入员额制 85%以上在办案一线]," https://www.chinacourt.org/article/detail/2016/07/id/2022503.shtml.

———. 2018. "Continuing the Judicial Reform and Moving Forward [坚持司法改革不停步]," https://www.chinacourt.org/article/detail/2018/03/id/3244680.shtml.

China Law Society. 2018. *Annual Report on the Construction of the Rule of Law in China (2018) [中国法治建设年度报告(2018)]*.

China Justice Observer. 2020. "How Chinese Courts Perform: a Close Look at World Bank Group's Doing Business Report 2020". https://www.chinajusticeobserver.com/a/how-chin

ese-courts-performs-a-close-look-at-world-bank-groups-doing-business-report-2020   (last visit on 2 August 2022).

China News. 2008. "The Second Trial of Yang Jia's Case Will Continue Today or the Verdict Will be Handed Down, The Press Waited at the Door [杨佳案今日继续二审或将宣判 媒体门口等候采访]," https://www.chinanews.com.cn/sh/news/2008/10-20/1417524.shtml.

———. 2013. "The First Overhaul of the Administrative Procedure Law in 23 Years Focuses on Solving the 'Trilemma' of People Suing Officials [行政诉讼法23年来首次大修 着力解决民告官"三难"]," https://www.chinanews.com/fz/2013/12-24/5656550.shtml.

———. 2014. "Enhancing Career Security to Prevent Judicial Attrition [完善职业保障防止法官流失]," https://www.chinanews.com.cn/fz/2014/03-13/5944632.shtml.

———. 2022. "In 2021, Procuratorial Organs Disbursed More Than 610 Million Yuan in Judicial Relief Funds [2021年检察机关共发放司法救助金6.1亿余元]," https://www.chinanews.com.cn/gn/2022/03-06/9693803.shtml.

China Youth Daily. 2014. "How do People's Jurors Get out of the Situation of 'Accompanying but not Judging' [人民陪审员如何走出"陪而不审"]," http://zqb.cyol.com/html/2014-03/27/nw.D110000zgqnb_20140327_3-03.htm.

Chua, Lynette J. 2014. "Rights Mobilization and the Campaign to Decriminalize Homosexuality in Singapore." *Asian Journal of Law & Society* 1(1): 205–228.

Chua, Lynette J., and David M. Engel. 2019. "Legal Consciousness Reconsidered." *Annual Review of Law and Social Science* 15: 335–53.

Clarke, Donald C. 1996. "Power and Politics in the Chinese Court System: The Enforcement of Civil Judgments." *Columbia Journal of Asian Law* 10(1): 1–92.

———. 2022. "Order and Law in China." *University of Illinois Law Review*, https://illinoislawrev.web.illinois.edu/wp-content/uploads/2022/04/Clarke-.pdf.

Cloke, Kenneth. 1987. "Politics and Values in Mediation: The Chinese Experience." *Mediation Quarterly* 17: 69–82.

Cohen, Jerome A. 1997. "Reforming China's Civil Procedure: Judging the Courts." *The American Journal of Comparative Law* 45(4): 793–804.

Conley, John M., and M. O'Barr William. 1991. "The Culture of Capital: An Anthropological Investigation of Institutional Investment." *North Carolina Law Review* 70(3): 823–848.

CPC. 2014. Decision on Several Major Issues Concerning Comprehensively Advancing the Rule of Law (中共中央关于全面推进依法治国若干重大问题的决定), promulgated October 23, 2014. https://www.gov.cn/zhengce/2014-10/28/content_2771946.htm?ref=neican.org.

CPC. 2019. Opinions on Strengthening Comprehensive Management to Effectively Solve the Problem of Judgment Enforcement (关于加强综合治理从源头切实解决执行难问题的意见), July 14, 2019. https://www.moj.gov.cn/pub/sfbgw/qmyfzg/201908/t20190822_150361.html.

CPC. 2021. The Management of the Sources of Litigation (关于加强诉源治理推动矛盾纠纷源头化解的意见), The Central Office of the Party on Comprehensively Deepening Reforms, February 21, 2021.

CPC and State Council. 2009. Opinions on Assuring the Expenditure on Political and Legislative Works (关于加强政法经费保障工作的意见), the General Office of the Central Committee of the Party and the General Office of the State Council, 2009.

CPC and State Council. 2015. Regulations on Documenting, Reporting, and Sanctioning Interference with Judicial Activity by Government Officials (领导干部干预司法活动、插手具体案件处理的记录、通报和责任追究规定), the General Office of the Central Committee of the Communist Party of China and the General Office of the State Council, August 19, 2015. http://politics.people.com.cn/n/2015/0331/c1001-26774155.html.

Creemers, Rogier. 2020. "Ideology and Organisation in Chinese Law: Towards a New Paradigm for Legality" in *Law and the Party in China* 1–28. Cambridge: CUP.

Creutzfeldt, Naomi and Ben Bradford. 2016. "Dispute Resolution outside of Courts: Procedural Justice and Decision Acceptance among Users of Ombuds Services in the UK." *Law & Society Review* 50(4): 985–1016.

Cui, Wei. 2012. *A Long March in Administrative Litigation* [诉讼远征]. People's Court Press: Beijing.

———. 2016. "Does Judicial Independence Matter: A Study of the Determinants of Administrative Litigation in an Authoritarian Regime." *University of Pennsylvania Journal of International Law* 38(3): 941–998.

Cui, Wei, Jie Cheng, and Dominika Wiesner. 2019. "Judicial Review of Government Actions in China." *China Perspectives* 1: 35–44.

Damaska, Mirjan R. 1986. *The Faces of Justice and State Authority: A Comparative Approach to the Legal Process*. New Haven: Yale University Press.

———. 1997. *Evidence Law Adrift*. New Haven: Yale University Press.

Daum, Jeremy. 2018. "Plea Leniency Pilot Overview." *China Law Translate*, 25 April 2018, https://www.chinalawtranslate.com/en/plea-leniency-pilot-overview/.

———. 2021. "A Plea for Greater Reform and Engagement." *China Law Translate*, 28 June 2021, https://www.chinalawtranslate.com/en/a-plea-for-greater-reform-and-engagement/.

DeLisle, Jacques. 2017. "Law in the China Model 2.0: Legality, Developmentalism and Leninism under Xi Jinping." *Journal of Contemporary China* 26(103): 68–84.

DeLisle, Jacques, and Guobin Yang. 2022. *The Party Leads All: The Evolving Role of the Chinese Communist Party*. Brookings Institution Press: Washington, DC.

Deng, Xiaoping. 1984. *Selected Works of Deng Xiaoping, vol. III*. Beijing: Foreign Language Press.

Ding, Chunyan. 2019. "How Much Do Expert Opinions Matter? An Empirical Investigation of Selection Bias, Adversarial Bias, and Judicial Deference in Chinese Medical Negligence Litigation." *Brooklyn Journal of International Law* 45: 139–192.

Ding, Chunyan, and Huina Xiao. 2021. "A Paper Tiger? Prosecutorial Regulators in China's Civil Environmental Public Interest Litigations." *Fordham Environmental Law Review* 32(3): 323–379.

Ding, Wei. 2014. *Qinyao Court: The Practical Logic of Grassroots Justice [秦窑法庭——基层司法的实践逻辑]*. Beijing: Joint Publishing.

Du, Guodong. 2018. "Why Chinese Courts Put so Much Emphasis on Enforcement of Civil Judgments?" https://www.chinajusticeobserver.com/a/why-chinese-courts-put-so-much-emphasis-on-enforcement-of-civil-judgments.

Dui Hua Foundation. 2019. "The Execution of Wo Weihan," https://duihua.org/the-execution-of-wo-weihan-2/.

Durkheim, Émile. 1952. *Suicide: A Study in Sociology*. Routledge & Kegan Paul Ltd.

———. 1993. *The Division of Labor in Society*. Free Press: New York.

Edin, Maria. 2003. "State Capacity and Local Agent Control in China: CCP Cadre Management from a Township Perspective." *The China Quarterly* 173: 35–52.

The Economist. 2013. "Strike Less Hard," https://www.economist.com/china/2013/08/03/strike-less-hard.

———. 2017. "For Some Plaintiffs, Courts in China Are Getting Better," https://www.economist.com/china/2017/09/30/for-some-plaintiffs-courts-in-china-are-getting-better.

El-Ghobashy, Mona. 2008 "Constitutionalist Contention in Contemporary Egypt." *The American Behavioral Scientist* 51(11): 1590–1610.

Erie, Matthew S. 2007. "China's (Post-)Socialist Property Rights Regime: Assessing the Impact of the Property Law on Illegal Land Takings." *Hong Kong Law Journal* 37(3): 919–950.

———. 2016. *China and Islam: The Prophet, the Party, and Law*. Cambridge: CUP.

Ewick, Patricia, and Susan S. Silbey. 1998. *The Common Place of Law: Stories from Everyday Life*. Chicago: University of Chicago Press.

Fang, Siyuan. 2015. "Constructing the System of the Circuit Tribunals of the Supreme People's Court [最高人民法院巡回法庭的制度建构]." *Science of Law (Journal of Northwest University of Political Science and Law)* [法律科学] 33(2): 61–69.

Fang, Wang, and Guo Liang. 2019. "Do Confessions Contribute to Lenient Punishments in China: An Empirical Study Based on Crimes-of-Intentional-Injury Trials." *Tsinghua China Law Review* 12(1): 57–85.

Fei, Xiaotong. 1992. *From the Soil: The Foundations of Chinese Society*, translated by Wang Zheng. Berkeley: University of California Press.

Felstiner, William L.F., Richard L. Abel, and Austin Sarat. 1981. "The Emergence and Transformation of Disputes: Naming, Blaming, Claiming." *Law & Society Review* 15(3–4): 631–654.

Feng, Jing. 2024. "The Dissemination of Law and the Perception of Justice: An Empirical Study of the Influence of Rule of Law Propaganda on the Legal Consciousness of Litigants in Civil Litigation [法的传播与正义感知——法治宣传影响民事诉讼当事人法律意识的实证研究]." Manuscript on file with author.

Feng, Yuqing, and Qing Cao. 2014. "Popularized Judiciary in Rural China: Paternalistic Approaches and Enchanted Legal Consciousness." *Hong Kong Law Journal* 44(2): 651–77.

Feng, Yuqing, and Xin He. 2018. "From Law to Politics: Petitioners' Framing of Disputes in Chinese Courts." *The China Journal* 80(1): 130–149.

Feng, Yuqing, and Qing Xu. 2021. "The Evolution of *Guanxi* Dynamics in the Chinese Legal System: A Perspective of Career Mobility." *Hong Kong Law Journal* 51(3): 1131–1154.

Feng, Yuqing, and Yu Zeng. 2022. "Stability Justice: Petitioners versus Non-petitioners in China's Criminal Adjudication." *Law & Society Review* 56(4): 555–579.

Finder, Susan. 2020a. "What is the Impact of the SPC's Circuit Courts?" *Supreme People's Court Monitor*, https://supremepeoplescourtmonitor.com/2020/06/10/what-is-the-impact-of-the-spcs-circuit-courts/.

———. 2020b. "Supreme People's Court Starring on Court TV," *Supreme People's Court Monitor*, https://supremepeoplescourtmonitor.com/2016/07/14/supreme-peoples-court-starring-on-court-tv/.

———. 2021. "The Long March to Professionalizing Judicial Discipline in China" in *Disciplining Judges*, edited by Richard Devlin and Sheela Wilderman, 78–106. Cheltenham: Edward Elgar.

Fisher, George. 2000. "Plea Bargaining's Triumph." *Yale Law Journal* 109(5): 857–1086.

Fraenkel, Ernst. 1941. *The Dual State: A Contribution to the Theory of Dictatorship*. Oxford: OUP.

Friedman, Lawrence M. 1998. *American Law: An Introduction*. 2nd ed. New York: W.W. Norton.

———. 2016. *Impact: How Law Affects Behavior*. Cambridge, MA: Harvard University Press.

Fu, Hualing. 2003. "Putting China's Judiciary into Perspective: Is it Independent, Competent and Fair?" in *Beyond Common Knowledge: Empirical Approaches to the Rule of Law*, edited by Erik G. Jensen and Thomas C. Heller, 193–219. Stanford, CA: Stanford University Press.

———. 2018. "The July 9th (709) Crackdown on Human Rights Lawyers: Legal Advocacy in an Authoritarian State." *Journal of Contemporary China* 27(112): 554–568.

———. 2019. "Duality and China's Struggle for Legal Autonomy." *China Perspectives* 1: 3–9.

———. 2023. "High Policing and Human Rights Lawyering in China" in *Regime Type and Beyond: The Transformation of Police in Asia*, edited by Weitseng Chen and Hualing Fu, 53–86. Cambridge: CUP.

Fu, Hualing, and Michael Palmer. 2015. "Mediation in Contemporary China: Continuity and Change." *Journal of Comparative Law* 10: 1–24.

Fu, Hualing, and Richard Cullen. 2011a. "From Mediatory to Adjudicatory Justice: The Limits of Civil Justice Reform in China" in *Chinese Justice: Civil Dispute Revolution in Contemporary China*, edited by Margaret Y.K. Woo and Marry E. Gallagher. New York: CUP.

———. 2011b. "Climbing the Weiquan Ladder: A Radicalizing Process for Rights-protection Lawyers." *China Quarterly* 205: 40–59.

Fu, Yulin. 2006. "Report on the Situation of the Law Services at the Basic Level in China [中国基层法律服务现状与发展——以农村基层法律服务所为窗口]" in *Research on Rural Law Service at the Basic Level [农村基层法律服务研究]*, edited by Fu Yulin, 3–55. Beijing: China University of Politic Science and Law Press.

———. 2021. "Dimensions and Contradictions of Judicial Reforms in China" in *Chinese Courts and Criminal Procedure: Post-2013 Reforms*, edited by Björn Ahl, 59–83. Cambridge: CUP.

Fu, Yulin and Randall Peerenboom. 2010. "A New Analytic Framework for Understanding and Promoting Judicial Independence in China" in *Judicial Independence in China: Lessons for Global Rule of Law Promotion*, 95–133. Cambridge: CUP.

Galanter, Marc. 1974. "Why the 'Haves' Come Out Ahead: Speculations on the Limits of Legal Change." *Law & Society Review* 9(1): 95–160.

———. 1985. "A Settlement Judge, not a Trial Judge: Judicial Mediation in the United States." *Journal of Law and Society* 12(1): 1–18.

———. 1986. "The Emergence of the Judge as a Mediator in Civil Cases." *Judicature* 69(5): 25–62.

———. 2004. "The Vanishing Trial: An Examination of Trials and Related Matters in Federal and State Courts." *Journal of Empirical Legal Studies* 1(3): 459–570.

Gallagher, Mary. 2006. "Mobilizing the Law in China: 'Informed Disenchantment' and the Development of Legal Consciousness." *Law & Society Review* 40(4): 783–816.

Gallagher, Mary, and Yuhua Wang. 2011. "Users and Non-users: Legal Experience and its Effect on Legal Consciousness" in *Chinese Justice: Civil Dispute Resolution in Contemporary China*, edited by Margaret Woo and Mary Gallagher, 204–233. Cambridge: CUP.

Gao, Qicai, Weiping Zhou, and Zhenye Jiang. 2009. *Rural Justice: An Empirical Study of the People's Tribunal at Village Yang in the Social Evolution [乡土司法：社会变迁中的杨村人民法庭实证分析]*. Beijing: Law Press.

Gao, Tongfei. 2021. *Research on the Substantive Reform of Chinese Jurors [中国陪审员实质性改革研究]*. Beijing: *China University of Political Science & Law Press*.

Garoupa, Nuno, and Tom. 2015. *Judicial Reputation: A Comparative Theory*. Chicago: The University of Chicago Press.

Ge, Lin. 2008. *Research on Criminal Reconciliation (刑事和解研究)*. Beijing: University of Police Press.

Geng, Baojian. 2016a. "Review and Prospect of the Implementation of the New Administrative Procedure Law [新《行政诉讼法》实施一年回顾与展望]." Journal of Law Application [法律适用] 8: 8–14.

———. 2016b. "The Settlement of Administrative Disputes under "Pan-judicalization—Discuss the Revision Path of 'Administrative Review Law' [泛司法化]下的行政纠纷解决——兼谈《行政复议法》的修改路径]." *China Law Review* [中国法律评论] 3: 229–237.

Geng, Baojian, and Mi Zhou. 2016. "Abuse and Limitation of Prosecution Right in Field of Government Information Publicity: Concurrently on Information Publicity Case Value of Lu Hongxia vs. Nantong Municipal Development and Reform Commission [政府信息公开领域起诉权的滥用和限制——兼谈陆红霞诉南通市发改委政府信息公开案的价值]." *Administrative Law Review* [行政法学研究] 3: 32–40.

Ginsburg, Tom, and Tamir Moustafa. 2008. *Rule by Law: The Politics of Courts in Authoritarian Regimes*. New York: CUP.

Givens, John Wagner. 2014. "Sleeping with Dragons? Politically Embedded Lawyers Suing the Chinese State" *Wisconsin International Law Journal* 31(3): 734–770.

Gong, Ting. 2004. "Dependent Judiciary and Unaccountable Judges: Judicial Corruption in Contemporary China." *China Review* 4(2): 33–54.

Granovetter, Mark S. 1973. "The Strength of Weak Ties." *American Journal of Sociology* 78(6): 1360–1380.

Gu, Weixia. 2021. *Dispute Resolution in China: Litigation, Arbitration, Mediation and their Interactions*. London: Routledge.

Gu, Yongzhong and Peiquan Xiao. 2017. "Observations in Person, Thoughts and Suggestions for 'Perfecting Plea Leniency' (完善认罪认罚从宽制度"的亲历观察与思考、建议)" *Rule of Law Research* [法治研究] 1: 56–70.

Gu, Qian. 2021. "On the Application Scope of Administrative Litigation Mediation [论行政诉公调解的适用范围]." *Administrative Law Science Study* [行政法学研究] (3): 163–176.

Guangzhou Daily. 2021. "96.85% of Prosecutorial Suggested Sentences Confirmed by Courts for the first 11 months," http://news.ycwb.com/2021-12/20/content_40463829.htm.

Guarnieri, Carlo. 2001 "Judicial Independence in Latin Countries of Western Europe" in *Judicial Independence in the Age of Democracy: Critical Perspectives from around the World*, edited by Peter H. Russell and David M. O'Brien, 105–124. Charlottesville, Virginia: University Press of Virginia.

Guo, Zhiyuan. 2021. "Live Witness Testimony in the Chinese Criminal Courts" in *Chinese Courts and Criminal Procedure: Post-2013 Reforms*, edited by Björn Ahl, 183–207. Cambridge: CUP.

Hand, Keith J. 2011. "Resolving Constitutional Disputes in Contemporary China." *University of Pennsylvania East Asia Law Review* 7(1): 51–159.

Hans, Valerie P. 2008. "Jury Systems around the World." *Annual Review of Law and Social Sciences* 4: 276–297.

Harvard Law Review. 2020. "Making Chinese Court Filings Public? Some Not-So-Foreign American Insights." *Harvard Law Review* 133(5): 1728–1749.

Haynie, Stacia L. 1994. "Resource Inequalities and Litigation Outcomes in the Philippine Supreme Court." *Journal of Politics* 56(3): 752–772.

He, Dongqing. 2021. "Learn and Use the 'Ma Xiwu Trial Method', Carrying Forward the Fine Tradition of People's Justice [学好用活"马锡五审判方式" 继承发扬人民司法优良传统]." *People's Court Daily*, Oct. 1, 2021.

He, Haibo. 2018. "How Much Progress can Legislation Bring? The 2014 Amendment of the Administrative Litigation Law of PRC." *University of Pennsylvania Asian Law Review* 13: 137–190.

———. 2022. *Administrative Law[行政诉讼法]*. Beijing: The Law Press.

He, Jiahong. 2016. *Back from the Dead: Wrongful Convictions and Criminal Justice in China*. Manoa: University of Hawaii Press.

He, Qisheng. 2013. "Public Policy in Enforcement of Foreign Arbitral Awards in the Supreme People's Court of China." *Hong Kong Law Journal* 43(3) 1037–1060.

He, Xin. 2004. "Ideology or Reality? Limited Judicial Independence in Contemporary Rural China." *Australian Journal of Asian Law* 6(3): 213–230.

———. 2007. "Why did they not Take on the Disputes? Law, Power and Politics in the Decision-making of Chinese Courts." *International Journal of Law in Context* 3(3): 203–225.

———. 2008. "The Financial Incapability of Chinese Courts and Judicial Corruption [中國法院的財政不足與司法腐敗]." *Twenty-First Century [二十一世紀]* 105: 12–23.

———. 2009a. "Enforcing Commercial Judgments in the Pearl River Delta of China," *American Journal of Comparative Law* 57(2): 419–456.

———. 2009b. "Court Finance and Court Responses to Judicial Reforms: A Tale of Two Chinese Courts". *Law & Policy* 31(4): 463–486.

———.2009c. "Administrative Law as a Mechanism for Political Control in Contemporary China" in *Building Constitutionalism in China*, edited by Stéphanie Balme and Michael W. Dowdle, 143–161. New York: Palgrave Macmillan US.

———. 2011. "Debt Collection in the Less Developed Regions of China: An Empirical Study from a Basic-level Court in Shaanxi Province." *China Quarterly* 206: 253–275.

———. 2012. "Black Hole of Responsibility: The Adjudication Committee's Role in a Chinese Court." *Law & Society Review* 46(4): 681–712.

———. 2013. "Judicial Innovation and Local Politics: Judicialization of Administrative Governance in East China." *China Journal* 69(1): 20–42.

———. 2014. "Maintaining Stability by Law: Protest-supported Housing Demolition Litigation and Social Change in China." *Law & Social Inquiry* 39(4): 849–873.

———. 2016. "Double Whammy: Lay Assessors as Lackeys in Chinese Courts." *Law & Society Review* 50(3): 733–765.

———. 2017. "'No Malicious Incidents': The Concern for Stability in China's Divorce Law Practice." *Social & Legal Studies* 26(4): 467–489.

———. 2020. "(Non)legality as Governmentality in China," https://papers.ssrn.com/sol3/papers.cfm?abstract_id=3612483.

———. 2021a. *Divorce in China: Institutional Constraints and Gendered Outcomes*. New York: New York University Press.

———. 2021b. "Pressures on Chinese Judges under Xi." *The China Journal* 85(1): 49–74.

———. 2022. "The Judge as a Negotiator: Claims Negotiating and Inequalities in China's Judicial Mediation." *Law & Social Inquiry* 47(4): 1172–1200.

———. 2023. "From Hierarchical to Panoptic Control: The Chinese Solution in Monitoring Judges." *International Journal of Constitutional Law* 21(2): 488–509.

He, Xin and Jing Feng. 2021. "Unfamiliarity and Procedural Justice: Litigants' Attitudes Toward Civil Justice in Southern China." *Law & Society Review* 55(1): 104–1238.

He, Xin, and Yuqing Feng. 2016. "Mismatched Discourses in the Petition Offices of Chinese Courts." *Law & Social Inquiry* 41(1): 212–241.

He, Xin, Luoyun Li, and Yuqing Feng. 2017. "The Mediatory versus Legalistic Discourse in Chinese Courts." *PoLAR: Political and Legal Anthropological Review* 40(2): 326–341.

He, Xin, and Fen Lin. 2017. "The Losing Media? An Empirical Study of Defamation Litigation in China." *China Quarterly* 230: 371–398.

He, Xin, and Kwai Hang Ng. 2013a. "Inquisitorial Adjudication and Institutional Constraints in Chinese Civil Justice." *Law & Policy* 35(4): 290–318.

———. 2013b. "In the Name of Harmony: The Erasure of Domestic Violence in China's Judicial Mediation." *International Journal of Law, Policy and the Family* 27(1): 97–115.

———. 2017. "'It Must be Rock Strong!' *Guanxi*'s Impact on Judicial Decision Making in China." *American Journal of Comparative Law* 65(4): 841–871.

He, Xin, and Yang Su. 2013. "Do the 'Haves' Come out Ahead in Shanghai Courts?" *Journal of Empirical Legal Studies* 10(1): 120–145.

He, Xin, Lungang Wang, and Yang Su. 2013. "Above the Roof, Beneath the Law: Perceived Justice behind Disruptive Tactics of Migrant Wage Claimants in China." *Law & Society Review* 47(4): 703–738.

He, Yongjun. 2018. *Fracture and Persistence: The Development of the People's Court (1978–2005)* [断裂与延续：人民法院建设（1978–2005）] Beijing: China University of Political Science and Law Press.

Heinz, John P., and Edward O. Laumann. 1982. *Chicago Lawyers: The Social Structure of the Bar.* New York: Russell Sage Foundation.

Henderson, Dan Feeno. 1965. *Conciliation and Japanese Law: Tokugawa and Modern.* Washington: University of Washington Press.

Hendley, Kathryn and Peter H. Solomon. 2023. *The Judicial System of Russia.* Oxford: OUP.

Hendley, Kathryn. 2004. "Business Litigation in the Transition: A Portrait of Debt Collection in Russia." *Law & Society Review* 38(2): 305–348.

———. 2007. "Are Russian Judges Still Soviet?" *Post-Soviet Affairs* 23: 240–274.

———. 2017. *Everyday Law in Russia.* Ithaca: Cornell University Press.

Hessick, Carissa B. 2021. *Punishment without Trial: Why Plea Bargaining is a Bad Deal.* New York: Abrams Press.

Hessler, Peter. 2015. "Travels with my Censor" *The New Yorker.* Mar. 9, 2015.

Hilbank, Lisa. 2007. *Judges beyond Politics in Democracy and Dictatorship: Lessons from Chile.* 1st ed. Cambridge: CUP.

Hou, Meng. 2011. "The Attitude and Expression of the SPC Petitioner [最高法院访民的心态与表达]." *Peking University Law Journal [中外法学]* 23(3): 648–659

———. 2012. "Social Management of Petitioning in Beijing—Starting from the Phenomenon of 'Black Prison' [进京上访的社会管理—从'黑监狱'现象切入]." *Law Science[法学]* 5: 115–120.

———. 2021. *Process of Justice* [司法的运作过程]. Beijing: China Legal Publishing House.

Hou, Xiaoyan, and Yongjie Xing. 2019. "Practical Observation of Excluding Witness Testimony as Illegal Evidence in China's Criminal Justice [我国证人证言排除的刑事司法实务观察]." *Journal of National Prosecutors College [国家检察官学院学报]* 27(4): 122–139.

Hou, Xuebin, and Yueou Chen. 2020. "The Campaign-style Governance Preference of the People's Court: Based on the Analysis of its Solution to the Problem of Difficult Enforcement [人民法院的运动式治理偏好—基于人民法院解决"执行难"行动的分析]." *Jilin University Journal Social Sciences Edition [吉林大学社会科学学报]* 60(6): 70–84.

Howson, Nicholas Calcina. 2010. "Corporate Law in the Shanghai People's Courts, 1992–2008: Judicial Autonomy in a Contemporary Authoritarian State." *East Asia Law Review* 5(2): 303–442.

Hu, Changming. 2019. *Research on Protections for Judicial Professionals* [中国法官职业保障研究]. Beijing: China Social Sciences Press.

Huang, Philip C. 1996. *Civil Justice in China: Representation and Practice in the Qing.* Stanford, CA: Stanford University Press.

———. 2005. "Divorce Law Practices and the Origins, Myths, and Realities of Judicial 'Mediation' in China." *Modern China* 31(2): 151–203.

———. 2010. *Chinese Civil Justice, Past and Present.* Lanham, MD: Rowman & Littlefield.

Huang, Qihui. 2013. "Research on the Trial Status of First Instance of Administrative Litigation – Based on Statistical Analysis of 2,767 Judgment Documents of 40 Courts [行政诉讼一审审判状况研究——基于对40家法院2767份裁判文书的统计分析]." *Tsinghua Law Journal [清华法学]* 7(4): 73–85.

Ip, Eric and Kelvin Kwok. 2017. "Judicial Control of Local Protectionism in China: Antitrust Enforcement against Administrative Monopoly on the Supreme People's Court." *Journal of Competition Law & Economics* 13(3): 549–575.

Ivkovic, Sanja Kutnjak. 2007. "Exploring Lay Participation in Legal Decision-making: Lessons from Mixed Tribunals." *Cornell International Law Journal* 40(2): 429–454.

Jacobs, Andrew. 2012. "Daring Circle, Now at Risk, Aided Activist's Flight in China." *New York Times,* April 29, 2012.

Jiang, Bixin (ed.). 2005. *Perfection of China's Administrative Litigation System* [中国行政诉讼的完善]. Beijing: Law Press.

Jiang, Hua. 1989. *Literatures on Judiciary by Jiang Hua* [江华司法文集]. People's Court Press: Beijing.

Johnson, David T., and Franklin E. Zimring. 2009. *The Next Frontier: National Development, Political Change, and the Death Penalty in Asia.* Oxford: OUP.

Johnson, Ian. 2017. "When the Law Meets the Party." *New York Times,* August 17, 2017.

Keith, Ronald C., Zhiqiu Lin, and Shumei Hou. 2014. *China's Supreme Court.* Oxon: Routledge.

Kellogg, Thomas E. 2009. "Constitutionalism with Chinese Characteristics? Constitutional Development and Civil Litigation in China." *International Journal of Constitutional Law* 7(2): 215–246.

Kinkel, Jonathan J. 2015. "High-end Demand: The Legal Profession as a Source of Judicial Selection Reform in Urban China." *Law & Social Inquiry* 40(4): 969–1000.

Kinkel, Jonathan J., and William J. Hurst. 2015. "The Judicial Cadre Evaluation System in China: From Quantification to Intra-state Legibility." *The China Quarterly* 224: 933–954.

Komaiko, Richard, and Beibei Que. 2009. *Lawyers in Modern China.* New York: Cambria Press.

Kritzer, Herbert M. 2004. "Disappearing Trials? A Comparative Perspective." *Journal of Empirical Legal Studies* 1(3): 735–754.

Krygier, Martin. 2012. "Rule of Law" in *The Oxford Handbook of Comparative Constitutional Law,* edited by Michel Rosenfeld and Andras Sajo. Oxford: OUP.

Lampton, David M. 1992. "A Plum for a Peach: Bargaining, Interest, and Bureaucratic Politics in China" in *Bureaucracy, Politics, and Decision Making in Post-Mao China,* edited by Kenneth Lieberthal and David M. Lampton. Berkeley: University of California Press.

Landry, Pierre F. 2008. *Decentralized Authoritarianism in China: The Communist Party's Control of Local Elites in the Post-Mao Era.* New York: CUP.

Landsman, Stephen and Jing Zhang. 2008. "A Tale of Two Juries: Lay Participation Comes to Japanese and Chinese Courts." *UCLA Pacific Basin Law Journal* 25, 179–227.

Legal Daily. 2014. "It is Unrealistic to Detain Officials for not Enforcing Administrative Judgments [行政机关不执行判决可拘留官员规定不现实]." February 4.

_____. 2016. "Report: Stepping into the Year of Ruling the Country by Law, Political and Legislative Institutions Progressively Improved their Capability of Dealing with the Public Opinion [报告: 依法治国开局之年 我国政法机关舆情处置能力稳步提升]," http://www.cac.gov.cn/2016-01/25/c_1117887637.htm.

Lempert, Richard O. 2007. "The Internationalization of Lay Legal Decision-making: Jury Resurgence and Jury Research." *Cornell International Law Journal* 40(2): 477–488.

Li, Yinhe. 2015. "Keynote Speech: Sexuality in China," https://www.brookings.edu/wp-content/uploads/2015/03/20150403_china_gender_sexuality_transcript.pdf.

Li, Enshen. 2010. "Li Zhuang Case: A Coincidental Incident or A Deliberate Event?" *Columbia Journal of Asian Law* 24(1): 129–169.

———. 2018. *Punishment in Contemporary China: Its Evolution, Development and Change.* London: Routledge.

———. 2022a. "Haste Makes Waste: Why China's New Plea Leniency System is Doomed to Fail." *Asian Journal of Comparative Law* 17: 76–105.

———. 2022b. "Chinese Courts' New Plea Leniency System: Scrutinizing the Efficacy of Mandatory Defense Counsel." *The China Journal* 88(1): 78–99.

Li, Feng. 2013. "Analysis of the Influence Mechanism of Judicial Trust: An Empirical Study Based on Shanghai Data [司法信任的影响机制分析——基于上海数据的实证探讨]." *Gansu Social Sciences [甘肃社会科学]* 6: 140–143.

Li, Hao. 2013. "Let Mediation be Mediation, Let Adjudication be Adjudication: Separating Mediation and Adjudication in Civil Trial [调解归调解，审判归审判: 民事审判中的调审分离]." *China Legal Science [中国法学]* 3: 5–18.

Li, Hongjiang. 2006. "The Implementation of Criminal Reconciliation Should be Slowed Down (刑事和解应缓行)." *The Chinese Procurators (中國檢察官)* 5: 13–14.

Li, Ji. 2013. "Suing the Leviathan—An Empirical Analysis of the Changing Rate of Administrative Litigation in China." *Journal of Empirical Legal Studies* 10(4): 815–846.

Li, Ke. 2015. "'What He Did Was Lawful': Divorce Litigation and Gender Inequality in China." *Law & Policy* 37(3): 153–179.

———. 2022. *Marriage Unbound: State Law, Power, and Inequality in Contemporary China.* Stanford, CA: Stanford University Press.

Li, Ke, and Sara Friedman. 2016. "Wedding Marriage to the Nation-state in Modern China: Legal Consequences for Divorce, Property, and Women's Rights" in *Domestic Tensions, National Anxieties: Global Perspectives on Marriage, Crisis, and Nation,* edited by Kristin Celello and Hanan Kholoussy, 147–169. Oxford: OUP.

Li, Li, and Peng Wang. 2019. "From Institutional Interaction to Institutional Integration: The National Supervisory Commission and China's New Anti-corruption Model." *The China Quarterly* 240: 967–989.

Li, Lianjiang, Mingxing Liu, and Kevin J. O'Brien. 2012. "Petitioning Beijing: The High Tide of 2003–2006." *China Quarterly* 210: 313–334.

Li, Ling. 2011. "Performing Bribery in China: *Guanxi*-practice, Corruption with a Human Face." *Journal of Contemporary China* 20(68): 1–20.

———. 2012. "The 'Production' of Corruption in China's Courts: Judicial Politics and Decision Making in a One-party State." *Law & Social Inquiry* 37(4): 848–877.

———. 2019. "Politics of Anticorruption in China: Paradigm Change of the Party's Disciplinary Regime 2012–2017." *The Journal of Contemporary China* 28 (115): 47–63.

Li, Xilian. 2019. "A Rethinking of the Relation of Trial and Mediation in China's Civil Trial [我国民事审判中调审关系的再思考]." *Science of Law [法律科学]* 37: 142–152.

Li, Yan, and Xingge Gao. 2021. "On the Protection of Human Rights in the Civil Enforcement Procedure [论民事执行程序中的人权保障]." *Journal of Chongqing University (Social Science Edition) [重庆大学学报(社会科学版)]* 28(6): 258–271.

Li, Yedan, Joris Kocken, and Benjamin Van Rooij. 2018. "Understanding China's Court Mediation Surge: Insights from a Local Court." *Law & Social Inquiry* 43(1): 58–81.

Li, Yedan. 2016. "From 'Access to Justice' to 'Barrier to Justice'? An Empirical Examination of Chinese Court-annexed Mediation." *Asian Journal of Law and Society* 3(2): 377–397.

Li, Yuwen. 2014. *The Judicial System and Reform in Post-Mao China.* Farnham: Ashgate.

Li, Zheng. 2012. "The Current Situation of Civil Enforcement in China [中国民事执行的当下境遇]." *Tribune of Political Science and Law [政法论坛]* 30(2): 48–59.

Li, Zhiyu. 2018. "Innovation through Interpretation: How Judges Make Policy in China." *Tulane Journal of International and Comparative Law* 26(2): 327–380.

Liang, Bin, and Ni He. 2014. "Criminal Defense in Chinese Courtrooms: An Empirical Inquiry." *International Journal of Offender Therapy and Comparative Criminology* 58(10): 1230–1252.

Liang, Bin, Ni Phil He, and Hong Lu. 2014. "The Deep Divide in China's Criminal Justice System: Contrasting Perceptions of Lawyers and the Iron Triangle." *Crime, Law and Social Change* 62(5): 585–601.

Liang, Bin. 2008. *The Changing Chinese Legal System, 1978–Present: Centralization of Power and Rationalization of the Legal System.* New York: Routledge.

Liao, Yong'an and Shenggang Li. 2005. "The Current Operational Status of the System of Litigation Fees in China: Case Study of a Basic Court in a Poor Area [我国民事诉讼费用制度之运行现状：以一个贫穷地区基层法院为分析个案]." *Peking University Law Journal* [北大法律评论] 17(3): 304–327.

Liao, Yongan, and Jiang Fengming. 2018. "Reflection and Correction of the Reform Goal of the People's Jury System—Taking the Two Pilot Courts in City A as an Example [人民陪审制改革目标的反思与矫正--以 A 市两试点法院为例]." *Journal of Huaqiao University: Philosophy and Social Sciences Edition [华侨大学学报:哲学社会科学版]* (1): 67–77.

Liao, Yongan, and Fangyong Liu. 2014. "The Alienation of the Goals of the People's Assessor System and its Reflection—An Investigation Based on the Practice of the People's Assessor System in a City in Hunan Province [人民陪审员制度目标之异化及其反思——以湖南省某市人民陪审员制度实践为样本的考察]." *Study of Law and Business[法商研究]* (1): 85–92.

———.2018. *Whose assessment: Survey on People's Assessment of China [谁的陪审？：人民陪审访谈录].* Beijing: China Renmin University Press.

Lieberthal, Kenneth. 1992. "Introduction – The 'Fragmented Authoritarianism' Model and its Limitations" in *Bureaucracy, Politics, and Decision Making in Post-Mao China,* edited by Kenneth Lieberthal and David Lampton, 1–32. Berkeley: University of California Press.

Liebman, Benjamin L. 2006. "Innovation through Intimidation: An Empirical Account of Defamation Litigation in China." *Harvard International Law Journal* 47 (1): 33–109.

———. 2008. "China's Courts: Restricted Reform." *The China Quarterly* 191: 620–638.

———. 2011. "A Populist Threat to China's Courts?" in *Chinese Justice: Civil Dispute Resolution in Contemporary China,* edited by Margaret Woo and Mary Gallagher, 269–313. Cambridge: CUP.

———. 2015. "Leniency in Chinese Criminal Law: Everyday Justice in Henan." *Berkeley Journal of International Law* 33 (1): 153–228.

———. 2017. "Authoritarian Justice in China: Is there a 'Chinese Model'?" in *The Beijing Consensus? How China has Changed Western Ideas of Law and Economic Development,* edited by Weitseng Chen, 225–248. Cambridge: CUP.

Liebman, Benjamin L., Margaret E. Roberts, Rachel E. Stern, and Alice Z. Wang. 2020. "Mass Digitization of Chinese Courts Decisions: How to Use Text as Data in the Field of Chinese Law." *Journal of Law and Courts* 8(2): 177–201.

Lin, Delia, and Susan Trevaskes. 2019. "Creating a Virtuous Leviathan: The Party, Law, and Socialist Core Values." *Asian Journal of Law and Society* 6(1): 41–66.

Lin, Lihong, and Guotao Song. 2013. "Knowing and Doing of China's Administrative Adjudication Judge—Investigation Report on Administrative Litigation Law Implementation · Judge [中国行政审判法官的知与行—《行政诉讼法》实施状况调查报告·法官卷]." *Administrative Law Review [行政法学研究]* (2): 49–62.

Lin, Yimin. 2002. "Beyond Dyad Social Exchange: *Guanxi* and Third-party Effects" in *Social Connections in China: Institutions, Culture, and the Changing Nature of Guanxi,* edited by Thomas Gold, Doug Guthrie, and David Wank, 57–74. New York: CUP.

Lind, E. Allan, and Tom R. Tyler. 1988. *The Social Psychology of Procedural Justice.* Berlin: Springer Science & Business Media.

Linz, Juan J. 1978. *The Breakdown for Democratic Regimes: Crisis, Breakdown, and Reequilibration.* Baltimore: The Johns Hopkins University Press.

Liu, Bin. 2015. "From the Phenomenon of Judges' 'Resignation', Exploring the Underlying Logic of the Reform of Judge Quota System [从法官'离职' 现象看法官员额制改革的制度逻辑]." *Law Science* [法学] 10: 47–56.

Liu, Fangyong, and Yongan Liao. 2016. "An Empirical Study on the Operation of the People's Assessor System in China – Taking a County-level City in Central China as an Sample [我国人民陪审员制度运行实证研究—以中部某县级市为分析样本]." *The Jurist* [法学家] (4): 53–70.

Liu, Fangyong. 2016. "Role Conflict and Adjustment of People's Jurors [人民陪审员角色冲突与调适]." *Science of Law* [法律科学] 2: 155–166

Liu, Jie. 2006. *Courthouse on Horseback* [马背上的法庭]. Beijing Children's Art Theater production.

Liu, Jingdong, and Lulu Wang. 2018. "An Empirical Study of China's Recognition and Enforcement of Foreign Arbitral Awards under the 'Belt and Road Initiative' ['一带一路"下我国对外国仲裁裁决承认与执行的实证研究]." *Journal of Law Application* [法律适用] 5: 31–39.

Liu, John Zhuang. 2021. "Public Support for the Death Penalty in China: Less from the Populace but More from Elites." *The China Quarterly* 246: 527–544.

Liu, Lawrence J., and Rachel E. Stern. 2021. "State-adjacent Professionals: How Chinese Lawyers Participate in Political Life." *The China Quarterly* 247: 793–813.

Liu, Qian. 2023. "Relational Legal Consciousness in the One-child Nation." *Law & Society Review* 57(2): 214–233.

Liu, Qinghui. 2007. "Focusing on the Practice of Trial System of People's Assessors [对人民陪审制运行过程的考察]." *Peking University Law Review* [北大法律评论] 8(1): 15–38.

Liu, Renwen. 2012. "Retrospect and Prospect of China's Death Penalty Reforms [中国死刑改革的回顾与展望]." *Journal of Henan University of Economics and Law* [河南财经政法大学学报] 27(2): 1–8.

Liu, Sida. 2008. *The Lost Polis: Transformation of the Legal Profession in Contemporary China* [失落的城邦：当代中国法律职业变迁]. Beijing: Peking University Press.

———. 2011 "Lawyers, State Officials and Significant Others: Symbiotic Exchange in the Chinese Legal Services Market." *The China Quarterly* 206: 276–293.

———. 2013. "The Legal Profession as a Social Process: A Theory on Lawyers and Globalization." *Law & Social Inquiry* 38: 670–93.

———. 2017. *The Logic of Fragmentation: An Ecological Analysis of the Chinese Legal Services Market (Revised Edition)* [割据的逻辑：中国法律服务市场的生态分析]. Beijing: Yilin Press.

Liu, Sida, and Terence C. Halliday. 2016. *Criminal Defense in China: The Politics of Lawyers at Work.* Cambridge: CUP.

Liu, Zhewei. 2008. "The Present and the Future of the People's Assessor System [人民陪审制的现状与未来]". *Peking University Law Journal* [北大法律评论] 20(3): 433–447.

Liu, Zhong. 2012a. "Scales and Inner Governance: The Transformation of the Personal Quota of China's Court in Past Thirty Years [规模与内部治理：中国法院编制变迁三十年]." *Law and Social Development* [法制与社会发展] 18(5): 47–64.

———. 2012b. "The Appointment of Court Presidents under Tiao-Kuai Relations [条条与块块关系下的法院院长产生]." *Global Law Review* [环球法律评论] 34(1): 107–125.

———. 2016. "Unfinished 'Equality of Arms': Cultivating the Non knowledge Technical Rationality of Criminal Defense Lawyers [未完成的"平等武装"刑辩律师非知识技艺理性的养成]." *Peking University Law Journal* [北大法律评论] 28: 410–446.

———. 2019. "Internal Governance Shift in Chinese Judicial Reform: A Re-evaluation Based on Reasons for Judge Resignations [中国法院改革的内部治理转向—基于法官辞职原因的再评析]." *Studies in Law and Business* [法商研究] 36(6): 76–88.

Liu, Zuoxiang. 2003. "Criticism on the Local Protectionism in Chinese Judiciary: Also on the Guideline of Judicial Reform by 'Nationalization of Judicial Power' [中国司法地方保护主义之批判—兼论'司法权国家化'的司法改革思路]." *Chinese Journal of Law* [法学研究] (1): 83–98.

Lo, Carlos Wing-Hung, and Ed Snape. 2005. "Lawyers in the People's Republic of China: A Study of Commitment and Professionalization." *American Journal of Comparative Law* 53(2): 433–455.

Long, Cheryl Xiaoning, and Jun Wang. 2015. "Judicial Local Protectionism in China: An Empirical Study of IP Cases." *International Review of Law and Economics* 42: 48–59.

Lora-Wainwright, Anna, Yiyun Zhang, Yunmei Wu, and Benjamin Van Rooij. 2012. "Learning to Live with Pollution: The Making of Environmental Subjects In A Chinese Industrialized Village." *China Journal* 68(1): 106–124.

Lu, Haitian, Hongbo Pan, and Chenying Zhang. 2015. "Political Connectedness and Court Outcomes: Evidence from Chinese Corporate Lawsuits." *The Journal of Law and Economics* 58(4): 829–861.

Lu, Hong, and Terance D. Miethe. 2002. "Legal Representation and Criminal Processing in China." *British Journal of Criminology* 42 (2): 267–280.

———. 2007. "Provincial Laws on the Protection of Women in China: A Partial Test of Black's Theory." *International Journal of Offender Therapy and Comparative Criminology* 51(1): 25–39.

Lu, Yuguang. 2021. "Comparative Research of the Plea Leniency System of China." PhD dissertation, Indiana University.

Lubman, Stanley. 1999. *Bird in a Cage: Legal Reform in China after Mao*. Stanford, CA: Stanford University Press.

Ma, Chao, Zhaoyou Zheng, and Haibo He. 2021. "China's Experiment of Administrative Court: A Study Based on 240000 Judgments [行政法院的中国试验—基于24万份判决书的研究]." *Tsinghua University Law Journal [清华法学]* 15(5): 192–206.

Ma, Huaide. 2022. "Reform of Administrative Reconsideration System and Amendment of the Administrative Reconsideration Law [行政复议体制改革与《行政复议法》修改]." *Justice of China [中国司法]* 2: 61–64.

MacCoun, Robert J. 2005. "Voice, Control, and Belonging: The Double-edged Sword of Procedural Fairness." *Annual Review Law and Social Science* 1: 171–201.

Machura, Stefan. 2001. "Interaction between Lay Assessors and Professional Judges in German Mixed Courts." *Revue Internationale De Droit Pénal* 72(1): 451–479.

———. 2003. "Fairness, Justice, and Legitimacy: Experiences of People's Judges in South Russia." *Law & Policy* 25(2): 123–150.

Mao, Wenzheng, and Shitong Qiao. 2021. "Legal Doctrine and Judicial Review of Eminent Domain in China." *Law & Social Inquiry* 46(3): 826–859.

Markovits, Inga. 2002. "Justice in Lüritz." *American Journal of Comparative Law* 50: 819–874.

Martin, James. 1998. *Gramsci's Political Analysis: A Critical Introduction*. Houndmills, Basingstoke: Macmillan Press.

Mather, Lynn and Barbara Yngvesson. 1980–1981. "Language, Audience, and the Transformation of Disputes." *Law and Society Review* 15(3–4): 775–821.

McAdam, Doug. 1983. "Tactical Innovation and the Pace of Insurgency." *American Sociological Review* 48(6): 735–754.

McConville, Michael, Satnam Choongh, Pinky Choy Dick Wan, Eric Chui Wing Wong, Ian Dobinson, and Carol Jones. 2011. *Criminal Justice in China: An Empirical Inquiry*. Cheltenham; Northampton, MA: Edward Elgar.

McIntosh, Wayne. 1981. "150 Years of Litigation and Dispute Settlement: A Court Tale." *Law and Society Review* 15(3): 823–848.

Meng, Ye. 2023. "The Limits of Judicial Reforms: How and Why China Failed to Centralize its Court System." *The China Quarterly* 255: 753–767.

Merry, Sally E. 1990. *Getting Justice and Getting Even*. Chicago: University of Chicago Press.

Merry, Sally Engle, and Neal Milner (eds.). 1993. *The Possibility of Popular Justice*. Ann Arbor: University of Michigan Press.

Miao, Michelle. 2013a. "The Politics of China's Death Penalty Reform in the Context of Global Abolitionism." *British Journal of Criminology* 53(3): 500–519.

———. 2013b. "Capital Punishment in China: A Populist Instrument of Social Governance." *Theoretical Criminology* 17(2): 233–250.

_____. 2021a. "Democratizing Courts in an Authoritarian Polity? Using an Interest-based Bargaining Theory to Explain China's Pilot Reform on its People's Assessor System". *Washington University of Global Study Law Review* 20(2): 431–468.

———. 2021b. "Performance Evaluation in the Context of Criminal Justice Reform: A Critical Analysis" in *Chinese Courts and Criminal Procedure: Post-2013 Reforms*, edited by Björn Ahl, 235–257. Cambridge: CUP.

Michelson, Ethan. 2006. "The Practice of Law as an Obstacle to Justice: Chinese Lawyers at Work." *Law & Society Review* 40(1): 1–38.

———. 2022. *Decoupling: Gender Injustice in China's Divorce Courts*. Cambridge: CUP.

Migdal, Joel S. 1997. "Studying the State" in *Comparative Politics: Rationality, Culture, and Structure*, edited by Mark Irving Lichbach and Alan Zuckerman, 208–235. Cambridge: CUP.

Mingpao. 2022. "Burn the Tibetan Female Influencer to death, the Ex-husband was Executed Death Penalty [烧死藏女纲红 前夫执行死刑]," http://www.mingpaocanada.com/Tor/htm/News/20220724/tcac1_r.htm.

Ministry of Education of the PRC. 2023. "Number of Regular Students for Normal Courses in HEIs by Discipline," http://www.moe.gov.cn/jyb_sjzl/moe_560/2022/quanguo/202401/t20240110_1099511.html.

Ministry of Human Resources. 2017. Notice by the Political and Law Committee of Issues concerning Establishment of Working Allowance Scheme (关于建立政法委机关工作津贴有关问题的通知)," 2017. https://blog.sina.com.cn/s/blog_72e358450102yz16.html.

MOJ. 2021. "The Statistical Analysis of Lawyers and Grassroots Legal Services in 2020 [2020年度律师、基层法律服务工作统计分析]," http://www.moj.gov.cn/pub/sfbgw/zwxxgk/fdzdgknr/fdzdgknrtjxx/202106/t20210611_427394.html.

———. 2022. "The Home Page of Lawyers' Party Building," http://www.moj.gov.cn/pub/sfbgw/zwgkztzl/ztzlbwcxgdz/bwcxgdzdjgzld/djgzldlsdj/.

Minzner, Carl F. 2006. "Xinfang: An Alternative to the Formal Chinese Judicial System." *Stanford Journal of International Law* 42: 103–179.

———. 2009. "Judicial Disciplinary Systems for Incorrectly Decided Cases: The Imperial Chinese Heritage Lives On." *New Mexico Law Review* 39 (1): 63–88.

———. 2011. "China's Turn against Law." *The American Journal of Comparative Law* 59(4): 935–984.

_____. 2013. "The Rise and Fall of Chinese Legal Education." *Fordham International Law Journal* 36: 334–395.

Mnoonkin, Robert, and Lewis Kornhauser. 1979. "Bargaining in the Shadow of the Law: The Case of Divorce." *Yale Law Journal* 88(5): 950–997.

MOJ. 2012. Decision on Establishing an Oath System for Lawyers (关于建立律师宣誓制度的决定), February 3, 2012. https://www.moj.gov.cn/policyManager/policy_index.html?showMenu=false&showFileType=2&pkid=8e0990af38db42029a62f8968d498864.

_____. 2017. Measures on Administering Grassroots Legal Service Workers(基层法律服务工作者管理办法), December 25, 2017. https://www.moj.gov.cn/policyManager/regulationDetail.html?showMenu=false&showFileType=1&pkid=32221f6b656040b38a6c63f686e2609e

Morley, John. 1886. *Rousseau*. 2nd ed. London: Macmillan.

Mou, Yu. 2020. *The Construction of Guilt in China: An Empirical Account of Routine Chinese Injustice*. Oxford: Hart Publishing.

Moustafa, Tamir. 2007. *The Struggle for Constitutional Power: Law, Politics, and Economic Development in Egypt*. Cambridge: CUP.

———. 2008. "Law and Resistance in Authoritarian States: The Judicialization of Politics in Egypt" in *Rule by Law: The Politics of Courts in Authoritarian Regimes*, edited by Tom Ginsburg and Tamir Moustafa, 132–155. Cambridge: CUP.

Moustafa, Tamir and Tom Ginsburg. 2008. "Introduction: The Functions of Courts in Authoritarian Politics" in *Rule by Law: The Politics of Courts in Authoritarian Regimes*, edited by Tom Ginsburg and Tamir Moustafa, 1–22. New York: CUP.

MPS. 2012. Provisions on the Procedures for Handling Criminal Cases by Public Security Organs (公安机关办理刑事案件程序规定), December 13, 2012. https://www.gov.cn/gongbao/content/2013/content_2332778.htm.

National Court Judicial Statistics Bulletin [全国法院司法统计公报]. 2015. http://gongbao.court.gov.cn/Details/27e1cd92304feeeffd132e8244441a.html.

Nebehay, Stephanie. 2018. 'U.N. Says it has Credible Report that China Holds Million Uighurs in Secret Camps.' *Reuters*, August 10, 2018. https://www.reuters.com/article/us-china-rights-un/u-n-says-it-has-credible-reports-that-china-holds-million-uighurs-in-secret-camps-idUSKBN1KV1SU.

Nesossi, Elisa. 2017. "Wrongful Convictions: The Useful Injustice?" in *Justice: The China Experience*, edited by Flora Sapio, Susan Trevaskes, Sarah Biddulph, and Elisa Nesossi, 141–167. Cambridge: CUP.

Ng, Kwai Hang. 2019. "Is China a "Rule-by-Law" Regime?" *Buffalo Law Review* 67(3): 793–821.

Ng, Kwai Hang, and Xin He. 2014. "Internal Contradictions of Judicial Mediation in China." *Law & Social Inquiry* 39(2): 285–312.

———. 2017a. *Embedded Courts: Judicial Decision-making in China*. Cambridge: CUP.

———. 2017b. "The Institutional and Cultural Logics of Legal Commensuration: Blood Money and Negotiated Justice in China," *American Journal of Sociology* 122 (4): 1104–1143.

NPC Standing Committee. 2004. On Improving the People's Assessors System (全国人民代表大会常务委员会关于完善人民陪审员制度的决定), promulgated on August 28, 2004. https://www.gov.cn/gongbao/content/2004/content_62980.htm.

NPC Standing Committee. 2016. Decision on Authorizing the Pilot Work on a System of Leniency for Guilty Plea in Criminal Cases in Certain Regions (Draft)(关于授权在部分地区开展刑事案件认罪认罚从宽制度试点工作的决定(草案)), September 2, 2016. https://www.spp.gov.cn/zdgz/201609/t20160903_165677.shtml.

O'Barr, William M. 1994. "Juju Atkinson: Blurring the Distinction between Mediation and Adjudication" in *When Talk Works: Profiles of Mediators*, edited by Deborah Kolb, 359–374. Jossey-Bass: San Francisco.

O'Barr, William M. and John M. Conley. 1988. "Lay Expectations of the Civil Justice System." *Law & Society Review* 22(1) 137–161.

O'Brien, Kevin J., and Lianjiang Li. 2006. *Rightful Resistance in Rural China*. Cambridge: CUP.

Ohnesorge, John. 2023. "Regulation of the Legal Profession in China: A Historical Review." *China Law and Society Review* 9: 1–37.

Ong, Lynette H. 2018. "Thugs and Outsourcing of State Repression in China." *The China Journal* 80(1): 94–110.

Osnos, Evan. 2012. "The Love Business" *The New Yorker*. May 14, 2012.

Packer, Herbert L. 1964. "Two Models of the Criminal Process." *University of Pennsylvania Law Review* 113(1): 1–68.

Palmer, Alex W. 2017. "'Flee at Once': China's Besieged Human Rights Lawyers." *The New York Times Magazine*. July 25, 2017.

Palmer, Michael. 2014. "Mediating State and Society: Social Stability and Administrative Suits" in *The Politics of Law and Stability in China*, edited by Susan Trevaskes, Elisa Nesossi, Flora Sapio, and Sarah Biddulph, 107–126. Cheltenham: Edward Elgar.

———. 2017. "Domestic Violence and Mediation in Contemporary China" in *Mediation in Contemporary China: Continuity and Change*, edited by Hualing Fu and Michael Palmer, 286–318. London: Wildy, Simmonds & Hill Publishing.

Pan, Jianfeng and Niu Zhenghao. 2021. "The Socialized Cooperative Execution Mechanism from the Perspective of 'Fengqiao Experience' in the New Era—An Empirical Research Based on J Provincial Court [新时代'枫桥经验'视域下的社会化协同执行机制——基于J省法院的实证研究.]" *Dongyue Tribune* [东岳论丛] 42(3): 171–181.

Papagianneas, Straton. 2023. "Automating Intervention in Chinese Justice: Smart Courts and Supervision Reform." *Asian Journal of Law and Society* 10(3): 463–489.

Papagianneas, Straton and Nino Junius. 2023. "Fairness and Justice through Automation in China's Smart Courts." *Computer Law & Security Review* 51: 1–13.

The Paper [澎湃]. 2017. "The Supreme People's Court: In Comparison with the Statistics Last Year, the Number of Judges Nationwide Has Declined 60 Percent, While the Number of Cases Resolved on this First Half Year has Increased Around 10 Percent [最高法：全国法官人数少4成，今年上半年结案量同比升近1成]," July 31, 2017, http://m.thepaper.cn/newsDetail_forward_1747748.

———. 2021. "File an Administrative Lawsuit in Bad Faith or be Listed on the Yellow List? Zhengzhou Central People's Court Retracts Related Opinions [恶意提起行政诉讼或被列入黄名单？郑州中院撤回相关《意见》]," December 25, 2021, https://www.163.com/dy/article/GS36039H0514R9P4.html.

Peerenboom, Randall. 2001. "Seek Truth from Facts: An Empirical Study of Enforcement of Arbitral Awards in the PRC." *American Journal of Comparative Law* 49(2): 249–328.

———. 2002. *China's Long March towards Rule of Law.* Cambridge: CUP.

———. 2009. "Judicial Independence in China: Common Myths and Unfounded Assumptions" in *Judicial Independence in China: Lessons for Global Rule of Law Promotion*, edited by Randall Peerenboom, 69–94. New York: CUP.

———. 2010. "Introduction" in *Judicial Independence in China: Lessons for Global Rule of Law Promotion*, edited by Randall Peerenboom. New York: CUP.

Pei, Minxin, Guoyan Zhang, Fei Pei, and Lixin Chen. 2010. "A Survey with Corporate Litigants in Shanghai" in *Judicial Independence in China*, edited by Randall Peerenboom, 221–233. New York: CUP.

Peng, Xiaolong. 2011. "The Recovery and Practice of the People's Jury System: 1998–2010 [人民陪审员制度的复苏与实践]". *Chinese Journal of Law* [法学研究]. 1: 15–32.

Peng, Zhen. 1991. *Selected Works of Peng Zhen (1941–1990)* [彭真文选 (1941–1990)], edited by the Editorial Committee on Party Literature of the Central Committee of the Communist Party of China, 509–519, Beijing: People's Publishing House.

People's Daily. 2004. "Half of China's Civil Court Rulings Remain on Paper," http://en.people.cn/200403/13/eng20040313_137390.shtml.

———. 2019. "The People's Assessor Law Has Been in Effect for Nearly a Year. A Reporter Visited Yunnan: Juries are More Standardized and Perform their Duties More Conscientiously [人民陪审员法施行近一年，记者在云南探访：陪审更规范，履职更认真]," http://cpc.people.com.cn/n1/2019/0331/c64387-31004848.html.

———. 2020. "Making Execution Difficult No Longer 'Difficult' [让执行难不再是'老大难']," http://www.court.gov.cn/zixun-xiangqing-214241.html.

———. 2021. "In the Three Years Since the People's Assessor Law was Implemented, People's Assessors have Participated in the Trial of More than 1.553 Million Criminal Cases [人民陪审员法实施3年来人民陪审员共参审刑事案件155.3万余件]," http://society.people.com.cn/n1/2021/0723/c1008-32166978.html.

People's Court Daily [人民法院报], "How Many Judges are Sufficient [法官多少才够用]," http://rmfyb.chinacourt.org/paper/html/2013-06/07/content_64729.htm?div=0; 2012-2013.

Philips, Susan U. 1990. "The Judge as Third Party in American Trial Court Conflict Talk" in *Conflict Talk: Sociolinguistic Investigations of Arguments in Conversations*, edited by Allen D Grimshaw, 197–209. Cambridge: CUP.

Pils, Eva. 2006. "Asking the Tiger for his Skin: Rights Activism in China." *Fordham International Law Journal* 30(4): 1209–1287.

———. 2014. *China's Human Rights Lawyers: Advocacy and Resistance.* London: Routledge.

———. 2018. "The Party's Turn to Public Repression: An Analysis of the '709' Crackdown on Human Rights Lawyers in China." *China Law and Society Review* 3(1): 1–48.

Potter, Pitman B. 1995. *From Leninist Discipline to Socialist Legalism: Peng Zhen on Law and Political Authority in the PRC*, Stanford, CA: Stanford University Press.

———. 2002. "*Guanxi* and the PRC Legal System: From Contradiction to Complementarity" in *Social Connections in China: Institutions, Culture, and the Changing Nature of Guanxi*, edited by Thomas Gold, Doug Guthrie and David Wank, 179–196. New York: CUP.

Ramseyer, J. Mark, and Eric B. Rasmusen. 2001. "Why is the Japanese Conviction Rate so High?" *The Journal of Legal Studies* 30(1): 53–88.

Ren, Jianxin. 1989. "Adhere to the System of Open Adjudication, Prevent Local Protectionism: President Ren Jianxin's Response to Journalists [坚持公开审判制度杜绝地方保护主义—任建新院长答本刊记者问]." *People's Judicature* [人民司法] (7): 8–9.

———. 2005. *Fifty Years of Political-legal Work: Selected Literatures by Ren Jianxin* [政法工作五十年：任建新文选]. Beijing: People's Court Press.

Renhelaw. 2008. "Zhou Yongkang's Speech at the Seventh National Lawyers' Congress [周永康在第七次全国律师代表大会上的讲话]," http://bjlaw.org/bbs/dispbbs.asp?boardid=5&Id=1349.

Rennig, Christoph. 2001. "Influence of Lay Assessors and Giving Reasons for the Judgment in German Mixed Courts." *International Review of Penal Law* 72(1): 481–494.

Resnik, Judith. 1995. "Many Doors? Closing Doors? Alternative Dispute Resolution and Adjudication." *Ohio State Journal on Dispute Resolution* 10(2): 211–265.

Rousseau, Jean-Jacques. 1762 (1968). *The Social Contract*. London: Penguin Publishing Group.

Ruan, Fangfu. 1991. *Sex in China: Studies in Sexology in Chinese Culture*. New York: Plenum Press.

Ruskola, Teemu. 2002. "Legal Orientalism." *Michigan Law Review* 101(1): 179–234.

Scheingold, Stuart, and Austin Sarat. 2004. *Something to Believe in: Politics, Professionalism, and Cause Lawyering*. Stanford, CA: Stanford University Press.

Selznick, Philip. 1966. *TVA and the Grass Roots: A Study in the Sociology of Formal Organization*. New York: Harper & Row.

Shangrao Court. 1996. *Chronicle of the Court at Shangrao Region* [上饶地区法院志]. Internal publication [内部发行].

Shapiro, Martin. 1981. *Courts: A Comparative and Political Analysis*. Chicago: University of Chicago Press.

———. 2008. "Courts in Authoritarian Regimes" in *Rule by Law: The Politics of Courts in Authoritarian Regimes*, edited by Tom Ginsburg and Tamir Moustafa, 326–336. Cambridge: CUP.

Shavell, Steven. 2004. *Foundations of Economic Analysis of Law*. Cambridge: Harvard University Press.

Shen, Kui. 2021. "The Stumbling Balance between Public Health and Privacy amid the Pandemic in China." *The Chinese Journal of Comparative Law* 9(1): 25–50.

Shen, Wei, and Shu Shang. 2020. "Tackling Local Protectionism in Enforcing Foreign Arbitral Awards in China: An Empirical Study of the Supreme People's Court's Review Decisions, 1995–2015." *China Quarterly* 241: 144–168.

Silbey, Susan S., and Sally E. Merry. 1986. "Mediator Settlement Strategies." *Law & Policy* 8(1): 7–32.

Silverstein, Gordon. 2008. "Singapore: The Exception That Proves Rules Matter" in *Rule by Law: The Politics of Courts in Authoritarian Regimes*, edited by Tom Ginsburg and Tamir Moustafa, 73–101. Cambridge: CUP.

Sina News. 2004. "Guangxi High Court Will Not Accept the Following 13 Types of Cases Awaiting the Government to Deal with [广西高院下文不受理13类案件 希望政府出面处理]," https://news.sina.com.cn/c/2004-08-12/02233375229s.shtml.

———. 2010. "The Police Disclosed that the Associate Professor Was Suspected of Gathering Fornication and the Arrest Process [警方披露副教授涉嫌聚众淫乱案发及抓捕经过]," https://news.sina.com.cn/s/2010-04-07/101017335163s.shtml.

———. 2012. "Zhejiang Nail Households Have Clung to their Neighbors for 10 Years to Make their Lives Easier [浙江钉子户固守10年 官方为其生活便利未拆邻家]", https://news.sina.com.cn/c/2012-12-03/220825720643.shtml.

Smith, Tobias Johnson. 2019. "Harsh Justice?" https://madeinchinajournal.com/2019/10/25/harsh-justice/.

———. 2020. "The Contradictions of Chinese Capital Punishment." PhD dissertation, University of California, Berkeley.

Sohu. 2003. "The Old Couple Killed Themselves in Front of the Court, the Judge is on Trial for Negligence [老夫妇败诉法院门口自杀 法官涉嫌玩忽职守受审]," http://news.sohu.com/09/32/news208793209.shtml.

Solinger, Dorothy J. 1999. *Contesting Citizenship in Urban China: Peasant Migrants, the State, and the Logic of the Market.* Berkeley: University of California Press.

Solomon, Peter H. 1996. *Soviet Criminal Justice under Stalin.* Cambridge: CUP.

———. 2012. "The Accountability of Judges in Post-Communist States: From Bureaucratic to Professional Accountability" in *Judicial Independence in Transition*, edited by Anja Seibert-Fohr, 909–935. New York: Springer.

Song, Yinghui. et al. 2008. "Empirical Analysis on Criminal Reconciliation" (我国刑事和解的实证分析). *China Legal Science [中国法学]* 5: 123–135.

Songer, Donald R., and Reginald S. Sheehan. 1992. "Who Wins on Appeal? Upperdogs and Underdogs in the United States Courts of Appeals," *American Journal of Political Science* 36(1): 235–258.

SPC. 1998. Stipulations on the Reform of Civil and Economic Trial Methods (最高人民法院关于民事经济审判方式改革的若干规定), July 6, 1998. https://www.faxin.cn/lib/Zyfl/Zyfl Content.aspx?gid=A192068.

———. 2001. Several Rules Relating to Civil Litigation Evidence (关于民事诉讼证据的若干规定), December 21, 2001. http://gongbao.court.gov.cn/Details/0d82ddc253c5a8a44fbea92 ea600bb.html.

———. 2010. "2006–2010 the Trend of the Clearance Rate of Judicial Cases and the Number of Judges [2006年–2010年审执结案件数量与法官人数走势情况]," http://www.court.gov.cn/fabu-xiangqing-2409.html.

———. 2014. The Interpretations of the CiPL of the PRC (《中华人民共和国民事诉讼法》的解释), December 18, 2014. https://www.spp.gov.cn/spp/flfg/sfjs/201502/t20150205_90222.shtml.

———. 2015a. Opinions on Comprehensive Deepening of Reform of People's Courts – The 4th Five-year Outline for Reforming People's Courts (2014–2018) (最高人民法院关于全面深化人民法院改革的意见 –人民法院第四个五年改革纲要 (2014-2018)), 2015. https://www.chinacourt.org/article/detail/2015/02/id/1557989.shtml

———. 2015b. "Opinions on Perfecting the Judicial Responsibility System [最高人民法院关于完善司法责任制的意见]," http://gongbao.court.gov.cn/Details/58f02f7ad96f8dcb0e75b8c 7e08999.html.

———.. 2016a. Opinions on Further Deepening the Reform of Diversified Dispute Resolution Mechanisms in People's Courts（关于人民法院进一步深化多元化纠纷解决机制改革的意见）, June 28, 2016. *People's Courts Daily*, June 30, 2016.

———. 2016b. Work Program on Solving "Difficulties of Judgment Enforcement" within Two to Three Years (关于落实"用两到三年时间基本解决执行难问题"的工作纲要), April 29, 2016. http://xndtfy.qhfy.gov.cn/article/detail/2018/08/id/3476696.shtml.

———. 2017a. Opinions on Accelerating the Construction of Smart Courts (最高人民法院关于加快建设智慧法院的意见), December 4, 2017. http://gongbao.court.gov.cn/Details/5de c527431cdc22b72163b49fc0284.html.

———. 2017b. Opinions of the Supreme People's Court on Strengthening the Work of Case-handling by Presidents and Division Heads of the People's Courts at Various Levels (Trial) (最高人民法院关于加强各级人民法院院庭长办理案件工作的意见(试行)), May 1, 2017. http://gongbao.court.gov.cn/Details/8086e6256dc454a1e4441e7de4fb65.html.

———. 2017c. Provisions on Pre-reporting of Arbitration Cases under Judicial Review (最高人民法院关于仲裁司法审查案件报核问题的有关规定), December 26, 2017. http://gong bao.court.gov.cn/Details/d17983803cada81e2fb2d3e16c4f4f.html.

———. 2017d. Provisions on Several Issues Concerning Judicial Review Arbitration-Related Cases (最高人民法院关于审理仲裁司法审查案件若干问题的规定), December 26, 2017. http://gongbao.court.gov.cn/Details/5f3c604478ea374abcb71a940579ec.html.

———. 2017e. Opinions of the Supreme People's Court on the Implementation of the Judicial Accountability System (Trial Implementation) (最高人民法院司法责任制实施意见(试行)), September 22, 2017. http://gongbao.court.gov.cn/Details/37c4426c4862a07d0efad453869 0c7.html.

———. 2018. The Interpretations of the Administrative Procedure Law of the PRC (《中华人民共和国行政诉讼法》的解释), February 8, 2018. https://ipc.court.gov.cn/zh-cn/news/view-397.html.

———. 2019a. Interpretations on Several Issues Concerning the Application of the LPA (最高人民法院关于适用《中华人民共和国人民陪审员法》若干问题的解释), May 1, 2019. http://gongbao.court.gov.cn/Details/5e0bcb73349075bf4145d9b40b57ca.html.

———. 2019b. *Judicial Reform of Chinese Courts 2013–2018* [中国法院司法改革2013–2018]. https://www.court.gov.cn/zixun/xiangqing/389751.html.

———. 2020. Opinions on Deepening the Reform of the Mechanism for "Separation of Cases, Pre-trial Mediation, Fast-tracking and Summary Procedures for Simple Cases" in People's Courts (最高人民法院关于人民法院深化"分调裁审"机制改革的意见), February 10, 2020. http://gongbao.court.gov.cn/Details/165debc9eea5369dac05ab189b0046.html.

———. 2021a. The Guiding Opinions on Strengthening and Improving the Assessment of Judges (关于加强和完善法官考核工作的指导意见), October 12, 2021. https://www.chinalawtranslate.com/en/judge-evaluations/.

———. 2021b. Guiding Opinions of the Supreme People's Court on Accelerating the Integration of People's Court Mediation Platforms into Rural Areas, Communities, and Grids (最高人民法院关于加快推进人民法院调解平台进乡村、进社区、进网格工作的指导意见), October 18, 2021. https://www.court.gov.cn/zixun/xiangqing/326931.html.

———. 2021c. Opinions of the Supreme People's Court on Promoting the Reform of Separating Complex and Simplified Administrative Litigation Procedures (最高人民法院关于推进行政诉讼程序繁简分流改革的意见), May 18, 2021. http://gongbao.court.gov.cn/Details/07f12b1170d38b8de1bde94606df4c.html.

———. 2022a. Explanation of the Draft Civil Compulsory Enforcement Law of the PRC (关于《中华人民共和国民事强制执行法（草案）》的说明), June 25, 2022. http://www.sdcourt.gov.cn/lymyfy/402898/402899/402923/402890/9276199/index.html.

———. 2022b. Report on the Construction of the People's Court's One-stop Multiple Dispute Resolution and Litigation Service System (2019–2021) (人民法院一站式多元纠纷解决和诉讼服务体系建设(2019–2021)), February 24, 2022. https://www.court.gov.cn/zixun/xiangqing/346691.html.

SPC Information Department. 2023. "Person-in-charge of the SPC's Civil Division Addressed the Journalists Regarding the Fourth Publication of Typical Cases about the Construction of 'One Belt One Road' [最高人民法院民四庭负责人就发布第四批涉'一带一路'建设典型案例相关问题答记者问]." *Tianjin Second Intermediate Court*, https://mp.weixin.qq.com/s/6Ei2zjocFGy7WYsDx1o90A.

SPC Work Reports.various years. http://gongbao.court.gov.cn/.

SPC and MOJ. 2018. On Expanding the Scope of the Pilot Program of Full Coverage of Defense by Lawyers in Criminal Cases (最高人民法院、司法部关于扩大刑事案件律师辩护全覆盖试点范围的通知), December 27, 2018. https://www.moj.gov.cn/pub/sfbgwapp/zwgk/tzggApp/202105/t20210517_395668.html.

SPC and MOJ Notice. 2020. "Notice on the Situation after the People's Assessor had been Implemented for Two Years [最高人民法院、司法部通报人民陪审员法实施两周年工作情况]," https://www.court.gov.cn/shenpan/xiangqing/264241.html.

SPC and MOJ Reply. 2020. Reply to Several Issues in the Implementation of the LPA (《中华人民共和国人民陪审员法》实施中若干问题的答复), August 11, 2020. https://www.moj.gov.cn/pub/sfbgw/zlk/202010/t20201019_174542.html

SPC, SPP, MPS, MSS, and MOJ. 2017. Regulations on the Exclusion of Illegal Evidence (关于办理刑事案件严格排除非法证据若干问题的规定), June 20, 2017. https://www.spp.gov.cn/zdgz/201706/t20170627_194051.shtml.

_____. 2019. Guiding Opinions on Implementing the Plea Leniency System (关于适用认罪认罚从宽制度的指导意见), promulgated on October 24, 2019. https://www.spp.gov.cn/spp/xwfbh/wsfbh/201910/t20191024_435829.shtml.

SPP. 2019. "The 2019 Work Report of the Supreme People's Procuratorate [最高人民检察院工作报告]," https://www.spp.gov.cn/spp/tt/201903/t20190312_411422.shtml.

———. 2020. "SPP guiding cases: the 22nd batch [最高检第22批指导性案例.]," https://www.spp.gov.cn/spp/xwfbh/wsfbt/202012/t20201208_488360.shtml#2.

Stern, Rachel E., and Lawrence J. Liu. 2020. "The Good Lawyer: State-led Professional Socialization in Contemporary China." *Law & Social Inquiry* 45(1): 226–248.

Stern, Rachel E., Benjamin L. Liebman, Margaret Roberts, and Alice Z. Wang. 2021. "Automating Fairness? Artificial Intelligence in the Chinese Court." *Columbia Journal of Transnational Law* 59: 515–553.

Stevenson, Alexandra. 2021. "China Sentences Former Bank Chief to Death in Rare Move." *New York Times*, January 5, 2021.

Stone Sweet, Alec. 1999. "Judicialization and the Construction Governance." *Comparative Political Studies* 32(2): 147–184.

Stone Sweet, Alec., and Trevor T.W. Wan. 2023. "Global Constitutionalism and the People's Republic of China: Dignity as the 'fundamental basis' of the Legal System?" *International Journal of Constitutional Law* 21(2): 433–460.

Su, Li. 2000. *Sending Law to Rural Communities: Studies on Grassroots Legal Institutions in China [送法下乡：中国基层司法制度研究]*. Beijing: China University of Political Science and Law Press.

Su, Liyin and Jiang Yuan. 2017. "Research on Grand Panel Mechanism: Taking Beijing Second Intermediate People's Court as a Sample [大合议庭陪审机制研究:以北京市第二中级人民法院为样本]." *The People's Judicature [人民司法]* 7: 38–42.

Su, Xinjian. 2014. "The Influence of Procedural Justice on Judicial Trust: An Empirical Study Based on Subjective Procedural Justice [程序正义对司法信任的影响—基于主观程序正义的实证研究]." *Global Law Review [环球法律评论]* 36(5): 21–32.

Su, Yang, and Xin He. 2010. "Street as Courtroom: State Accommodation of Labor Protest in South China." *Law & Society Review* 44(1): 157–184.

Sun, Changyong, and Wenjun Tian. 2021. "An Empirical Research on the Sentencing Recommendation Mechanism in the Case with the Accused Pleading Guilty and Accepting Punishment: Based on Cases Tried by the Two-instant Courts in City A [认罪认罚案件量刑建议机制实证研究——以A市两级法院适用认罪认罚从宽制度审结的案件为样本]." *Journal of Southwest University of Political Science and Law* [西南政法大学学报] 23(5): 3–16.

Sun, Changyong. 2018. "The Standard of Proof in the Pleading Guilty and Accepting Punishments Cases [认罪认罚案件的证明标准]." *Chinese Journal of Law [法学研究]* 40(1): 167–187.

Sun, Ying, and Hualing Fu. 2022. "Of Judge Quota and Judicial Autonomy: An Enduring Professionalization Project in China." *China Quarterly* 251: 1–22.

Svolik, Milan W. 2012. *The Politics of Authoritarian Rule*. Cambridge: CUP.

Tang, Weijian, and Tianyu Qi. 2012. "Drift of Chinese Civil Mediation System [漂移的中国民事调解制度]." *Journal of Comparative Law [比较法研究]* 5: 78–90.

Tang, Yingmao, Zhuang Liu, and Kangyun Bao. 2022. "Is Trial Fairness Affected in Live Broadcast? Preliminary Evidence from a Court in China." *China Review* 22(3): 107–136.

Tarrow, Sidney. 2011. *Power in Movement: Social Movements and Contentious Politics*. Cambridge: CUP.

Teng, Biao. 2016. *Report on the 709 Crackdown [709大抓捕报告]*. Hong Kong: China Human Rights Lawyers Concern Group.

Thaman, Stephen C. 1999. "Europe's New Jury Systems: The Cases of Spain and Russia." Law and Contemporary Problems 62(2): 203–232.

Thibaut, John W., and Laurens Waler. 1975. *Procedural Justice: A Psychological Analysis*. Hillsdale: L. Erlbaum Associates.

Thio, Li-Ann. 2004. "The Rule of Law within a Non Liberal Illiberal 'Communitarian' Democracy: The Singapore Experience" in *Asian Discourses of Rule of Laws: Theories and Implementation of Rule of Law in Twelve Asian Countries with Comparisons to France and the U.S.*, edited by Randall Peerenboom, 183–224. London/New York: Routledge Curzon.

Tian, Yanmei, Kaiyue Xu, and Jian Wei. 2021. "Factors Influencing Court Decisions: Mediating Effect of Party Resources and Litigation Ability [法院判决的影响因素——当事人资源与诉讼能力的中介效应]." *Tsinghua University Law Journal [清华法学]* 15(5): 163–176.

Toharia, José Juan. 1975. "Judicial Independence in an Authoritarian Regime: The Case of Contemporary Spain." *Law & Society Review* 9(3): 475–496.

———. 2003. "Evaluating Systems of Justice through Public Opinion: Why, What, Who, How and What For?" in *Beyond Common Knowledge: Empirical Approaches to the Rule of Law*, edited by Erik G. Jensen and Thomas C. Heller, 21–62. Stanford, CA: Stanford University Press.

Trevaskes, Susan. 2007. *Courts and Criminal Justice in Contemporary China.* Lanham: Lexington Books.

———. 2010a. *Policing Serious Crime in China: From Strike Hard to Kill Fewer.* London: Routledge.

———. 2010b. "The Shifting Sands of Punishment in China in the Era of 'Harmonious Society'." *Law & Policy* 32(3): 332–361.

———. 2011. "Political Ideology, the Party, and Politicking: Justice System Reform in China." *Modern China* 37(3): 315–344.

———. 2013. "China's Death Penalty: The Supreme People's Court, the Suspended Death Sentence and the Politics of Penal Reform." *British Journal of Criminology* 53(3): 482–499.

Trevaskes, Susan, Elisa Nesossi, Flora Sapio, and Sarah Biddulph (eds.). 2014. *The Politics of Law and Stability in China.* Cheltenham: Edward Elgar.

Tyler, Tom R. 1990. *Why People Obey the Law.* New Haven: Yale University Press.

———. 2007. "Procedural Justice and the Courts," *Court Review* 44(1/2): 26–31.

Upham, Frank K. 2009. "From Demsetz to Deng: Speculations on the Implications of Chinese Growth for Law and Development Theory." *NYU Journal of International Law and Politics* 41(3) 551–602.

van den Bos, Kees, Riel Vermunt, and Henk Wilke. 1997. "Procedural and Distributive Justice: What is Fair Depends More on what Comes First than on what Comes Next." *Journal of Personality and Social Psychology* 72(1): 95–104.

Walder, Andrew G. 1986. *Communist Neo-traditionalism: Work and Authority in Chinese Industry.* Berkeley: University of California Press.

Wang, Alex. 2006. "The Role of Law in Environmental Protection in China: Recent Developments." *Vermont Journal of Environmental Law* 8(2): 195–224.

Wang, Hongyan. 1999. "On the Separation of Investigation and Trial in Civil Litigation [试论民事诉讼中的调审分立]". *Law Review [法学评论]* 3: 108–115.

Wang, Hsiao-Tan. 2019. "Justice, Emotion, and Belonging: Legal Consciousness in a Taiwanese Family Conflict." *Law & Society Review* 53(3): 764–790.

Wang, Jing. 2021. "Judicial Review of Regulatory Documents in Administrative Litigation in China." *University of Pennsylvania Asian Law Review* 16: 328–373.

Wang, Liming. 2009. "Characteristics of China's Judicial Mediation System." *Asia Pacific Law Review* 17: 67–74.

Wang, Lusheng. 2015. "Horse-picking and Horse-racing: An Empirical Study on the Appointment Mechanism of Judges in China [相马与赛马: 中国初任法官选任机制实证研究]." *Law and Social Development [法制与社会发展]* 21(2): 41–53.

———. 2020. "The Non-equilibrium Dilemma of the Effectiveness of People's Assessors Reform and its Countermeasures—Big Data Mining Based on Criminal Judgments [人民陪审改革成效的非均衡困境及其对策——基于刑事判决书的大数据挖掘]." *Criminal Science [中国刑事法杂志]* (4): 137–154.

Wang, Qinghua. 2007. "Administrative Litigation in China: Polycentric justice [中国行政诉讼：多中心主义的司法]." *Peking University Law Journal [中外法学]* 5: 513–533.

———. 2011. *Justice in Politics[政治中的司法].* Beijing: Tsinghua University Press.

Wang, Shengjun. 2009. "Thoroughly Learn and Practice the Scientific Outlook on Development, Persist to Serve the Big Picture and Judiciary for the People [深入学习实践科学发展观 坚持为大局服务为人民司法]." *Qiushi [求是]* (4): 9–11.

———. 2011. "Some Knowledge about the Socialist Judicial System with Chinese Characteristics [关于中国特色社会主义司法制度的几点认识]." *Qiushi [求是]* (5): 13–16.

Wang, Shitao. 2021. "The Normative Analysis and Institutional Reflection of Administrative Person Appearing in Court [行政负责人出庭的规范分析与制度反思]." *Southeast Law Review [东南法学]* (1): 70–85.

Wang, Shucheng. 2022. *Law as an Instrument: Sources of Chinese Law for Authoritarian Legality*. Cambridge: CUP.

Wang, Tao. 2016. "China's Pilot Judicial Structure Reform in Shanghai 2014–2015: Its Context, Implementation and Implications." *International Law and Disputes Resolution Review* 24: 53–84.

Wang, Xiang, and Xiaohong Yu. 2013. "An Empirical Study on the Impact of People's Assessors [人民陪审员参审效能的实证分析]." *The Jurist [法学家]* 3: 30–44.

Wang, Xiaoqiang. 2015. "Controlling '*Guanxi*' Cases through Faces—Based on Game-of-Survival Wisdom of Multiple Parties [透过面子的关系案控制—以多方生存性智慧博弈为基础)]." *Xiangjiang Law Review [湘江法律评论]* 12: 249–265.

Wang, Yanan. 2018. "China's Disappeared: A Look at Who Went Missing in 2018," https://www.apnews.com/55bf0e55b551480f86bf2721ce0ab3f7.

Wang, Yanling. 2021. "Effective Defense in Death Penalty Cases: An Empirical Analysis Based on 6517 Verdicts [死刑案件的有效性辩护——基于6517份判决书的实证分析]." *Journal of South China Normal University [华南师范大学学报]* (6): 134–149.

Wang, Yaxin, and Yulin Fu. 2015. "Country Report: China [中国国别报告] " in *Comparative Researches on Case Management in Civil Litigation in China and Europe*, edited by Fu Yulin and van Rhee, 195–221. Beijing: Law Press.

Wang, Yongqiang. 2003. "Chief of the State Petition Bureau: Investigations Revealed that 80% or Above of the Petitions are Grounded [国家信访局局长：调查显示80%以上的上访有道理]." *Banyuetan Zhazhishe [半月谈杂志社]*, https://news.sina.cn/sa/2003-11-20/detail-ikkntiak8641842.d.html.

Wang, Yueduan. 2020a. "Overcoming Embeddedness: How China's Judicial Accountability Reforms Make its Judges More Autonomous." *Fordham International Law Journal* 43(3): 737–766.

———. 2020b. "Pre-empting Court–Civil Society Synergy: How China Balances Judicial Autonomy and Legal Activism." *Hong Kong Law Journal* 50: 1081–1106.

———. 2021. "'Detaching' Courts from Local Politics? Assessing the Judicial Centralization Reforms in China." *The China Quarterly* 246: 545–564.

———. 2024. "Embedded Supervision: China's Prosecutorial Public Interest Litigation against Government". Manuscript on file with author.

Wang, Yueduan, and Ying Xia. 2024. "State-sponsored Activism: How China's Law Reforms Impact NGOs' Legal Practice." *Law & Social Inquiry* 49(1): 451–477.

Wang, Yuhua. 2018. "Relative Capture: Quasi-experimental Evidence from the Chinese Judiciary." *Comparative Political Studies* 51(8): 1012–1041.

Wang, Yuhua, and Carl Minzner. 2015. "The Rise of the Chinese Security State." *The China Quarterly* 222: 339–359.

Wang, Vivian. 2024. "Xi Jinping's Recipe for Total Control: An Army of Eyes and Ears." *The New York Times*, May 24.

Weber, Max. 1954. *Max Weber on Law in Economy and Society*. Cambridge, MA: Harvard University Press.

Wheeler, Stanton, Bliss Cartwright, Robert A. Kagan, and Lawrence M. Friedman. 1987. "Do the Haves Come out Ahead? Winning and Losing in State Supreme Courts, 1870–1970," *Law & Society Review* 21(3): 403–445.

Woo, Margaret Y.K. 2003. "Shaping Citizenship: Chinese Family Law and Women." *Yale Journal of Law and Feminism* 15(1): 99–134.

Woo, Margaret YK, and Yaxin Wang. 2005. "Civil Justice in China: An Empirical Study of Courts in Three Provinces." *American Journal of Comparative Law* 53(4): 911–940.

Worth, Heather et al. 2019. "There Was No Mercy at All": Hooliganism, Homosexuality and the Opening-up of China." *International Sociology* 34(1): 38–57.

Wu, Ruozhi. 2007. "On the Practice of the Family Law System in Contemporary China—South China's R County as an Example [当代中国家事法制实践研究—以华南R县为例]." PhD dissertation, Renmin University of China.

Wu, Yuhao, and Zhuang Liu. 2023. "How does Public Opinion Affect the Measurement of Penalty?—Taking the Crime of DWI as a Point [民意如何影响量刑?—以醉酒型危险驾驶罪为切入]." *China Law Review* [中国法律评论] (1): 179–196.

Wu, Yuhao. 2020a. "Is a Plea Really a Bargain? An Empirical Study of Six Cities in China." *Asian Journal of Criminology* 15(3): 237–258.

———. 2020b. "Empirical Studies of the Effects of Legal Reforms on the Criminal Justice System in China." PhD dissertation, University of Pennsylvania.

Xi, Jinping. 2014. "Facilitating Social Fairness and Justice, Safeguarding People's Happy Livelihood." (促进社会公平正义，保障人民安居乐业), http://munich.china-consulate.gov.cn/zgzt/xjpzglz/201410/t20141028_3968363.htm.

———. 2015. "Strengthen the Construction of Laws and Regulations against Corruption and Advocating Integrity to Fully Release the Power of Legal System [加强反腐倡廉法规制度建设 让法规制度的力量充分释放]." *People's Procuratorate* [人民检察] (13): 1.

Xi, Chao. 2022. "How the Chinese Judiciary Works: New Insights from Data-driven Research." *China Review* 22(3): 1–8.

Xia, Jisen. 2018. "An Empirical Study on the Professional Identity of Judges in the Sight of Judicial System for Specified Number of Personnel [员额制下法官的职业认同实证研究—基于在安徽省某市法官员额制试点法院的调查]." *Law Science Magazine* [法学杂志] 1: 109–116.

Xian, Yifan. 2015. "Grassroots Judges of China in the Resurgence from Adjudicatory to Mediatory Justice." *Journal of Comparative Law* 10 (2): 126–141.

Xiang, Miao, and Liangcong Fan. 2021. "An Empirical Study on the Implementation Effect of Administrative Litigation Jurisdiction System in Different Places [行政诉讼异地管辖制度实施效果的实证研究]." *Governance Studies* [治理研究] 37(1): 117–126.

Xiao, Yang. 1999. "The Legal Safeguard of Human Rights in China [中国的人权法律保障]." *Qiushi* [求是] (6): 18–21.

———. 2003. "Court, Judge and Judicial Reform [法院、法官與司法改革]." *The Jurist* [法学家] (1): 3–10.

———. 2006. "Fully Exercise the Positive Effect of Judicial Mediation in Constructing the Socialist Harmonious Society [充分发挥司法调解在构建社会主义和谐社会中的积极作用]." *Qiushi* [求是] (19): 5–8.

Xie, Lu. 2022. "Who is the Haves in the Foreign-related Commercial Litigation?" PhD dissertation, City University of Hong Kong.

Xin, Xin. 2014. "Are Chinese Courts Undermining People's Rights through Judicial Mediation? A Critical Evaluation with Special Reference to Divorce Cases." PhD dissertation, City University of Hong Kong.

Xing, Shiwei. 2016. "Secretary of the Central Political and Legal Commission: Conducting the Pilot of the System of Leniency on Admission of Guilty and Acceptance of Punishment [中央政法委书记：试点认罪认罚从宽制度]." *The Beijing News*. January 1, 2016, http://news.sina.com.cn/c/2016-01-22/doc-ifxnuvxc1651648.shtml.

Xinhua Net [新华网]. 2017. "In Dong'an, Hunan, the Judge was Held Accountable for Seven Mistakes Made in the Judgment, Including the Information about the Place, Name and the Gender [地名、姓名、性别都写错 湖南东安"七错裁判文书"涉事法官被问责]," http://m.xinhuanet.com/2017-11/12/c_1121943097.htm.

———. 2016. "Who is Interfering with Judicial Work? The Central Party Political Commission Again Publishes 7 Typical Cases Involving 20 People [谁在干预司法？中政委再次通报7起典型案例，20人涉案]." February 1, 2016, http://www.xinhuanet.com/local/2016-02/01/c_1117960559.htm.

———. 2017. "Experimental Establishment of Judge Quotas is Basically Completed [我国法院法官员额制改革试点工作基本完成]," http://www.xinhuanet.com/2017-02/13/c_1120459608.htm.

———. 2021. "The Changsha Procuratorate Reported 'Murder of Female Judge Case': Criminal Xiang was Arrested in Batches [长沙检察机关通报"女法官遇害案":犯罪嫌疑人向某被批捕], http://www.xinhuanet.com/2021-01/19/c_1126997224.htm.

Xinhua News. 2014. "习近平：确保刀把子牢牢掌握在党和人民手中," https://m.huanqiu.com/article/9CaKrnJGT95.

Xinhua News. 2024. "China's GDP Increased by 5.2% in 2023 [2023年中国GDP同比增长5.2%]," http://www.xinhuanet.com/20240117/4fbac004043a47bf924fcdf1baad6a6f/c.html.

Xiong, Hao. 2015. "The Feasibility of Court Mediation in the Grassroots Society of Southwest China: A Case Study from Yunnan." *Hong Kong Law Journal* 44(1): 277–302.

Xiong, Moulin, and Michelle Miao. 2017. "Miscarriage of Justice in Capital Cases in China." *Hastings International and Comparative Law Review* 41(3): 271–342.

Xu, Jian. 2020. "The Role of Corporate Political Connections in Commercial Lawsuits: Evidence from Chinese Courts." *Comparative Political Studies*, 53(14): 2321–2358.

Xu, Jiaxin. 2017. "Responding to Questions Related to the Judicial Responsibility System and the Comprehensive Reform Pilot [徐家新就司法责任制等综合改革试点工作答问]," http://www.court.gov.cn/fabu-xiangqing-49802.html.

———. 2018. "Promoting the Personnel-system Reform and Strengthening the Team Building [推进司法人事制度改革 加强队伍建设]." *The Supreme People's Court of the People's Republic of China[中华人民共和国最高人民法院]*, http://www.court.gov.cn/shenpan-xiangqing-85662.html.

Xu, Xiaoqun. 2020. *Heaven Has Eyes: A History of Chinese Law*. Oxford: OUP.

Xu, Xin and Lu Tian. 2011. "Violent Defiance against the Law: 1983–2009 [法院执法中的暴力抗法：1983–2009]." *Law and Social Development [法制与社会发展]* 17(1): 3–28.

Xu, Xin. 2006. *Dispute Resolution and Social Harmony [纠纷解决与社会和谐]*. Beijing: Law Press.

Xu, Zhenhua, and Xingguang Wang. 2017. "A Probe into the Progressive Model of Judges' Responsibility for Handling Cases [法官办案责任追责的递进式模式研究]," *Journal of Law Application [法律适用]* 7: 14–20.

Yan, Zhaohua. (2020) "Procuratorial Organs' Dominant Status: The Rational Construction of Procedure Mode of Giving Leniency for Pleading Guilty and Accepting Penalty [检察主导:认罪认罚从宽程序模式的构建]." *Modern Law Science* 42(4): 37–51.

Yang, Jianshun. 2014. "It is not Compulsory for the Executive Head to Appear in Court to Answer the Lawsuit [行政首长出庭应诉不宜强制]." *Sinanews*, May 28, 2014, https://news.sina.com.cn/o/2014-05-28/062030245397.shtml.

Yardley, Jim. 2005. "A Judge Tests China's Courts, Making History." *New York Times*, November 28, 2005.

_____. 2007. "With New Law, China Reports Drop in Executions." *New York Times*, June 9, 2007.

Ye, Bin and Xiong Bingyuan. 2018. "Comparative Study on the Results of Civil Judgments and Criminal Judgments [刑事和民事判决结果的比较研究]". *Hebei Law Science [河北法学]* 36(8): 130–144.

———. 2020. "Judicial Local Protectionism in Enterprise Contract Dispute Cases [企业合同纠纷案件中的司法地方保护主义]." *Research on Financial and Economic Issues [财经问题研究]* 11: 22–31.

Yi, Shenghua. 2013. *Don't Cry in Strange Land: A Record of a Lawyer [别在异乡哭泣：一个律师的成长手记]*. Beijing: Peking University Press.

Yin, Bo. 2018 "Effectiveness of Criminal Defense for the Death Penalty Cases: Situations，Dilemmas and Solutions [死刑案件辩护有效性研究:状况、困境与出路]." *Law Science [法学杂志]* 39(3): 116–124.

———. 2021. "Impact and Restraint of Performance Appraisal Indexes upon Criminal Procedure [绩效考核指标对刑事程序法治的冲击与反制]". *Legal Forum [法学论坛]* 36(2): 143–151.

Yin, Bo, and Yu Mou. 2023. "Centralized Law Enforcement in Contemporary China: The Campaign to "Sweep Away Black Societies and Eradicate Evil Forces." *China Quarterly* 254: 366–380.

Yngvesson, Barbara. 1988. "Making Law at the Doorway: The Clerk, the Court, and the Construction of Community in a New England Town." *Law & Society Review* 22(3): 409–448.

Young, Alwyn. 2000. "The Razor's Edge: Distortions and Incremental Reform in the People's Republic of China." *Quarterly Journal of Economics* 115(4): 1091–1135.

Yu, Ping. 2002. "Glittery Promise vs. Dismal Reality: The Role of a Criminal Lawyer in the People's Republic of China after the 1996 Revision of the Criminal Procedure Law." *Vanderbilt Journal of Transnational Law* 35: 827–864.

Yu, Longgang. 2020. "Enforcement Ecology and Imbalanced Enforcement of Basic Courts [基层 法院的执行生态与非均衡执行]." *Chinese Journal of Law [法学研究]* 42(3): 102–122.

Yu, Wenguang. 2013. "The Theoretical Basis and System Construction of Administrative Litigation Mediation [行政诉讼调解的理论基础与制度建构]." *Journal of the East China University of Political Science and Law [华东政法大学学报]* 1: 3–16.

Yu, Xiaohong. 2021. "The Meandering Path of Judicial Reform with Chinese Characteristics" in *Chinese Courts and Criminal Procedure: Post-2013 Reforms*, edited by Björn Ahl, 29–58. Cambridge: CUP.

Yu, Xiaohong, and Wang Xiang. 2022. "Caught between Professionalism and Populism." *China Review* 22(3): 167–209.

Yu, Xiaohong, and Zhaoyang Sun. 2022. "The Company they Keep: When and Why Chinese Judges Engage in Collegiality." *Journal of Empirical Legal Studies* 19(4): 936–1002.

Yu, Yongcheng and Wei Jian. 2017. "The Mutation of Litigants' Resource Theory in the Judicial Practice of China: An Empirical Research Based on the First Instance Judgment of Contractual Dispute Cases [当事人资源理论在中国司法实践中的变异——基于合同纠纷案一审判决书的实证研究]." *Journal of Guangdong University of Finance & Economics [广东财经大学学报]* 32(1): 87–98.

Yue, Liling. 2001. "The Lay Assessor System in China." *Revue internationale de droit penal* 72(1): 51–56.

Zeng, Hui, and Zheng Wang. 2007. "People's Assessor System with Problems: The People's Assessor System Covered by 'the Elementary Court's Needing' [困境中的陪审制度—— "法院需要"笼罩下的陪审制度解读]." *Peking University Law Review [北大法律评论]* 8(1): 39–61.

Zhang, Jiajun. 2015. "People's Assessor: Empirical Analysis and System Reconstruction [人民陪审制度: 实证分析与制度重构]." *The Jurist [法学家]* (6): 1–14.

Zhang, Jian, and Ruoyu Wang. 2022. "Empirical Analysis and System Perfection of Administrative Litigation of Archival Information Disclosure: Take 109 Administrative Litigation Cases as Samples [档案信息公开行政诉讼的实证解析与制度完善—以109起行政诉讼案件为样本]." *Archives Science Study [档案学研究]* (3): 44–51.

Zhang, Jikun. 2020. "Study on the Substantive Trial in Civil Jurisdiction [民事审判庭审实质化问题研究]." *Law Science Magazine [法学杂志]* 41(7): 114–120.

Zhang, Jun. 2019. "Several Issues about the Procuratorate Work [关于检察工作的若干问题]." *Journal of National Prosecutors College [国家检察院学报]* (13): 3–12.

Zhang, Qing. 2019. "Case Pressures and Solutions in Basic Judicature after the Reform of Judge Quota System: Take Three Typical Courts in Y-Province as Example [员额制改革后基层司法的案件压力及其应对: 以Y省三个典型基层法院为例]." *Journal of China University of Political Science and Law [中国政法大学学报]* (69): 96–108.

Zhang, Taisu, and Tom Ginsburg. 2019. "Legality in Contemporary Chinese Politics." *Virginia Journal of International Law* 59: 307–390.

Zhang, Wei. 2022. "An Assessment on Judicial Reforms in Tibet [西藏地区司法体制改革的整体性评估与展望]." *Journal of Tibet Minzu University [西藏民族大学学报]* 43(1): 90–98.

Zhang, Weiping. 2001. "Court Investigation and Debate: An Inquiry of Division or Union [法庭调查与辩论:分与合之探究]." *Law Science [法学]* 4: 44–51.

Zhang, Wusheng. 2015. "Reviewing and Remodeling Chinese Civil Case Trial Procedure and Means [我国民事案件开庭审理程序与方式之 检讨与重塑]." *China Legal Science [中国法学]* 184(2): 66–80.

Zhang, Xuehua, Leonard Ortolano, and Zhongmei Lü. 2010. "Agency Empowerment through the Administrative Litigation Law: Court Enforcement of Pollution Levies in Hubei Province." *The China Quarterly* 202: 307–326.

Zhang, Yixiong. 2018. "Construction of China's Administrative Litigation Mediation System Under the Background of Multi-dispute Resolution [多元纠纷解决背景下我国行政诉讼调解制度之构建]." *Jianghai Academic Journal [江海学刊]* (6): 219–223.

Zhang, Yonghe and Jia Yu. 2009. *People's Assessor System in Wuhou District [武侯陪审]*. Beijing: Legal Press.

Zhang, Yuxia, and Zhuang Liu. 2024. "The Rise of the Chinese Judiciary and its Limits: Administrative Litigation in the Reform Period." *China Quarterly*, forthcoming.

Zhang, Zhiyuan. 2022. "Guiding the New Development of the Administrative Trial System with Xi Jinping Thought on the Rule of Law [以习近平法治思想引领行政审判制度新发展]" *Chinese Journal of Law [法学研究]* 44(4): 3–19.

Zhao, Yan. 2016. "I Became the Judge's Assistant [我成了法官的判案助手]" in *Assessors' Stories in Beijing [京城陪审故事]*, edited by Yuhua Li, China University of Political Science and Law Press.

Zhejiang Daily. 2019. "The Automatic Compliance Rate of Court Rulings Nationwide Rose to 57%, Increasing 12% in Three Years [全国法院判决自动履行率升至近57% 3年提升12%]," https://baijiahao.baidu.com/s?id=1623234509572515211&wfr=spider&for=pc.

Zheng, Bochao. 2020. "The System of Leniency on Admission of Guilty and Acceptance of Punishment: 'Chinese Approach' to Realize Impartial and Efficient Justice [认罪认罚从宽制度：实现公正高效司法的'中国方案']," https://www.spp.gov.cn/spp/zdgz/202010/t20201013_481731.shtml.

Zheng, Chengliang, and Wenjie Li. 2016. "People's Assessor Practice: Considerations and Reflections in the Context of China's Rule of Law—A Study Based on the Operation of People's Assessor in the Three Districts of Shanghai [人民陪审实践:法治中国语境下的考量与反思——基于上海三区法院陪审运行之研究]." *Law Science [法学杂志]* (11): 77–88.

Zheng, Chunyan, Jiahui Ai, and Sida Liu. 2017. "The Elastic Ceiling: Gender and Professional Career in Chinese Courts." *Law & Society Review* 51(1): 168–199.

Zheng, Ruoting, and Jieren Hu. 2020. Mediating State–society Disputes in China: Outsourced Lawyers and their Selective Responses. *China Information* 34(3): 383–405.

Zheng, Tianxiang. 1994. *Records of the Travel [行程纪略]*. Beijing: Beijing Press.

Zheng, Yongliu, Xiehua Ma, and Qicai Gao. 1992. "Realistic Changes of Chinese Farmers' Legal Consciousness—An Empirical Study from Hubei Countryside [中国农民法律意识的现实变迁—来自湖北农村的实证研究]." *China Legal Science [中国法学]* (6): 92–101.

Zhong Jianhua, and Guanghua Yu. 2003. "Establishing the Truth on Facts: Has the Chinese Civil Process Achieved this Goal?" *Journal of Transnational Law & Policy* 13(2): 393–446.

Zhong, Lena Y., and Mengliang Dai. 2019. "The Politics of Wrongful Convictions in China." *The Journal of Contemporary China* 28 (116): 260–276.

Zhou, Li'an. 2017. *Local Governments in Transition: Official Incentives and Governance [转型中的地方政府: 官员激励与治理]*. Shanghai: Gezhi Press.

Zhou, Qiang. 2017. "Explanations on the LPA[对《中华人民共和国陪审法(草案)的说明]," http://www.npc.gov.cn/zgrdw/npc/lfzt/rlyw/2018-04/27/content_2054204.htm.

Zhou, Xueguang. 2022. *The Logic of Governance in China*. Cambridge: CUP.

Zhu, Jingwen (ed.). 2007. *Report on China Law Development [中国法律发展报告]* Beijing: China Renmin University Press.

Zhu, Suli. 2010. "The Party and the Courts" in *Judicial Independence in China: Lessons for Global Rule of Law Promotion*, edited by Randall Peerenboom, 52–68. Cambridge: CUP.

Zhu, Jingwen (ed.). 2012. *Report of China Law Development 2012 [中国法律发展报告2012]* Beijing: China Renmin University Press.

Zou, Meiqing. 1997. "Solving the Problem of Local Protectionism Should Start from the Courts Themselves [解决地方保护主义问题应从法院自身做起]." *Law and Social Development [法制与社会发展]* (4): 61–63.

Zuo, Weimin. 2017. "How to be Lenient on Admission of Guilty and Acceptance of Punishment: Misunderstanding and Rectification [认罪认罚何以从宽: 误区与正解]." *Chinese Journal of Law [中国法学]* 39(3): 160–175.

———. 2022. "Empirical Study on the 'Difficult Enforcement' Response Model in China: An Analysis Based on Regional Experiences [中国'执行难'应对模式的实证研究 基于区域经验的分析]." *Peking University Law Journal [中外法学]* 34(6): 1445–1463.

Zuo, Weimin, and Jinghua Ma. 2012. "Effect and Paradox: An Empirical Study on the Mechanism of Criminal Defense in China—A Case Study of D County, S Province [效果与悖论:中国刑事辩护作用机制实证研究—以S省D县为例]." *Tribune of Political Science and Law [政法论坛]* 30(2): 60–73.

Case Cited

Brady v. United States, 397 U.S. 742 (1970).

Laws Cited (in chronological order)

NPC Standing Committee. 1980. Interim Regulations on Lawyers of the PRC (中华人民共和国律师暂行条例), promulgated on August 26, 1980.

NPC Standing Committee. 1982. Civil Procedure Law of the PRC (Trial) (中华人民共和国民事诉讼法（试行）), promulgated on August 3, 1982.

National People's Congress. 2017. The Administrative Litigation Law (ALL) of the PRC, promulgated on April 4, 1989. Last amended on June 27, 2017.

NPC Standing Committee. 2017. The Arbitration Law of the PRC (中华人民共和国仲裁法), promulgated on August 31, 1994, amended on September 1, 2017.

Ministry of Justice. 2017. Measures on the Administration of Grassroots Legal Service Workers (基层法律服务工作者管理办法), promulgated on March 30, 2000, amended on December 25, 2017.

NPC Standing Committee. 2018. The Law of People's Assessors of the PRC (中华人民共和国人民陪审员法), promulgated on April 27, 2018.Ministry of Justice. 2018. Measures on the Selection of People's Assessors(人民陪审员选任办法), promulgated on August 22, 2018.

National People's Congress. 2018. Criminal Procedure Law of the PRC (中华人民共和国刑事诉讼法), promulgated on July 1, 1979, amended on October 26, 2018.

NPC Standing Committee.2018.Organic Law of the People's Courts of the PRC (中华人民共和国法院组织法), promulgated on May 7, 1979, revised on October 26, 2018.

NPC Standing Committee.2019.The Judges Law of the PRC [中华人民共和国法官法], promulgated on February 28, 1995, amended on April 23, 2019.

National People's Congress. 2020. The Law on Administrative Sanctions on Civil Servants (公职人员政务处分法), promulgated on June 20, 2020.

National People's Congress. 2020. Criminal Law of the PRC (中华人民共和国刑法), promulgated on July 1, 1979, amended on December 26, 2020.

National People's Congress. 2021. Civil Procedure Law of the PRC (中华人民共和国民事诉讼), promulgated on April 9, 1991, amended on December 24, 2021

Central Committee of the Party and the State Council. 2022. Statutes on Handling Petitions (信访工作条例), promulgated on February 25, 2022.

NPC Standing Committee. 2023. The Administrative Reconsideration Law (ARL) of the PRC (中华人民共和国行政复议法), promulgated on August 27, 1999, amended on September 1, 2023.

Index